Performing Virginity and Testing Chastity in the Middle Ages

Performing Virginity and Testing Chastity in the Middle Ages opens with a survey of classical and medieval medical treatises that offer advice on verifying female virginity – and sometimes suggest ways to fake it. Then, proofs of virginity as they recur throughout Christian hagiography (particularly when the virgin is threatened with rape) are discussed, as well as the chastity test or 'ordeal' as it is represented in vernacular romance. The representation of the male virgin in hagiography and romance is also analysed. Finally, the author explores examples from contemporary fiction, television and film in which testing virginity is a theme.

Performing Virginity and Testing Chastity in the Middle Ages presents a compelling and provocative study of virginity, which challenges the belief that female virginity can be reliably and unambiguously defined, tested and verified.

Kathleen Coyne Kelly is Associate Professor of English at Northeastern University, Boston. She is the editor, with Marina Leslie, of *Menacing Virgins: Representing Virginity in the Middle Ages and Renaissance* (1999).

Routledge Research in Medieval Studies

Performing Virginity
and Testing Chastity
in the Middle Ages

Kathleen Coyne Kelly

London and New York

First published 2000
by Routledge
2 Park Square, Milton Park, Abingdon, Oxon, OX14 4RN

Simultaneously published in the USA and Canada
by Routledge
270 Madison Ave, New York NY 10016

Reprinted 2002

Transferred to Digital Printing 2005

Routledge is an imprint of the Taylor & Francis Group

© 2000 Kathleen Coyne Kelly

The right of Kathleen Coyne Kelly to be identified as the Author of this
Work has been asserted by her in accordance with the Copyright, Design
and Patents Act 1988

Typeset in Baskerville by
HWA Text and Data Management, Tunbridge Wells

British Library Cataloguing in Publication Data
A catalogue record for this book is available
from the British Library

Library of Congress Cataloging in Publication Data
Kelly, Kathleen Coyne.
     Performing virginity and testing chastity in the Middle Ages /
Kathleen Coyne Kelly.
          p. cm. – (Routledge research in medieval studies)
     Includes bibliographical references (p.) and index.
     1. Literature, Medieval–History and criticism. 2. Virginity–
Religious aspects–Christianity–History of doctrines–Middle Ages,
600–1500. 3. Christianity and literature–Europe–History–To
1500. 4. Romances–History and criticism. 5. Virginity in
literature. 6 Christian hagiography. I. Title. II. Series.
PN682.V56K45 2000   99-40601
809´.93353–dc21   CIP

ISBN 0-415-22181-1

Contents

Acknowledgments

Harvard University has a rather famous collection of nineteenth-century glass flowers in the Peabody Museum, which were designed for botany students so that they could study reliable and durable specimens. The flowers are much bigger than life-size in order to show the details of pistils and stamens (words, I suspect, that have held an erotic charge for most people since they took natural science in high school). When I visited the collection, I was struck by the fact that one can determine when a bee has visited a "closed" flower, such as a sweet-pea. It seems that after the bee has insinuated itself into the flower, it leaves a distinct signature as it backs out, widening the passage as it goes. In effect, it is possible to observe not the deflowering of virgins, but the devirginizing of flowers. It is such twists on the material and metaphorical signification of the virgin and the virginal that led me to become a virginologist in the first place. I owe much to friends and colleagues who have had to listen to this anecdote and numerous others as I was working on this book, and I am happy to acknowledge such debts here, as well as to thank all of those who contributed in more substantial ways.

Northeastern University was generous in granting me release time from teaching to work on the book, as well as in funding library privileges at Widener Library at Harvard and my travel to conferences in the US and abroad. I especially want to thank the Interlibrary Loan staff at Northeastern University, Ives Hyacinthe and Loreen Esser, who were always patient and speedy in responding to requests. My colleagues in the Department of English at Northeastern supported my research with plenty of intellectual enthusiasm and good humor. Wayne Franklin was particularly supportive at a crucial time in the making of this book.

Helen Lemay graciously lent me her photocopies of *De secretis mulierum* texts and of the works of Guilielmus de Saliceto. Monica Green was very prompt in responding when she received a book chapter and a long list of questions from a stranger, and her comments proved very useful and incisive. Timothy D. Barnes, James A. Brundage, and Jacqueline Murray were also helpful in their correspondence. My notes demonstrate how much I owe to these scholars and to others who work in areas outside of my own specialty, which is Middle English literature.

I have profited from many conversations, sometimes in unexpected places and contexts, and I'd like to thank Glenn Adelson, Tim Cockey, S. Jean Emans, Maureen Fries, La Vinia Jennings, Mary Loeffelholz, Vince LoRusso, Sarah

Stanbury, Bonnie Wheeler, Wendy Barrie-Wilson, and Susan Yager for their valuable input over dinner, on the phone, and between conference sessions. I thank Lynn Dornink, Deanne Harper, Matt Noonan, Diane Putnam, Cindy Richards, and Ellen Sharfenberg for their help with certain obscurities of pop culture in *fin de siècle* America. I am grateful to Frank Blessington for his patience and help with Greek and Latin. Any errors that remain are my own, of course.

Cindy Carlson, Kathryn Lynch, Guy Rotella, Susan Wall, and Angela Jane Weisl read parts of the manuscript as it evolved. I hope they see the degree to which their comments made a difference. Laurie Finke and Martin Shichtman were lively and insightful readers, and I am grateful for their advice.

I especially want to thank Marina Leslie, fellow virginologist and treasured colleague, who made many wise suggestions for revision. My greatest debt, however, is to Barry Hoberman, bibliographer extraordinaire and my toughest and best reader.

Finally, this book is for my mother, Elizabeth Irene.

A note on translations, editions, and previously published material

In the body of the text, I give the original Middle English together with a translation into modern English; except in a few instances, all noted, all translations are mine. Similarly, when I quote phrases or short passages from other languages, I provide translations. When the passage is substantial or proves unwieldy for the page, I give the translation in the main body of the text and provide the original language in the notes. For the most part, I use translations that have already been published in standard editions, and give full attribution. Biblical quotations in English are taken from the New Revised Standard Version.

Part of Chapter 4 previously appeared in *Menacing Virgins: Representing Virginity in the Middle Ages and the Renaissance* as "Menaced Masculinity and Imperiled Virginity in Malory's *Morte Darthur.*" I thank the University of Delaware Press for permission to reuse this material. A version of Chapter 2 appeared as "Unrepresentable Rape and the Represented Church in Medieval Saints' Lives," in *Literary Constructions of Widowhood and Virginity in the Middle Ages*, ed. Cindy L. Carlson and Angela Jane Weisl, and I thank St. Martin's Press for permission to reprint. I also thank *Arthuriana* for permission to reprint portions of my article, "Malory's Body Chivalric."

Abbreviations

EETS	Early English Text Society
PG	Patrologiae Graeca
PL	Patrologiae Latina
PMLA	Proceedings of the Modern Language Association of America

Preface

Holden: "So you're still a virgin then."

Alyssa: "Noooo."

"But you've only been with girls."

"So you're saying a person is a virgin until they've had intercourse with a member of the opposite sex?"

"Isn't that the standard definition?"

"Again with your standards! I think virginity is lost when you make love for the first time."

"With a member of the opposite sex."

"Why? Why only then?"

"Because that's the standard, let me tell ya."

"So if a virgin is raped, then she is still a virgin."

"No, of course not."

"But rape is not the standard. So she's had sex, but not the *standard* idea of sex. And according to your definition, she'd still be a virgin."

"OK, fine, I'll revise. Virginity is lost when the hymen is broken."

"Well then I lost my virginity at ten."

"Really?"

"Hmmm. Cause you see I fell on a fence post when I was ten and broke my hymen."

"OK ... second revision. Virginity is lost through penetration."

"Physical or emotional?"

Chasing Amy (1997, Kevin Smith)

As the above exchange illustrates, the concept or condition of virginity often resists definition and verification in surprising ways – surprising because, if pressed, most people believe that they would be able to define virginity with some confidence. The frustration that Alyssa and Holden share here reveals the degree to which virginity is contingent upon cultural, not physiological, criteria, on "standards" that only apply to female bodies and that serve to establish heterosexuality as the norm. Such standards are reproduced through the persistence of a number of unexamined assumptions about the body – chief among them, the idea that the body will yield up its secrets to empirical investigation and study.

This book is intended to challenge the belief that virginity can be reliably and unambiguously defined and verified. I examine a variety of medieval and modern narratives across a number of genres in which virginity is ostensibly tested, and argue that even at the point at which virginity seems to be most visible, most susceptible to verification, it successfully evades any conclusive confirmation.

There are many possible paths into such a study of virginity as I undertake here – paths variously determined by academic discipline (anthropology, folklore, history, history of medicine, literary studies, sociology), by historical era (classical, medieval, modern) and by geography (Eastern, Western). Because I am a medievalist by training, I focus on Western European legal, medical, historical, and literary discourses from around 1200 to 1500 in order to provide as textured a reading of virginity and its verifications in this period as I can. But the testing and verifying of virginity has a history all its own, and therefore I also attempt to document part of that history by surveying the classical antecedents to medieval discourses on the body and virginity. I devote the final chapter to modern representations of verifying virginity in various media – film, television, and literature – in order to demonstrate some of the continuities and discontinuities between the Middle Ages and contemporary Anglo-American culture. More than any other history of a given physiological or psychological "fact" about women, the study of attitudes toward and beliefs about virginity makes obvious the workings of how the female body is regulated by patriarchy. The gendered nature of virginity has been an inescapable feature of Western discourses on the body for more than two thousand years. How one goes about defining and verifying virginity may change over time, but the general belief that the body is readable, and virginity is verifiable, has remained fairly consistent.

As I hope to suggest by coining the word *hymenologies* in my title for Chapter One, the hymen is but one sign of virginity that we attempt to read and to rely on. Yet because of its inherent instability as a sign, the hymen has been regularly supplemented by other means of verification deriving not only from the "scientific" medical knowledge of a given time and place, but also from the domains of religion, folklore, and magic. Thus such signs as a woman's behavior and dress, the color of her urine, the direction in which her breasts point, and her ability to drink from a magic cup or to carry a sieve full of water have served as proofs of virginity in different eras and societies. The reasons for such a plethora of signs are complicated; most important, I think, is the idea that virginity operates as much more than a material "fact" of the body. Virginity, the virgin, and the virginal also have great metaphorical and mythical power, and are capable of generating and representing a whole complex of cultural beliefs. For example, virginity is often figured as wholeness, intactness, perfection, and the virgin as a conduit to the divine and/or an earthly prize to be won or bestowed. The lure of the pure (extra virgin olive oil, virgin wool, virgin snow) and of the new and untried (maiden voyage, virgin territory, Virgin Airlines) is an enduring one.

In what follows, by focusing on virginity and its verifications, I explore how bodies come to have meaning – more precisely, how a specific part of a gendered body, the hymen (and its cultural analogues) functions as both metaphor and metonym for an array of ideas and beliefs about women, women's relations with and to men, and relations between men in cultural systems in which women figure as objects of exchange.

Introduction

Castitas/Virginitas

It is the hymen that desire dreams of piercing, of bursting, in an act of violence that is (at the same time or somewhere in between) love and murder.

Jacques Derrida, "The Double Session"

The virgin ...

"I'm a teaching assistant, and one of my assignments is to lecture first-year engineers on the history of science and technology. ... I was telling them about the Vestal Virgins, and how they could prove their virginity by carrying water from the Tiber in a sieve. I challenged the handful of girls in my immense class of a hundred and forty to try it, and some of them were good sports and did – and couldn't. Big laughs. Then I carried some water about twenty paces in a sieve without spilling a drop, and when they Oohed and Aahed at that I invited them to examine the sieves. Of course mine was greased, which proved that the Vestal Virgins had a practical understanding of colloid chemistry."[1]

This is a clever story that the fictional scholar Maria tells in Robertson Davies' *The Rebel Angels*, and I open with it in order to illustrate that, in any given narrative, at the very moment virginity can be asserted, it can also be denied. The paradox of bodily and spiritual integrity as both presence and absence is the subject of this book.

The concept of virginity (and/or chastity; distinctive as the meanings of these two terms are, they are sometimes blurred together, as I discuss below) is developed within and across a number of different discourses in the Middle Ages: medical and scientific treatises (and their classical antecedents), patristic writings and the medieval commentaries on them, legal records and documents, and literary texts. My focus is the representation of virginity and its verifications in these discourses (mainly texts of the thirteenth through the early fifteenth century), with a special emphasis on literary texts. However, I do not read other discourses merely as sources for literary texts. Medical treatises, for example, discuss virginity and tests of virginity in great detail, but this material does not appear in imaginative literature. On the other hand, the discourse of the judicial ordeal parallels, and sometimes underpins, several of the chastity tests found in vernacular romance. These discourses are best imagined in relation to each other as parts of a Venn diagram, overlapping only in their preoccupation with female virginity and in their anxiety about verifying it. And as in a Venn diagram, there is no center, no fixed point, at which virginity/chastity is sited.

Virtually all the tests of chastity and fidelity that I have been able to locate in medical and imaginative literature are designed for, or wished upon, women. (The major exception is the story of Galahad and the Holy Grail, which I discuss in Chapter 4.) Consequently, a large portion of this book is devoted to the study of the gendering of virginity within religious and secular culture in the late Middle Ages.

This book is intended as a contribution to the growing number of studies on the body in the Middle Ages and in contemporary Western culture.[2] The represented "body," of course, is never quite the same thing through time and across space, but is instead the construct of complex and contradictory knowledges. What does not seem to change, however, is the notion that the body is a *readable* body; that is, while interpretations of the body are contingent upon culture, the body itself is persistently identified as a site or depository of information. By focusing on virginity and its verification, located in the body but inextricable from its relation to spirit (or soul, or mind) and its social expression, I explore how bodies come to have meaning – more precisely, how a specific part of a gendered body, the hymen and its analogues, as it were, functions as both metaphor and metonym for an array of ideas and beliefs about women, women's relations with and to men, and even relations *between* men. This book should at least suggest (following Caroline Walker Bynum) that the dualist concept of body/ mind or body/soul that we sometimes impose on the Middle Ages is just that: an imposition. Virginity and its verifications, chastity and its confirmations, demonstrate that bodies and spirits are not easily separated in medieval practice.

In these introductory remarks, it is hardly possible to survey the entire history of virginity that underpins and runs through late medieval texts. Nor is it necessary to do so, given the many excellent studies that examine virginity in its specific historical contexts, particularly with respect to the cult of Mary, the virgin *par excellence* in the writings of the Church Fathers and in later medieval commentaries.[3] In fact, it is the legend of Mary that underwrites what may be the most famous example of a chastity test: the legend of the unicorn who eludes all hunters but comes willingly to lay his head in the lap of a virgin. (This story has taken on a life of its own beyond the confines of religious and scholarly interest, while the unicorn itself has achieved the status of a pop icon.) In the present study, because of the wealth of scholarship on virginity in its mystical and religious valences, rather than focus on the many representations of the Virgin and her influence, I take Mariology as a given, as a starting point for exploring virginity and the various ways in which it has been subject to verification or proof. What I will try to do in what follows is to survey the ways in which virginity and chastity have been defined, and to show how Western Christianity's attitudes toward ascertaining virginity remained fairly consistent from late antiquity, when they were first formulated by the Church, through the Middle Ages. I hope that what emerges is the sense that virginity was (as it apparently still is) such an unstable and relative concept that it had to be repeatedly defined and described by early patristic writers and their medieval commentators.

In *The Rebel Angels*, Father Darcourt tells Maria that chastity is "a quality of the spirit," while virginity is "a physical technicality."[4] For the most part, this distinction between the terms *castitas* and *virginitas* holds true throughout early patristic literature and later medieval commentaries. It is repeatedly asserted that spiritual chastity is superior to physical virginity. For Christian authors, the body – a flawed "clay jar" in which we keep our "treasure," as Paul put it (2 Cor. 4: 7) – is an abject object that must be disciplined and subdued.

The Bible provides the spiritual and theological underpinnings for defining chastity, and the writings of the Church Fathers provide the detailed exposition. The earliest patristic writers follow Paul in his insistence on the necessity of both bodily and spiritual integrity ("the unmarried woman and the virgin are anxious about the affairs of the Lord, so that they may be holy in body and spirit" [1 Cor. 7: 34]). Yet the writings of Ambrose, Jerome, Augustine, and others do not furnish us with an ideologically uniform, internally consistent body of thought on the subject of virginity.[5] Depending on the context, the patristic authors and their later commentators who use the terms *castitas* and *virginitas* may be referring either to one's never having experienced coitus (that is, a "virgin" in one, purely physical sense); *or* to an individual's commitment to the celibate religious life (regardless of whether that individual was single, married, or widowed); *or* to sexual faithfulness in a monogamous marriage.

That the definitions and descriptions of virginity and chastity so vary (but also overlap) reveals the degree to which these concepts were negotiable within the evolving institution of the early Church, when virginity became a key issue in the struggle to consolidate ecclesiastical authority. The conflict is not over the nature of virginity (which has no existence as a pre-cultural condition), but over the issue of who gets to "speak" it. One might say that the early Church aimed to create a monopoly on virginity.

John Chrysostom's *De Virginitate* (c. 380–90) is a classic statement of a political and theological strategy of regulation and containment of virginity/chastity. In this influential text, Chrysostom eloquently praises virginity/chastity and its heavenly rewards, arguing that true virginity can be achieved only if the celibate life is chosen freely.[6] But encomia are not his only agenda: Chrysostom also attacks certain Gnostic sects that condemn marriage as inherently evil. Such a heretical view makes chastity no choice at all, and diminishes the sacrifice that a true virgin makes when she (emphatically *she* in this text) renounces the world and dedicates her body and soul to God. "The virginity of the heretics," says Chrysostom, "has no reward"; that is, it is not recognized in heaven.[7] The heretical virgins are false virgins, not because they have lost physiological virginity – Chrysostom does not doubt their physical integrity – but because they practice, as it were, their virginity outside of the Church hierarchy. Chrysostom thus politicizes virginity, using it as a weapon against the perceived enemies of the Church. *De Virginitate* is a formative document in an emerging policy that makes the Christian Church the only institution with the power to define, recognize, and reward virginity.[8]

Chrysostom says: "Even if [a virgin's] body should remain inviolate the better part of her soul has been ruined: her thoughts. What advantage is there in the wall having stood firm when the temple is destroyed?" Later, he elaborates:

> It is not enough to be unmarried to be a virgin. There must be spiritual chastity, and I mean by chastity not only the absence of wicked and shameful desire, the absence of ornaments and superfluous cares, but also being unsoiled by life's cares.[9]

By enumerating – if not inventing – the characteristics of virginity, Chrysostom establishes it as an orthodox state, arguing that consecrated virginity has value only within the boundaries created by the institutionalized Church.

In another treatise, *On the Necessity of Guarding Virginity* (also known by its Latin title, *Quod regulares feminae viris cohabitare non debeant*) Chrysostom again takes up virginity in order to reserve for the Church the authority to recognize it. In the early Church, men and women who had taken vows of chastity sometimes shared the same household. Such an arrangement had its advantages, but it could also prove hazardous to one's spiritual health, as Chrysostom, Tertullian, Cyprian, Jerome, and others made quite clear in their condemnation of such households.[10] In *On the Necessity of Guarding Virginity*, for example, Chrysostom affirms that physiological virginity and spiritual chastity are not necessarily the same thing. He says:

> When a virgin learns to discuss things frankly with a man, to sit by him, to look at him, to laugh in his presence, to disgrace herself in many other ways … the veil of virginity is destroyed, the flower trampled underfoot.[11]

Spiritual chastity takes precedence over its bodily analogue, and it is extremely fragile: true virginity is even endangered by verbal intercourse.

Jerome's *Ad Jovinianum* (393) is another early patristic text in which the regulating of virginity is made to serve institutional ends. As does Chrysostom, Jerome glosses Paul (the original advocate for the institutionalization of virginity), but he also quotes extensively from other Scriptural and even classical authorities. Jovinian had argued that the chastity of virgins, wives and widows was equally admirable and deserved the same heavenly reward. In his response to Jovinian, Jerome – who says he was asked to "crush [Jovinian] with evangelical and apostolic vigour" – takes up the challenge to prove the superiority of virginity over marriage.[12] The interest in *Ad Jovinianum*, not only that of Jerome's immediate successors, but of later scholars and readers (including the Wife of Bath, who was particularly interested in Jerome's borrowings from a certain Theophrastus), has been focused on the misogynist arguments that Jerome marshals against marriage. What is relevant to the present study, however, is the way in which Jerome reaffirms the Church's power to name and to hierarchize virginity.

Most patristic writers and their later commentators echo the opinion that bodily integrity counts for nothing if the soul or spirit is not chaste.[13] In *De Virginitate* (377), Ambrose declares that "mere physical virginity does not gain merit, but rather, the integrity of the mind."[14] The spirit, in fact, is more easily corrupted than the body. According to the logic of the Church Fathers, a woman could retain her chastity even if her body is violated, so long as she did not consent to the sexual act. Yet that same woman could lose her chastity through her lascivious dress or actions or thoughts – or even if she were simply the focus of the male gaze. In *Adversus Helvidium* (383), Jerome constructs chastity as a fragile state that can be maintained only in isolation, declaring, for example: "I certainly do not know if she who is engaged in the shopkeeping business remains a virgin in body, but I do know that she does not remain a virgin in spirit." Here, the market-place stands in for the secular world, which is full of dangers for even the most resolute of virgins.[15] Augustine, in *De Civitate Dei* (begun in 413, finished in 425), puts a great deal of emphasis on the will, saying that "no one, however magnanimous and shamefast, has it always in his power to decide what shall be done with his flesh, having power only to decide what he will in his mind accept or refuse."[16] By the time the English abbot Aldhelm writes *De Virginitate* (late seventh century), the privileging of spiritual chastity over physical integrity has the ring of received opinion, the fixedness of a trope, such as when Aldhelm asserts that "carnal integrity is in no way approved of, unless spiritual purity is associated with it as companion."[17]

If defining and claiming virginity in the early, formative centuries of the Church helped to consolidate Church authority, then the renascence of interest in virginity in the twelfth century might be said to represent a crisis in that authority. As John Bugge chronicles in *Virginitas: An Essay in the History of a Medieval Ideal*, the twelfth century was marked by, as he puts it, "opposition between monastery and cathedral."[18] The issue of clerical celibacy (that is, male virginity) was at the heart of the great monastic reform movement, led by Bernard of Clairvaux and others. Reformers argued that the only road to spiritual perfection was through virginity and the cloistered life. However, extolling the virtues of the contemplative life for all proved to be impractical, given the very material and prominent role the Church had taken in world affairs. Those of the "cathedral," while not rejecting the importance of virginity, repositioned it within an ecclesiastical hierarchy of values. In accordance with such a move, proponents of the new scholasticism began to pose quite different questions about virginity from those of their patristic predecessors, such as whether and how to classify chastity and virginity as virtues.[19] To ask, as Augustine so urgently did, whether chastity and virginity were qualities of body, mind, or spirit, tended to become a mere exercise in classification and systemization in the twelfth century.

In his superb *Bridling of Desire: Views of Sex in the Later Middle Ages*, Pierre Payer stresses that no single monologic definition of chastity/virginity dominated the religious thought of twelfth- and thirteenth-century Western Europe. With respect to thirteenth-century usage, Payer says that:

> *continentia* connotes self-restraint in general, but is often used with a marked sexual reference; *castitas* connotes restraint from illicit sexual behaviour; *pudicitia* [purity] connotes areas tangential to sex such as touches, looks, and kisses, but it is sometimes taken to be synonymous with chastity.[20]

Even with a variety of specialized terms at their disposal, many theologians recognized that it was difficult to identify absolutely the parameters of chastity/virginity. One had to be willing to recognize degrees or types of virginity. "[T]here are cases," Payer says,

> in which physical integrity would be lost and we would not want to say that virginity was lost, or in which women could have sexual experience and retain physical integrity and we would want to say that virginity was lost. Then there is male virginity, which has no meaningful physical integrity associated with it. It must have been considerations such as these that led many medieval writers to distinguish among types of virginity in order to highlight the virginity that has moral and spiritual worth.[21]

Albertus Magnus, as Payer discusses in some detail, carefully distinguishes among four types of virginity in his *Quaestiones de Bono: De Castitate* (c. 1240): first, that of infants before the age of reason who possess innate virginity; second, that of individuals who possess virginity without having taken a religious vow; third, that of individuals who possess virginity and have taken a religious vow; fourth, that of individuals who possess virginity, but behave foolishly in their overbearing piety or inappropriate manner and dress – who might even look and behave like prostitutes, as a matter of fact.[22] The third type of virginity is the most admirable, of course. Like Augustine, Albertus Magnus locates virginity ("incorruption") in the will. Payer notes that in doing so, Albertus Magnus intends "to obviate a conception of virginity that would locate its essence in a requirement of physical intactness."[23]

We find a similar impulse in the writings of Thomas Aquinas. In the *Summa Theologiæ* (c. 1269–74), under the heading "Temperance," Aquinas discusses abstinence, continence, chastity, and virginity (in the *Summa*, virginity, along with purity, is a subset of chastity). These commentaries illustrate some of the problems – and opportunities – for defining these terms. Aquinas says that *castitas*

> has a proper and a metaphorical meaning. Properly speaking, it is a special virtue having its own well-defined material, namely the desires for pleasure of sex. Metaphorically speaking it is broader.[24]

The virtue of chastity, along with its opposite, the vice of lechery, may be located in the "commingling of bodies" (*corporis commixtione*). But Aquinas moves to the broader metaphorical meaning of chastity when he argues that it is possible to speak of *spiritualis castitas* (which is "refrain[ing] from enjoying things against [God's] design"), and its opposite, *spiritualis fornicatio*, (which is "delighting in things against God's order.")[25] Aquinas also says, citing Augustine, that "*Virginitas* implies a certain purity" ("pudicitiam quamdam importat"), and dwells in the soul; it "does not consist in a bodily condition" ("non consistit in carne incorruptione.")[26]

By defining virginity/chastity primarily as a spiritual quality, patristic and scholastic writers reconfigured the limits of the physical body. However, the fact that virginity may exceed bodily boundaries and actually reside in a given discourse did not prevent various writers from attempting to locate virginity in the flesh – female flesh, that is, for it is invariably women who are praised for their chastity or condemned for their lack thereof. The tension between a constructed, immutable chastity and an equally constructed, mutable body is one that informs most of the texts that I have examined for this book.

... and the test

The signs of virginity vary considerably in the texts under consideration in this study, depending upon the discursive tradition in which a test or proof or ordeal is found. Generally speaking, medical discourse addresses the physical body itself, while other discourses approach the physical body only obliquely: the body is present only through a fetishized object or externalized symbol. It is worth repeating that there is virtually no overlap or cross-influence between tests found in medical discourse and those found in imaginative literature (in the latter, the "test" is really a cross between a test and an ordeal, as I discuss in more detail in Chapter 3.) As Mary Wack has shown in *Lovesickness in the Middle Ages: The Viaticum and its Commentaries*, the physical signs of lovesickness as they were constructed in medical treatises were transferred wholesale to literary texts depicting the lovesick hero or heroine.[27] Such is not the case with medical tests of chastity, which apparently had no place in the discourse of romance. We can immediately identify a very pragmatic reason for this lack of crossover: urinalysis, a common medieval medical test for virginity, is decidedly unromantic (both in the modern and generic senses of the word). Moreover, the medical test is a private affair, while the ordeal is staged as a public event. While a husband may have very sound reasons for wanting to know if his new bride is a virgin or if his wife has kept her marriage vows, in the romance, the question of marital fidelity is often framed as an issue of communal interest, in a society in which "adultery, the secret deed *par excellence*, automatically becomes a matter of public policy," as R. Howard Bloch puts it.[28] The virginal or sexually faithful female body may occupy the same position in medical and literary texts, but it seems to have a different, genre-specific, discursive force in each.

Given the unreliability of the physical indicators of virginity – an abstract idea residing in an anatomical metonym – it is not surprising that a society like that of medieval Western Europe, so invested in the concept of chastity in both the religious and secular realms, turned to other means of verifying female virginity, given that virginity is a prerequisite and corollary to that other crucial but equally unknowable condition, paternity. And both virginity and paternity are essential to the workings of a feudal society that held the bulk of its wealth in private, aristocratic hands and passed on such wealth from father to son. Biological facts do not always correspond to cultural needs, and therefore biology must be supplemented in some way. Moreover, as Ellen Ross and Rayna Rapp argue,

> sexuality's biological base is always experienced culturally, through a trans-
> lation. The bare biological facts of sexuality do not speak for themselves;
> they must be expressed socially.[29]

As a social expression of a biological uncertainty – or, better, of a desire for certainty over biology – tests of chastity have a rich textual history. Folklorists and literary scholars have long collected and attempted to classify the numerous examples of chastity tests and ordeals that are found throughout medieval imaginative literature, in such languages as Arabic, English, French, German, Icelandic, Latin, Persian, Sanskrit, Spanish, and Welsh.[30] There is no distinct *ur*-test from which all others spring: rather, we find a nexus of tales that have their origins in oriental, classical, and Celtic texts (the last is most likely the immediate source for the motif in French romances, in turn the source for German and English romances). The thirteenth-century Middle English romance, *Floris and Blauncheflur*, is a fine example of the chastity-testing motif, illustrating how literary discourse represents the testing of virginity, and how biology is "translated" into the social sphere. In the poem, the Sultan of Babylon owns a magic fountain, about which we are told:

> Yif a woman com that is forlaught
> And she be do to the streme
> For to weshe her hondes clene
> The water wille yelle as it were woode
> And bicome red as bloode.[31]

> [If an unchaste woman comes down to the fountain in order to wash her
> hands clean, the water will scream out as if it were completely mad and
> become red as blood.]

In *Floris and Blauncheflur*, the chastity test is framed as an ordeal: the maiden who fails is put to death. Taken out of its narrative context, the episode of the magic fountain becomes just another static entry in the *Motif-Index of Folk-Literature*, ready to be counted alongside all the other curious tests and ordeals of chastity that are found in literatures around the world. However, as is true of many other chastity tests found in medieval vernacular romances, the fountain in *Floris and Blauncheflur* is actually an extremely compromised and complicated object when examined within the larger context of the narrative.

In an interesting mix of eastern custom and western mores, the Sultan of

Babylon has a harem at his disposal, but he does not browse among his many choices night after night. Instead, he marries a new maiden at the end of each year, discarding the previous one. He uses the magic fountain to weed out unsuitable brides. This fountain, which runs with blood and screams, is thus capable, apparently, of impersonating the young woman at the precise moment of penetration, as it were; that is, what caused her to shed the blood of virginity. (The screaming does not only alert those who may not be able to see the blood, but also suggests that first intercourse is necessarily painful. As we shall see, pain often constitutes evidence of virginity.)

Once the maidens have passed the first test, they must undergo a second test, which is, as we would say today, rigged. Growing alongside the magic fountain in the Sultan's private garden is another wonder, called "þe tree of loue" (631). The chosen virgins are led under this tree, and the one on which the blossoms fall is made the next Queen. However:

> ȝif any mayden þer is
> þat þe Amyral telleþ of more pris,
> þe flour shal be to her sent
> þrouȝ art of enchauntement. (637–40)

> [If there is a particular maiden that the Sultan considers to be the worthiest (or "the most valuable"), the blossom shall be sent to her by magical art.]

In other words, this tree is not at all magical, but is manipulated by the Sultan's own "art" – and desire. This passage follows so quickly upon the description of the magical fountain that it ought to give a reader pause: what are we to think of the efficacy of the fountain, if the tree is obviously a fraud perpetrated by the Sultan? The two signifiers, fountain and tree, participate in a destabilizing exchange by virtue of their narrative juxtaposition. That a signifier can be so patently false as the tree casts doubt on the signifier immediately preceding it – namely, the fountain. The story of the fountain and the tree in *Floris and Blauncheflur* demonstrates how a literary test of virginity is sited not in the private and physical (feminine) body, but in material objects that apparently have already undergone reification, and now function as completely separate from the psyche, individual and/or collective.

Hymenologies

It may be helpful at this point to anticipate part of the argument in Chapter 1, "Hymenologies: the multiple signs of virginity." Today, the primary physiological "sign" of virginity in women is considered to be the "unbroken" hymen; "proof" of first intercourse is the flow of hymeneal blood. I use scare quotes here to emphasize that even at the end of the twentieth century, the hymen is commonly figured in ways that do not coincide with the known medical facts. Considered to be the physiological mark *par excellence* of virginity, the hymen is in fact a notoriously unstable and ambiguous concept, with an anxious and uncertain history. The basic assumption that the presence of the hymen is proof of virginity hardly varies across a wide range of discourses and registers today, from technical medical texts to popular oral lore to representations of the virgin in literature (high and low), films, and television.

In medieval medical treatises, however, the hymen was recognized as but one of many physiological signs of virginity. The concept of the hymen, the notion that it was a normal feature of female anatomy, did not have the same sort of currency in the medical literature of antiquity and the Middle Ages that it has in today's gynecology. One way to approach the "discovery" or "invention" of the hymen is to ask to what degree it has been recognized as a discrete structure in female anatomy. This is not to say that the structure was not always "there," but to suggest that its meaning or import *as* a structure was not always in operation. In the ancient Greek medical and natural historical corpus (that is, in Aristotle's works, the texts now known as the Hippocratic corpus, and in those texts attributed to Galen), we find no description of the hymen as it is defined and illustrated in, for example, *Gray's Anatomy*, or in the more popular *AMA Encyclopedia of Medicine* and *The New Our Bodies Our Selves: A Book By and For Women*. (The word *hymen* does appear in one medical text of antiquity, but this is a special case. See Chapter 1 for further discussion.) *Gray's Anatomy* defines the hymen as "a thin fold of mucous membrane ... the internal surfaces of the fold are normally folded to contact each other and the vaginal orifice appears as a cleft between them," and goes on to add that the hymen "has no established function."[32] According to the most recent *AMA Encyclopedia of Medicine*, the hymen is the "thin fold of membrane surrounding the vaginal opening. The hymen has a central perforation that is usually stretched or torn by the use of tampons or during first sexual intercourse."[33]

In recent years, in response to the growing number of child sexual-abuse cases in which expert testimony is called for, a small, quite technical, body of literature has evolved in which the hymen is described, measured, and classified according to what strikes a non-medical person as an arcane morphology. In this literature, the hymen is described as "annular," "crescentic," "fimbriated," "septated," or "cribriform," terminology that attests to the fact that the size, shape, and thickness of the hymen can vary remarkably from girl to girl, woman to woman.[34] It may be barely discernible, simply a thin ridge of tissue that edges the vaginal opening, or a more obvious tissue with one or more perforations.[35] In rare cases, a woman may be found to have an imperforate hymen, a condition that requires surgical attention. Given the pronounced variations in size and shape from woman to woman, perhaps it would be more accurate to identify the hymen as a *site* than as an anatomical *part*. To make an analogy: we all have insteps, but to identify precisely where the "top" of the instep is would be very difficult. However, if identifying the exact location of the top of the instep were, in some Swiftian fashion, crucial to social identity, then insteps would become the subject of much controversy indeed.

In her elegant study, *Greek Virginity*, Giulia Sissa says, "as an organ of virginity, the hymen of imagination is a cover."[36] She continues:

The hymen today is a part of the body whose function as sign or *signaculum*, hence as seal, is alleged to be valued and whose actual existence is not questioned. It is a sort of biological undergarment protecting the female genitals. ... the conviction [is] that this membranous veil is as natural a part of the female body as the clitoris and that its rupture is universally acknowledged to be a bloody injury ... Is the hymen perhaps a hypostasis, a fetish, an article of faith? Neither mariology nor psychoanalysis nor forensic medicine nor erotic literature can renounce belief in this material token of female intactness.[37]

In a way, the hymen *had* to be invented. How else to read the figurative language in the Song of Songs ("A garden locked, a fountain sealed" [4: 12])? How else to understand Ambrose on the nature of virginity ("And close your vessel discretely ... Lock it with the key of integrity" and "open your mind, preserve your seal"[38])? The hymen is *not* a seal; it cannot be broken, pierced, or perforated. But the hymen *is* a seal; it is an (ideological) barred door, a sealed fountain, the gateway to a *hortus conclusus*. We have stepped into metaphor, and only as a metaphor can a hymen be "broken" or "lost": the figural has shifted into the pseudo-factual. As we shall see, the many attempts to fix virginity in/on the body are inevitably compromised by recourse to metaphors and metonyms – tropes which make visible not only virginity's constructed character, but its gendered and heterosexualized nature as well.

The paradox of virginity

Mary Louise Pratt argues that "people and groups are constituted not by single unified belief systems, but by competing self-contradictory ones."[39] While we no longer view the "Middle Ages" as a product of a unified, monologic discourse or as a set of fixed polarities, Pratt's point is worth remembering as we examine the construction and representation of virginity in medieval culture. Verifying virginity is a theme that recurs across a number of discourses, but how it is represented can vary immensely. I try to capture this variety and its conflicts by reading a wide assortment of texts in English, French, German, and Latin. Though my methodology sometimes has much in common with the survey or *Toposforschung* of traditional medieval scholarship, I move beyond the conventions of the traditional survey in order to interpret selected texts, using feminist criticism and gender studies as a frame and a guide.

The motif of the chastity test (and/or ordeal) antedates the corpus of medieval texts under consideration here. Thus a chastity test often has a curious ahistorical feel to it. In vernacular romance, for example, the test sometimes seems to have been included merely because it was available as a trope. While it may have a crucial intratextual function, the episode of the test rarely connects to or reflects the immediate cultural and historical moment that produced the romance in the first place. Donna Haraway, in a very different context, observes that:

Technologies and scientific discourses can be partially understood as formalizations, i.e., as frozen moments, of the fluid social interactions constituting them, but they should also be viewed as instruments for enforcing meanings.[40]

Always an effect of a confluence of discourses and generic constraints, the chastity test may be seen as an example of such a "formalization" or "frozen moment" functioning as an "instrument" that defines and constructs female virginity/chastity. Its very repetition from text to text, a repetition that links an episode in one text to another episode in another text in a hermeneutic (and performative) chain, attests to the chastity test's continuing value in activating complex narratives about female virginity and its cultural uses.[41] Yet as we saw in *Floris and Blaunche-flur*, such "instruments" for verifying virginity are themselves not foolproof and absolute, but subject to manipulation – a fact which is repeatedly foregrounded in almost all of the texts that I consider here. This is one reason that, while I occasionally move from history to literary text and back again, my primary interest lies in the troping of virginity/chastity as a paradox. In this respect, the (sometimes-oppositional) theories of Jacques Derrida and Jacques Lacan have proved useful (though their theories rarely appear in full orthodox force). By interrogating the very systems that are predicated upon its verifiability, virginity defies close scrutiny and resists definition. Thus virginity contains within it the seeds of its own deconstruction; it is an "absence of event," to borrow a phrase from Derrida.[42] My borrowings from Lacan are less quotable and more abstract: in formulating the operations of desire as presence and absence, he has provided me with a language that best captures the paradox that is virginity.

In Chapter 1, "Hymenologies: the multiple signs of virginity," I examine embodied virginity/chastity as it is discussed in medical treatises of antiquity and the Middle Ages, from Soranus (second century AD) to Avicenna (eleventh century) and Averroës (twelfth century), to pseudo-Albertus Magnus (thirteenth century). In classical and medieval texts, the uterus was thought to be the single most important part of female anatomy. While this chapter is primarily intended to be a survey, I argue that the Greek model of the uterus – an open vessel with a constricted neck – was central to the idea of virginity in Greek medical texts. Though the Greeks did not discuss the constriction or relaxation of the uterus as an index of virginity (that is, as something that would indicate the presence or absence of chastity), medieval authors explicitly cite the shape or condition of the uterus as one such sign. In fact, it is the condition of the uterus, not the hymen, which is the sign of virginity *par excellence* in medieval texts, with the blood of first intercourse being a more important sign than the hymen. (In medieval gynecology, the presence of blood did not *ipso facto* indicate a hymen.) I also discuss other methods for verifying virginity that appear in medieval medical literature, such as examining the urine, observing the effects of certain decoctions and fumigations, and even reading astrological signs.[43]

One finds, as well, numerous recipes for faking virginity in medical texts. I argue that the sheer variety of ways to test virginity – and of ways to cheat on a test – undermines rather than supports the idea of a stable, readable, knowable female body. Finally, I discuss what the early patristic writers and medieval scholiasts have to say about verifying female virginity. All of these churchmen express concern, and often disdain, for the idea that virginity can be subjected to medical scrutiny. (However, as we shall see, medieval canonists often called for physical examinations in certain legal cases.) As Ambrose puts it, a *virgo intacta* is not the same as a *virgo integra*. For the scholars of the Church, the proof of virginity/chastity is not to be located in the body physical, but in the body ecclesiastical.

The body ecclesiastical is the subject of Chapter 2, "'Armour of Proof': the virgin and the church in hagiography," in which I discuss proofs of virginity as they have been conventionalized in the discourse of hagiography. The "proofs" under discussion have little in common with the medical and magical tests for physiological virginity or marital fidelity that are treated in Chapter 1. Here, I make what I hope is a useful distinction between a "test" of virginity, which suggests that the subject's virginity is in doubt, and a "proof" of virginity, which is a public affirmation of the "fact" of virginity/chastity. Though I cite a number of examples of such proofs from various late antique and medieval sources, my main focus is the thirteenth-century *Legenda Aurea* and its retellings of the stories of Agatha, Agnes, and Lucy, celebrated virgin martyrs of late antiquity.

When Eusebius makes the statement that a certain pagan governor, frustrated in his attempts to break the virgins he has consigned to torture, was thus "always defeated by women," he suggests its obverse: Christianity is defended – shielded – by women.[44] I explore how and why the virgin body comes to function as a metonym – a rhetorical shield – for the Church, particularly in the tale of circumvented rape. In this tale, a consecrated virgin is threatened by a pagan official (or frustrated lover) or sent to the brothel, but is protected by a miracle. The miracle serves as proof that the menaced girl or woman is indeed a virgin; however, it also affirms, even celebrates, the power of the Church to identify and legitimate the paradigmatic Christian virgin while obscuring the sources of that power. Moreover, the narrative of circumvented rape paradoxically makes most visible that which should be most hidden from view; that is, the virgin body, while masking (or avoiding) the historical and material facts of rape. This rhetoric of simultaneous display and disguise seeks to remove the virgin martyr from history in order to re-place her in an idealized, transcendent narrative more in keeping with the Church's image of itself.

I move to the discourses of romance and the *lai* in Chapter 3, "'Love's Traces': The Lady and the Test in Romance," in order to examine the literary representation of the ordeal of chastity, in which marital chastity, that is, sexual fidelity, is the subject of proof. I read Heinrich von dem Türlin's *Diu Krône* (1215–20); Robert Biket's *Lai du Cor* (third quarter of the twelfth century); Jean Renart's *Romance of the Rose*, also known as *Guillaume de Dole* (early thirteenth century); the Italian *Tristan* (*La Tavola Ritonda*, second quarter of the fourteenth century); and Malory's retelling of the Tristan story in the *Morte Darthur* (completed c. 1470; printed by Caxton in 1485). Once again, it is necessary to be precise about terminology, for a chastity "ordeal," while it may have much in common with the proofs of virginity as discussed in Chapter 3, is emphatically a matter of performance – in both the Butlerian and the theatrical sense – as the faithful wife must swear an oath, and/ or successfully complete an impossible, magical, or dangerous task in order to demonstrate her chastity.

In vernacular romance and the *lai*, the chastity ordeal typically depends upon a fetishized magical object – a drinking horn, a cloak, or other common article – and, in the case of the equivocal oath, upon fetishized language itself. On first impression, the ordeal seems to function as a didactic lesson, if not a warning, for women; however, the ordeal as it appears in these texts has a curious habit of boomeranging on the men who have insisted upon it in the first place. In Lacanian terms, the ordeal, a quite literal example of the Law of the Father, reinforces the bar separating the Imaginary from the Symbolic; at the same time, the chastity-testing story and its ambiguous ending undermines the very idea of any such Law functioning absolutely.

In Chapter 4, "Oxymoronic bodies: male virgins in hagiography and romance," I discuss the figure of the male virgin. Building upon Chapter 2, I distinguish between the proofing of virginity and the *assaying* of virginity: in the corpus of late antique and medieval hagiography, women are invariably threatened with rape; men, however, are threatened with seduction; that is, with the temptations of the flesh, not with sexual assault. I argue that the rhetoric of seduction found in the tale of the assayed male virgin is designed to direct our attention away from the male virgin (ostensible object of desire) and toward his seductress (ostensible instrument of desire), a strategy that checks the trajectory of the potentially fragmenting (and socially feminizing) gaze, leaving masculine subjectivity intact. In fact, it seems that male virginity is made intelligible only by reference to an elaborate feminized and feminizing signifying system. This is particularly evident in the tenth-century legend of Pelagius, in which Pelagius, as the object of the caliph's desire, is represented under the sign of the feminine.

I then turn to medieval romance, to Malory's *Morte Darthur*, arguing that the male virgin in this text can best be recognized or represented through a semiotics of the feminine. When the male body is threatened with penetration and fragmentation – that is, at the very moment when we would expect it to be most visible – either the fetishized female body is substituted for it, or the male body is feminized. Thus masculinity, along with the code of knighthood that constitutes it, remains protected from critique. I also consider what is perhaps the most famous medieval example of assayed male chastity: the episode of Gawain and the Lady in *Sir Gawain and the Green Knight* (c. 1400), arguing that Gawain's resolute adherence to his vow of chastity further compounds the problem of masculine identity as it is represented in this text.

In Chapter 5, "Multiple Virgins and Contemporary Virginities," I move from the Middle Ages to the present and explore modern ideas about verifying virginity and chastity. I opened this Introduction with a scene from *The Rebel Angels* in which Maria demystifies the legend of the Vestal Virgin and the sieve for her undergraduates while illustrating a chemistry lesson. She then tells the story to a group of sophisticated academics, who go on to intellectualize the problem of ascertaining virginity. Yet one can imagine Maria's first audience, those engineering students, gleefully staging the sieve trick at the next fraternity party, thereby restoring this ancient "test" to the mix of contemporary popular lore about virginity. It is from this stock of popular lore (film, television, popular fiction, and personal narrative, including responses to a Web site that I created on the subject of verifying virginity) that I draw my examples in this chapter.

When we – that is, we as inheritors of Western European culture, whether we are scholars or not – look back on the Middle Ages, we are faced with two equally alluring but mutually exclusive temptations: to see medieval people as very much like ourselves, or to see them as radically different. In late twentieth-century America, no one would think of trying to ascertain if a woman has had intercourse by looking at which way her breasts point or by administering a urine test. These methods strike us as ludicrous and ignorant. Yet there are many today, from purveyors of pornography to Christian fundamentalists, who still believe (or make a tactical decision to believe) that verifying virginity is necessary, important – and possible. The methodology for ascertaining virginity may have changed, but the desire to do so has not, and for many of the same reasons medieval people wanted to verify virginity. In fact, we can still find traces of certain "medieval" ideas circulating in contemporary popular culture: for example, it is commonly believed, as it was in the Middle Ages, that in comparison to the vagina of a sexually experienced woman, a virgin's vagina is "tighter," and a virgin will inevitably (and perhaps should) experience pain at first intercourse. This motif surfaces quite regularly in modern romance novels, in which the heroine triumphantly and happily bears her pain, making a perverse gift of it to her lover. Moreover, in contemporary popular culture, as in the Middle Ages, running parallel to the narrative of verifying virginity is the narrative of faking or simulating virginity: in fact, as I will discuss, women today may avail themselves of hymen "reconstruction" surgery in order to do so.

One fact that quickly emerges in an examination of late twentieth-century American ideas about virginity is the degree to which virginity, in addition to being gendered feminine, is the product of a dominant heterosexual paradigm; that is, "loss" or absence of virginity is usually defined in terms of the penetration of a vagina by a penis. This is a subtext that runs through earlier chapters: in the final chapter, I address this issue more explicitly, examining the ways in which representations of gendered virginity in popular culture help to secure what Adrienne Rich calls "compulsory heterosexuality." Both respecting and transgressing the boundaries of the female virgin body are actions and ideologies that attempt to fix identities through biological and social difference, while sanctioning the "opposite" sex as the object of desire. These two distinct and contradictory narratives – one in which female virginity is praised and revered, the other in which female virginity is "lost" or "taken" – valorize heterosex while suppressing gay and lesbian constructions of sex and desire.

Virginity matters

Judith Butler, in *Bodies that Matter: On the Discursive Limits of "Sex"*, describes how she initially made an attempt to "fix bodies as simple objects of thought." However, she found that

> Not only did bodies tend to indicate a world beyond themselves, but this movement beyond their own boundaries, a movement of boundary itself, appeared to be quite central to what bodies "are."[45]

There is no better example of the body exceeding its own physical boundaries than that of virginity, which exists on the cusp between the body and culture. By definition, virginity is an abstraction greater than the sum of body parts.

1 Hymenologies
The multiple signs of virginity

Ne jompre ek no discordant thyng yfeere,
As thus, to usen termes of physik
In loves termes ...
> *Troilus and Criseyde* II. 1037–39

[Don't jumble together jarring things – medical terms, for example, don't fit the language of love ...]

The virgin and the test

"J'ai nom Jehanne la Pucelle," said Jeanne the peasant girl when she first met Charles VII. And she has been known as *la Pucelle* – the Maid – ever since. To the modern sensibility, the virginity of Jeanne d'Arc would seem to be the least of her attributes, not one worth immortalizing, at least when compared to her ability to wield a sword, devise military strategies, and persuade men to follow her into battle – let alone her ability to communicate with St. Michael, St. Catherine, and St. Margaret. However, Jeanne herself, and the soldiers, captains, dukes, kings, priests, and bishops who met Jeanne, believed that all of her gifts, and especially her visions, were the result of or at least connected to her virginity.

According to the testimony at Jeanne's Trial of Rehabilitation (1456), as Jeanne waited for her first audience with the King in Poitiers in 1429, Queen Yolande of Sicily (mother-in-law to Charles VII), Madame de Gaucourt (wife of the Governor of Chinon), and Madame de Trèves (wife of Robert le Maçon) were charged with determining Jeanne's virginity.[1] Jeanne's squire Jean d'Aulon testified that

> the said Maid was seen, visited and privately looked at and examined in the secret parts of her body, but after they had seen and looked at everything which ought to be looked at in such a case, the aforesaid lady [Yolande] said and related to the king that she and the said ladies found that she was certainly a true and entire maid, in whom could be found no corruption nor mark of violence.[2]

At Rouen, after Jeanne was captured by the English, she was examined again, either by Anne of Burgundy (Duchess of Bedford) or by Anne's women.[3] The Duke of Bedford, so the story goes, witnessed this examination through a spyhole.[4] Jeanne was declared a *virgo intacta*, but it was noted that she must have injured herself at some time in the past, perhaps by sitting astride her horse.[5]

The physician Guillaume de la Chambre also testified on Jeanne's behalf at her posthumous Rehabilitation: "I know, in so far as one can know by the art of medicine, that she was a virgin and intact. For I saw her almost naked ... I felt her loins, and her flesh was very firm, so far as I could see by the look of it."[6] Marguerite la Touroulde, who sheltered Jeanne at Bourges in 1429, also testified at this time, saying: "I saw her several times in the bath and in the hot-room, and so far as I could see I believe that she was a virgin."[7]

Culled from the first- and second-hand reports that make up the documents of the Rehabilitation, these statements raise more questions for modern readers than they answer. How was Jeanne examined? *What* was examined? What sort of visual or physical evidence sufficed?

In this chapter, I hope to fill in the gaps in the narrative of Jeanne's examination by tracing out what medieval people believed about testing or verifying virginity. I will begin my survey by discussing how female physiology, especially "virginal" physiology, was represented in classical and medieval medical texts. As we shall see, it was the condition of the uterus, not the presence or absence of the hymen, that was believed to be the most reliable sign of female virginity. In fact, as my chapter title suggests, the hymen is just one of many signs of virginity detailed in medieval medical treatises: other methods for verifying virginity run the gamut from the medical to the pseudo-medical to the magical and the miraculous.[8] In addition to discussing various tests for virginity, I also examine the many recipes for faking virginity. The sheer variety of ways to test virginity – and of the ways to cheat on a test – calls into question the idea of a stable, readable, knowable female body. I argue that, in the end, all tests for verifying virginity are inherently flawed. Finally, I consider patristic commentary on the physical signs of virginity. According to the Church, the body is not the only, much less the ideal, carrier of the "meiðhades merke," as the author of *Hali Meiðhad* puts it.[9] The Church Fathers who refer to medical lore and the bodily proofs of virginity do so only to dismiss such proofs. The body cannot be trusted, but "virginal" or "chaste" behavior can, particularly when that behavior is dictated by the Church. By locating virginity/chastity in *disciplina ecclesiastica præscripta* ("precepts of ecclesiastical discipline"[10]), as Tertullian says, patristic commentators make clear that they thought of virginity not as a pre-cultural essence lodged in the physical body, but as a series of acts and identifications that must constantly be performed according to an institutionalized "discipline."

An archaeology of virginity

"The Jews disdain the beauty of virginity ... the Greeks admire it in amazement, but only the Church of God praises it," declares John Chrysostom in *De Virginitate*, summing up what was for him the essential difference between Christian culture and its antecedents.[11] Chrysostom's opinion notwithstanding, we find plenty of evidence that virginity – that is, female virginity – was highly valued in ancient Israel, albeit only as a temporary state before marriage. In fact, it seems that the Israelites and, later, the Jews of the Talmudic era, esteemed female virginity enough to attempt to verify its presence or absence – if, that is, the handful of chastity-testing narratives recorded in the Pentateuch and the Talmud reflect actual tests administered to women and are not simply literary inventions. Even literary inventions, of course, have their cultural significances and uses, and are therefore worth noting here.

One passage in particular would seem to highlight the cultural importance of virginity among the ancient Israelites, and, in its narrative discontinuities, to serve as an example of how a given culture may mystify virginity and its proofs. According to Deuteronomy 22: 13–20, if a man believes that his wife was not a virgin at the time of marriage, he may declare publicly that he did not find, as the Hebrew has it, *betulim*, "evidence of virginity," or, better, "virginness." (Jerome translates *betulim* as *signa virginitatis* in the Latin Vulgate, and Wycliff translates it as "þe tooknes of here maydyn-hood.") It is up to the bride's parents to furnish such "tokens": they are directed to "spread the garment [Hebrew *simla*, 'garment,' 'blanket'; Vulgate, *vestimentum*] before the elders of the city" so that the elders may adjudicate the case.[12] A modern reader may reasonably conclude that such "tokens" refer to traces of blood on the garment (or wedding sheet), yet the text itself does not furnish the basis for such a conclusion. It is difficult to say whether such phrasing in the original Hebrew assumes an informed audience or if it is intended to be obscure, or perhaps merely euphemistic.

The Babylonian Talmud (generally believed to have been redacted around AD 500; it certainly contains materials of more ancient provenance) records several cases in which husbands "put forward the claim of blood" after the wedding night.[13] I cite the Talmud with some caution, since parts of Deuteronomy antedate parts of the Talmud by anywhere from five hundred to a thousand years. We do not know how ancient Israelites constructed female physiology at the time Deuteronomy 20: 13–20 was written, though we do know that in many Near-Eastern societies, the display of the wedding sheet is an ancient custom that continues to this day (see Chapter 5).[14] And while scholars have long noted the influence of Hellenistic thought on the Talmud, we cannot determine what the redactors of the Talmud may have absorbed about Hellenistic medicine and constructs of the body to incorporate into their commentaries. In fact, as we shall see, Hellenistic medicine has very little to say about the signs of physical virginity. The point I want to make is that the Israelites of the pre-Hellenistic period and the Jews of the Talmudic era may have recognized blood as evidence of virginity, but that does not mean that they recognized what we call the hymen as the *source* of such blood.

While the redactors of the Talmud recorded cases in which the sign of blood is adduced as proof of virginity, they also recognized that blood could be an unreliable sign of virginity. One case is cited in which a man married into a family in which the women "have neither blood of menstruation nor blood of virginity."[15] In another case, it was noted that the bride was suffering from malnutrition, and therefore could not produce the blood of virginity.[16] Finally, it was acknowledged in the Talmud that it is possible for a woman to injure herself in some way unrelated to intercourse (as the Talmud euphemistically puts it, a woman may have injured herself with "a piece of wood," thereby causing the blood of virginity to flow). In such cases, according to the rabbis, the absence of blood at first intercourse would not "prove" that the woman had previously lost her virginity.[17]

In fact, the rabbis of the Talmud, though they believed that female virginity was valuable and, in general, verifiable, never maintained that the "proofs" of bodily virginity were infallible. Perhaps this is why we find another kind of "evidence" for virginity in the Talmud: in tractate *Kethuboth*, it is recorded that Rabbi Gamaliel performed a virginity test, calling for "two handmaids, one who is a virgin and one who had intercourse with a man." The two women were placed upon a cask of wine. The Rabbi, we are told, was able to smell the fumes of the wine through the mouth of the nonvirgin; however, the wine was undetectable on the breath of the virgin.[18] Elsewhere, in the same tractate, in speaking to an indignant husband who had failed to find evidence of his wife's virginity, Rabbi Gamaliel suggests: "perhaps you moved aside"; that is, had coitus without causing the woman to bleed. The Rabbi goes on to develop an elaborate metaphor of the vagina as a barred door, telling the story of a certain man who "came to his house and found the door locked. If he moves aside the bolt of the door, he finds it locked." The "bolt" is the penis, the "door" the vagina, and the "bar" on the door presumably a material or metaphorical hymen.[19] As a matter of fact, loss of virginity is sometimes expressed in the Talmud by saying that the new husband has found an "open opening" – written with scare quotes in the Soncino Press translation of the Babylonian Talmud, thus attesting to the difficulties of translation – a particularly ambiguous expression that captures the conflation of the literal and the metaphorical, and that furnishes a construct of the female body that is both permeable and impermeable.[20] Such imagery, taken together with the claustral metaphors of the Song of Songs (dated anywhere from the tenth to the third century BC), might tempt us to conclude that the Jews of late antiquity believed in a sealed, hermetic, virginal body. However, it may be more accurate to say that the Jews sometimes chose to represent the female body as closed. In some contexts, the image of a sealed body may simply have been more productive, resonating in a much more dramatic way than the image of an opened or openable body. Patristic writers may have borrowed this image of a claustral body – or (re)invented it – when they came to describe the bodily integrity of the Virgin Mary. I will return to the notion of a sealed body when I discuss medical texts, below.

Whatever Chrysostom's opinions on the Jews, he is partially correct when he speaks of Greek "amazement" at virginity (though whether he means the amazement expressed in traditional Hellenistic thought or that of his contemporaries is not clear). As Giulia Sissa has demonstrated in *Greek Virginity*, female virginity (*parthenia*) had its sacred aspect in Greek (and later Roman) society, but was not so tied to physical fact (and therefore subject to change or loss) as it was to essence or being. Representations in Greek literary texts of the loss of virginity do not necessarily mark a physiological event; more often, they document a social event: the initiation of the girl into the roles and responsibilities of adulthood. The "tokens of virginity" were many and varied in Hellenistic culture, and could be found in the body *and* outside of it, within the matrix of the culture that created the "body" in the first place.

Certainly no attitude of amazement toward virginity can be detected in the medical treatises known collectively as the Hippocratic Corpus (fifth/fourth centuries BC). Generally speaking, Greek physicians were more concerned about pregnancy and childbirth and their attendant dangers and diseases than about virginity, which had its own etiology. According to humoral theory, sexual abstinence was presumed to upset the balance of hot and cold, moistness and dryness, a balance believed necessary to health in both men and women. Because it was thought to open up the vaginal passageway and stimulate a woman's humors, intercourse was considered to be an efficacious remedy if certain symptoms were presented by a patient; pregnancy might also be prescribed for some women.[21] In Greek and Roman society in which marriage was the norm, the "ills" of virginity were only temporary.

The Hippocratic texts, and, later, the important medical treatises authored by Soranus of Ephesus and Galen of Pergamon (both second century AD), contain information about the differences between the virginal body and the body of a woman who has experienced intercourse. While such data are usually found in general discussions of health, and are not necessarily provided with virginity tests in mind, it is easy to see how such information could be applied toward the (actual or hypothetical) testing of virginity.

Before I continue, I should say a few things in general about the dominant – and often contradictory – paradigms that shaped the construction and experience of the body in antiquity, especially since these paradigms are reproduced with few alterations in medieval medicine. Medieval physicians and natural philosophers knew that the Latin translations, epitomes, and summaries of Greek texts (some of which came to them directly from Greek sources before the eleventh century, and then indirectly from Greek to Arabic to Latin) did not constitute a monolithic, unproblematic body of knowledge.[22] Many medieval writers recorded the contradictions that they found in their sources without comment, while others attempted to synthesize and reconcile theories that were obviously at odds with each other. Moreover, some medieval authors felt obliged to adjust or delete certain material in order to bring it into line with prevailing Christian mores.

Medieval physicians and natural historians accepted the classical notion that ontology both determines and transcends biology.[23] The medicalization of sex difference in antiquity and the Middle Ages was based not so much on empirical observation of the human body, but on adducing the "facts" of cultural experience, in which the male and the masculine were considered the ideal. The male body was the uncorrupted base text, as it were; the female, an imperfect copy. For example, when Galen describes female anatomy, he does so by using male anatomy as the standard: "all the parts ... that men have, women have too, the difference between them lying in only one thing, ... in women the parts are within [the body], whereas in men they are outside."[24] He adds that one should be able to "turn outwards the woman's [genitals], turn inward, so to speak, and fold double the man's, and you find them the same in both in every respect."[25] By quoting Galen, I do not mean to imply that his theory of sex "difference" was the only one available in antiquity and the Middle Ages, but to acknowledge that it certainly was an influential one. Neither am I arguing for a dominant or singular "one-sex" model as Thomas Laqueur does in *Making Sex: Body and Gender from the Greeks to Freud*.[26] However, I would like to stress the power and pervasiveness of the rhetoric of analogy that underpins not only Galen's conception of the human body but also Aristotle's notion of the superior, perfected man and inferior, flawed woman. In this model, body heat, as Gail Kern Paster puts it, serves as an "attribute of sex difference."[27] According to Aristotle, the male body is more perfect than the female because it is hotter and drier, and thus better equipped to achieve the proper balance of humors necessary to good health. The female body, in comparison, is colder and moister; therefore, a woman is more prone to physical ailments and mental disorders.[28]

Partially located within this model of physiology-by-analogy, but not completely contained by it, is another set of competing ideas specifically concerned with human reproduction: the Aristotelian "one-seed" theory that asserted that only males contributed the necessary materials for making a new life, while females simply served as a vessel for the man's seed; and the Galenic "two-seed" theory, in which both males and females supplied the crucial matter in equal amounts.[29] Both the one-seed and two-seed theories have implications for defining and determining virginity, as we shall see; for example, one of the commentators on the thirteenth-century text *De secretis mulierum* (attributed to Albertus Magnus in the Middle Ages) avers that one "true sign [signum uerissimus] of virginity is if the man feels the woman's seed flow abundantly."[30]

The medicalization of virginity

In classical and medieval texts, the uterus was thought to be the single most important part of female anatomy. How this organ was constructed was central to the medical idea of virginity in Greek texts. Sissa says that the female body in medical texts is described as always potentially open at both ends, with two sets of lips at rest against each other. The labia majora and minora are not the "lips" Greek physicians had in mind; rather, the mouth that they imagined is found further in, at the entrance to the uterus, that is, what Galen calls the "neck."[31] Sissa cites Aristotle's *Historia Animalium* and the anonymous *On Generation*, in which certain verbs recur that describe the uterus as closing like a mouth; she also quotes from the Hippocratic *Diseases of Women*, which refers to the entrance of the uterus as "the mouth of the uterus." Oribasius, who compiled numerous Hippocratic works in the fourth century AD, also says that the uterus leads to the genitals, just like a mouth.[32] These medical metaphors are consistent with Greek literary depictions of virginity. The virginal oracle at Delphi, for example, open to the god but closed to men, is imagined as a conduit.[33]

Ann Ellis Hanson agrees with Sissa, but argues that classical medical descriptions of the entrance to the uterus as a closed mouth, a set of pursed lips, are shadowed by another image, that of the uterus closed off by an imperforate membrane: uterus as sealed vessel. She says that this concept – the uterus as "an upside-down jug" with a stopper – may be what is left of a pre-Hippocratic, popular (vs. learned) anatomy.[34] As support for such an idea, she cites a variety of literary allusions, as well as the existence of classical amulets which "often picture a uterus equipped with a lock at the mouth."[35] As an illustration in a tenth-century medical MS demonstrates, the idea that the uterus was shaped like a jug survived at least into the early Middle Ages: in this MS, the uterus looks very much like an upside-down amphora, with a distinctive neck and flattened rim.[36] Is the patristic representation of female anatomy, in which the sealed womb is so crucial to the doctrine of the Immaculate Conception, a revival of pre-Aristotelian and pre-Hippocratic medicine? Hanson, in her response to Guilia Sissa's work, sees no connection between the two.[37] And while Peter Brown has documented the many examples of the image of the *hortus conclusus* or *vas clausum* in patristic texts and has examined the ideological motivations behind the development of such metaphors, he is silent on any sort of continuity between popular classical medical ideas or Near-Eastern notions as evidenced in the Talmud and Christian imagery.[38] Such a history, beyond the scope of the present study, remains to be written.

Galen describes the "neck" (that is, the cervix) of the uterus as capable of opening and closing, expanding and contracting, depending on need – it opens to receive semen (both male and female) during coitus, but closes once conception takes place in order to retain and protect the fetus.[39] The neck of the uterus is "crooked and winding ... when the semen is not passing in or the fetus passing out."[40] During intercourse or childbirth, the neck straightens out, but then returns to its earlier state; that is, the state before first intercourse. The medical literature assumes that the opening and closing of the uterus has some effect on its elasticity; once the uterus expands to allow the menses to pass out, receive seed, or carry a fetus, it never contracts back to its original state.[41] This more relaxed condition can be discerned either visually or manually by a physician or midwife – or even, in some cases, "felt" by the male partner during intercourse.

In the Hippocratic text *Diseases of Young Girls*, it is said that adolescent girls may suffer from a buildup of blood that cannot be released. Such a girl may become delirious and violent, throw herself about, or even attempt to strangle herself. "My advice to young girls ... is to marry as soon as possible," says the author, adding, "in effect, if they get pregnant, they will be cured."[42] In the text known as *Diseases of Women II*, a host of remedies are prescribed for this problem in widows, including manual palpitation, binding the abdomen, and oral and vaginal suppositories; the widow is also advised to become pregnant. Different remedies are recommended for virgins, but physicians are advised to encourage young girls to marry.[43] In short, such remedies are predicated upon the notion that the uterus is capable of constriction and relaxation.

The idea that the womb could open and close is also found quite commonly in medieval medical texts. One commentator on *De secretis mulierum* says (following Isidore of Seville), that "the vulva [that is, vagina] is named from the word *valva* because it is the door of the womb" ("vulua dicitur quasi valua, quia est ianua ventris"). He adds that the womb is capable of closing up "like a purse" ("clauditur sicut vna bursa").[44] In a fourteenth-century English text, it is said that when a woman has conceived "þe inner resceyuer is closyd þat þer may no sed entere þerinne tyl che be delyuered" ("the inner reservoir is closed so that no seed can enter until a woman has given birth").[45]

The concept of the open body/open uterus influences the medieval understanding of and treatment for "suffocation of the womb," an affliction that receives a good deal of attention in medieval gynecological treatises. The medieval descriptions of and cures for this illness are worth dwelling upon because they indicate that the medical female body was not constructed as completely closed or sealed, in spite of the metaphorical and literary construction of the impermeable female body. (The Song of Songs contains the most famous and influential example of such a figurative construction: the lover's body is described as "a garden locked, a fountain sealed" [4. 12].) Traces of the Galenic two-seed model are discerned in medieval medical texts when the cause of "suffocation" is attributed either to the retention of the menses or of female seed; in the one-seed model, the uterus may be suffocated because of the retention of menses alone.[46] Heterosexual intercourse was the most efficacious cure in either case, but fumigation, the application of ointments, or even massage was also prescribed, especially for virgins and widows, for whom intercourse was theoretically not an option. In a fifteenth-century English text, the author makes a distinction between suffocation caused by the retention of menses and that caused by the retention of seed. In the latter instance, he advises that:

> it is profitable to haue company with man. But þus vunderstonde: in lawefull company, as with her housebandes and with none other; for in certayn it were better for a man other for a woman to haue þe grettest sekenesse of þe body the whiles þei leven than to ben helyd thorough a dede of lechery other ony other dede ayenst goddis hestys.

> [It is helpful to have relations with a man. But understand what I have to say: the relations must be lawful, such as with her husband and no other; for certainly it is better for man or woman to have the greatest physical illness while they live than to be healed through a deed of lechery or any other deed against God's commands.][47]

If suffocation were caused by the retention of menses, the application of ointments or massage could cause no harm; however, if the disease were caused by the retention of seed, then physicians faced a dilemma, for the expulsion of seed, which is supposed to happen during intercourse, may cause "corruption" in the virgin, as "loss" of virginity is so often expressed in medieval treatises. Aware of this problem, Albertus Magnus asserts that "the hand does not defile or corrupt these [women], but rather cures them" ("manus illas polluere eas vel corrumpere, sed potius medicare eis").[48] Albertus Magnus is not thinking of a break or a rupture of a membrane that would indicate "corruption," but of an emission of seed, which is one crucial way a woman *or* a man could lose virginity. In fact, any emission is innocent if it does not occur during sexual arousal, Albertus Magnus argues in *De Castitate*.[49]

Hymeneal variations

As we have seen, the treatment of certain female diseases in antiquity and then later in the Middle Ages was predicated upon the idea that the female genitals were not sealed or obstructed, either partially or completely. Such a construction of the female body does not rule out the possibility that physicians and midwives either theorized or observed a ridge of tissue inside the vagina – that is, what we today call the hymen – yet the medical writers of antiquity did not name it, include a description of it, or furnish an explanation for its purpose in any of the treatises on female anatomy that we have. Aristotle, for example, who has a good deal to say about the membranes of the body, is silent on the existence of any "virginal membrane." Galen makes no mention of a hymen or membrane covering the entrance of the vagina in his description of the uterus. The references that we do find in ancient and medieval medical and gynecological treatises to an obstructing membrane or ridge of tissue treat such tissue as a medical problem. It is not a part of every woman's physiology, and it is not described as physical proof of virginity.

Soranus is the only writer of antiquity who raises the possibility – only to deny it – that virgins are somehow naturally "sealed." He declares that

> it is a mistake to assume that a thin membrane [ὑμένα, "hymen"] grows across the vagina, dividing it, and that this membrane ... bursts in defloration.[50]

Given the absence of written evidence, it is not clear if such an idea of a membranous seal is a rhetorical red herring, or if it actually circulated within traditional and/or nontraditional medical circles (see Hanson's argument about the image of the uterus as a sealed jug in ancient medical and literary texts, discussed above).

Soranus goes on to say that if there were such a membrane:

> in virgins, the probe ought to meet with resistance (whereas the probe penetrates the deepest point)... . if this membrane, bursting in defloration, were the cause of the pain, then in virgins before defloration excessive pain ought necessarily to follow upon the appearance of menstruation and no more in defloration.[51]

In other words, the onset of menses ought to break this membrane – if it existed. Aline Rousselle, in *Porneia: On Desire and the Body in Antiquity*, argues that arranged marriages, especially of prepubescent girls to older men, skewed the understanding of female anatomy in a number of ways, and may have led to a confusion of the first blood of intercourse with menstrual blood. Because girls often married before the onset of their first menses, it was sometimes thought that coitus "opened" the uterus to allow menstruation.[52]

Soranus offers the following explanation for the blood of first intercourse:

> In virgins the vagina is flattened and comparatively narrow, since it possesses furrows held together by vessels which take their origin from the uterus. And when the furrows are spread apart in defloration, these vessels burst and cause pain and the blood which is usually excreted follows.[53]

At first glance, when we compare Soranus' description of the hymen with modern medical descriptions, they seem quite similar. However, as Ann Hanson and Monica Green point out, what Soranus describes as "furrows" [or "folds," ϲτολιϲι] and "vessels" [ἀγγείων] refers to the sides of the vagina, not to a hymeneal membrane.[54] Soranus denies that the word ὑμένα denotes a specific, discrete part of female anatomy that functions as a seal or veil. By talking about "furrows," he does not identify a *structure* so much as he describes a *site*. In effect, he is not describing what we today call the hymen. Soranus frames his observations on the female genitals not by whether a woman is a virgin or not, but by her age and reproductive status. For example, Soranus says that both the uterus and the vagina change in size in relation to age, and that the neck of the uterus "elongat[es] like the male genital" during intercourse.[55]

Soranus, in denying the existence of a hymen-as-seal, incidentally furnishes two other ways to verify physiological virginity: first, by the shape of the uterus, and second, by the evidence of blood that follows penetration, which is not the result of a broken membrane *per se*, but of tissue sensitive to contact. When, for example, Soranus says that virgins "in their prime of puberty" have smaller uteruses when compared to "women who are older and have already been deflowered," and that the vagina of a virgin is "soft and fleshy" compared to women who have borne children, such statements could be used to determine virginity.[56] Presumably, such a judgment could be made by palpitation, either by a midwife or physician.

We do find descriptions of a ridge of tissue rich in blood vessels which may well refer to the hymen in a handful of influential Arabic texts which were translated into Latin in the Middle Ages. Esther Lastique and Helen Rodnite Lemay are two scholars who argue that the concept of the hymen (that is, the hymen as we recognize it today) originated in the Arabic medical tradition, which was then incorporated into the texts of the Latin West in the early Middle Ages. Lastique and Lemay cite the writers Rhazes (late ninth/early tenth century), Avicenna (eleventh century), and Averroës (twelfth century), all of whom furnish an explanation for the blood of first intercourse. Rhazes describes the vulva as a wrinkled surface covered with veins that break at first intercourse.[57] Avicenna discusses certain delicate membranes full of veins that are destroyed at intercourse.[58] In his *Colliget*, Averroës also declares that "the opening of the vulva of a virgin is wrinkled."[59] In the *Summa conservationis et curationis* (1285), Guilielmus de Saliceto follows Avicenna when he describes the "knot of virginity" ("nodus virginitatis") as "tightly woven together veins and arteries, clearly wrinkled in texture" ("constrictum contextum venis & artariis manifestus rugatum in cuius textura").[60] Such descriptions of the female genitals are still used by gynecologists today, and, like Soranus' description of the uterus and the vagina, speak more to the age of the woman than to her virginal state.

Lastique and Lemay also cite a passage in Albertus Magnus' *De Animalibus*, which most likely reflects the influence of Avicenna and Averroës:

> before corruption, in the neck and at the mouth of the womb of virgins are membranes [*panniculi*] made of a tissue of veins and very fragile ligaments. These are the proven signs of virginity when observed, and which are destroyed by intercourse or even by the penetration of fingers, at which the small amount of blood in them flows out.[61]

However, such evidence for the hymen conceived of as an actual structure must be weighed against Hanson and Green's point about what Soranus meant by the word *hymen*, discussed above. Is Soranus the only extant representative of a lost Western tradition? Did he influence Islamic writers? Was his work then re-transmitted back to the West? Did Arabic writers develop their own descriptions of the hymen – structure or site – independently?[62] Western scholars have just begun to examine, classify, and analyze the corpus of Arabic and Byzantine medical texts that underpin or influence Western medieval medicine. When this work is done, we will have a much clearer understanding of the transmission of medical and gynecological knowledge in the Middle Ages and the part that Soranus' seemingly unique discussion of the hymen and the uterus plays.

If we return to *De secretis mulierum*, we find that the author speaks of "a certain skin [*pellicula*] in the vagina and the bladder" which is broken at first intercourse ("Alia autem causa coadiuuans, quia est quædam pellicula in vulua & vesica quae corrumpitur").[63] This description is consistent with Soranus' description of what he calls "hymen," and with the descriptions of "hymen" in the Arabic texts cited above. A commentator (most likely writing in the fourteenth century) on *De secretis mulierum* adds:

> [A]ll virgins, when they first consort with men, have a certain membrane [*pellicula*] broken, called the hymen [*himen*], and this is the guardian of virginity. It is located near the bladder and the opening of the womb above the vulva. ... it is found in all women when they are first corrupted.[64]

Here, metaphor constructs the hymen: it is "the *guardian* of virginity" ("*custos uirginitatis*"). Moreover, at the very moment the hymen is determined to exist, namely, at the moment of first intercourse, it *ceases* to exist. The author and commentators do not mention blood in this passage; rather, they go on to describe the pain that results from the breaking of this *himen*, adding that "the more [women] have sex, the more they become accustomed to it."[65] In fact, more than one medieval author notes that a woman's pain or difficulty can be read as one of the signs of virginity.

At this point, it may be worth recalling the Galenic model of the human body, in which female reproductive organs are described as analogous to male organs: the ovaries correspond to the testes and the uterus to the scrotum, and so on.[66] (When Soranus compares the neck of the uterus to the penis, above, he has this model in mind.) If one were working within this model, one might conclude that, since men do not have a hymen – that is, a membranous seal – women also should not. This is an important point, though admittedly problematic, given that Soranus and then Avicenna and Averroës describe *something* as unique to female anatomy. Yet we should keep in mind that writers of antiquity and the Middle Ages did not always follow either a Galenic or an Aristotelian model to the exclusion of the other, but sometimes conflated the two.

To men and women in the Middle Ages, what was more pertinent than the existence or exact nature of the hymen was the fact that first intercourse for a woman often resulted in bleeding. The evidence of blood was crucial to the medieval understanding of loss of virginity – more crucial, in fact, than the precise details of female anatomy. But people in medieval times were well aware that bleeding could also result from manual penetration of, or injury to, the female genitals. It was understood, at least by some, that the hymen (however defined) and hymeneal blood ultimately could not serve as a reliable sign of virginity or chastity.

Here and in the Introduction, I have tried to make the point that the hymen has a history: what we recognize as the hymen today was not always considered as such, and even now there is often a considerable gap between learned and popular knowledge about this part of female anatomy. If we trace the etymology of the word *hymen* from Greek through Latin to English, we can observe how the word progressively narrows in meaning, first denoting any sort of bodily membrane, then referring to the womb, and finally coming to mean almost exclusively "virginal membrane" in the early modern period.[67] In fact, in both England and France during the sixteenth and seventeenth centuries, a period in which the number of both learned and popular medical treatises multiplies dramatically, we find a number of physicians and others discussing and describing the hymen – and, often, ardently debating its existence.[68] I cannot stress enough the degree to which the hymen is an overdetermined, widely misunderstood sign precisely because it has never been a fixed part of anatomy – as obvious, say, as other body parts, such as the eyes or the heart (both of which have their own cultural histories, of course). I make this point here because I will have reason to return to the hymen both as an anatomical part and as a metonym throughout this study.

Fail-safe testing?

The thirteenth-century physician Guilielmus de Saliceto understood that blood at first intercourse is an ambiguous sign of virginity. Thus he warned his readers that one should examine the consistency of the blood in order to distinguish between virginal and menstrual blood, for "the blood of the corruption of virginity is less in quantity when compared to the menses; it is much lighter in color and does not pour out."[69] Given that the hymen may not be present in a virgin in the first place, or that it may have been destroyed through some trauma unrelated to sexual intercourse, and that blood itself is not a reliable sign, it is not surprising that we find other ways to verify virginity in medical treatises. It is the opening and closing, open *but* closed, uterus (especially with respect to the emission of seed), which is more often subjected to tests in medical texts.

In his enumeration of ways to tighten the vagina (it was thought that a tight vagina was not only a sign of virginity, but necessary to conception), Guilielmus de Saliceto also suggests that the shape and size of the vagina or cervix can be read as an index of chastity.[70] In *De secretis mulierum*, the author says that, in some cases, if a man can enter a virgin "without any pain to his member [*sine dolore sui membri uirilis*] … [it] is a sign that the woman was first corrupted."[71] One commentator adds, "the vagina [*vulua*] of a virgin is always closed," which would explain the difficulty in penetration.[72]

The presence or absence of a hymen and/or blood, the constriction or relaxation of the uterus, are but three of the many accepted signs of female virginity described in medieval medical and gynecological literature. For example, the author of *De secretis mulierum* recommends that, if a man wants to determine if a particular woman is a virgin, he should examine her urine. The urine of virgins is "clear and lucid, sometimes white, sometimes sparkling."[73] The reason given: "Corrupted women have a muddy urine because of the rupture of the aforementioned skin [*pelliculae*], and male sperm appear on the bottom."[74] In other words, "muddy urine" results when the blood of first intercourse and male sperm "contaminate" the urine. (In the two-seed paradigm, the emission of female "sperm" can also affect the urine.) In *Summa conservationis et curationis*, Guilielmus de Saliceto also advises his readers to perform a urine test. According to Saliceto, a virgin "urinates with a subtle hiss, and indeed takes longer than a small boy" ("cum mingit sibilat subtilius mingit longius quasi quidem puer").[75]

In *De passionibus mulierum*, the fifteenth-century Italian physician Niccolò Falcucci describes a very complicated chastity test involving urinalysis. I quote it in full in order to illustrate the empirical method of the day:

> [I]f a woman is covered with a piece of cloth and fumigated with the best coal, if she is a virgin she does not perceive its odor through her mouth and nose; if she smells it, she is not a virgin. If she takes it in a drink, she immediately voids urine if she is not a virgin. A corrupt woman will also urinate immediately if a fumigation is prepared with cockle. Upon fumigation with dock flowers, if she is a virgin she immediately becomes pale, and, if not, her humor falls on the fire and other things are said about her [et dicuntur etiam alia].[76]

De secretis mulierum contains a similar recipe:

If you want to determine of a virgin has been corrupted, grind up the flowers of a lily and the yellow particles that are in between the flowers, and give her this substance to eat. If she is corrupt, she will urinate immediately.[77]

These tests are not as farfetched as they may first seem, given the medieval construction of the female body. As I mentioned earlier, a number of gynecological remedies called for some sort of fumigation (inhaling sweet or foul odors through the nose and mouth, or allowing such fumes to pass through the vagina) all of which suggest that the female body possesses passages that are not sealed, but merely constricted. Depending upon the illness, a cure by fumigation would facilitate the closing or opening the womb.[78]

A commentator on *De secretis mulierum* repeats a story found in Averroës' *Colliget* about a young girl who was impregnated after bathing in water in which a man had ejaculated. She asks Averroës for help in clearing her name, and indeed, he says that it is possible and natural for the uterus to "extract" semen under such conditions. But the commentator seems to be somewhat dissatisfied with this conclusion,[79] adding:

> The question that arises is, was this girl a virgin or not? We reply briefly that there are two types of corruption. The first takes place through the emission of seed. The second takes place through a wound in the skin of virginity, that is, when the hymen is broken. Thus I would say she was corrupted in the first way because she attracted and emitted seed, but in the second way she was not, for her skin was not broken.[80]

In other words, the girl was not corrupted by penetration, but she *was* corrupted both by the man's and her own emission of seed. If medieval people gave this story any credence, they would have had to imagine the hymen as permeable, for the man's seed can apparently pass through it, without a penis "breaking" it.[81] Once again, we are dealing with a construct of the uterus as constricted and not sealed. This is borne out by the fact that classical and medieval authors took for granted that menstrual blood could be expelled easily enough; if not, there was a pathological reason for the retention of menstrual blood.

De secretis mulierum also lists signs of chastity/virginity that have nothing to do with the physiological or the anatomical, such as exhibits of "shame, modesty, fear, a faultless gait and speech, casting eyes down before men and the acts of men" ("verecunda, timor, cum casto incessu, & loquela, cum despectu applicans se viris & virorum actibus").[82] Such signs derive from a patristic tradition (discussed below) in which the body is viewed as suspect and unreliable; the character, on the other hand, because it is shaped by religious teaching, is much more dependable.

Lapidaries, while not part of the medieval medical mainstream *per se*, also offer suggestions for verifying virginity. In his *De Mineralibus*, Albertus Magnus includes under the description of *gagates* (jet) this chastity test: "if water in which [jet] has been washed is strained and given with some scrapings [of the stone] to a virgin, after drinking it she retains it and does not urinate; but if she is not a virgin, she urinates at once."[83] John of Trevisa, in his translation (fourteenth century) of Bartholomaeus Anglicu s' *De Proprietatibus Rerum* (thirteenth century), includes quite a dramatic chastity test. It seems that *magnete*,

> ysette vnder hede of a chaste wyf makeþ hire sodeinliche to byclippe hire housbonde, and if sche is a spousebreker, sche schall moeue hire out of þe bedde sodeynliche by drede of fantasye.[84]

> [placed under the head of a chaste wife, makes her suddenly embrace her husband, and if she is a "spousebreaker," she will take herself out of the bed suddenly because of a frightening vision.]

In one twelfth-century gynecological MS (Bern Codex 803) we find a "recipe" for "Vt mulier dormiens interroganti verum dicat de adulterio" ("How to question a sleeping woman so that she tells the truth about adultery"):

> Write the names [of the Seven Sleepers] (Aiohel, Deomedius, Eugenius, Probatus, Sabatus, Stephanus, Quiriacus) on clean paper; place between her breasts while she sleeps; [she will then] name all adulteries.[85]

Astrological treatises translated from the Arabic were another source of information for determining chastity. The conjunction of the stars might tell a man if a woman has had intercourse – or even if a woman has had impure thoughts. Abenragel, in the eleventh-century *Liber in iudiciis astrorum* (translated into Latin in the thirteenth century), asserts: "If the ascendent and the moon are in fixed signs ... the woman is a virgin and free from all suspicion; if they are in mobile signs, she is corrupt."[86] John of Seville (twelfth century), in his translation of a ninth-century Arabic astrological text which came to be known as *De interrogationibus*, includes a series of questions under the heading "Questio de muliere si sit virgo vel corrupta."[87]

Guido Bonatti, in his *Decem tractatus astronomie* (thirteenth century), describes how the stars can reveal degrees of corruption in a woman. It can be known if a woman

> was tempted, but did not give in to tempting words.... . she was tempted, and is still tempted ... at some point embraced and kissed a certain one ... [or if the lover] touched the woman's private parts.[88]

If the stars reveal that a woman has ejaculated her seed "by her own hands or by another's" ("solo tactu manus suæ uel alienae"), she is corrupt – up to a point, that is. Thus it seems that a "hierarchy" of corruption is not only possible but knowable, as the author of *De secretis mulierum* and, earlier, Averroës suggested (see the case of the girl in the bath, above). As Helen Lemay points out, Bonatti is concerned about the social (and decidedly secular, not spiritual) effects of such knowledge. If an astrologer reads a degree of corruption in a young girl's stars – she may have, Bonatti says euphemistically, "laughed and played with another" ("riserit uel luserit cum aliquo") – but that does not necessarily mean that the astrologer is obligated to share his knowledge, for the girl surely will be considered as corrupt "as if she had been with a man" ("si egisset cum uiro").[89] We can imagine that any number of advantageous matches and marriage contracts might be endangered by a too-rigid reading of such "evidence."

Finally, one may be, apparently, just a little bit *devirginatam*, but of course one cannot be just a little bit pregnant. The one incontrovertible test for the presence or absence of virginity – though one has to wait a number of months for the results – is pregnancy.[90] In the meantime, one commentator on *De secretis mulierum* advises: "If a girl's breasts point downwards, this is a sign that she is corrupted," because when she is impregnated, "the menses move upwards to the breasts and the added weight causes them to sag."[91]

Cheating on the test: medical advice and literary exempla

The author of *De secretis mulierum* warns that some women who are no longer virgin are clever enough to "resist detection" by simulating modesty.[92] (It is at this point that he recommends urinalysis, a seemingly much more reliable index of chastity.) Guilielmus de Saliceto also warns his readers that a woman might feign virginity; in this case, she may be ingenious enough to use certain ointments (for which Saliceto provides the recipe) in order to tighten her genitals. Saliceto adds that a woman might put a dove's intestine filled with blood in her vagina, designed to break at the climactic moment.[93] In one of the medical texts traditionally attributed to Trotula (second half, eleventh century), we find two recipes under the rubric of "De virginitate restituenda sophistice," the tone of which is quite cynical and quite out of keeping with other "Trotula" texts:

> This remedy will be needed by any girl who has been induced to open her legs and lose her virginity by the follies of passion, secret love, and promises … When it is time for her to marry, to keep the man from knowing, the false virgin will carefully deceive [blind] the husband as follows. Let her take ground sugar, the white of an egg, and alum and mix them in rainwater in which pennyroyal and calamint have been boiled down with other similar herbs. Soaking a soft and porous cloth in this solution, let her keep bathing her private parts with it. … But best of all is this deception: the day before her marriage, let her put a leech very cautiously on the labia, taking care lest it slip in by mistake; then blood will flow out here, and a little crust will form in that place. Because of the flux of blood and the constricted channel of the vagina, thus in having intercourse the false virgin will deceive the man.[94]

We find a similar description of the uses of leeches in the *Breviarum Practice*: certain brides of Naples are said to feign virginity on their wedding night in the same way.[95] Recall that de Saliceto tells his readers that one must examine the blood of virginity in order to tell it apart from menstrual blood: a bride might attempt to arrange the nuptials so that she would be menstruating on the wedding night.

Literary texts also include tales of faking virginity (as well as stories about what happens when a woman fails a "test" or ordeal, as we shall see in Chapter 3). The story of the bride substitute is one example of how a woman might deceive her spouse, as in Gottfried von Strassburg's *Tristan*. But not every bride has a loyal handmaiden such as Brangæne, and therefore a bride must depend on other means. The seventh story of the second day of Boccaccio's *Decameron* records a tale of resourcefulness: the Sultan's daughter Alatiel marries the King of Algarve, and "despite the fact that eight separate men had made love to her on thousands of different occasions, she entered his bed as a virgin and convinced him that it was really so."[96] Her methodology is left to the reader's imagination.

Technologies of virginity

For the most part, patristic writers such as Tertullian, Ambrose, Jerome, and Augustine – who invented the concept of virginity/chastity as it came to be understood in the Middle Ages – make it very clear that their subject is *female* virginity.[97] Though these authors and others extol virginity as the ideal state for both men and women, they write either directly *to* women or to men *about* women. Moreover, patristic writers provide copious advice on how to behave, speak, walk, dress, and pray, and even tell the vowed virgin what to eat. The "machine required can be constructed," says Foucault of the creation of the modern docile, useful body, and this remark can be applied to the making of the virgin body in patristic texts.[98] Jerome's "Ad Eustochium" (Epistola XXII) and "To Laeta" (Epistola CVII), as well as Ambrose's *De virginibus ad Marcellinam sororem*, suggest that virginity was constructed as a series of acts that must be performed. "Ad Eustochium," for example, includes a series of hortatives and imperatives addressed to the virgin: avoid wine and delicacies, avoid vainglory, practice humility, be industrious, spend time in prayer, "walk not often abroad," "let your dress be neither elegant nor slovenly," do not imitate those women who use affected speech – who lisp and clip all their words."[99] Thus virginity is produced and maintained in a *discursive* space that takes precedence over the actual *physical* space that it may be said to occupy. The interest of patristic writers in maintaining such a distinction between the discursive "body" and the physical body is made particularly clear in their critique of the physical examination as a way to ascertain virginity. As Ambrose declares: "the case is going badly when the body has to be consulted for stronger proof than the mind."[100] And in *De Civitate Dei*, Augustine says: "The holiness of the body lies not in the integrity of its parts" ("Neque enim eo corpus sanctum est, quod eius membra sunt integra").[101]

Cyprian (d. 258) may have been the first to undermine explicitly the veracity of medical wisdom in order to establish the primacy of spiritual integrity over the merely physical. Pomponius, Bishop of Dionysiana, wrote to Cyprian for advice on how to proceed in the case of certain vowed virgins who had been living with men, and even sharing their beds. Cyprian recommends that those women who are affirmed in their virginity after an examination by a midwife are to do penance and to be received back into the church. However, those who are no longer virgin are to do penance as an "adulteress, not against a husband but against Christ" ("non mariti, sed Christi adultera est"[102]), and then to be admitted back into the church. Yet Cyprian also acknowledges that a physical examination for virginity is not always reliable:

> both the hands and the eyes of the midwives are often deceived so that, even though [a woman] may have been found an incorrupt virgin in that part in which a woman can be, she may yet have sinned in some other part of the body which can be corrupted and yet cannot be examined.[103]

In other words, a physical examination may show that the woman is intact, yet such a finding is not a guarantee that she did not sin. What "part" of the body "can be corrupted and yet cannot be examined" by a midwife? Perhaps this is a reference to that "part" in which the will or the spirit resides (here reified for rhetorical effect), a "part" subject to examination by a priest – surely a higher authority than a midwife, and an authority that Cyprian chooses to endorse.

In a letter to Syagrius, Bishop of Verona, Ambrose rejects the idea that the physical proof of virginity has any validity. Apparently, one Indicia was accused of breaking her vow of chastity by her brother-in-law. Ambrose is sympathetic to her position, averring that her enemies, moved by envy, slander her. When Ambrose hears that she was examined by a midwife (the nature of this examination is not specified), he exclaims: "when the accusations are without proof, will it be allowable to demand an inspection of the private parts, and will holy virgins always be handed over to sport of this sort, which is horribly shocking to the eye and ear?"[104] He faults Syagrius' choice of a midwife, whom he refers to as a "cheap slave, a shameless … slave" whose "shameless services" can only "prostitute the other's modesty." Yet even "one of the most skillful and wealthy women of this profession" (the profession of midwifery) is subject to error and susceptible to bribery.[105] Moreover, the presence of a midwife at the house of a consecrated virgin is capable of broadcasting another message altogether to her neighbors: that the young woman might be in childbirth. (It is tempting to identify in such condemnations a few of the seeds of the hostilities that physicians came to direct against midwives, hostilities resulting in medieval and early modern legislation that elevated the status of physicians at the expense of midwives.) Ambrose continues: "The virgin of the Lord is weighed on her own scales in giving proof of herself … And no inspection of hidden and secret parts, but modesty, evident to all, gives proof of her integrity."[106] In actuality, *modestia* is not a quality "discovered" in the conse-crated virgin; it does not have an *a priori* existence "evident to all." The virgin is not "weighed on her own scales"; she is judged according to the standards that Ambrose and others were attempting to work out in their many treatises on virginity. Jerome, for example, describes such standards in his letter addressed to the matron Laeta, in which he lays out a program of education for her daughter

Paula. Jerome declares that a future temple of God must "be trained" (*erudienda*); the best way to do so is to keep the virgin from the world, both from its pleasures and its evils.[107] Her maids and attendants must be carefully chosen, "lest they render their evil knowledge worse by teaching it to her."[108] By playing with the right sort of girls (and never frolicking with boys), reading the right books, memorizing and reciting Scripture, learning to weave, and never going about in public unaccompanied, Paula will soon "become" the virgin that Jerome is busily inventing.

Like Cyprian, Ambrose doubts the veracity of medical opinion: "What of the fact that medical experts say that the trustworthiness of an inspection is not clearly understood and this has been the opinion of older doctors of medicine?"[109] (It is unfortunate that we cannot recover Ambrose's actual medical reading or knowledge.) He goes on to say: "Why should we take suspect and doubtful measures when there are greater documents and proofs for testing the truth?"[110] These "greater proofs" include pregnancy on the one hand, and, once again, "maidenly modesty and holiness" ("virginalis pudoris et sanctitatis") on the other.[111] Chrysostom is another who expresses concern about the reliability of medical evidence. In *On the Necessity of Guarding Virginity*, he decries "the daily running of midwives to the virgins' houses ... in order to discern who is violated and who is untouched." Those who imagine that virginity is proved on the body, or is only of the body, must constantly turn for reassurance to a daily ritual of verification. Such runnings back and forth reveal a deep distrust of the virgin. Chrysostom defends the virgin as he defends the prerogative of the Church to define and determine spiritual virginity. Chrysostom continues:

> One virgin readily consents to the examination but another resists it and by her very refusal goes out disgraced even if she has not been deflowered. The one was convicted, the other not, but she for her part is shamed no less than the first, insofar as she was unable to demonstrate her trustworthiness by her character but required the testimony afforded by minute examination.[112]

Chrysostom's expertise is not that of the midwife's, but that of the churchman, and it is as a churchman that he wants to establish authority over virginity. Chrysostom uses "character" as a measure of spiritual virginity, the absence of which is more telling than any sort of physical inspection.

A little over a hundred years later, Augustine also condemns the practice of relying on medical examinations in attempting to verify virginity. He tells the story of how "a midwife, as she investigated the maidenhead [*integritatem*] of a certain virgin, destroyed it either by ill intent or clumsiness or accident during examination."[113] Augustine, it seems, would have had no trouble understanding Heisenberg's uncertainty principle: whatever one sets out to examine is subject to change or destruction by the very act of examination. In sum, for the Church Fathers, a medical or magical test of virginity is an operation performed *on* the body; such evidence can never be as legitimate as an operation performed *by* the body through prayer, dress, diet, gesture, or ritual.

In spite of such early condemnations of verifying virginity, there is evidence that such tests of physical virginity were mandated, and sometimes actually performed, throughout the Middle Ages. In fact, those clerics – the direct inheritors of the patristic tradition – who wrote, compiled, revised, and refined the foundational texts of medieval canon law, often required the testimony of what came to be called "juries of matrons," women who, because of their demonstrated probity, came to replace midwives as expert witnesses in many legal cases.[114] Virginity, however, was never a black-and-white matter under the law and in the medieval court. For example, James Brundage cites a manuscript of the *Glossa Palatina* (attributed to Laurentius Hispanus, d. 1248) in which a distinction is made between "corruption" caused by masturbation or foreplay and that caused by penetration by a penis ("secus si membro uirili"): only a woman who had experienced the former, as Brundage puts it, "still counted as a virgin for ecclesiastical purposes."[115] The woman who actually experienced coitus must resign herself to the place of a lay sister.

Nor was verifying the signs of virginity before a court completely dependent on a physical examination. The English cleric and jurist Henry de Bracton (d. 1268) includes a section, "Si raptus virginum" ("Where there is rape of virgins") in *De Legibus et Consuetudinibus*; he lists "indicta certa" ("certain signs") by which rape can be known, including "huthesium levatum ... et ruptum vestimentum, et si non ruptum, sanguine tamen intinctum" ("where the hue has been raised ... or her garments are torn, or if not torn, stained with blood").[116] It is not clear if the blood here refers to hymeneal blood, or to the blood that may result from a violent attack. The other signs – the hue and cry, the torn garments – point to evidence of resistance on the virgin's part, not necessarily to virginity. However, in *De Legibus*, physical examination is called for when it must be determined if a woman is pregnant or not. In such cases, Bracton recommends that the court rely on the testimony of "discretis mulieribus" ("responsible matrons").[117]

On the other hand, ecclesiastical law on marriage and divorce sometimes called for verifying virginity in a way that most likely depended on a physical examination. For example, "expert witness" testimony was sometimes necessary in divorce proceedings based on a claim of non-consummation of the marriage. Brundage speaks of the "peculiarly difficult evidential problems"[118] in determining impotence in divorce actions, and cites Gratian's *Decretum* (c. 1140) in which a physical examination of both parties by midwives is recommended, including examining the wife for signs of virginity.[119] The *Liber Extra*, a 1234 supplement to the *Decretum*, in speaking of a specific case, notes: "a matronis bonae opinionis, fide dignis, ac expertis in opere nuptiali dictam fecistis inspici mulierem" (you have had the said woman inspected by matrons of good reputation, worthy of trust, and experienced in the work of marriage).[120] However, we are not told just what is to be inspected.

Jacqueline Murray cites a divorce case in Pisa in 1241, in which a certain Ricca sues her husband Gaitanus for divorce, and is granted her petition by the Archbishop after she is examined by "bonas et honestus mulieres" who swear that she is a virgin.[121] Murray also cites a case in Cerisy in 1317, in which one Thomassia

Blancvilain successfully sued her husband, Thomas Osmeul, for divorce on the ground of impotence. The details of this case are a bit more ambiguous, for, as Murray points out, it is not clear whether Thomassia or Thomas was the subject of examination by midwives.[122]

We may have evidence for a chastity test in Jean Froissart's *Chroniques*, in his gossipy description of the "courtship" of Isabel of Bavaria by Charles VI in 1385. Froissart says that the initial negotiations were quite secret because Isabel lived so far way, which apparently made certain official interventions, as it were, difficult:

> It is the custom in France for any lady, however great her family may be, whom it is intended to marry to the King, to be seen and examined by ladies in a completely naked state [qui il convient que elle soit regardée et avisée toute nue par dames], to decide [savoir] whether she is fit and properly formed to bear children [propise et fourmée à porter enfans].[123]

Perhaps we should take the phrase *propise et fourmée* as a collocation, referring only to bearing children. However, if we read *propise* as a separate quality, we may well ask what, precisely, makes a prospective Queen "suitable." I would suggest that it is virginity. Of course, Froissart's language occludes the actual practice of the *dames* – and perhaps deliberately so. (The language of Jeanne d'Arc's witnesses is equally vague.) Yet there is other evidence in Froissart's reconstruction of the nuptial negotiations that suggests that more is at stake than health and fertility. At one point, Froissart reports that Duke Stephen, Isabel's father, has certain worries, saying to his brother Frederick: "there is that examination to be passed before she could become the wife of a king [si i a trop grant regard à faire une roïne et femme dou roi]. I should feel exceedingly offended if, having sent my daughter to France, she was then brought back to me."[124] This could indeed refer to a concern about Isabel's child-bearing ability, crucial to the continuity of a dynastic line. A page or two later, Froissart says that Stephen raises the issue again with his brother, anxious that "if the King of France does not want [Isabel], she will be disgraced for the rest of her life. So think carefully what you are doing, for if you bring her back here you will have no worse enemy than me."[125] Granted, the King could have rejected Isabel on the basis of her looks, or for a host of other reasons. That would have been embarrassing – but not a cause for disgrace. Froissart's dwelling upon Stephen's fears – his narrative repetition – in this short account of Isabel and Charles VI's marriage arouses a suspicion that something is being suppressed – or better, euphemized.

In the Middle Ages, medical and magical tests of virginity existed alongside the earlier arguments of the Church Fathers against such tests. In part, the tension that existed between medical discourse and theological discourse mirrors the larger struggle that went on between secular and religious interests with respect to the changing status and significance of the family and marriage.[126] Joan Cadden captures the complexities of the medical and theological positions when she says that

> in the case of virginity, medicine sometimes upheld the prevailing values and sometimes responded to social circumstances that failed to conform with

those values. Medicine's complicity with the insistence on virginity is compromised by its role in a conspiracy to replace the substance of virginity with a mere shadow. Yet medicine is by no means at war with the values it evades, since the very act of counterfeiting (and the social circumstances that require it) must be based on the recognition of virginity as the true currency.[127]

In the context of my argument here, I would characterize the "conspiracy" that Cadden refers to as the collective attempt of the early Church to regulate bodies as it saw fit within the evolving discourse of Christian asceticism. By defining virginity as an abstraction greater than the sum of body parts, patristic writers and their later commentators were able to reconfigure the boundaries of the physical body, extending the "space" of the virgin body into ecclesiastical space. Yet throughout the medieval and early modern period, in spite of this concept of virginity – and, perhaps, because of it – we can also document many attempts to return to the body as the site of the burden of proof.

As we shall see in Chapters 3 and 4, the vernacular romance is a particularly fertile ground for exploring what can and cannot be known about virginity. The magical tests found so often in these literary texts reflect an abiding hope that, if manipulated correctly, the body will indeed offer up its secrets. Arguments for the superiority of spiritual virginity over bodily prove inadequate for those with interests and investments in virginal brides and faithful wives.

An epistemology of virginity

We do not know if the women who examined Jeanne – Queen Yolande, Madame de Gaucourt, and Madame de Trèves – would have known how to conduct a manual examination of Jeanne; there is no evidence in the historical record that any of them had experience as midwives, though they most likely would have overseen a number of births on their own estates. Certainly this noble jury of matrons could have used their knowledge of their own bodies as a guide. They may have examined Jeanne for a hymen, but this would have been just one of many physical signs they might have attempted to verify. The women would have tried to determine if Jeanne had given birth some time in the past; they would have tried to determine if she were currently pregnant. (Jeanne was certainly incarcerated long enough for any pregnancy to show.) They would have checked the size of the uterus and attempted to ascertain whether it seemed open or constricted. Supposedly, the condition of the uterus also could have told her examiners if Jeanne had had an emission of seed, though the women could not have said if this emission occurred during heterosexual intercourse.

And what would the Duke of Bedford, watching through his peephole, have seen? That the women conducted an expert and fair examination? That Jeanne's flesh was indeed, as the physician Guillaume de la Chambre put it, "firm"? That Jeanne appeared appropriately modest, with eyes cast down, during her examination?

In the records of the Rehabilitation of Jeanne d'Arc, there is no indication that any evidence was brought before the court that Jeanne was *not* a virgin. This does not mean that Jeanne was not accused of immorality; many believed that Jeanne could not possibly be chaste or a virgin, given the way that she behaved; after all, she spent a great deal of time in the field with rough soldiers – and she wore men's clothing. However, all of those who testified to the virginity of Jeanne did so with great assurance. Jeanne was examined primarily to ascertain the validity of her visions. In the end, there was simply too much at risk for both sides for Jeanne to be declared a fraud: the French could accept the leadership of, and the English could accept defeat by, a divinely-inspired girl; neither the French nor the English could have tolerated the leadership of a witch or a whore.

Perhaps Jeanne did not have visions because she was a virgin; perhaps she was a virgin because she had visions. Jeanne's examiners were so confident, I would suggest, because they were culturally disposed to believe in her virginity rather than to doubt it. In the hagiographical tradition – a tradition very familiar to Jeanne and her contemporaries – virgins often possess unusual gifts, including extraordinary eloquence, imperviousness to pain, and prophetic and visionary powers.[128] In addition to these qualities, Jeanne was also a fine military strategist and soldier, thus embodying the Greek ideal of *aretē*, "male virtue" or "manliness," a virtue that was often transferred approvingly to female martyrs in the earliest hagiographies. Such gifts not only mark the virgin as God's chosen one, but, as I discuss in the next chapter, serve as proofs of the power of virginity and of virginity itself.

2 "Armour of proof"
The virgin and the church in hagiography

In the Golden Legend the martyrdoms of the saints are no more dwelt upon than are the trivial incidents of their lives; it is as though all human experience, measured against one supreme spiritual adventure, were of about the same importance.
Willa Cather, Letter of 23 November 1927 to the editor of *Commonweal*

Ultimately, to be a saint is to be a saint *for others*, to acquire the reputation of saint from others and to play the role of saint for others.
Pierre Delooz, *Sociologie et Canonizations*

The personal is political

Jeanne d'Arc, certified virgin and visionary, apparently possessed a remarkable power: while on the road and sleeping alongside of her soldier-companions, she was able to deflect any prurient thoughts that they might be having about her. At Jeanne's posthumous Rehabilitation, the Duke of Alençon said that, even after seeing *la Pucelle's* breasts – "quæ pulchræ erant" ("which were beautiful") – he was not sexually aroused.[1] One of the King's men, Gobert Thibault, testified that he had questioned a number of soldiers, who asserted that "they never felt sensual desire when they saw her."[2] Jeanne's squire Jean d'Aulon concurred:

> [S]ometimes when I was dressing her wounds I have seen her legs quite bare, and I have gone close to her many times – and I was strong, young and vigorous in those days – never ... was my body moved to any carnal desire for her, nor were any of her soldiers or squires moved in this way, as I have heard them say and tell many times.[3]

Jeanne's virginity was thus not confined to the contours of her physical body, but was realized in the realm of the social as a force capable of dampening the potential ardor of the men around her. In other words, the men who came into contact with Jeanne came to "know" her virginity through narrativizing its public "effects" as an absence of desire. Anthropologists sometimes classify cultures by the degree to which they are driven by an honor/shame dichotomy; in such cultures (usually organized by patriarchy), female virginity often serves as a metonym for the honor of the entire community. As Sherry B. Ortner puts it, certain "male-defined structures represent themselves and conceptualize their unity and status through the purity of their women."⁴ Geraldine Brooks expresses this idea more trenchantly when she speaks of "the dangerous female body" that has been forced "to carry the heavy burden of male honor."⁵ In Jeanne's case, it could be said that her power resided not so much in her body, emanating outward, but in the *response* to it, a response located in public space, shaped by shared notions about sanctity and femininity (and apparently masculinity, in d'Aulon's case). Jeanne's virginity had a communal function, taking on symbolic value, not so much for herself, but for those who bore witness to it.

The testimony of Jeanne's companions has been absorbed into the larger narrative of *la Pucelle*'s life, details in a hagiography, or "sacred biography," as Thomas Heffernan prefers to call it,⁶ that reproduces the sacred and secular value and power of virginity. The story of Jeanne's virginal force-field also illustrates the uneasy relationship of hagiography to history, for certain elements of hagiographical narrative resist a post-Enlightenment, positivist notion of history. In his critique of traditional historiography, Hayden White distinguishes between fiction and history by arguing that the forms ("systems of meanings production," or "modes of emplotment") are the same, but the content ("'real' rather than 'imaginary' events") is different.⁷ Yet as his scare quotes demonstrate, "real" and "imaginary" are problematic adjectives, and this is particularly true with respect to the content of the saint's life. While White does not specifically discuss hagiography, this hybrid genre furnishes a fine test case for his theories, particularly when White argues that, in the historical narrative, "experiences distilled into fiction as typifications are subjected to the test of their capacity to endow 'real' events with meaning." He adds: "it would take a *Kulturphilistinismus* of a very high order to deny to the results of this testing procedure the status of genuine knowledge." Indeed, hagiography functioned and still functions as "genuine knowledge" for many communities worldwide. Though the nature of that knowledge has changed over time, hagiography continues to be a productive mode of representation for its redactors and readers, figuring, as White would put it, "another order of reality."⁸ In the present chapter, while my chief interest is in proofs of virginity and how they function as the sign of the "docility-utility" (Foucault's words) of virginal bodies in the hagiography of late antiquity and the Middle Ages, I also consider how the hagiographic blend of history, biography, panegyric, and allegory privileges meaning over event and the general and exemplary over the specific (even in narratives that are markedly detailed and localized) in order to produce "useful" virgins.⁹

Most obviously, the saint's life is "useful" in that it serves as a model, however idealized, for Christian behavior. But the saint and the saint's virgin body also came to represent the "body" of the Church metonymically, serving as the first line of defense, the lightening rod, the decoy, as it were, for the institution behind it. Ever since Christ said "this is my body," the way was cleared to construct parallels (both actual and hierarchical) between the individual body and the collective Church. In fact, the *female* virgin body, produced through a series of mystifications as closed, sealed, intact – both a wall and a door, as the Song of Songs puts it (8: 9) – came to function as the most apt homology between the self and the institutionalized Church, even when that self was gendered male.

The body of the female virgin and the body of the Church came to be equated often enough in patristic texts on female virginity. Jerome avers that "no vessel of gold or silver was ever so dear to God as the temple of a virgin's body"; Ambrose says that the virgin is a living *templum Dei.*[10] In commenting upon Song of Songs 4. 12, Ambrose also says that "Christ says this [that is, "Hortus conclusus, soror mea, sponsa, Hortus conclusus, fons signatus"] to the Church which He wishes to be a virgin, without spot, without wrinkle. ... And no one can doubt that the Church is a virgin."[11] With such rhetorical equations in mind, historian Peter Brown calls the early virgins of the Church "human boundary-stones," whose presence marked a "privileged, sacred space."[12] A violation of a consecrated virgin could thus be construed as a violation of the Church, both literally and figuratively. In fact, rape is precisely the story that is suppressed in the hagiography of late antiquity and the later Middle Ages. Inviolate virginity was produced as essential – and I use this word in both its traditional and current critical senses – to the construction and continuance of the Christian Church.

Menaced virgins

The "proofs" of virginity under discussion in this chapter have little in common with the medical and pseudo-medical tests for physiological virginity or marital fidelity discussed in the last chapter; moreover, it is important to distinguish between a "test" of virginity, which suggests that one's virginity is in doubt, and a "proof" of virginity, which is a public affirmation of the "fact" of one's virginity/ chastity. Such an affirmation of virginity is most visible in what I call the tale of circumvented rape or near-rape, which invariably includes two parts: 1) the threat of rape, and 2) the prevention of rape, usually by miraculous means. In this type of tale, a pagan official or suitor either attempts to rape a consecrated virgin himself, or he sends her to the brothel to be raped. However, the rape is never committed, for a miracle prevents it. Bunyan's Pilgrim says, "I was clothed in Armour of proof," and the menaced virgin is clothed in similar armor of proof when she must face her accusers, torturers, and would-be rapists. In the legends in which circumvented rape surfaces as a trope, the consecrated virgin may lose her limbs or her life, but never her virginity. *Virginity* always outlasts the *virgin*. In every society, says Foucault, the body finds itself "in the grip of very strict powers, which imposed on it constraints, prohibitions or obligations."[13] The female virgin body carried severe obligations indeed, as its very public, agonistic proofs attest.

A few words about rape are in order at this point, for the subject of rape has recently received a good deal of scholarly attention, both as a historical phenomenon and a literary trope. Kathryn Gravdal's *Ravishing Maidens: Writing Rape in Medieval French Literature and Law* is one example of such attention, and has led me to call a rape a rape: no more circumlocutions such as "he forced his attentions on her" or "he attempted to seduce her."[14] In the scores of saints' legends that I have read for this study, it is very clear that rape is indeed the issue. However, so far as I have been able to determine, there are no extant saints' lives in which a virgin is actually raped by a Roman consul or in a brothel; I have never read a narrative which describes rape, or says that rape was committed, or even creates a "before and after" scenario, as in, for example, Richardson's *Clarissa* and Hardy's *Tess of the D'Urbervilles*. It is possible to argue that rape is "represented" in hagiography through a rhetoric of silence, if not displacement and substitution, but the fact remains that there are no direct narratives of rape in hagiography. As we shall see, the unrepresentability of rape is a correlative to the unrepresentability of virginity. At the point at which the two converge in the saint's life is precisely and paradoxically the moment when the female body becomes most visible – subject to narrativization – while the actual circumstance or moment recedes into the background.

In the first half of this chapter, I examine the evidence for near-rape and rape that exists outside of the traditional hagiography of late antiquity. I am defining "traditional" or "standard" hagiography as any narrative that *plots* the story of a saint or saints, as opposed to a summary of or reference to a story. For example, Augustine and others acknowledge that many vowed virgins were subjected to rape, but they provide only reports, not direct, consciously-plotted narratives. In the second half of the chapter, I examine the hagiographical legends themselves. Stories of near-rape exist in a number of different permutations (ranging from short anecdotes to substantial narratives in verse and prose) from late antiquity to the end of the Middle Ages. However, most tales of circumvented rape, and the most sensational of them, were first recorded from the second to the fourth centuries, at a time when the Church was under particular assault both within the Roman Empire and at its ideological margins. The fourth century in particular marks the institutionalization of a number of foundational saints' legends, which are then recycled and reshaped over and again in the Middle Ages. I begin with the earliest-known accounts of the legend of Agnes in order to emphasize its syncretic features and to identify the role narrative plays in its development. I then turn to the fully-narrativized legend of Agnes as told by Jacobus de Voragine in the *Legenda Aurea*, and also discuss his version of the legends of three other menaced virgins of late antiquity: Agatha, Euphemia, and Lucy. The *Legenda Aurea*, most likely completed before 1267, gathers together tales from a range of sources, and includes over one hundred and thirty saints' lives from the second to the thirteenth centuries. The *Legenda Aurea* becomes the major source for subsequent retellings, surviving in over eight hundred Latin MSS alone.[15] This compilation highlights the more prominent features of conventional hagiography, and it is the conventions of the genre, those elements that come to define it, which are my particular concern as I examine the ubiquitous motif of circumvented rape. As Simon Gaunt observes, "[h]agiography creates the illusion of a united textual community, unchanging over time, for whom differences of gender (or class, for that matter) are entirely naturalized," but he does so in order to read against such effects in his study, *Gender and Genre*.[16] However, I am interested in reading *with* such effects, in reading the illusion itself, in order to explore how this illusion might function in/as Christian ideology. I argue that the menaced virgin in the near-rape narrative is more useful as a metonym, as an inviolate body that stands in for the Church, than as an actual, historical person. Hayden White argues that metonymy is "reductive"; it allows one to "simultaneously distinguish between two phenomena and reduce one *to the status of a manifestation of the other*" (emphasis mine).[17] The virgin indeed figures as a "manifestation" of the Church, but does so most effectively when she is lifted out of her historical moment and textualized in the discourse of hagiography. I am not so concerned with contextualizing the "facts" of a given saint's life, and how such facts were originally established (an almost impossible task), collected, and interpreted at various times. Rather, I am concerned with interrogating the assumptions and conventions of hagiography in order to discover what the genre can reveal about the uses of the female virgin martyr in the early Church, and how and why the trope of near-rape persists into the Middle Ages, long after its immediate historical context is lost. While it would be a mistake to assume that the legends of Agatha, Agnes, and Lucy were read throughout the Middle Ages in the same way that they were read in late antiquity, it is clear that the story of the menaced virgin continued to resonate outside of the particular confines of the beleaguered Christian community of late antiquity. Joyce Wogan-Browne points out that most collections of saints' lives in medieval England were produced for women in religious houses (whose reading pleasure may have been as much vicarious as instructive), and notes that the figure of the virgin martyr was especially popular in the vernaculars of the twelfth and thirteenth centuries. She argues:

> If [violence] is a literary convention necessary for the posing of obstacles for the heroine to overcome, it is a convention which a contemporary audience was able to accept as a true representation of the life of someone known to them.[18]

Jeanne d'Arc prayed to the virgin martyrs Catherine and Margaret (who "spoke" back), and took them as models for her own behavior on the battlefield and on trial. Medieval hagiographers often drew comparisons between their subjects and the virgin martyrs of antiquity. The trope of near-rape remained a productive, if not central, episode in subsequent retellings.

Real women, real rape

Perhaps the earliest hagiographical tale of divine intervention can be found in the *Acts of Paul and Thecla* (c. AD 185–95). Thecla of Iconium endured a number of trials because of her vow of chastity: first, her own mother condemns her to be burned because she will not marry, but a rainstorm miraculously extinguishes her bonfire. Then when a certain Alexander attempts to rape her, she fights him off. Brought before the courts for her presumption, she is condemned to the beasts, but time after time they refuse to harm her. Thecla is humiliated by being stripped in public view, but the crowd is prevented from seeing her naked by a "cloud of fire" that surrounds her. Finally Thecla is left in peace, and she goes off to live as a hermit in a cave. When she is around ninety years old, a group of men appear, with rape evidently their intention. However, her prayers open a rift in the rocks and she vanishes within, never to be seen again.[19] Another early tale of circumvented rape can be found in the *Acts of Saint John* (ca. mid-second century to mid-third century). Here, the pious Drusiana dies from shame when the obsessed (if not diabolically possessed) Andronicus threatens her with rape.[20] Andronicus goes so far as to break into Drusiana's tomb in order to have intercourse with her dead body, but is prevented by an angel from doing so.

R. G. Collingwood said that the "scientific historian never asks himself [sic]: 'Is this true or false?' ... The question he asks himself is: 'What does this statement mean?' ... the scientific historian does not treat statements as statements but as evidence."[21] Yet I *do* want to know if Thecla, when sentenced to the arena to be devoured by beasts, actually "asked of the governor that she might remain a virgin until she should fight the beasts." Was she really turned over to Queen Tryphaena for the safeguarding of her virginity until then?[22] I am perfectly willing to discount the miracles in the tale, but I want to know if there is a kernel of truth in her plea for protection. Yet even Tertullian and Jerome argued that the *Acts of Paul and Thecla* was spurious, though the cult of Thecla survived for centuries afterward. (The Vatican finally decanonized her in 1969.) Perhaps there was no "historical" Thecla, but did the textual "Thecla" have sisters now lost to history? Were consecrated virgins really threatened with rape, or actually raped? During the Great Persecutions, were Christian women who refused to sacrifice – thus making themselves candidates for execution (as decreed by the Edicts of Diocletian) – actually sent to the brothel to be raped? We can cite examples from twentieth-century history in which rape is made a part of a program of oppression: one of the hard lessons of Bosnia is the fact that the Bosnian Serbs have used rape routinely as a terrorist tactic. And consider the case of the hundreds of Korean women who recently initiated suits against the Japanese government for the actions of Japanese troops during World War II. Some 100,000 women were kidnapped, raped, and forced into prostitution in order to serve Japanese soldiers in occupied countries from Korea to Indonesia. Such women were known as *ianfu*, "comfort women."[23]

The documentation that we have for these contemporary events has no equivalent in late antiquity or the Middle Ages. When we look outside standard hagiographies for "evidence" of rape and near-rape, we must turn to such invested and interested writers as Lactantius, Eusebius, Jerome, Ambrose, and Augustine (some of these, also wrote standard hagiography, of course). In his accounts of martyrs in the *Ecclesiastical History* (written c. 300, and revised c. 313 to 326) and *The Martyrs of Palestine*, Eusebius, who, along with Lactantius, chronicled the organized persecutions of Christians under the fourth-century emperors Diocletian and Maximian, suggests that rape (or the threat of rape) of a condemned consecrated virgin was all too routine in the days of the early Church. In the *Ecclesiastical History*, Eusebius reports that the women were not less manly than the men in behalf of the teaching of the Divine Word: as they endured conflicts with the men, and bore away equal prizes of virtue. And when they were dragged away for corrupt purposes, they surrendered their lives to death rather than their bodies to impurity.[24]

Eusebius tells of the many Christian women in Thebais who "were bound by one foot and raised aloft in the air by machines, and with their bodies altogether bare and uncovered, presented to all beholders this most shameful, cruel, and inhuman spectacle."[25] He also reports the story of a woman of Antioch and her two daughters, who drown themselves rather than submit to "the things terrible to speak of that men would do to them – and the most unbearable of all terrible things, the threatened violation of their chastity."[26] In the *Martyrs of Palestine*, Eusebius recounts how one Ædesius attempted to intervene when a judge of Alexandria "consign[ed] women of greatest modesty and even religious virgins to procurers for shameful treatment."[27] Eusebius does shift from reportage to direct narrative in one instance: Potamiæna, says Eusebius in the *Ecclesiastical History*, was "famous ... for the many things which she endured for the preservation of her chastity and virginity. For she was blooming in the perfection of her mind and her physical graces." The judge Aquila, frustrated in the face of her unwavering faith, after "having inflicted severe tortures upon her entire body, at last threatened to hand her over to the gladiators for bodily abuse."[28] At this point, instead of relating a stock story of divine intervention, Eusebius tells us that, "being asked for her decision [to renounce Christianity], she made a reply which was regarded as impious. Thereupon she received sentence immediately."[29] Potamiæna may have been saved from rape by her "impious" remarks (perhaps a condemnation of pagan worship[30]), but she was not saved from death: she was killed by having burning pitch poured over her body.

Throughout the *Ecclesiastical History* and *The Martyrs of Palestine*, Eusebius focuses not on miracles, but on the strength and perseverance of the Christian martyrs, many of whom he himself saw tortured and put to death. Scholars today judge Eusebius to have been a reliable historian, especially given the standards of his day, yet he undeniably had an agenda – which is not say, of course, that there is such a thing as a historian without an agenda. For example, Eusebius says of Book VIII of his *History* that he will "introduce into this history in general only those events which may be useful to ourselves and afterwards to posterity. ... the sacred conflicts of the witnesses of the Divine Word."[31] Eusebius shapes the stuff of history to support a Christian teleology, and in the process, the virgin martyr is transformed into a social document, "useful" for those who would read such a "text." As I will argue in more detail, rape is not a "useful" narrative in a semiotic system in which the inviolate virgin functions as a metonym for the institution of the Church.

In *On the Preservation of Virginity* (*De Vera Virginitatis Integritate*, between 336 and 364) Basil, Bishop of Ancyra (modern Ankara), also records that vowed virgins were raped, in a passage worth quoting at length:

In the time of the persecutions virgins who had been pursued because they remained faithful to the Husband and were given to impious men managed to preserve their bodies from being defiled for He for whom they had suffered paralyzed and struck with impotence the violence those impious men tried to use on their bodies, and He preserved their very bodies, I tell you, completely free of corruption by an astonishing miracle, or else if they had been taken by violence, as their soul took no part in the fleshly pleasures, they seemed to mock their dead bodies and they gave their soul, which had refused to give in to the sensual pleasure of the one who had outraged them, to their true Husband, pure and more shining in its fidelity and virginity.[32]

Basil not only attests to the miracles that saved certain virgins from rape, but asserts that the virgin who did not consent to sexual assault remained miraculously uncorrupt, even after bodily death.

Ambrose, Jerome, and Augustine each embed stories about menaced virginity in their respective exhortations to chastity, yet they use the saint's life in the service of another project: to formulate doctrine on whether or not suicide in order to preserve virginity is justified. At the same time, these writers use the near-rape narrative to affirm that it is not the body that sins, but the will, and that spiritual virginity is not only more valuable than physical, but also impervious to corruption. For example, in *De Virginibus*, Ambrose tells the story of "a virgin at Antioch" who is consigned to the brothel, but who is saved by a soldier who switches places with her. He declares:

> The Virgin of Christ can be exposed to shame, but she cannot be contaminated. Everywhere she is the Virgin of God, and the Temple of God: houses of ill-fame cannot injure chastity, but chastity does away with the ill-fame of the place.[33]

Though not unsympathetic, Ambrose is more interested in the story for its power to inspire: "Listen, ye holy virgins, to the miracles of the martyr, forget the name of the place."[34] Offered up as a model to be emulated, the martyr counts far more than her historical moment. As Ambrose said of Agnes, the virgin of Antioch (whose very name is forgotten, or at least thought not worth recording) represents a "new kind of martyrdom!" ("Novum martyrii genus") – that is, a new kind of *witnessing*, as in the original sense of μάρτυρ – a witnessing that works on and through the abstracted virginal body.[35]

In *De Civitate Dei*, Augustine acknowledges that Christian women, even *quasdem sanctimoniales* (certain consecrated virgins), were raped in the attack on Rome by the Goths. His announced subject is "whether the violation of captured virgins, even those consecrated, defiled their virtuous character, though their will did not consent."[36] His audience is other Christians: "Nor are we here concerned so much to deliver a reply to those not of our kind as to bring comfort to our own people themselves."[37] This careful designation of audience strikes me as an instance of paradigm-building. While Augustine's comment may be intended to dismiss pagans as unworthy of hearing his message and to draw in the already converted, it also reveals a conscious attempt to use these women as *exempla* only, as fodder for the fashioning of doctrine. Augustine goes on to argue that "no matter what anyone else does with the body or in the body that a person has no power to avoid without sin on his own part, no blame attaches to the one who suffers it," for "purity is a possession of the soul, [and not] lost when the body is violated."[38] This is, apparently, the only *consolatio* available for believing Christians.

Pope Leo (d. 461) takes up the nature of violated virginity in a letter to the Bishops of Africa about a number of consecrated virgins who had apparently been raped. The women were anxious about their continued status as virgins. While Leo regrets that these women ("handmaids of the lord who lost their perfect virginity because they were violated by barbarians") can no longer compare themselves to "undefiled virgins," he adds, "although all sin has its source in the will, and a mind which did not yield could remain uncorrupted by the pollution of the flesh, it will hinder [the women] less if they grieve over having lost even in their bodies what they could not lose in their minds."[39] According to patristic writers, the proper object of discipline is the mind or spirit, not the body; therefore, these women should take comfort in the fact that they did not consent, even though they must undergo a reduction in heavenly rank.

As far as I can determine, there are no Roman – that is, non-Christian – sources that attest to the rape or attempted rape of the consecrated virgin during the persecutions of Christians in late antiquity. Not surprisingly, we must rely on the persecuted, not the persecutors, to tell this story. However, we do find evidence of laws against, or at least limiting, forced prostitution, which suggests that consignment to a brothel was not entirely a fiction in imperial Rome.[40] Let us also consider an intriguing remark that Ambrose makes in *De Virginibus* that leads us, albeit circumstantially, to an alleged custom in certain state executions. He says that, at the time of her martyrdom, the virgin Agnes was "not yet of fit age for punishment but already ripe for victory" ("Nondum idonea poenæ, et jam matura victoriæ").[41] According to Ambrose, Agnes was twelve years old when she died. In Roman society, a "fit age" for a woman was marked by the onset of the menses and/or the loss of virginity. Perhaps Ambrose had in mind the idea, or more likely the myth, that virgins could not or should not be executed by the Roman state. In the *Annals* (c. AD 116–18), Tacitus tells a story about the over-ambitious but doomed Sejanus, a prefect under Tiberius from AD 14–31 Tiberius ordered Sejanus' family to be killed, including his young daughter. Tacitus says carefully: "It is recorded by authors of the period that, as it was considered an unheard-of thing for capital punishment to be inflicted on a virgin, she was violated by the executioner."[42] Suetonius also recorded this story in *The Lives of the Caesars* (AD 120); however, he is less careful and more sure about rape as a general practice: "Since ancient usage made it impious to strangle maidens, young girls were first violated by the executioner and then strangled."[43] This story was intended to illustrate the cruelty and depravity of Tiberius. To be sure, it is tenuous evidence for any sort of Roman "policy" on rape. However, it does suggest that rape as an instrument of humiliation and punishment had the status of an open secret (to borrow a phrase from D. A. Miller) in imperial Rome and its provinces.[44]

Based on what little evidence we have for the historicity of near-rape and rape, we might construct the following scenario: in the cities of the Mediterranean in late antiquity, chastity came to be one of the more obvious practices and symbols of all that set Christians apart from pagans. The identity of the young woman and that of the Christian community she represented depended upon her professed and visible virginity. If one were a pagan official, one might conclude that the best way to undermine a Christian woman's faith and demoralize her family and friends would be physical violence and sexual assault. Tertullian suggests as much in the *Apologeticum*, when he rhetorically addresses Roman officials: "Nam et proxime ad *lenonem* damnando Christianam *potius quam ad leonem* confessi estis labem pudicitiae apud nos atrociorem omni poena et omni morte reputari" (emphasis mine). The striking phrasing works just as well in English, as the following translation demonstrates: "Yes, but lately, when you condemned a Christian girl to the *pander rather than the panther*, you admitted that we count an injury to our chastity more awful than any penalty, any death" (emphasis mine).[45] In his *Peristephanon* (usually dated 405), Prudentius steps into the mind of Agnes' tormenter (*trux tryannus*), having him declare that, while Agnes "scorns life as of little worth, still the purity of her maidenhood is dear to her. I am resolved to thrust her into a public brothel."[46] Tertullian's and Prudentius' narratives of the brothel are indeed much stylized, but they also carry the ring of psychological truth for the emerging Christian community.

Fictional women, fictional rape

The question of the historicity of the near-rape narrative is further complicated by the fact that hagiographical accounts of threatened but divinely protected chastity have their analogues, if not their partial origins, elsewhere. For example, in his *Controversiae* (first quarter of the first century), Seneca the Elder offers for debate the story of a virgin "captured by pirates and sold; she was bought by a pimp (*lenone*) and made a prostitute."[47] (Seneca does not say whether this story is true or not.) The Greek prose romance or novel, sometimes referred to as a "chastity romance,"[48] furnishes ample evidence that the motif of the threat of rape and divine or magical intervention, or, in some cases, a creaking *deus ex machina*, circulated before the bulk of late antique hagiography was written down. Scholars have long noted that the earliest hagiography has much in common with the Greek novel of antiquity;[49] in fact, the plot lines are often very similar. In Xenophon's *An Ephesian Tale* (mid-second century AD?), for example, the heroine Anthia is sold to a brothel, but she avoids rape by faking epilepsy; in Heliodorus' *Aethiopica* (third–fourth century AD?), the heroine Chariclea is saved time and again from rape by a number of deus ex machinations. In Achilles Tatius' *Leucippe and Cleitophon* (third quarter, second century AD), Leucippe at one point declares:

"Bring on the instruments of torture: the wheel – here, take my arms and stretch them; the whips – here is my back, lash away; the hot irons – here is my body for burning; bring the axe as well – here is my neck, slice through! Watch a new contest: a single woman competes with all the engines of torture and wins every round."[50]

The hyperbolic language in this passage parallels the more serious rhetoric found in the earliest hagiography. (As we have seen, Ambrose speaks of a "new kind of martyrdom"; compare this to Tatius' phrase, "a new contest." In fact, writers of hagiography often compared the martyr to the athlete in the arena.) This passage raises the possibility that Tatius knew the conventions of some saints' lives well enough to caricature them, and, given the urbane and mannered tone of *Leucippe and Cleitophon*, such a parody is a likely possibility. However, it must be said that comparing the dates of the Greek novel with the earliest hagiographical accounts of the menaced virgin presents a number of problems. Without a way to recover oral tradition and transmission, charting the flow of influence, from novel to hagiography, or hagiography to novel, is extremely difficult. These novels, long neglected by mainstream classicists, are just now beginning to receive serious attention. As we learn more about them, their readership, and their dissemination, we will surely learn more about the origins of the menaced virgin of late antique and medieval hagiography. Suffice it to say that the story of female chastity under assault seems to have been a perennial popular subject, and remains so today, as hundreds of Barbara Cartland novels attest.

In the Greek novel, highly entertaining and often self-consciously sensational fictions, the story of menaced virginity is easily consumed as just one more titillating tidbit. Indeed, the same can be said of the hagiographical tale – what differs (what is supposed to differ) is the context in which one reads the story. Yet what ties the two genres together are shared assumptions about the uses and significations of the virgin. The ideology that structured the virgin's tale in the Greek novel also shaped the parallel plot in the emerging literature of the Christian Church. In both contexts, the virgin functions as an originary figure, as an occasion, for a number of very specific social structures and regimes. (In fact, as the story of Lucrece and countless tales of gods and their sexual interest in mortal women attest, the rape narrative also has the potential for inaugurating change in social relations.[51]) Sherry Ortner, in "The Virgin and the State," even hypothesizes a connection between the rise of the state and

the ideological linkage of female virginity and chastity to the social honor of the group, such chastity being secured by the exertion of direct control over women's mobility to the point of lifetime seclusion, and/or through severe socialization of fear and shame concerning sex.[52]

Ortner defines the state as any development of a central locus of power and the attendant administration to support it. Not only would such a definition apply to the Greco-Roman state of the second through fourth centuries (in its various permutations), but also to the early Church (a syncretic institution shaped by Greco-Roman/Judaic/Middle-Eastern values). It seems that virgins and their proper supervision and disbursement required a complicated bureaucratic infrastructure as well as heavily-regulated customs and rituals in both the profane and the sacred spheres.

Both the Greco-Roman state and the early Church could count a wealth of virgins among their assets, though how they choose to deploy such assets differed radically, of course. In the secular realm of late antiquity, the virgin was not only an object of exchange between men, but also served as a sign that the homosocial system was functioning properly. In the context of the early Church, however, the consecrated virgin came to figure very differently. As Peter Brown has shown in *The Body and Society*, as a treasure saved up, exempt from marriage (however humble or dynastic), the Christian virgin came to be seen as undermining the authority of the state, which hitherto had had sole power over virtuous bodies, their manners and their management. However, as the interests of the Church and the state gradually merged, or at least came to be reconciled, the vowed virgin secured a respected place in the larger culture, serving as an important and powerful symbol in both fiction and history.

Local heroines

In Robertson Davies' novel, *Fifth Business*, the main character Dunstan Ramsay is a "saint-hunting, saint-identifying, and saint-describing" scholar. "There is a saint," Ramsay says, "for just about every human situation."[53] In fact, female saints and martyrs do exist for every occasion in the hagiographical legends of late antiquity and their retellings and additions in the Middle Ages. Women may be represented as heroic and proactive; other times, they may be depicted as helpless victims. Sometimes women martyrs are silent; sometimes they speak out; they may be young girls, often still children, or quite advanced in age; they may be noble and wealthy or poor and humble; they live in rural areas, in cities, and come from every country. Women saints may be virgins, wives, mothers, widows, transvestites, and even reformed prostitutes. It simply is not possible to generalize about the representation and function of the female saint. Influenced by feminism and cultural studies, many scholars (Amy Hollywood, Elizabeth Petroff, Elizabeth Robertson, and Karl Uitti, among others) have demonstrated how diverse the hagiographical corpus can be, especially in the late Middle Ages. In doing so, they are often reacting against earlier studies in hagiography that tended to produce a grand Theory of Everything, ignoring gender difference in the process. Yet it is important to remember that hagiography itself is invested in working out an overarching teleology, in spite of the fact that it employs no uniform strategies of representation: legends may be quite detailed, anchored to particular places and times, or be quite abstract and stylized. Moreover, a given saint's life often changes function and direction in the hands of different redactors and readers, gaining or losing detail and clarity.[54] Such changes cannot always be charted as a case of chronological, narratorial "evolution," though one can discern quite a difference between the hagiography of late antiquity (however much recycled in the Middle Ages) and the "sacred biographies" written in the Middle Ages about contemporary figures. Just why this is so is complicated, but I would like to offer one reason here: as violence against Christians lessened – when, for example, state persecutions ceased with the accession of Constantine in AD 306 – new narratives, reflecting new and different challenges to the Church, developed alongside stories of torture and near-rape. In fact, not many new accounts of near-rape and miraculous intervention were added to the store of legends after the fourth century (though, of course, the legends of late antiquity were retold over and again), but we can find a few scattered examples, such as the story of Jutta de Huy (born c. 1160). Widowed early – after wishing to remain a virgin in the first place – she is attacked by a friend of her dead husband's. Her biographer adds a dramatic flourish to the story:

> What should she do? … To whom should she turn? If she wished to escape there was no place to go. If she tried to resist, the man was stronger. If she cried out, she was afraid the aggression would become public and the ensuing scandal would compromise both of them forever.[55]

As events near crisis, a woman Jutta takes to be the Blessed Virgin appears; though the young man cannot see her, the sound of footsteps scares him off, and Jutta is saved.

Other medieval tales in which divine intervention plays a part are not so much about the menaced virgin as they are about the man who menaces her. In the *Gemma Ecclesiastica* (c. 1190), Geraldus Cambrensis tells two stories of divine intervention. In the first, a cleric carries a girl into St. Mary's Church in order to rape her, but the statue of Mary takes a candelabrum in hand and strikes him with it; in the second, another cleric is killed by a falling crucifix while attempting to rape a young girl.[56] However, Geraldus intends these anecdotes to serve as a lesson to men on the swift and just retribution of God, not as a celebration of female virginity.

More often, the motif of divine intervention is much diminished or disappears altogether by the medieval period. The story of Christina of Markyate (d. c. 1155–66) is a good example of rape prevented by pluckiness and perseverance rather than by miracle. According to her *Life*, when Christina was assaulted by the Bishop of Durham, she used a ruse to lock him in a room, thus saving herself from his embraces. Attempting to force her to marry, Christina's own parents unceasingly tried to arrange her rape (or, at least, her abduction) by her suitor. At one point, she chose confinement in a closet-sized cell for four years in order to avoid attacks upon her virginity.[57]

We also find tales of virgins of late antiquity and the Middle Ages who wished to avoid marriage who were granted not the grace of stamina and bravery, but that of a physical deformity, such as blindness, leprosy, or tumors. The legend of Wilgefortis (a tale whose origins may well be traced to Gregory the Great in the sixth century) is particularly sensational in this regard. Purportedly the daughter of a pagan king of Portugal, she took a vow of chastity, and then was betrothed to the King of Sicily. She prayed to become ugly, and, miraculously, grew a beard. The lover gave up his suit, and the girl's enraged father had her crucified.[58]

There are other medieval tales in which the virgin takes a more active part in protecting her chastity, either through self-mutilation or through suicide (a common motif found alongside the motif of circumvented rape in late antique martyrologies.) Jane Tibbets Schulenberg provides a number of medieval examples of self-mutilation, and recounts the story of two sisters who place rotted chicken parts between their breasts to stave off attacks on their virginity. She also tells the story of St. Ebba and the other members of her convent who cut off their noses and lips to deter the intentions of Danish invaders. Horrified by the sight, the Danes lose all interest in rape, and settle for burning the convent and all its inhabitants.[59] Schulenberg has done a marvelous piece of detective work in identifying the historical foundations for such horrifying tales. An analogue to the tales that Schulenberg has collected can be found in the Middle English *An Alphabet of Tales*: a prince, we are told, sends his men to kidnap an unnamed nun who has refused his advances. When she asks why she alone arouses the prince's lust, the soldiers tell her that the prince thinks her eyes are beautiful. She immediately plucks them out and puts "þaim in a dissh" to be presented to the prince.[60] This tale came to be attached to Saint Lucy in the Middle Ages, because, as Hippolyte Delehaye explains, Lucy was often depicted as carrying two eyes on a platter – or, at least, what medieval people thought were eyes.[61] As this anecdote demonstrates, such tales have a way of migrating from their historical moment into legend, there to be diffused and used over and again.

In order to explain this phenomenon, it may be helpful to borrow M. M. Bakhtin's distinction between centripetal and centrifugal forces in language and apply it to the heterogeneous genre that we call hagiography. It sometimes seems that hagiography is constituted of two contrary desires – the first a centripetal impulse, to create and maintain a homogenized, authoritative discourse (by flattening difference and privileging universality), and the second a centrifugal impulse, to interrogate or critique the power of such a discourse (by registering difference and highlighting the particular). In fact, the *study* of hagiography is made up of similar conflicting centripetal and centrifugal desires. Such fluctuations and fashions suggest that Graham Pechey, in "Bakhtin, Marxism and Post-Structuralism," is correct when he asserts: "There are no monologic texts ... only monological readings."[62] Authoritative discourse (formed by centripetal forces) and its opposite, internally-persuasive discourse, do not necessarily represent innate qualities of discourse; they indicate functions or roles that discourse assumes in a social context. At certain points and in some places, when the centripetal forces of hagiography prevail, the universalized and de-historicized virgin is a more useful figure than the local version. I would argue that, in the first four centuries of the Church, when its founders and defenders were working most actively to establish and secure ecclesiastical authority, the tale of the menaced virgin was constructed in such a way as to remove the virgin martyr from history and re-place her in an idealized, transcendent narrative. Such a move, which aestheticizes and displaces real pain and suffering, expedited an untroubled, unproblematized identification between the virgin (and through her, every believing Christian) and the Church. Medieval redactors of hagiography, as they adapted legends in which the trope of near-rape appears for their own purposes and particular audiences, also inherited and preserved this identification of virgin and Church.

Universalized symbols

Our earliest extant version of the legend of St. Agnes is Ambrose's account in his sermon, *De Virginibus* (377). Here, the trope of menaced virginity as I have described it is barely discernible. Ambrose gives us not a narrative of what "happened" to Agnes, but an abstract panegyric that focuses on her bravery and eloquence in the face of her executioner. The closest he comes to suggesting that her virginity may have been threatened is found in the following passage:

> What threats the executioner used to make her fear him, what allurements to persuade her, how many desired that she would come to them in marriage! ... She both remained a virgin and she obtained martyrdom.[63]

Similarly, no trace of threat can be found in two other early accounts; first, in the hymn, *Agnes beatae virginis*, dated later than Ambrose's sermon (and sometimes attributed to him), but written before the end of the fourth century, and second, in what is known as the inscription of Saint Damasus (Pope 366–84), thought to have been composed in between Ambrose's sermon and the hymn.

As we have already seen, Prudentius provides us with a quite explicit reference to the threat of the brothel in the *Peristephanon* on the cusp of the fifth century. Prudentius gives us a fully-plotted narrative, complete with dialogue and differing points of view. The miraculous is prominently featured. In his thorough and invaluable study of the origins of the Agnes legend, A.J. Denomy points out that we do not know if these early texts represent separate threads of the legend, or if they form part of a common genealogy.[64] It strikes me that Prudentius' embellishments must have come out of a very different rhetorical context than that in which Ambrose, Damasus, and the writer of Agnes' hymn are writing. It may be that Prudentius was influenced by a tradition represented by the Greek *Passio of Saint Agnes*, which also includes a reference to the threat of the brothel. Again, we are unable to identify clearly the trajectory of influence; i.e., which text, the *Passio* or the *Peristephanon*, antedates the other. I would argue that it is likely that the conventions of the Greek novel influenced the writer of the *Passio* and/or Prudentius. Our next account, the Latin *Gesta sanctae Agnes*, is usually dated as fifth century or early sixth, with some seventh-century additions. Its sources are thought to be diverse, including Ambrose's and Prudentius' accounts, and, perhaps, the Greek *Passio*. The *Gesta* is the source for the legend of St. Agnes that we find in the *Legenda Aurea*.[65]

If one examines all of these versions of the legend, one might plausibly argue that the seeds of the near-rape narrative can be found in Ambrose's sermon. So

Denomy suggests, though he concludes that the origins of this episode are pagan and classical. The number of miraculous details increases from redaction to redaction, which certainly gives the legend more coherence, if less veracity. Jody Enders recently observed that "the New Historicist tendency to revel in indeterminacy proves just as problematic as the Old Philologist tendency to try to resolve it," and trying to solve the problem of the origins of the near-rape episode in the legend of St. Agnes as well as in other, similar legends of late antiquity using Old Philology to make a New Historicist argument is tricky indeed.[66] I quoted Donna Haraway in the Introduction, and her words are worth repeating here:

> Technologies and scientific discourses can be partially understood as formalizations, i.e., as frozen moments, of the fluid social interactions constituting them, but they should also be viewed as instruments for enforcing meanings.[67]

The trope of near-rape is an excellent example of a "formalization" or "frozen moment"; not a matter of fact, but of fiction, a result of a teleocentric Christian "technology." While the original impetus or inspiration (mainly irrecoverable, though available to speculation) for the narrative is lost, its effects remain beyond the particular historical moment of its creation.

Let me now turn to the legend of St. Agnes in the *Legenda Aurea*, which, despite Voragine's rhetorical arrangements and innovations, still serves as a fine example of a "formalization," and a formalization which served as a primary source for the bulk of vernacular saints' lives throughout the Middle Ages. The tale begins with a proprietary gaze: a prefect's son sees Agnes on her way home from school, and falls in love with her. He offers marriage to Agnes, but she spurns him in no uncertain terms: "Go away, you spark that lights the fire of sin, you fuel of wickedness, you food of death! I am already pledged to another lover!"[68] The boy then sinks into lovesickness, and his father seeks out Agnes to find out who her betrothed is. Once it is made clear to him that Agnes is talking about Christ, he orders her to sacrifice to the virgin goddess Vesta, or else she will be sent to a brothel. She refuses to sacrifice, and, when she is stripped, her hair miraculously grows long enough to cover her entire body (this detail is first found in the *Gesta sanctae Agnes*).[69] An angel throws a mantle of light around her once she enters the brothel, and this light is enough to deter anyone who approaches her. The prefect's son urges his companions to "take their pleasure" with her, but they are too terrified (I.103).[70] The prefect's son then "in a fury rushe[s] in to force himself upon Agnes" and is struck dead (I.103).[71] Though Agnes restores him to life, the prefect, too cowardly to set her free in the face of public opinion, turns her over to a deputy, who orders her to be burnt. The flames do not harm her. She is subjected to more tortures, and finally dies with a dagger through her throat.

Let us consider a few more examples of what we might call centripetal narratives – that is, narratives that dramatize the miraculous and the global at the expense of the historical and local – in the *Legenda Aurea*. In the legend of Euphemia, the judge Priscus sends Euphemia to prison for refusing to sacrifice to the gods, and there tries to rape her. However, as Voragine says, she resisted manfully, and the power of God paralyzed his hand. Priscus thought he was under some kind of spell. He sent his head steward to promise her all sorts of things if she would do his will, but the man was unable to open the jail door with keys or to break into it with an ax, and finally was seized by a demon, screamed, tore his own flesh, and barely escaped with his life. (II.182)[72]

The Romans then try to behead her, but are unsuccessful. Priscus consequently orders that the city's ruffians be rounded up in order to "enjoy her as long as they liked, until she dies exhausted" (II.182).[73] But when Priscus' chancellor goes to Euphemia's cell, he is miraculously converted and refuses to give her over to the waiting crowd. After several attempts to torture her, all of which fail, Euphemia is finally stabbed to death by a follower of Priscus', who does so "in order to avenge the offence given to his master" – that is, the apparent frustration Priscus felt at his inability to break Euphemia (II.183). It is significant that no torture, however ingenious, is able to have an effect on her physical body; for example, Euphemia was to be "crushed like an olive between great millstones," but the stones turn to harmless powder. That the virgin saint can only be killed by the (phallic) sword or knife is a motif repeated over and over in hagiographical legend.[74] It is very tempting to read this and other deaths as a displacement, as a rhetorical substitution for the act of rape itself. In a way, death is less complicated than rape, for it is a "discourse" that prevents any further traffic with the virgin/ virgin body; it is an end to a narrative, an end to change and exchange. As the Church Fathers warned over and over again, so long as the virgin is in circulation, she is in danger. It is also possible that the depiction of the virgin's death functioned as a cathartic moment for its original audience, whose sense of what was at stake in the near-rape narrative would have been much greater than our own. Better the virgin lose her life and keep her virginity, for her reward in heaven would be that much more.

Stories of overt sexual humiliation and torture (another strategy of displacement and substitution) are frequently found in the near-rape narrative; for example, according to their legends, Agatha, Candida, and Febronia were first publically stripped and then had their breasts removed as part of their torture.[75] The story of Agatha is particularly well-known in the West. (Though Jerome includes Agatha in his martyrology, it is likely that her martyrdom is completely fictitious.) Depending on the version of the story, her breasts were cut off, ripped off, or, in the *Legenda Aurea*, twisted off. In each version, Agatha's breasts are miraculously restored. A detail that anticipates (and promises) the resurrection of the body at the Last Judgment, the restoration of Agatha's breasts also focuses the reader's attention on gender and how it matters: it is as if Agatha's sex must be initially asserted and foregrounded in order for it to be fully recuperated when she is later saved from rape through divine intervention.

In the *Legenda Aurea*, before Agatha is tortured, she is handed over to a brothel by the consul Quintianus. Voragine inserts some sound psychologizing at this point: Quintianus is "determined to get [Agatha] in his grasp. Being of low degree, he would gain respect by lording it over a noble, her beauty would satisfy his libido, he would steal her riches to feed his avarice, and, being a pagan, he would force her to sacrifice to the gods" (I.154).[76] Quintianus gives the prostitute Aphrodisia a month to debauch Agatha – by what means Voragine doesn't say. Predictably, in the face of Agatha's prayers and incessant weeping, Aphrodisia fails, declaring: "It would be easier to split rocks or reduce iron to the softness of lead than to move or recall that girl's mind from its Christian intention" (I.154).[77] The "miracle" is not so much an example of divine intervention as it is of divine protection. However, whatever the form of the miracle, here, as in other tales, only virginity is saved, not the body itself: after being rolled naked over broken pots and live coals, Agatha dies in prison. Abstract virginity counts far more than the specific, fleshly body, according to a logic in which the soul's eternity supersedes the body's chronicity. When particular bodies are effaced, only the abstract idea remains, transcending and transmuting the historical moment into a universalizing, identificatory experience. The paradox inherent in the hagiographical narrative is that this operation takes place when the virgin body is at its most visible and vulnerable to the gaze – that is, when the virgin is narrativized most explicitly and vividly as a female body.

Lucy, my next example of the menaced virgin, is unhappily betrothed. (Lucy is supposed to have died in 304, in the persecution ordered by Diocletian. We can trace the earliest evidence of her cult to an inscription of c. 400.) She begins to give away her possessions, which alarms and angers her intended. After all, what she distributes to the poor was to be his. (We can discern traces of an antique pagan *realpolitik* in this tale of an unauthorized distribution of wealth.) He turns her over to the consul Paschasius, who in turn summons procurers: "invite a crowd to take their pleasure with this woman, and let them abuse her until she is dead" (I.29).[78] However, when they try to carry her off, she remains fixed to the ground. Even a thousand men and a thousand oxen cannot move Lucy. Finally, as in the story of Euphemia, "the consul's friends, seeing how distressed he was, plunged a dagger into the martyr's throat" (I.29).[79] Yes, how distressed *he* was: just as Priscus was so disturbed by Euphemia's steadfastness, so is Paschasius at his wit's end because he cannot harm the virgin Lucy. Once again, what cannot be violated by the act of rape is penetrated by a phallic weapon. In fact, that Lucy is stabbed in the throat (*guttur*) may well be significant, for in the gynecology of late antiquity, the throat was considered to be homologous to the neck of the uterus.[80] What cannot be narrated directly is merely suggested through a substitution of body parts. Moreover, that the throat is the site of the voice is surely significant. In this respect, death has a double valence, for while it protects Lucy from her would-be rapists, it also silences her so that she is no longer able to speak to and against her oppressors. It is also worth noting that hanging, not the sword, was "the privileged instrument of female death" in ancient Greece; in Rome, hanging was described as "a feminine death, unworthy of a man," whose only honorable death lay in the sword. In this and other hagiographical tales, it may be that death by the sword actually honors the female virgin martyr by recognizing her *aretē* (that is, manliness, which is a quality of the spirit, not the body).[81]

These and other stories of near-rape chronicle the resistance to early Christianity within the cultures of the eastern rim of the Mediterranean, but also capture a deep anxiety about how one defines and determines virginity itself. Perhaps more than other notions about human sexuality, virginity is perceived as a "natural" condition, an ideal that resides somewhere in the body and spirit. This belief underpins a number of fundamental assumptions about the ties that bind a society together. Female virginity in particular serves as an important counter in homosocial relations among men. As Patricia Klindienst Joplin provocatively puts it, "the virgin's hymen must not be ruptured except in some manner that reflects and ensures the health of the existing political hierarchy."[82] The Church, in fact, monopolizes the homosocial bond by monopolizing the hymen, by refusing to allow its goods on the market at all.[83] Perpetual virginity is valued precisely because the virgin remains perpetually *un*exchanged.

Gender and genre

In *The Second Sex*, Simone de Beauvoir notes: "Most female heroines are oddities: adventuresses and originals notable less for the importance of their acts than for the singularity of their fates."[84] This is certainly true of the Christian heroines I have discussed in this chapter. Hagiography specializes in singular fates that take on symbolic, universal significance, as many a medieval hagiographer knows. The Abbot of Bonne-Esperance, for one, is well aware of this feature of the saint's life. In his life of the blessed Oda of Hainault (d. 1158; the Abbot was writing soon after), he describes how she cut off her own nose on the day of her wedding in order to preserve her chastity. Oda's story is unusual in that she is not martyred in attempting to save her virginity; she lives to become a nun and ultimately a prioress. This deviation from the conventions of the saints' life seems to disturb the Abbot's sense of order. He argues that Oda's act of self-mutilation, which had obviously been done out of love for God, is indeed a kind (*genus*) of martyrdom. "Martyr igitur & Virgo Oda est, quia virginitas esse non potest sine martyrio" (Oda is martyr and virgin, because virginity is not possible without martyrdom), he declares.[85] Almost a century later, Thomas Aquinas offers support for the Abbot's position in a *sic et non* disquisition on martyrdom. In the *Summa Theologiæ*, he asks, "is death essential to the idea of martyrdom?" ("utrum mors sit de ratione martyrii?").[86] Citing Jerome and Gregory, Aquinas first answers:

> We read that certain women held their lives in praiseworthy contempt in order to preserve their physical virginity ... there are occasions on which persons are robbed of that physical virginity, or an attempt is made to rob them of it, because they confess the Christian faith. ... *So it appears that the term martyrdom should be used rather for a woman's loss of her physical virginity*

for belief in Christ, than for the further loss of her bodily life. (51, 53, emphasis mine)[87]

In this regard, Aquinas specifically mentions Agnes and Lucy. Argued in this way, then, the answer is no: death is not necessary to martyrdom, for rape is a kind of martyrdom in itself. On the other hand, the answer is yes: "the perfect idea of martyrdom requires one to endure death for Christ's sake."[88] Yet this is a qualified yes, for Aquinas goes on to say that his authorities "speak of martyrdom figuratively" ("loquuntur de martyrio per quamdam similitudinem").[89] However, since one cannot know if a woman lost her virginity (through rape) for love of Christ, or because she did not value her virginity enough, the question is moot. In short, for many ecclesiastics, as R. Howard Bloch has observed, "the only real virgin ... is a dead virgin."[90] As I suggested earlier, death is the ultimate form of monologic discourse, the only real insurance against tampering with the borders and boundaries of the body – individual or ecclesiastical.

The Abbot of Bonne-Esperance transforms the stuff of Oda's life into a textual artifact, to be consumed by, and subsumed in, dominant ecclesiastical culture. Along with Aquinas, he asks us to focus not on the literal story, but on the figurative. Moreover, I would say that the Abbot impels us to contemplate the genre itself. In fact, I would argue that genre and consecrated virgin follow a very similar trajectory in the hagiographic tale of near-rape. Allon White says that certain genres are

> sealed off from heteroglossia ... immune from an intertextual interference. Nothing can intervene across their endless cycles of telling and retelling, production and consumption ... [a genre is] a kind of discursive economy which cannot expand its base because it has not developed a division of linguistic labour to any significant extent.[91]

We can substitute *virgin* for *genre* with uncanny ease: *virgins* are "sealed off from heteroglossia ... immune from an intertextual interference." And, as I said before, *virgin* is substituted for *church* with equal ease in the long history of Christianity. What Mary Douglas argues in *Purity and Danger* has special relevance here: "the body is a model which can stand for any bounded system. Its boundaries can represent any boundaries which are threatened or precarious ... the powers and dangers credited to social structure [are] reproduced in small on the human body."[92] Ambrose seems to be as mindful of the implications of Douglas' point as any modern anthropologist would be.

Even the names of the saints underscore the discursive designs of these tales of near-rape. For example, Wilgefortis "is" a *virgo fortis* (strong virgin), and goes under other names as well, including that of Liberata. She is called Uncumber in England: weighed down by superfluous hair on the one hand, she is equally free of a superfluous husband on the other.[93] Of course, I am not the first to notice the messages so blatantly foregrounded in these names; hagiographers themselves go on endlessly about them. Euphemia, Voragine tells us, may mean either "good woman" or "sweet sound" (*euphonia*).[94] Voragine provides a number of interpretations for Agatha: "saint of God," or "a 'goddess' who does not love earthly things," or "one who speaks perfectly," or "one in higher servitude" (that is, in the service of God), or "one who is solemnly consummated."[95] (On the other hand, the wicked Aphrodisia, whatever her powers in certain circles, does not live up to her name when it comes to her charge to corrupt Agatha. Perhaps we should read her name as an example of antiphrasis.[96]) These polysemous names, or, better, epithets, help to distance us from imagining real virgins and real rape: horror in these stories is successfully suppressed and aestheticized at the point at which we are directed to contemplate the figural, not the literal.

Unrepresentable rape and the represented church

At this juncture, I cannot resist the punning possibilities of the Abbot of Bonne-Esperance's name: he is indeed, like many another believing medieval Christian, in "good hope and expectation" that virginity is both a physical and mental condition that can somehow be recognized and measured, and therefore preserved. If rape is the aporia, the gap in the text, that hagiographers are determined to avoid, then the moment of divine intervention can be read as a moment of *anti*-aporia: an attempt to fix the textual/sexual body for all time.

Within the context of the Church, virginity, I have been arguing, is intended to function as the supreme expression of what Mikhail Bakhtin calls monologic or authoritative, discourse. Authoritative discourse is, Bakhtin says, "fully complete"; it

> has but a single meaning, the letter is fully sufficient to the sense and calcifies it … it demands our unconditional allegiance … authoritative discourse permits no play with the context framing it, no play with its borders, no gradual and flexible transitions.[97]

With Bakhtin's words in mind, let us return to the stories of Agatha and Lucy in the *Legenda Aurea*. It seems to me that Quintianus' lust for Agatha cannot be separated from the fact that he is both a) a representative of Roman authority and b) a pagan. The fight over Agatha's body is thus located firmly in the public sphere – both *his* desire and *her* virginity are politicized. But Agatha's spiritual resolve is stronger than rock or iron. In other words, as Aphrodisia says, "that girl's mind" – as well as her other body parts – is admirably, transcendently monologic. Agatha's virginity shores up the Christian Church and guards against the riot of *heteroglossia*, Bakhtin's term for multi-voiced and many-intentioned discourse. It is important to note that, in the hagiographical paradigm, in which the details of a particular virgin's martyrdom drive the narrative, a virgin may be tortured – the Syriac hagiographies are particularly graphic in this regard[98] – but she *must* remain intact, sexually inviolate. To imagine her otherwise is too much of a threat to the system. The raped virgin is a paradox, an oxymoron that would cause the whole system of stable, fixed signs to collapse.[99] In this closed literary and hagiographic economy, rape must remain *unrepresentable in order to insure* that the virgin may continue to function as the first line of defense of the monologic.

The superordinary weight of Lucy's body, in metonymic relation to the religious body, has a special resonance when we pursue this line of thought. Impervious to persuasion, rhetorical or otherwise, Lucy's resolve is both spiritual and literal: she simply cannot be moved. (In these stories of frustrated fathers, suitors, and political appointees, "over my dead body" becomes a literal place indeed.) The metaphors that cluster around the notion of weight are the same that cluster around authoritative discourse. Violation cannot exist in the same space.

Authoritative disorders

I have been arguing that the female virgin functions as a metonym for a monologic discourse that the early Church sought to erect around itself, and that the medieval redactors of saints' legends perpetuated. Rape, the ultimate literal and figurative violation, is absent in the hagiographical narrative because neither the idea of the virgin nor the institution of the Church can tolerate such a violation. Actually, it would be more accurate to say that the virgin represents *a desire for* an absolute, unambiguous, transcendent discourse – a desire that is actually frustrated in and by the very act of attempting to create such a discourse. Consider, for example, how these tales of near-rape skew the narrative focus toward the virgin's body in a way that invites readers and listeners to situate themselves as voyeurs or victims (depending on their subject position). Indeed, a number of scholars have suggested that the stories in which a virgin is stripped, tortured, and/or sent out to be assaulted and defiled, had a certain titillating appeal for medieval audiences – and has a similar appeal for modern readers, I should add. (By gathering together these stories, I am aware that I reproduce their titillating effects for yet another audience.) Elizabeth A. Castelli argues that, because the "practices and discourses of martyrdom" are "embedded in an androcentric framework ... the sexual objectification of women is in some measure predictable and is tied not only to the historical experience of martyrdom but to its retelling."[100] It is in this paradox of vicarious, recurring violation that I would locate a breach in the figuration of the monologic, inviolate virgin. In other words, the very circulation, the constant repetition of, the near-rape narrative – and the readerly enjoyment and consumption thereof – threatens and undermines a monologic discourse that hagiography tries to maintain/sustain as it works along its centripetal axis. As Tertullian and other patristic writers asserted over and over again – while violating their own admonitions to so argue – chastity is best maintained by a deliberate non-play of signifiers, by absence and silence. However, hagiography, in which the virgin is made subject to narration, which is inherently unstable and mutable, forces the virgin into play, and it is motion, not stasis, that puts her at risk.

In order to illustrate the point that the menaced virgin's tale often contains the seeds of its own deconstruction, let us return to the legend of Agnes in the *Legenda Aurea*. In defense of her chastity, Agnes uses language that depends upon an eroticized vision of love (recall: "Go away, you spark that lights the fire of sin, you fuel of wickedness, you food of death! I am already pledged to another lover!"). At one point, Agnes even declares to her distressed suitor: "The one I love is far nobler than you ... his love is chastity itself, his touch holiness, union with him, virginity ... Already his chaste embraces hold me close, he has united his body to mine" (I.102).[101] Agnes – so willing to speak and so willing to allow her words to be used against her – is produced by an appropriated discourse in which the language of carnal love is used to represent a purely spiritual ardor. Such words incite everyone who hears her, first to anger, then to lust, and finally to murder. (Agnes has a profane cousin in Iphigenia: both women sacrifice themselves on the altar of the monologic, for a cause that insists on their compliance and complicity.) The struggle for her body/the Church's body is explicitly located in a discourse that never fully escapes or suppresses its original context. This language actually compromises Agnes' inviolate position because of its profane resonances. In its often-eroticized narratives of torture, threatened sexual assault, and murder, the story of the menaced virgin often reveals – or at least hints at – that which it seeks to suppress. The near-rape narrative is a bait-and-switch game that always leaves the audience fully aware of the bait that has been withheld.

To paraphrase Clifford Geertz, the saint's life is a story that Christians of late antiquity and the Middle Ages told themselves about themselves.[102] And they told it over and over again, following a script first written on Christ's body. One of the effects of this repetitive performance is to elide "real" experience, real suffering, real death in order to privilege both an Imaginary and an imaginary past. Moreover, hagiography, its miraculous content and repetitive formulae, its borrowings (obvious to us in hindsight, but perhaps just as obvious to much of its original readership, or at least to a portion of its educated readership), its resistance to documentation and authentication, and its overt ideological intentions, interrogates history in its most empirical, transparent form. Put another way, *Christianity* is capable of resisting history – that is, human-made history – in order to privilege an eschatology in which truth-value is registered on a different scale altogether.

Art Historian Adrienne Auslander Munich says that "absolute virginity tells no story about itself but enables the story to be told."[103] "The story to be told" is not that of Euphemia, Agnes, Agatha, or Lucy, or of Thecla (or of Iconium, Agape, Chionia, Hirena, and other menaced virgins), but of the ecclesiastical body that subsumes theirs. Hagiography, in telling the story of the menaced virgin martyr, is really telling the story of a Church that reserved to itself the right to recognize, sanction, and reward virginity.

3 "Love's traces"

The lady and the test in vernacular romance

[W]e cling to the illusion that the signifier answers to the function of representing the signified, or better, that the signifer has to answer for its existence in the name of any signification whatever.

Jacques Lacan, "Agency of the Letter in the Unconscious"

Exemplary performances

The Book of Numbers contains a ritual known as the "law of the jealousies." This "law" allows a suspicious husband to bring his wife before a priest to determine if she has been faithful. The priest makes her swear an oath, and gives her the "water of bitterness that brings the curse." If she has been unfaithful, "her womb shall discharge, her uterus drop, and the woman shall become an execration among her people" (5: 24, 27).[1] Herodotus (fifth century BC) tells a story about young Libyan women who ritually battle each other with stones and sticks: "If any girl … is fatally injured and dies, they say it is a proof that she is no maiden [*pseudoparthenoi*]."[2] Valerius Maximus (first century AD) includes the tale of the virgin Tuccia in a collection of didactic aphorisms and anecdotes that was very popular in the Middle Ages. Accused of violating her sacred vow, Tuccia calls upon the goddess Vesta to give her accusers a sign of her chastity. She then is able to carry water from the river Tiber to the temple in a sieve.[3] Aelian (AD 170–235) tells a story of initiation in which a serpent in a cave accepts cakes only from the hand of a virgin.[4] In Achilles Tatius' *Leucippe and Cleitophon* (third quarter, second century AD), the suspicious Thersander challenges his wife Melite to take an oath and immerse herself in the waters of Styx; he also challenges Leucippe to be shut into Pan's cave, where, if she is proved a virgin, pan-pipes will be heard; if not, she will never be seen again. Charicleia and her lover Theagenes are to be sacrificed to the gods in Heliodorus' *Aethiopica* (third–fourth century AD?); in order to test their chastity and therefore their suitability, they are first made to walk across a golden grate that burns anyone who is impure. Both pass the ordeal – Charicleia even stands motionless on the grate to emphasize her chastity.[5] According to the Winchester Annals for the year 1043, the mother of Edward the Confessor, Queen Emma, was accused of adultery; to prove her innocence she walked across hot ploughshares without injury.[6] The eleventh-century Queen Cunegunda, it was said, lived in a chaste marriage with her husband, the Ottonian emperor Henry II. However, the devil circulated rumors that she was unfaithful. Cunegunda chose to walk over hot plowshares to prove her virginity, and her feet were left unscathed.[7] A widely-circulated twelfth-century story concerned the eighth-century Saint Gengulfus, whose wife's fidelity was apparently suspect. He asked her to retrieve a stone from the bottom of a certain cold spring; when she removed her arm, it was burned as if by fire, therefore proving that she had been unfaithful.[8]

As these stories demonstrate, the ordeal of chastity has a long and varied genealogy in the West, both mythical (that is, as preserved in folklore and literary texts) and historical (that is, as accounted for in early medieval law, such as in the trial by fire or water and/or the ritual oath). In what follows, I focus on the motif of the ordeal as it is found in the long, episodic romance and in the short *lai*. In both genres, the ordeal is usually used to verify what medieval Christians recognized as marital chastity; that is, fidelity to one's spouse – invariably, a wife's sexual faithfulness. An ordeal, as opposed to a test or proof, is a matter of performance: the virgin or faithful wife must swear an oath, and/or successfully complete an impossible, magical, or dangerous task in order to prove her chastity. The consequences of failure are immediate and irreparable for the accused: injury, banishment, or death.

As a public spectacle, the chastity ordeal and its rituals as they are played out in the romance and the *lai* have much in common with the public proof of virginity in the saint's legend. Just as the saint's virginity is both the property and proof of the Church, a wife's chastity is ornament and testimony to the honor of the husband and/or the community. While virginity functions as a measure of the body ecclesiastical, marital fidelity functions as a measure of the body politic: in both cases, the success, continuance, and integrity of the institutional body is proved upon the feminine body. The miracle that is the defining moment in hagiography is paralleled by magic in the romance, magic that resides in the cup that a woman must drink from without spilling a drop, or in the cloak that a woman must don in the hope that it fits her perfectly. There is, however, a crucial difference between the staging of the proof of virginity in hagiography and that of the ordeal in vernacular romance: the virgin saint is always triumphant in her purity, but the wife or lover usually fails the ordeal. On the occasions that a woman actually passes an ordeal, she does so as a paragon against which other wanting women are measured – or, more commonly and more notoriously, a woman triumphs through rhetorical or physical trickery.

Historians and literary critics have long considered the judicial ordeal to be the more privileged and productive site for investigation, treating the literary representation of the ordeal as derivative and secondary, as vestiges of a folkloric tradition that must be recuperated by history. More interested in the social formations that produced the ordeal, scholars have traditionally read the episode of the ordeal in the literary text as reflective of (and often critical of) real practice. (The ordeal found in many of the Tristan and Isolde romances is a case in point, as I will show in my discussion, below, of Gottfried von Strassburg's *Tristan*, in which Îsôt manages to trick her husband Mark, the entire court, and even God through a clever verbal ploy.) As a result, until recently,[9] the fundamental issue of gender in the tale of the ordeal has been suppressed in favor of its interest as a commentary on the evolving social institutions governing the relations between men during the Middle Ages.[10] The motif itself has escaped ideological analysis. In this chapter, while keeping in mind the historical context that shaped the literary representation of the ordeal, I read the ordeal as a trope on its own terms. I show how the ordeal, ostensibly about the women who are forced to undergo it, is really about the men who insist upon it. At first glance, the many literary depictions of the chastity ordeal seem intended to discourage women from breaking their marriage vows. I do think that a didactic lesson is often meant, and in some cases, it is a lesson backed up by an implied or quite blatant threat. However, after women fail the ordeal, our attention shifts to the men who must act on the results, and who then refuse to do so. Most men disavow the "evidence" of the ordeal, for to exile, divorce, or kill one's wife – someone's daughter, sister, or cousin – threatens the foundation upon which homosociality is built.[11] In effect, the narrative of the ordeal in the romance and the *lai* allowed its original audience to imagine what would happen if a community were to follow the ordeal to its logical conclusion – when, for example, King Mark in Malory's *Morte Darthur* orders his wife and the other women at court to be burned for treason after they fail a drinking horn test. More interestingly, when a wife fails a chastity ordeal in the romance or the *lai*, it seems to be not so much of a reflection on her (though it is) as it is a commentary on the precarious status of the husband, a status which is paradoxically dependent upon his wife's behavior. Allen Frantzen, in his analysis of early medieval penitentials in which women are usually punished more severely than men for adultery, argues:

> The canons concerning adultery are not about the act or the person who performs it; rather, they are about the husband's status and his vulnerability to [the wife's] acts. ... They also suggest that the male can be seen as occupying the weaker role, for his status is subject to his wife's behavior; her misconduct is more heavily assessed because her wrongdoing damages her husband's prestige and defies his power over her.[12]

Though realized within a different discursive system than that of the penitentials, the literary representation of a chastity ordeal is also concerned with the issue of a husband's prestige. The penitentials cannot always be taken as evidence of actual practice, yet we can understand that any attempt to assign a certain penance would have depended upon a wife's confession of wrongdoing – too late to prevent damage to a husband's honor. On the other hand, the narrative of the ordeal recuperates a husband's honor through denying, or suppressing, the very public evidence of a wife's guilt. Ultimately, the ordeal narrative reveals that the bonds that hold a community together are fragile indeed, capable of breaking if tested too severely. In fact, the ordeal makes it clear that such bonds are not at all natural and preordained, but constructed and contingent, and therefore in need of constant maintenance.

In discussing the medieval judicial ordeal, John Bowers says:

> The body of the accused afforded a kind of documentation synthesizing the past deed with the present trial in order to render a visible text of justification. The flesh itself became the litmus paper upon which the acid of guilt might be made legible.[13]

This is true in that the ordeal is predicated upon the notion that the body is a readable body. However, simply because the body is made the repository of truth does not mean that it actually holds or tells the truth. Thus I also argue that the ordeal confirms not the certainty of the body, but its dubiety. In a way, the narrative of the chastity ordeal parallels the logic of the Freudian fetish in that it is a narrative of desire predicated upon absence and loss. The magic drinking horn and the ritualized oath both obscure and reveal "facts" about the female body. "A fetish," as Robert Stoller famously put it, "is a story masquerading as an object," and the ordeal operates in a similar way in that it condenses within it an entire narrative of desire activated by the subject-supposed-to-know who suddenly finds himself not-so-in-the-know.[14]

The suggestion that the ordeal of chastity is structured like a fetish allows me to make another, more general point in this chapter about the problems and pleasures of signification in the text. It seems that virginity is so overdetermined that apparently just about anything can signify its presence or absence. A perusal of the *Motif-Index of Folk-Literature* amply illustrates this point: the magic object necessary to exposing infidelity or unchastity could be an apple, a bed and/or pillows, a bridge, a chair (an unchaste woman cannot sit on it), a cloak, a cup, a dog, a harp (it will play out of tune if a nonvirgin approaches), a lamp, a mirror, a pin (if a pin floats in water, the woman is chaste), a plant, a spring or a fountain, a statue, a stone, a swan, a tree, and even the dust of the Tabernacle. Ordeals are equally diverse, including catching a salmon with one's bare hands, holding the greased and shaven tail of a bull, holding a poisonous snake, passing through fire, or passing under a magic rod. "Indexes" (as the *Motif-Index* classifies them) of faithfulness or unfaithfulness include a number of material objects: a handkerchief, a picture, a ring, a shirt, a sword, uncooked meat, or various flowers. We even find Italian and Indian analogues of a story in which a woman's talking vulva betrays her. Under the classification of "illicit sexual relations," we find a South American Indian story about a young woman whose loss of virginity is exposed when her nipples turn black. In many chastity tests, the virgin is hypersensitive to touch or smell: if a feather is put on a lintel of a door, and a nonvirgin passes underneath, she will blush (recall the story of the Princess and the Pea). Virgins often possess special powers, the exhibition of which functions as proof of chastity: a virgin can make a ball of water, carry water in a sieve, raise a fallen elephant, or blow out one candle with one puff and re-light it with another.

Virginity is such a crucial concept in both lived experience and metaphorical representation that its signs are necessarily infinite and infinitely generative, migrating from body parts to objects and back again in an endless loop. A cup or a ring, objects somewhat analogous to the female body (particularly so in classical and medieval gynecology), makes some mimetic sense – but a dog? (It would be reductive to play match-the-symbol game: dog = fidelity.) Moreover, just as the signifier (that is, the material or linguistic component of the sign – the magic object or sworn oath) is capable of multiplying and shifting, the signified (that is, the idea – virginity/chastity) is almost as fluid and mobile, and could include "honor of the family," or "the status of a husband," "the assurance of a bloodline," "the character of a saint," "the body and spirit of the Church," or even "the integrity of the text." Just why virginity serves as such a crucial hinge, generating so many signifiers in one direction and signifieds in the other, is a complicated question, and one that may be answered according to the logic of more than one critical paradigm. In what follows, I find Lacan's concept of the Imaginary – a forever-lost place or condition that extends into the Symbolic as the Real – richly suggestive for reading the literary quest for the definitive signs of virginity/chastity. In invoking Lacan, I am mindful that feminists have thoroughly critiqued Lacan's systemic phallocentrism. However, it is precisely Lacan's phallocentric schema that helps us understand the narrative of the desire to verify virginity/chastity (whatever its historic and specific manifestations).

For Lacan, the sign always marks both presence (signifier) and absence (signified). This is a (linguistic, psychological) paradox that Tertullian seems fully aware of and finds useful for discussing virginity and its ontological instability when he declares: "For a virgin ceases to be a virgin from the time it becomes possible for her not to be one" ("Ex illo enim virgo jam desinit, ex quo potest non esse").[15] In other words, and according to the paradigm that Tertullian is building, virginity is so fragile a state, so vulnerable to the gaze, that as soon as it is recognized as such, it vanishes. Lacan's Imaginary follows a similar trajectory in that it also is subject to an infinite regress, receding further into the distance the more one attempts to approach. In what follows, I read the idea of virginity, always already feminized, and therefore in and of the Imaginary, as a way to figure the Imaginary. In such a scheme, the hymen – both the anatomical part and its many cultural analogues, such as cups, cloaks, and rings – could be read as constructed within the Symbolic as a bar intended to seal off the Imaginary. However, and simultaneously, the hymen is a breach through which the Imaginary continually leaks into the Symbolic. This paradox in part explains the obsessive and persistent need to return to the body, to insure that the hymen is "there" while suppressing the knowledge that it is not there. Moreover, the ordeal narrative repeatedly demonstrates that virginity cannot be subsumed in and proved by the Law of the Father – that, in fact, virginity continually calls into question the theoretical foundations of the Symbolic. We should not forget that virginity is a construct intelligible only according to a patriarchal script – a retrofitted ideal within the Symbolic, in Lacanian terms. As a signifier for a lost Imaginary, virginity actually derives its power from the Law of the Father; that is, it is not "really" of the Imaginary, but only of the Imaginary as the Imaginary can be opposed to the Symbolic within a phallocentric paradigm.

A turn to Lacan does not mean that one must turn away from history. Hayden White, in "The Value of Narrativity in the Representation of Reality," in fact casts the problem of the historical narrative in Lacanian terms when he says:

> The history ... belongs to the category of what might be called "the discourse of the real," as against the "discourse of the imaginary" or the "discourse of desire" ... we can comprehend the appeal of historical discourse by recognizing the extent to which it makes the real desirable, makes the real into an object of desire.[16]

In this context, we might read the narrative of verifying virginity as dramatizing a desire to return to a place that never existed in time, space, or psyche, a nostalgia for a time before history, as it were, before the very idea of "before" and "after" existed, before the binary of fiction and history was created by the Law of the Father. In attempting to establish the "history" of the feminine body to separate the fact of unchastity or infidelity from fiction, the ordeal only generates more anxiety, for it reveals how easy it is to substitute fiction for fact. The feminine body is enough of a provocation in and of itself within patriarchy, but it has also been constructed as the traditional *locus classicus* for the acting out of anxieties and desires about representationality. As R. Howard Bloch says:

> If the impossibility of locating virginity, which resides neither in the chaste body, nor in the body's desire, nor in the look, makes of it an abstraction equivalent to an Idea, the loss of virginity seems closest to what the medievals conceived as the loss of universality of an Idea through its expression. And since the paradox of virginity is, in essence, that of representation, any expression will do.[17]

Constructed knowledges, constructed ordeals

While historians have been able to locate references to the judicial ordeal in Western Europe in legal records as early as the fifth century, they have quite prudently refrained from attempting to account for its prehistoric origins.[18] The Western judicial ordeal seems to have originated among the Franks: as their power and influence spread, so did the practice of the ordeal. The pre-Christian uses of the ordeal came to be subsumed under the rubric of ecclesiastical authority, and the belief in supernatural intervention transformed into faith in God's omniscience.

Historians have not always agreed on how widely the trial by ordeal was actually practiced in Western Europe, but it seems to have been common enough for the Lateran Council to prohibit it in 1215. Generally speaking, the ordeal was used when evidence was ambiguous or nonexistent, and no witnesses were forthcoming.[19] Peter Brown and Paul Hyams have argued that the trial by ordeal functioned best in small communities in which consensus was paramount – as

Hyams puts it, "each man's personal character and standing are publicly known and affect the welfare of the rest."[20] On the other hand, Robert Bartlett argues in *Trial by Fire and Water: The Medieval Judicial Ordeal* that the ordeal also served the interests of lords who were intent on consolidating their power, and depended on ecclesiastical support to do so.[21]

No matter the context of the ordeal, scholars are agreed that the outcome of the ordeal was often recognized as ambiguous by those who used it. God may reveal the truth through the ordeal, but fallible – and interested – humans still had to interpret the signs. For example, in the trial of the hot iron, after the accused had grasped the iron, his or her hands would be bandaged for three days. Representatives from both sides of the dispute would then inspect the accused's hands in order to judge if they had healed properly; if so, the accused was innocent. The witnesses did not always agree on what they saw.[22] Such ambiguity, Brown argues, was not necessarily negative: "There was a built-in flexibility in the ordeal that enabled the group ... to maintain a degree of initiative quite contrary to the explicit ideology of the ordeal."[23]

Bartlett cites a handful of legal examples of the ordeal of the hot iron used in cases of alleged adultery, as well as in cases of sodomy, incest, bestiality, and disputed paternity.[24] And in two recent and invaluable articles that assess the impact of the juridical ordeal on literary texts, John Baldwin's "The Crisis of the Ordeal: Literature, Law, and Religion around 1200," and John Bowers' "Ordeals, Privacy, and the *Lais* of Marie de France," the authors focus on the use of the ordeal to uncover hidden or secret crimes. Baldwin in particular focuses on sexual transgressions: seduction, rape, and adultery. For Baldwin, the "crisis" of the ordeal lies in its inability to bring about closure; the ambiguity of the ordeal is simply too much for a given community to bear.[25] Yet it strikes me that it is precisely *because* of the difficulties inherent in determining the truth of certain crimes and acts that, as the actual use of the trial by ordeal goes into decline, the ordeal continues to survive in the medieval romance, where, as I have said, the (often pleasurable) tensions between fiction and reality are deliberately foregrounded.

Two texts that contain episodes that are either indebted to or closely parallel the judicial ordeal are Gottfried von Strassburg's *Tristan* (1200–1210) and Jean Renart's *Romance of the Rose*, also known as *Guillaume de Dole* (early thirteenth century). In both texts, the plot turns on the resourcefulness of a woman – or to put it in Lacanian terms, Gottfried's Îsôt and Renart's Liénor successfully challenge the Symbolic order by manipulating the Law of the Father that maintains it.

Gottfried von Strassburg's *Tristan* contains both the oath and the trial of the hot iron of the juridical ordeal. Yet the oath is actually a compromised oath, or equivocal oath – so worded that it is technically true, but also so worded that it obscures the truth of the matter. (Béroul is the first to attach the equivocal oath to the Tristan legend in *Le Roman de Tristan* [c. 1170].) As such, the equivocal oath is the narrativized equivalent of faking the medical (or pseudo-medical) virginity test. We find an early example of the equivocal oath in the late second-century romance, *Leucippe and Cleitophon*. Thersander, suspicious of his wife Melite, asks her to take the following oath:

> if Melite has not celebrated the communion rites of Aphrodite with this stranger *during the period of my absence*, and if she enters the waters of the holy Styx and swears to that, she will be acquitted of all charges.[26] (Emphasis mine)

The specificity of time that we see here ("during the period of my absence") is characteristic of the equivocal oath that we find in earlier, Eastern analogues and later Western medieval romances. Melite accepts the challenge to enter the Styx, saying that she will extend her oath to include: "I never allowed any man at all ... during the specified period."[27] This is indeed easy for Melite to swear to, for while she had taken a lover, she did so only after her husband had returned.

Gottfried von Strassburg's Îsôt also fulfils the letter, but not the spirit, of her oath, and consequently interrogates not only the concept of chastity (that is, marital fidelity), but the legal system – the codified Law of the Father – that depends upon juridical oath-taking.[28] Briefly, the story is as follows: discontents Melôt and Marjodo scheme to catch Îsôt and Tristan together, to "make trial of their intimacy" (*ursuoche leite*).[29] One evening, the King, Îsôt, Tristan, Brangæne, and Melôt are resting together in the royal bedchamber after having been bled. After Mark leaves the room, Melôt sprinkles flour between Îsôt's and Tristan's beds. Tristan, warned by Brangæne, avoids this trap by leaping from bed to bed; however, his vein opens, and he bleeds all over Îsôt's bed and then his own. Faced with this "evidence," what the narrator calls "Love's traces" (*minnen spor*[30]), Mark is uncertain how to proceed, for, as the narrator says, he has found evidence in his bed, "though not before it, and was thus told the truth and denied it."[31] The King takes his dilemma to his nobles, and the Bishop points out that, because the lovers are not caught *in flagrante delicto* – a crucial juridical requisite – there is no actual evidence of adultery.[32] Though she is not bound to do so by law, Îsôt agrees to undergo the ordeal by red-hot iron to clear her name. As many readers of the *Tristan* have noted, Gottfried/the narrator makes it very clear from the outset that his sympathies lie with the two lovers, whom he represents as bound together by an ennobling and transcendent passion. Thus it is not surprising that, during the episode of the ordeal, the narrator commiserates with Îsôt, even though he plainly acknowledges her guilt, saying at one point that the Queen gave away all her possessions "to win God's favour, so that He might overlook her very real trespasses."[33] He tells us that Îsôt is "harassed by the secret anxiety that she may have to whitewash her falseness," and so she "propounded to her secret self a ruse that presumed very far upon her Maker's courtesy."[34] So far, Gottfried/the narrator has more or less managed to defend Tristan and Îsôt's adulterous love against secular condemnation; here, he continues to save the appearances of the ideal love that he has chosen to celebrate, even when it offends against sacred law.

Îsôt plans things so that, on the day of her trial, Tristan comes to her ship disguised as a pilgrim. Îsôt declares that she will have no other carry her ashore. She whispers instructions to Tristan to stumble and drop them both to the ground, where he ends up in her arms. She then addresses Mark, fashioning her oath in the following way:

That no man in the world had carnal knowledge of me or lay in my arms or beside me but you, always excepting the poor pilgrim whom, with your own eyes, you saw lying in my arms.[35]

Just as in *Leucippe and Cleitophon*, the specificity of the oath helps to clear the Queen. Thus both Melite in the Greek romance and Îsôt in the *Tristan* turn the literalness of the Law of the Father – a literalness that is indeed an illusion – to their own ends.

The narrator of the *Tristan* then makes a speech that has troubled critics ever since:

Thus it was made manifest and confirmed to all the world that Christ in His great virtue is pliant as a windblown sleeve. He falls into place and clings, whichever way you try Him, closely and smoothly, as He is bound to do. He is at the beck of every heart for honest deeds or fraud. Be it deadly earnest or game, He is just as you would have Him.[36]

Critical reaction to this passage has been various and contradictory. I would like to note a few enduring interpretations. Some readers have argued that Gottfried/the narrator intended to criticize the practice of the judicial ordeal, already falling into disfavor as he was writing the *Tristan*. Others have argued that he intended Christ to represent a courtly figure, a champion of love – an interpretation that is not so far-fetched, given the narrator's overall treatment of the two lovers. Or, as still others have argued, perhaps the poet was simply committing blasphemy by turning Christ into Eros.[37] These and other arguments are premised upon the belief that Gottfried's poem has an internal, consistent coherence and design. Yet if we depart from this premise, we might read the narrator's speech as dramatizing a contradictory narrative in which the conflicts of private desires versus public responsibilities are not resolved, but foregrounded on the level of plot so that contradiction itself comes to function as a signifier. However, none of these arguments take into account that, in reducing Christ and his omniscience to the status of a magical charm or fetish, Gottfried may have been speaking ironically. Christ, the sacred embodied *logos*, is "just as you would have Him" ("er ist ie, swie so man wil"); he may or may not be an Eros figure, but he is certainly a sliding signifier.

Consider the chastity ordeal-cum-test in what is known as the First Continuation of Chrétien de Troyes' *Perceval*, in the episode (also known as the *Livre de Caradoc*) concerning a magic drinking horn. Guenievre, knowing that her infidelity is about to be revealed, prays aloud, asking for the horn to splash wine on Artus. When it does, Artus interprets the spill as a miracle, not as proof of the horn's efficacy – or, at least, Artus *says* that this is what he believes.[38] One sign system is thus substituted for another, and the ease with which it is done destabilizes both the "system" that the horn represents and the "system" that prayer represents. In fact, Guenievre actually has given Artus a convenient way out of his dilemma, a way to save face. In the same way, the literal becomes a loophole for Mark and his assembled nobles and clerics in Gottfried's *Tristan*. They get the chastity ordeal – and the results – which they deserve. In both cases, Artus and Mark would have had to face the consequences of failure: the infidelity of a wife may well be a private scandal, but the infidelity of a Queen threatens the whole realm, not only because a legitimate heir is essential to its continued stability, but also because the King embodies the State in a fundamental way. If the Queen can be accused of perfidy, then the King is open to critique as well, a critique that extends to the relations that he has built with those who have sworn allegiance to him. If a man cannot rule his wife – take his rightful place as head, to invoke St. Paul – how can he rule his kingdom or expect his lords to follow him? The answer to this question is one that most men in the vernacular romance seek to avoid.

In my next example of a literary depiction of a judicial ordeal, we find how, according to the internal logic of the text, a community actively participates in constructing and then reading the signifiers of virginity. In Jean Renart's *Guillaume de Dole*, the judicial ordeal is employed to prove not marital fidelity, but actual virginity. A brief synopsis of this romance may be helpful: after hearing his minstrel Jouglet tell a tale about a worthy knight and a beautiful lady, the Emperor Conrad is saddened because no such characters exist in real life. Jouglet tells him about Guillaume de Dole and his sister Liénor, who are remarkable in every way. Conrad falls in love with the very name of the lady, and desires to marry her. His jealous seneschal determines to thwart Conrad's plan, and visits Guillaume's house. (Interestingly, the seneschal, like many a romance heroine before and after him, remains nameless in a text that is very much interested in the politics of identity, naming, and accusing.) Though he never sees Liénor, the seneschal meets her foolish mother, who praises Liénor's beauty, confiding that the girl has a small rose on her thigh ("'No man who is capable of speech will ever see so great a marvel as the crimson rose on her soft white thigh.'"[39] The seneschal convinces Conrad that he "had had her virginity," citing his knowledge of the rose as proof.[40] (The recent drama played out in the media over Paula Jones' claim to know all about President Clinton's "distinguishing characteristics" has its fictional analogues.) Conrad halts all wedding plans. Her brother is too ill from shame to defend her, so Liénor goes to court on her own behalf. First, she sends a brooch, an embroidered belt, and an emerald ring to the seneschal, charging her messenger to say that they are from a lady who had previously rejected him, but now desires his love. He is to wear the gifts under his clothes. Liénor then goes before Conrad and accuses the seneschal of rape and theft, pointing to the jewels and belt as evidence. The seneschal takes an oath: "'May God strike me dead if I've ever seen her before!'"[41]

Liénor agrees to have the truth of her case adjudicated by an ordeal. The seneschal is immersed in holy water, and sinks to the bottom – the sign of his innocence. This is precisely the outcome Liénor hopes for. She then reveals her identity, reminding Conrad that the seneschal swore that he had never met her. She says: "'You have all seen how we were both exonerated by his ordeal; he did not have my virginity nor did he dishonor me.'"[42] The Emperor and Liénor marry.

Not surprisingly, recent readings of the *Romance* have focused on the role and function of language in the text, on what Laurence de Looze describes as "the interplay between art and reality."[43] Norris Lacy notes that Conrad falls in love because of a story told by his minstrel; in other words, he falls in love with a name – a signifier. Conrad comes to "know" Jouglet's Lady, not through experience, but through narrative.[44] Similarly, virginity, its presence or absence, is also made known to the seneschal (and then to the Emperor) through narrative. In the end, Lïenor proves to be the more able storyteller, outdoing the seneschal and even Jouglet; she "installs a new, more complex mode of fiction," as de Looze puts it; "her story becomes a laying bare of the discourse of fiction, an uncovering of the dialectic of truth and fable."[45] Renart's text is indeed a witty commentary on the instability of signs in general, and on how virginity resists verification in particular. As Helen Solterer says, "a wedge is driven between the linguistic representation of virginity and the physical form it takes. The discourse on the virgin does not correspond to the shape of a woman's body."[46]

By making the seneschal's body the object of the ordeal, *Guillaume de Dole* inverts the conventional subject/object positions of the chastity ordeal. As Solterer notes, it is the male body that is put on display, a reversal that she describes as "a delicious parody of the ritualized inspection of the virgin's body."[47] However, this reversal can only be taken so far, for it is still *female* virginity that is the object of scrutiny. In essence, the "signs" of *female* virginity are so overdetermined, so capable of migrating from site to site, that even the *male* body is capable of displaying them.

Within the mimetic but extra-real frame of the tale, what remains unquestioned is the ability of Conrad's court to agree upon a version/virgin. The rose on Lïenor's thigh is an already overdetermined sign, a flower with its origins in metaphor plucked from the Song of Songs (in which the beloved is a *flos*) and in the Latin and French verbs for "taking" or "losing" virginity: *deflorare* and *desflorer*. (Such associations are elaborated much more explicitly in that other, later, *Roman de la Rose*.) On one level, the rose is a fetishized mark that signifies a hidden, unknowable body part, a displaced, aestheticized hymen. The rose may or may not figure the physical "hymen" – that is, the "virginal membrane"; yet, as we have seen in Chapter 1, since the hymen is already compromised as a sign, physiologically and figuratively, the rose may well stand in for "any" hymen – that is, any sign of virginity.

On another level, the rose illustrates how knowledge is constructed and then disbursed/dispersed at Conrad's court. Lïenor's rose functions as a commodity in a verbal exchange – mother to seneschal, seneschal to Conrad, Conrad to court, and finally (restored) to Lïenor, who will, presumably, "give" it or "lose" it to Conrad. At the same time, such a "happy" ending also marks the end of circulating signs, of ambiguity itself. Once virginity is finally "disappeared," there is no story; however, so long as virginity remains in doubt, the narrative may continue. In this light, we might read *Guillaume de Dole* as a meditation on desire generated by a sign system *for* a sign system; within this tautology, the rose figures this desire. This point brings us from Freud's and Marx's technical uses of the word *fetish* to fetish-as-metaphor, as Jean Baudrillard prefers it. For Baudrillard, true fetishism resides in "the passion for the code," which is an ideological process, not a static thing. He sees fetishization as a preoccupation with the transcendent system ("the closed perfection of a system") that governs both subject and object. (The desire for a totalizing system in the first place creates the subject/object split.) In "Fetishism and Ideology: The Semiological Reduction," Baudrillard writes:

> the fetishist metaphor consists of analyzing myths, rites and practices in terms of *energy*, a magical transcendent power ... As a power that is transferred to beings, objects and agencies, it is universal and diffuse, but it crystallizes at strategic points so that its flux can be regulated and diverted by certain groups or individuals for their own benefit.[48]

The rose (the hymen) is one of those crystallized or reified "points," part of a pre- and inter-textual system of signs that all the players – Lïenor, the seneschal, Conrad, his court – collude in. It can be regulated (and even "diverted," as in the story of Îsôt's equivocal oath) by the ordeal, which is itself another sign in the continuous loop of the signifying chain.

We might also read the ordeals and their outcomes in these two romances as marking crucial moments in the history of two (albeit imaginary) dynasties: one that is passing away, and one that is about to be born. The Arthuriad is a story that, no matter how many times it is told, always ends badly. Tristan and Îsôt's ill-fated and illicit love, Mark's craven behavior, and the success of the equivocal oath function as signs of a social system in decline. On the other hand, if we project the "happily ever after" logic of *Guillaume de Dole* beyond its end point, we can predict that Conrad and his publicly-certified virgin bride will soon produce an heir, thus securing Conrad's throne and his lineage. These two texts – the first a cautionary tale, the second a fairy tale – reproduce and celebrate the values and aims of a social system dependent upon verified virginity and married chastity.

Truth or consequences

Foucault says: "Nothing in man – not even his body – is sufficiently stable to serve as the basis for self-recognition or for understanding other men."[49] The absoluteness of this statement and the absoluteness of Foucault's choice of grammatical gender help me make my argument in what follows. As we have seen in earlier chapters, the bodily signs of chastity ultimately remain unknowable in medical discourse, however they may be inscribed – the hymen, the shape and condition of the uterus, the appearance of the urine. Medieval religious and didactic discourse confirms that physical virginity is impossible to ascertain, preferring to locate its proofs and signs within the community formed by the faithful. In other words, identifying and defining "virginity" is always an effect and a function of the social. As such, female virginity and marital chastity carry a heavy burden of significance not only for women, but for men – and perhaps even more so for men, as I have been suggesting.

In medieval Western Europe, a woman's chastity served as an important token in homosocial exchange between men of the aristocracy, and strengthened the links between them. A married woman's fidelity not only reflected upon the husband, earning him admiration and respect, but, and more important, insured that his property and goods (even if he acquired them in the first place through his wife's dowry) were passed on properly, through blood. Among the nobility of medieval Europe, building alliances, allegiances, and empires was often predicated upon a strategic marriage and a secured lineage. In *The Knight, the Lady and the Priest*, Georges Duby says of marriage generally that it insures "the statue of heirs – that is, it gives the offspring ancestors, a name, and rights," and "regulates the transmission of wealth from one generation to another."[50] Assuring paternity depended upon assuring virginity. (It is ironic that both these conditions, so crucial to men's social relations, cannot be finally determined. Even DNA testing today is not fully dependable.)

Biket's *Lai du Cor* (third quarter of the twelfth century) is considered to be the oldest extant version of the motif of the fidelity horn in Western European literature, and aptly illustrates my argument that it is men (and the social code that they have created) who are ultimately tested, not women. Written just as Chrétien de Troyes began to compose his great Arthurian cycle (1170s through the 1180s), the *Lai du Cor* represents a different sensibility entirely. At Carlion, Artus' court is about to begin their feast. A squire arrives with a gift of a magical ivory horn for Artus, and leaves rather hastily, perhaps aware of the havoc his gift is about to create at court. Artus asks his chaplain to read the inscription on the horn, but the chaplain says that it is for Artus' ears only: "ne fu si grant oïe; / mais n'est lius qu'or le die" ("it ought not to be said here and now").[51] The king may have good reason, the chaplain suggests, for censoring the message of the horn. But Artus insists. Part of the inscription reads:

> Qui a cel cor bevra
> femme li estovra
> qui onques n'ait pensé –
> ne por deslealté
> ne por aveir conquerre
> ne por plus bel en terre –
> qu'ele de son seignor
> volsist aveir meillor.
> Se la soe est si veire,
> donc en porra li beire. (241–50)

> [Who would drink from this horn must have a wife who has never thought – out of disloyalty, out of desire for power, out of desire for gain – that she would take someone she thought better. If his wife is really true, then only such a one can drink from it.]

Hearing these words, *la reïne* – Guinevere is never named in the poem – sits with her head bowed. She can read this particular sign all too well, and seems to realize, along with the chaplain, that the very introduction of this challenge into the community will necessitate a response. Artus, angry at what the gift implies, calls for the horn to be filled "saveir se j'en bevrai" ("to know if I can drink from it," 280). Artus spills wine all the way "contreval des qu'as piez" ("down to his feet," 289). The amount of spilled wine suggests the extent and excess of Guinevere's infidelity. Note that it is the men, not the women, who must drink from the magic horn. This is not uncommon in the medieval analogues of the ordeal-cum-test. Just as in *Guillaume de Dole*, in which Lïenor's virginity is proved upon the senechal's body, in the *Lai du Cor*, wifely fidelity is proved upon the husband's body. Once again, our attention is drawn to the overdetermined nature of the signifier for female virginity/chastity, capable of traversing the boundaries of the gendered body.

My next example is the magic drinking horn found in Sir Thomas Malory's *Morte Darthur* (completed c. 1470; printed by Caxton in 1485). Intended for Gwenyver by Morgan le Fay, the horn is intercepted by Lamerok and sent to Mark instead. Lamerok says to Morgan's messenger: "For in the dyspyte of sir Tristrames thou shalt bere hit hym, that horne, and sey that I sente hit hym for to assay his lady, and yf she be trew he shall preve her."[52] Malory describes the horn as

> a fayre horne harneyste with golde, and the horne had such a vertu that there myght no lady nothir jantyllwoman drynke of that horne but yf she were trew to her husbande; and if she were false she sholde spylle all the drynke. (429)

In addition to its magical properties, and like the horn in the *Lai du Cor*, this horn is beautifully made. The narrator's description focuses our attention on it as an object in itself, fixing it as a fetish. And, as in the *Lai du Cor*, the challenge that the horn represents goads a king into using it. Mark insists that Queen Isode and all one hundred of her ladies drink, but "there were but four ladyes of all tho that dranke clene" (430).

So far, so good. The magic horn seems to be doing what it is designed to do: expose the secret infidelities of the women who drink from it. Now let us consider what happens after the women fail the test, when the men must confront the consequences. In the *Lai du Cor*, Artus threatens the shamed Queen with a dagger: "Or est pis!" ("this is intolerable!" 291), but his knights intervene. Ivain, conciliatory, says that there is no married woman who has not had a foolish thought. The Queen confesses to having given a ring to a young boy, a *danzel*, who had killed a giant, but that is the extent of her "infidelity." This "sin" is a minor transgression, even a charming transgression. Still not satisfied, Artus ("ja sols n'i avrai honte"; "I alone will not be shamed in this," 408) makes his guests – kings, counts, barons, and lesser folk – drink from the horn, and is restored to good humor only when they all spill the wine. The knight Garados is the only one who can drink without spilling a drop; he is the exemplar of the group, and the one whose success everyone chooses to ignore. His unnamed wife's fidelity serves to throw the infidelity of the rest of the women into sharper focus. Garados is given the horn to take home to Cirencestre – presumably as far from the court as possible. The embarrassed men claim that "car qui cest cor crerreit / sa muillier honireit" ("whoever credits this horn does no honor to his wife" 449–450). This is a stunning deconstruction of the premise that the men of the court were so willing to believe at first: that wifely fidelity can indeed be ascertained, and that the horn is the appropriate instrument for doing so.

The chastity-horn episode in the *Morte Darthur* has its origins in masculine anxieties about homosocial relations: earlier, Lamerok had challenged Tristram to a joust, but Tristram declined, saying it would not be fair or honorable, since Lamerok was too tired to fight. Mark commanded Tristram to fight Lamerok anyway. However, after knocking Lamerok off his horse, Tristram refused to fight him on foot. Lamerok is left feeling angry and ashamed. When he meets Morgan's messenger, he avails himself of the opportunity for revenge, which he almost achieves when Mark swears that Isode and the other women who failed the ordeal will be burned at the stake.[53] It seems that for Mark to desire to dispose of his own wife is one matter, but to presume to dispose of the wives of his men is quite another. His barons overrule him, nicely sidestepping the issue of infidelity and its consequences by arguing that "playnly they wolde not have tho ladyes brente for an horne made by sorcery ... For that horne dud never good, but caused stryff and bate" (430). As in the *Lai du Cor*, the infidelity is erased, and blame is transferred from the women to the now-maligned and untrustworthy object – and away from the possibility that Mark might do harm to his sworn men, or that the barons might actually revolt against their King. This is necessary, of course, for if the very bonds that hold society together are destroyed – that is, the oaths that bind men together, as well as the ties of wives, sisters, and daughters – the "stryff and bate" would be unbearable.

In both Biket's and Malory's treatment of the chastity ordeal, the homosocial equilibrium is restored through the construction of a narrative to explain the outcome of the ordeal. In this respect, the ordeal, like the fetish, is a narrative of discovery. The shock that the little boy experiences when he looks up his mother's skirts (or however one might want to narrativize the originary encounter with lack) parallels (if not reaffirms) the shock caused by the magic drinking horn or hot iron. Each suspicion of infidelity, each chastity ordeal, recapitulates the "inaugural" (but imaginary, as Lacan would say) search for a hymen that may not have existed in the first place. What is finally revealed through the ordeal is not necessarily the fidelity or infidelity of wife or lover, but the impossibility of knowing so. The female body, already constructed as fundamentally lacking, lacks once again: it lacks an icon, as it were, where one can simply point and click to reveal a menu of sexual experience. Though a reader may already know – from another text or tale, that is – that Biket's Queen and Malory's Isode each have a lover, the text at hand offers no real proof of outright infidelity *at the time of the test*. The chastity ordeal reveals the inadequacy of a system constructed as necessary to the regulation of female sexuality, in turn constructed as necessary to the maintenance of gender difference, in turn constructed as necessary to the realization of masculine subjectivity.

Critique?

The Italian *Tristan* (*La Tavola Ritonda*; second quarter of the fourteenth century) contains a version of the horn test that illustrates my point not through reinforcing the homosocial, but by interrogating it. Queen Isotta refuses to drink from the horn, saying, "chè per lo incantamento di questo corno, potrebbe fare a me inguiria e cosie ancora ad altre dame" ("The enchantment on this horn could do me injury and other ladies as well").[54] Marco replies: "Dama, poco vi varrà dire parole; chè, per la mia fè, voi prenderete lo corno e berrete" ("Lady, your words are worth nothing, for by my faith, you will hold this horn and drink from it"). Isotta and *six hundred and eighty-six other women* are unable to drink without spilling the wine. The narrator declares:

> I believe that such a thing happened in this country because the ladies were all such drunkards, liars, and gluttons, and were so fond of clothes, and more lecherous than other ladies. The men were handsome but cowardly, unskilled at arms and without valor, but they were very arrogant and greedy. (103)[55]

Such a commentary, which purports to expose the actual behavior of both ladies and knights at Marco's court, in effect obscures the specific judgment of the horn. Feminine infidelity is constructed as the symptom of a corrupt society, not as its cause. Marco, however, unable to distinguish between cause and effect, orders *all* of the women to be "dibruciate e arse, come false e meretrici" ("stripped and burned as false and lying women" (159; 103). (The word *meretrici* has more abusive force when we recall its Latin origin: *whore-like*). But Marco's seneschal Dinasso intervenes, saying:

> My lord, it does not seem just to me that our ladies be burnt because of an enchanted horn which was made on purpose to destroy some lady by great wrong and falseness. ... But Queen Isotta, even though she is not guilty, since it is for your pleasure and delight, let her be burnt. (104)[56]

Dinasso follows a strategy that we have already seen at work in *Lai du Cor* and the *Morte Darthur*. He deflects attention away from the results of the test to the questionable efficacy of the object. Marco, "tuto insuperbi" ("full of pride"), is taken in by this example of reverse psychology, and, for the sake of his "good" Queen, pardons all. In this text, the disruption of the social contract is so highly exaggerated (recall those six hundred and eighty-six ladies) that it opens up a space for the possibility of a critique of the homosocial. Keeping in mind the double-voicedness of the Italian *Tristan* – it simultaneously upholds and undermines medieval ideals of chivalry throughout – I do not think that this reading is far-fetched. The magic drinking horn functions metonymically here, pointing as it does to a breakdown of societal norms. Both women *and* men have transgressed their (assigned) roles. Marco's desire to punish the women is a displacement of his own political (if not personal) impotence, which says more about his character and his relationship with his men than it does about his wife's fidelity. However, Dinasso (that is, Dinadan of the Prose *Tristan*, a figure who represents bemused skepticism about the codes of chivalric behavior in many versions of the Arthuriad) possesses the sense and foresight that his King lacks, and understands that it is precisely Marco's tenuous hold on his crown and on his men's loyalty that cannot be discussed.

The hyperbolic *La Tavola Ritonda*, in which a rash and foolish King attempts to rule over an excess of unfaithful wives and unchaste maids, also suggests that the various medieval secular and ecclesiastical institutionalizations of punishment for adultery, however conceived of as amends or as deterrents, actually represent a failure of discipline, an inability to create absolutely docile female bodies. Once such a possibility is raised, it must be suppressed, and the scene in which men choose to ignore or nullify the results of the chastity ordeal effectively functions to deny the knowledge of such a failure in the homosocial system.

Crises of representation, crises of chastity

In the episodic romance, the ordeal is one of many embedded tales that function on what narratologists call the *hypodiegetic* level. The hypodiegetic level, on which the seemingly diversionary or digressionary is written, is framed by the main narrative, called the *diegetic* level. In the romances under discussion here, it appears that the diegetic narrative, foregrounds a narrative of relations between men that the hypodiegetic story – in this case, the tale of the ordeal – both reinforces and destabilizes. Paradoxically, what reinforces the homosocial bond among men with a vested interest in the outcome of a chastity ordeal is the very ambiguity of the results of the ordeal. This ambiguity directs our attention to yet another story, the instability of narrative itself (a theme that one might say operates on the *extra*diegetic level of the romance). Heinrich von dem Türlin's *Diu Crône* (*The Crown*, 1215–20), illustrates these narrative complexities quite well.

Heinrich von dem Türlin proves himself to be quite the *bricoleur* of Arthurian tales and themes. Heinrich seems determined to create something of his own out of the matter of Arthur, but cannot quite throw off the influence of his predecessors. As a result, his poem swerves away from conventional retellings, making strange the familiar core of tales. The tone of *Diu Crône* is very different from previous French and German romances: Heinrich prefers low comedy to high seriousness as a strategy for critiquing the values of his Artûs' court. For example, *Diu Crône* contains no Arthur-Lancelot-Guinevere triangle (Chrétien de Troyes is the first to make Lancelot the Queen's lover); instead, the narrative energy of this story is subverted and shunted into the episode of Gasozien, who abducts and rapes Ginover. The abduction episode draws its inspiration from the fabliau, not the romance: Heinrich describes Ginover's rape in a series of coy and coarse metaphors. Lewis Jillings captures many of the qualities of *Diu Crône* when he says that it is intended to offer a lively chivalric romance ... [and] in inherent contradiction to this, to understand chivalry from within by its satirical treatment of courtly figures and values. Features of Heinrich's romance which merit attention are the professional self-awareness of the poet and his competitive impulse; the considerable secularism which is evident in the work; the presentation of opportunism and a practical attitude in the romance, which displays some disdain for chivalric ideals; and the manner in which comic and satirical elements obtrude at the cost of any high moral significance.[57]

What Jillings calls "professional self-awareness" is embodied in the figure of Keiî (an Unferð crossed with a court jester) whose extradiegetic commentary runs alongside that of the putative narrator's, sometimes agreeing, sometimes contradicting. It is tempting to read Keiî and his acerbic exegesis on the action of the poem as representing Heinrich himself – an author who cannot resist his own ironic and powerful metacommentary.

The plotting of the chastity ordeal distinguishes *Diu Crône* in a number of ways. Heinrich probably knew Biket's *Lai di Cor* and the anonymous *Lai du Cort Mantel* (also called *Le Mantel Mautaillié*, c. 1200), and would have appreciated the humor and satire found in both, but Heinrich's reworking of the motif is much more trenchant than what we find in these two poems. In these and other medieval analogues, Arthur fails the ordeal along with everyone else. Yet in *Diu Crône*, Artûs is the only one who succeeds. (Actually, there are two ordeals/tests in the poem: one involving a magic tankard, the other involving a magic glove. Artûs, along with Gawein, passes this latter test as well.) While men are usually exempt from the chastity ordeal in the romance, both men and women must submit to the test in *Diu Crône*. (However, as we have seen, men are never exempt from the consequences of the ordeal; it is tempting to think that Heinrich intends to make explicit what has previously been implicit in the ordeal narrative.) In addition, compared to the often cursory treatment of the ordeal found in other romances, the story of the magic tankard (*kopf*) is an elaborate, detailed narrative in itself (almost two thousand lines of the 30,000-line poem) – a hypodiegetic tale that has both an intra- and inter-textual function.[58] That is, within the frame of *Diu Crône*, the episode is intended as an exposé of the hypocrisies and follies of the women and men at Artûs' court. However, Heinrich also moves out of the frame of the poem to other Arthurian fictions in order to critique their depiction of courtly life. Heinrich mounts an Aristotelian critique of representation – of the manipulation of words and images that results in, at least in his mind, a distortion of the truth. His target is *idealized* courtly conduct; that is, literary representations of courtly life that, in effect, function as propaganda. Thus Heinrich cites *textual* history, not actual history, as the site of problematized chivalry.[59] Heinrich treats the slippage between appearance and actuality as an essential characteristic of romance, and parodies such slippage in his own story-telling and in a series of rhetorical contradictions in *Diu Crône*.

Heinrich exploits the motif of the magic cup or horn in a way that earlier narratives could not have predicted, and those after him never quite match. *Diu*

Crône demonstrates that, as one attempts to survey the many examples of the chastity ordeal in medieval vernacular romance, there is no clear pattern or evolution of the tale – that is, a movement from a "primitive" version to a more sophisticated one. Malory's better-known and later episode is inert and lifeless by comparison; the story of Îsôt's equivocal oath in Gottfried's contemporaneous *Tristan* is clever, but not as multi-layered as is Heinrich's treatment of the ordeal.

Let us turn to the poem. Artûs and his court are assembled together on Christmas Day: "everyone was longing for something unusual [*gevienc*] to occur. Once expressed, this wish passed from table to table and took possession of all, so that they forgot themselves [*selber vergâzen*] ... and thought of nothing else."[60] (The origins of this longing are elided by the immediate narrative, but fully present in the convention of the Christmas-day "custom of the court" or *âventiure* [13]). A strange knight appears, riding a winged beast that is half-horse, half-dolphin; while dressed impeccably in the French style, the knight is more fish than human. He brings Arthur a magic tankard, a gift from King Priure, the King of the Sea. However, the gift has certain conditions attached to it.

It is as if Heinrich intended to reproduce Lacan's description of the workings of desire in this opening scene. We meet the court as it begins to move out of a sort of collective Imaginary and into the mirror-stage. The "mirror" of Lacan's mirror-stage is a trap and a decoy in which the subject's attention is captured, seized by a reflected image. The fairy knight, in effect, is that mirror. (That the knight is dressed in the latest French fashion might suggest that, for Heinrich, he symbolizes French romance and its allurements.) Desire is figured as enchantment – and once it is put into motion, desire cannot be resisted. It leaps from knight to knight until the entire court "forgets" itself. In classic Lacanian fashion, the court "forgets" its own agency in setting desire in motion – though what is forgotten will "return" as a symptom, and this symptom will be re-figured as cause. As we shall see, the desire for "something unusual" will return to haunt the entire court. "This is what I have called putting the rabbit into the hat," says Lacan, "so as to be able to pull it out again later."[61] The message returns as "news." In essence, the subject, like the magician, must forget the origin of his own trick in order to maintain the illusion of his subjectivity, which is now constructed as dependent on the other. The court's desire is powerful enough to conjure up the means of its fulfillment: the magic tankard.

Before enumerating the conditions of King Priure's gift, the messenger-knight declares: "My message is not really important unless everyone hears it, which is why I came: to see that it is made public" (14). The ordeal of chastity is thus explicitly structured as a public event. As we have seen, a public staging is integral to the workings of the ordeal plot. As the fairy messenger says, the test has no significance *unless* it is conducted in full view of the community – according to the Law of the Father, to which even Artûs must submit.

The *kopf*, continues the fairy knight, has a "valuable quality ... which causes both joy and pain":

It distresses many whose false heart is hidden by an honorable appearance, for no evil man can make full use of it. He who is mean spirited or deceives his sweetheart has this reward: when he lifts the tankard to his mouth, it at once spills wine all over him. And woman's modesty will not protect a lady, for the same thing will happen to her if she is deceitful. (15; ll. 1126–46)

In other chastity ordeals, as we have seen, the magic cup is employed as a test of marital chastity only. Here, the subject of the test seems to be chivalric virtue itself – of which chastity and fidelity to one's spouse or lover is a subset. This description of the properties of the tankard leads us in two directions, back to the conventional motif of the magic drinking cup, and forward to Heinrich's own adaptation of the motif.

The fairy knight requests that the tankard be passed around the hall, to all the ladies and knights. "Should there be a man or woman among them who the tankard serves and thus clears of deceit, it shall be yours," he says to Artûs (15). After the women are brought into the hall, they are invited to drink first. Since only the men of the court were present when the fairy-knight entered the hall, only they choose whether to accept or reject the ordeal – and then choose not to tell the women about the tankard's powers. That the women are left in ignorance (as is the case in the *Lai du Cort Mantel*) is often read as comical. I think that there is more to this detail than a pitch for a laugh. Access to knowledge about the test is made a defining characteristic of gender difference: men have and women have not. In Lacan's scheme, subjectivity is gendered because subjectivity is determined, more or less, by the subject's relation to the phallus, what he calls the "transcendental signifier." At the mirror stage, the female subject – who lacks the phallus – experiences language and coming into language in a fundamentally different way than does the male.[62] She is therefore put at a disadvantage; worse, she is made a symptom of (by being designated as the cause) of man's own troubled subjectivity.

The first lady to drink, the Queen of Lanphuht, "spill[s] so much wine that a broad stream ran down her" (16). All of the ladies blush for her – not because they know what the mishap signifies, but because such an accident is socially embarrassing. However, the reader, in the know and thus aligned with the knowing knights, can read this collective blush quite differently, as a suggestive (red) stain on the ladies' (white) honor. Keiî sneers:

It would be difficult for a giant to lift this mass of gold adorned with so many jewels.... How could a lady manage it without spilling claret all over herself? It would not have occurred if the lady had been stronger; weakness often brings woe. (16)

The ambiguity of this comment is, of course, lost on the ladies, who reasonably assume that the lidded tankard is extremely heavy. "Abashed and worried," Ginover takes her turn. (That the ladies blushed for Lanphuht and that Ginover is so worried might suggest that the women are responding to an intertextual cue: they know all about chastity tests because they have encountered them, after all, in "other" texts, outside of the one they happen to be "in.") The narrator tells us that "unfortunately a little wine, hardly enough to notice, spilled onto her lap [*schôz*]" (16). *Schôz* may well be a euphemism for the genitals: quite literally, the wine stains Ginover's sex, individual and collective. Keiî says to Ginover: "you moved too quickly at the last and thus revealed your shortcomings to everyone" (16). Next, Lady Flori, Gawein's *âmîen*, splashes the wine all over her face. "[T]here could be no denying the evil in her heart," says the narrator (16). And so it continues: Laudin, Enite, and Parthie all fail, and Keiî tells of some anecdote or tale associated with the lady and her lover that reflects badly on both. Even Keiî's lover, Galaida, fails; in fact, she cannot even pick up the vessel – her hands move uselessly back and forth in the air. Keiî blushes with shame, but he is only momentarily abashed. The trial continues, and Keiî resumes his commentary, sparing no one.

The drama played out at court after the tankard arrives allows Heinrich, through Keiî, to retell in compressed form several well-known episodes of French and German versions of the Arthuriad. In a way, the ordeal functions as a pretext for an intertext – or better, a hypertext: click here for the full story. The cup can only reveal the fact that those who attempt to drink from it are deceitful; it is Keiî who supplies the narrative "facts" behind the various failures.[63] Let me illustrate by quoting in full Keiî's reading of Laudin's failure, which may allude to Hartmann von Aue's *Iwein* (ca. 1205):

> Luck was with you at first ... And if you had had some of the power of the ring that saved Sir Iwein – the one Lady Lunete gave him after he killed your husband – then you probably could have drunk the wine; but your luck went lame. Perhaps the tankard shows that you regret loving Iwein so faithfully. To tell the truth, he learned to know this loyalty well and to his sorrow when your sudden anger and his fondness for you caused him to lose his mind and nearly die in the forest. (17)

The conventions of the chastity ordeal with which Heinrich was familiar do not prepare us for such an exegesis of Laudin's "fault." Moreover, Keiî's reading – and it is, I stress, an *interpretation* of *Iwein* – contradicts what the fairy knight tells us about the powers of the tankard. Hartmann von Aue's Laudine and Iwein are flawed in many ways, but they eventually overcome their failings and reconcile, their marriage the better for their trials. Marital infidelity, however, is not one of Laudine's faults. We find the same sort of gap between the fairy knight's description of the tankard and many of Keiî's other recitals: Enite's failure alludes to the prelude to Hartmann von Aue's *Erec* (ca. 1180–1200); Flori's (and perhaps Gawein's) to Wirnt von Grafenberg's *Wigalois* (ca. 1200–15); Blanscheflur's to Chrétien de Troyes' *Conte du Graal* (ca. 1150–90); Lanzelet's to Chrétien de Troyes's *Chevalier de la Charrette* (ca. 1180–90).[64] In all of these cases, at least according to Keiî's representation of them, marital infidelity is not the main issue; instead, infidelity serves as an occasion or pretext for a more wide-ranging polemic.

After all the ladies have failed the test, the narrator tells us: "All the men began to talk ... among themselves and laugh secretly because the tankard had clearly shown the ladies to be *untrue and inconstant* (18, "*[v]alches und unstæte*," l. 1431, emphasis mine). This comment returns us to the diegetic frame, but, as we have seen, it does not jibe with the hypertexts to which Keiî points. Keiî's allusions to the events of other Arthurian texts have nothing to do with infidelity; if guilty of anything, the ladies stand accused of loving too much. In *Wigalois*, Florie weeps when she marries Gawain – as if in anticipation of his leaving her. Later, she says to Wigalois: "How sorry I am that I ever chose him for a lover, since I lost him so strangely – I don't know how.... Having lost him thus, I must suffer grief and sorrow till I die."[65] Blancheflur may sin *with* Parzival in the *Conte du Graal*, but she is not unfaithful to him. Such contradictions between the hypodiegetic tale of the ordeal (an embedded or digressive narrative) and the diegetic frame (that is, the main narrative) seem to be deliberate on Heinrich's part: for example, he says early on that he intends to write about King Arthur, but really makes Gawein the central character. More on point, consider the ordeal of the magic glove, apparently the invention of Heinrich. By rendering various parts of the body invisible, the glove reveals the failings of the man or woman "whose heart has been corrupted by inconstancy" (259). Ginover tries on the glove, and the right side of her lips fade. Keiî says:

> she begrudged Sir Gasozein a kiss while they were together in the forest ... It happened even though she didn't want him to kiss her and wrestle with her. The mantle also fitted her well, and although the tankard was full, she did not spill wine on herself. (265)

Gasozein, we should remember, raped Ginover. And there is no mantle test in *Diu Crône*; in fact, the Queen fails the mantle test in all extant versions – in, for example, the *Lai di Cor*, the *Lai du Cort Mantel*, and *Der Mantel* (a poem which used to be attributed to Heinrich). Moreover, the Queen fails all cup ordeals as well (though, as we have seen in the *Livre de Caradoc*, she manages to turn her failure into a triumph – at least in her husband's eyes). Perhaps Keiî may have in mind the tankard episode in *Diu Crône* itself – though we know that Ginover did indeed spill wine on herself. Finally, recall that, in this episode, Keiî says to Ginover: "you moved too quickly at the last." He may be thinking of Chrétien de Troyes' *Chevalier de la Charrette*, the first account of the adulterous love of Arthur's Queen and Lancelot. The charge of moving too quickly may refer to the Queen's hasty judgment of Lancelot when she discovers that he has ridden to her aid in a cart. Yet there is also another possibility: perhaps Keiî refers to an episode that occurred *after* the chastity ordeal in *Diu Crône* – to Gasozein's rape of Ginover. In this episode, Heinrich suggests that the Queen did not move quickly enough at the outset, that her refusal of Gasozein was too little, too late. Has Heinrich nodded here, or is this a case of blatant misreading? Is this passage an example of Keiî's/ Heinrich's irony? Is the target Gasozein, Ginover, or the courtly institution that not only allowed Gasozein to go unpunished, but welcomed him back into the chivalric club?[66] If Heinrich is indeed referring to his own poem, such a narratorial anachronism seems in keeping with Heinrich's overall play throughout the poem. I would argue that Heinrich intends to misrepresent – or misremember – his own text in order to draw our attention to the problems of representation itself. Consider just one effect of these two passages: Heinrich creates a multiple, intertextual "Ginover/Guenièvre/Guenevere," a signifier that destabilizes all other like signifiers ranged along the signifying chain.

To return to the tankard episode: just as the laughing knights are beginning to feel superior to the ladies, the fairy messenger says that it is now the men's turn to drink from the tankard. After a few choice remarks from Keiî, the entire court begins to mutter and lament their fate, regretting the *âventiure* that they have invited into its midst. Except for Artûs (the one paragon Heinrich allows), all the members of the court spill the wine. The narrator takes over Keiî's exegetical role, saying that one Brisaz failed "because of a maiden whom he left in great distress without heeding her plea for help. Although he rescued her later, he still could not drink" (23). In other words, and as Keiî makes clear in his sly remarks, Brisaz had made the girl pregnant. The King of Ethiopia fails because, the narrator says, "his fickle heart was so strongly drawn to all sorts of worldly things that he could not control it" (23). Keiî then adds his own commentary on gluttony: "He knows how to drain tankards" (23). Lanzelet fails because he rode in a cart; Erec fails because he disgraced himself on his adventure with Enite; Parzival fails because of that "poor fisherman ... abandoned to his pain" (26).

In comparison, Gawein, says the narrator, is almost without fault, except "that he had once forgotten himself and been presumptuous about the proper favor of a lady" (23). He says: "As the tankard was offered to the warrior, a little stain concealed his great fame, a slight misdeed obscured his complete virtue" (24). The narrator seems unwilling to specify what Gawain did; however, we are left with the impression that Gawein had been indiscreet while in the company of his fellow knights. He either told a joke at a lady's expense, or, given Gawein's intertextual reputation as a lover, perhaps we can conclude that he had kissed and told. If we take *Wigalois* as the text to which Heinrich means to allude, we discover that when Gawain wanted to return to Arthur's court, he lied to Florie about the amount of time he planned to be away. The point is that Gawein's "slight misdeed" is not represented here, not articulated, but withheld, leaving the reader free to speculate endlessly about the exact nature of Gawein's fault.

Finally, Keiî, like his lover Galaida, spectacularly fails the test, upending the contents of the tankard over his head. He fails because, as the narrator says, he "had to pay for his habit of making fun of others" (30). It is tempting to read this comment as Heinrich's ironic reference to his own re-vision of Arthurian legend; indeed, Heinrich has had a good deal of fun at the expense of the greatest figures of fictional knighthood. It is also tempting to read Keiî's failure – a variation on the modesty *topos* – as Heinrich's awareness of his own embroilment in the imaginary world of chivalric romance.

As a reader of romance – as a literary critic, as it were – Heinrich is not that interested in the relation between *verbum* and *res*; he finds much more compelling the relation between *verbum* and *verbum*. "No signification can be sustained other than by reference to another signification," says Lacan, and it seems that Heinrich agrees wholeheartedly.[67] Heinrich appropriates what he sees as the received or authoritative discourse of romance, and by mixing it with elements of the fabliau, foregrounds the problem of representation, mis- or true, on the level of plot, which in turn draws our attention to the problem of representation that underwrites the poetic enterprise itself. In this context, we might view the magic tankard (an object on the diegetic plane) as, in Bakhtin's phrase, a "hybrid construction,"

> an utterance that belongs, by its grammatical (syntactic) and compositional markers, to a single speaker, but that actually contains mixed within it two utterances, two speech manners, two styles, two "languages," two semantic and axiological belief systems.[68]

In other words, the tankard (an "utterance" or signifier) has a monologic textual history that enacts a particular "belief system." In Heinrich's hands, the cup indeed represents a concern with chastity and constancy between spouses and between lovers, but it is also overwritten with another agenda. The idea of marital chastity becomes the ground upon which the larger idea of chivalric virtue is critiqued. Heinrich shifts the interest quite explicitly from the sexual body to the social body, particularly as that social body is constituted in the Symbolic. "Chivalric virtue" is exposed as an aesthetic construct, its roots in fiction, not in history.

History, fiction, virginity

The chastity ordeal as it is narrativized in vernacular romance and the *lai* can be read in a number of ways. Most obviously, the ordeal is intended as a warning to the unchaste wife. But as I have been arguing, the interest in, if not the obsession with, verifying virginity and confirming marital chastity is both an effect and a function of the homosocial in the Middle Ages. The ordeal, instead of cementing relations among men, has the opposite effect: it reveals the fault lines, the breaks and fissures that must be patched over through denying the *results* of the ordeal. Moreover, because the outcome of the ordeal is ultimately undecidable, the ordeal narrative opens up a space that allows us to examine the problem of representationality and asks us to attend to the nature of fiction and history and the relationship between the two.

Clearly, the homosocial, a modern concept and coinage, has been central to my argument in this chapter. I want to conclude by focusing on its historicity and relevance for the Middle Ages in order to emphasize that the fictional narratives in which verifying female virginity figure so prominently arose out of a very specific social context in which men had as much at stake as women. In 1985, in *Between Men: English Literature and Male Homosocial Desire*, Eve Sedgwick coupled the terms *homosocial* and *desire* in an attempt to capture the paradox inherent in the bonds that men develop among themselves to insure their own dominance – bonds, she argues, that are both compromised and strengthened by the threat of same-sex desire. Since then, medievalists have found the concepts of the homosocial and of homosocial desire extremely useful in describing medieval social systems in which power circulates chiefly among men of the land-holding class. For example, Carolyn Dinshaw, in her reading of the late fourteenth-century society that produced and read *Sir Gawain and the Green Knight*, argues that "a society that retains the structure and forms of feudal relations, even as feudal relations were diminishing in significance, can be described as bonded by homosocial desire."[69] But as Sedgwick notes, the term *homosocial* on its own had been used previously in the social sciences as a way to describe the phenomenon more popularly known as "male bonding"; that is, any activity that might strengthen the ties, allegiances, and obligations among men.[70]

The life of Guillaume le Maréchal (c.1145–1219) as it is related in the *L'histoire de Guillaume le Maréchal* serves as a very material example of such bonds among men of the noble class (and of the conflation of the historical and the fictional as well). The *Histoire* is a poem of 19,214 lines written within ten years of Maréchal's death, and is partly a romance, partly a chronicle, and, even by modern standards, fully a biography. The anonymous poet attests to the workings of homosociality as it operated in the Middle Ages and to the degree to which women served to bond men homosocially.

As the fourth son of John fitz Gilbert, marshal to the court of Henry I, Maréchal had no hope of an inheritance. Like other younger sons before him, Maréchal was expected to make his own way in the world in the one "noble" profession open to him: warfare. (Of course, many younger sons also became clerics.) Maréchal amassed property and wealth first through feats of arms and second through his strategic marriage to Isabel of Striguil, daughter of the Earl of Pembroke. He eventually rose to the position of Regent to Henry III, wielding extraordinary influence over the young king and therefore over the affairs of England. As the *Histoire* reveals, Maréchal treated his own youngest son, Anselm, in much the same way that his father had treated him. On his deathbed in 1219, as Maréchal distributed his considerable wealth among his family and retainers, he was inclined to leave Anselm nothing.[71] Anselm, as his father declared, "must ride errant till he win honor; then he will find someone who will cherish him and do him great honor, more than any other."[72] Here, deeds performed in the realm of the masculine are inextricable from their reward in the realm of the feminine. One, however, must precede, or lead to, the other.

Maréchal was a professional soldier, initially learning his craft in the *mesnie* (military household) of young Henry, son of Henry II. As he grew more accomplished on the field and in council, Maréchal also learned about the customs of the noble household, typically made up of a number of mercenaries gathered together under the leadership of one man. As Georges Duby notes, Henry was the only married man in the company to which Maréchal belonged, "not only because there were no firstborn males among them but because these groups, these *mesnies*, were identified with noble houses built around a single conjugal pair."[73]

The lord and his lady dominated such households; all social activities revolved around them. Every night, as the knights gathered in the hall, they were free to observe – and envy – the couple who sat at the high table. The lady represented what all bachelor knights desired: land, stability, and the opportunity to found their own line and to pass on their newly-acquired wealth to their sons. And, because the lady was expected to display her beauty, her body adorned in finery acquired through the largesse of her husband, she also represented erotic reward and fulfillment as well. Yet the wife was the one woman forbidden to the knights. This state of affairs was exacerbated by the fact that, as Duby dryly puts it, these young knights, committed to a "search for a rich girl with a fine establishment," faced a persistent problem: an "uncertain supply of suitable quarry."[74] In a market in which supply and demand were markedly out of balance, the lady on the dais thus looked even more desirable. When we recall the many admiring descriptions of women in medieval romances, the clichéd head-to-toe catalogues of physical attributes, what may often strike us as a tired rhetorical device takes on new significance when we imagine the actual scene in which men were permitted to look, but not to touch, the lady of the *mesnie*. The relationship between the bachelor knight and his lord's lady can be described as a sort of apprenticeship – sometimes sublimated, sometimes consummated – until the knight could afford a wife of his own. Indeed, we have an extensive body of troubadour poetry that attests to such a relationship, representing the bachelor knight as hopelessly devoted to a married woman (*dompna*) who remains forever out of his reach.[75] The troubadours, says Duby, were the spokesmen for those young men who "wanted to break into the erotic circle [of husband-wife-married lover] to the advantage of 'youth.'"[76] Whatever the historical realities of courtly love, there is plenty of evidence for *fin amor*.

Duby says that Maréchal kept watch over Isabel "as over the most precious treasure in the world," since

> All the power he claims to possess ... emanates from the person, from the "head" of Isabel; it is indispensable that his wife be seen there at his side, that every eye recognize her as his, acknowledging that he shares her bed, that they make one flesh, that consequently homage must be paid to this husband, who must form his own court and safeguard his honor in every fashion.[77]

Safeguarding Maréchal's honor translates into safeguarding the person of Isabel. This is made abundantly clear when Maréchal goes to England and leaves his wife behind at Kilkenny in 1207. He arranges a public, ritualized leavetaking:

> Vez la contesse que j'amain
> Ici devant vos par la main:
> Vostre dame naturalment,
> Fille al conte qui bonement
> Vos fefa tuz par sa franchise,
> Quant il out la terre conquise.
> Entre vos enceinte remaint.
> Dusqu'a tant que Dex me remaint,
> Vos pri a toz que bonement
> La gardez e naturalment,
> Qui vostre dame est, ce savon[78]

[See the countess whom I hold here before you by the hand: she is your natural lady, the daughter of the good count who gave you your fiefs when the land was first conquered. She remains among you, with child. Until the time that God restores me, I beg you all to guard her with care and according to nature, she who is your lady.]

By handing over his wife to his *mesnie* in this manner, Maréchal seems to exploit the symbolic power of the vows of the wedding ceremony. Given the staged feel of this scene, we may well believe that the author of the *Histoire* was being disingenuous when he earlier declared that "[a] history that is true should have perforce nothing in it of falsity."[79] But "every historical narrative," argues Hayden White, "has as its latent or manifest purpose the desire to moralize the events of which it treats."[80] Embellished or invented, the image of Maréchal and Isabel in the *Histoire* is still able to provide a powerful commentary on twelfth-century homosocial relations and expectations. We see, for example, how Maréchal takes an essentialized view of male-male relations *vis-à-vis* his wife in his appeal to "nature": it is according to the order of things that the men of his household take Isabel for their lady and promise to protect her.

Here, not only is a married (and obviously fertile) woman put on display, but she is also put on notice. In this ceremonial and symbolic exchange, her sexual availability is foregrounded along with, paradoxically, her chastity and *un*availability. (Consider the temptation scenes in *Sir Gawain and the Green Knight* in this respect.) I would argue that, in effect, the literal lady and her metaphorical function have been confounded, and confounded to the benefit of the homosocial. The ordeal narrative acknowledges, consciously or not, such a confounding, which in turn reveals the degree to which men have been complicit in creating a social system that best operates covertly.

In his remarks about history, truth, and falsity, the author of the *Histoire* reveals a desire for a history made up of disambiguated signs – in spite of the fact that he probably had a part in inventing such signs. In his biography of Maréchal, the poet produces a naturalized and very particular history of homosociality in which the figure of the chaste but desirable wife is crucial to the continuance of the *mesnie* – the homosocial unit, as it were. The ordeal narrative, which draws attention to the desirability of the wife – and only sometimes to her chastity – represents a similar desire for history: it purports to make evident the "history" of the woman's chaste body, which in turn confirms the legitimate history of the dynastic line.

Instead of satisfying a desire for a incontestable history, the ordeal actually calls our attention to the undecidability of history, to the slippage between *verbum* and *res* that inevitably characterizes all speech acts – oaths, agreements, promises, and contracts (and the written records of them). Since chastity (that is, sexual fidelity) is unable to be located on/in the body, marital fidelity (predicated upon an agreement between wife and husband that is sanctioned by the Church and upheld by secular law) is the perfect subject for the ordeal, for the proof of fidelity is precisely that which falls into the gap between *verbum* and *res*. To come at this problem from a different angle: chastity's very indeterminacy creates a desire to make it knowable, which in turn creates a social machina to do so. In effect, within a Lacanian paradigm, virginity figures as a nostalgic metonym for wholeness, intactness, of a time before the individuated and therefore alienated self – of a time before history.

The chastity ordeal is a device designed to assert the Law of the Father but instead dramatizes the limits of the Symbolic in which "woman" has been made into a symptom (though designated as the cause) of man's own troubled subjectivity, which homosociality is designed to buttress and protect. The motif of the chastity ordeal enacts in small the larger crisis of representation to which the medieval romance repeatedly returns (in various plots and across different registers) as it attempts to negotiate between fictionalized history and historicized fiction, and dramatizes the impossibility of doing so.

4 Oxymoronic bodies
Male virgins in hagiography and romance

I write woman: woman must write woman. And man, man ... it's up to him to say
where his masculinity and femininity are at.

Hélène Cixous, "The Laugh of the Medusa"

Do men have a hymen?

In *De virginibus velandis* (211), Tertullian states: "Seeing and being seen belong
to the self-same lust" ("Ejusdem libidinis est videri, et videre").[1] He insists that
consecrated virgins must be veiled not only for their own protection, but also for
the protection of others whose chastity may be imperiled by looking. In this
polemical text, Tertullian speaks forcefully about the female virgin: "Impose a
veil externally upon her who has (already) a covering internally," a statement
which may allude to a metaphorical and/or a very material hymen.[2] Thus a woman's
sartorial veil is made as integral to feminine and virginal identity as her hymeneal
"veil." At the same time, Tertullian must confront certain consequences of such a
semiotics of gender difference (rooted in Judaic and Hellenistic custom, and here
appropriated for Christianity). He argues that the veiled virgin should not be
honored for such an obvious sign of her virginity (that is, the veil itself), first
because women are subject to men, and second because such honor would not be
fair to "so many men-virgins" ("viri autem tot virgines"), voluntary eunuchs
("spadones voluntarii") who must necessarily "carry their glory in secret" ("cæco
bono suo incedant").[3]

There is much to unpack here, particularly because we so rarely find explicit
discussions of the male virgin as such in patristic writings, but I will focus on a
few points only. Tertullian consciously appropriates the Latin word *virgo*,
grammatically and denotatively feminine, in order to identify the male virgin –
hence the locution, *viri autem tot virgines*, "so many men-virgins." (*Virgo* may
denote either an unmarried girl or a girl who has never had intercourse; there was
no corresponding Latin term for a sexually inexperienced man. But *virgines* could
be either a feminine or masculine plural. Tertullian apparently wants to avoid
any ambiguity.[4]) The consecrated male virgin represents a new ontological category
with which Rome had had little previous experience, and for which Latin had no

words. By calling his readers' attention to this fact, Tertullian reproduces virginity as a naturalized feminine attribute, one that must be taken out of its context in order to be applied to men. Monique Wittig's charge that "the mark of gender" is always feminine, never masculine, is founded upon such assumptions as Tertullian's.[5] Thomas Laqueur describes the mark of gender in the following way:

> it is *always* woman's sexuality that is being constituted; woman is the empty category. Woman alone seems to have "gender" since the category itself is defined as that aspect of social relations based on difference between sexes in which the standard has always been man.[6]

Thus male sexuality, at least until recently, remains unmarked and under-examined. Female sexuality, on the other hand, has been historically so overdetermined that Shirley Ardener argues for the linguistic term "back-formation" to describe the process of applying terms of female sexuality to "similar" facts of male sexuality.[7] In the same way that contemporary expressions like "male model" and "male nurse" foreground certain expectations about gender roles, Tertullian's qualifier in the phrase "male virgin" reveals a number of gender-driven assumptions about virginity that are still in force today.

De virginibus velandis is just one example of, if not an origin for, how the female (and virgin) body has figured prominently as site, as meeting-place for ideological conflict, in both religious and secular relations between men. That the female body is employed in such a way is an old and oft-told story, shaped as much by the texts that we read as it is by the critical methodologies that we bring to them. For example, when Laqueur speaks of the image of the "problematic, unstable female body" versus the "unproblematic, stable male body" as they were constituted in the medical discourse of antiquity, he describes not only a historically-attested way of figuring difference, but his own construction of difference as well.[8] However, in the past few years, in the wake of post-Foucauldian feminist readings of the female body and under the rubrics of gender studies, gay/lesbian studies, and the study of masculinities, scholars have begun to challenge such monologic representations of the male body.

In this chapter, I hope to contribute to this project by examining representations of the male virgin and the male virgin body, first in medieval hagiography (except for one remarkable legend, the tale of Pelagius, these tales have their origins in late antiquity), and then in two late Middle English romances, Malory's *Morte Darthur* (completed c. 1470; first printed 1485) and *Sir Gawain and the Green Knight* (c. 1400). (I read these two romances out of chronological order because Malory relies on sources older than *Gawain* and gives us a version of the whole Arthuriad, of which *Gawain* is but one part. *Sir Gawain and the Green Knight*, extant in a single manuscript, has remained relatively unknown and unread until the twentieth century, and therefore has contributed little to the intertextual history of Arthurian legend.) As I examine these texts, I am primarily interested in the following questions: if virginity, or the lack thereof, is so crucial to female sexual and gender identity in the era of the early Church and later on throughout the

Middle Ages, what role did virginity play in male identity? If the "fact" of a woman's virginity could be subjected to a test or ordeal, what about a man's virginity? What sort of narrative strategies were available to an author who wanted to represent or dramatize male virginity? How is it that the female body has been constructed as a *readable* body, subject to endless explication, while the male body has so often been figured as something closed to interpretation, and male virginity as being exempt from verification? Paul Smith, in *Discerning the Subject*, furnishes a way to answer this last question when he identifies what he calls the "claustrophilic tendency" of certain discourses, which "seek the closure of that which they have opened" so that the "'subject' can revindicate its control which, ideally, should never have been in doubt."[9] Smith's metaphors of opening and closing are particularly useful here, since virginity is so often figured as a movement from sealed to open, from *integritas* to *corruptio* – in short, as a set of operations on a feminine or feminized body. In general, the discourse of virginity does attempt to close that which it has opened; when we consider the oxymoron of the male virgin, such a "claustrophilic tendency" is even more pronounced. Each text that I examine in this chapter can be read as "opening" the subject of the male body, risking exposure – and revision – of the privileged masculine subject, only to shut down any real dialogue in the end. I argue that, to the degree to which female virginity is overdetermined, male virginity is underdetermined, and can be made intelligible only by reference to an elaborate feminized and feminizing signifying system. In effect, these texts broach the subject only to change the subject, as it were, from masculine to feminine.

Habeas corpus

Before discussing male virgins as they appear in hagiographical texts, I wish to make a few observations about male virginity that may strike the reader as being patently obvious. However, it is our ready acceptance of the "obviousness" of the male body that continues to render the male virgin invisible while casting the female virgin into sharp relief. It should come as no surprise that classical and medieval medical texts are silent on the subject of the signs and proofs of male virginity; there was – and is – no recognized anatomical part associated with male virginity, no procedure for testing male virginity.[10] In the context of classical and medieval humoral theory (according to which both men and women must achieve a proper balance of hot and cold, moist and dry, to enjoy good health), discussions of male virginity are limited to the possible deleterious effects of abstinence on the one hand, or too much sexual activity on the other. In antiquity, as in the Middle Ages, there was no cultural imperative to verify and safeguard male virginity. Patriarchy, for which assured paternity and secured lineage and property are so crucial, depends upon maintaining *female*, not *male*, virginity and marital fidelity. (In fact, while female virginity is accorded greater or lesser importance across a number of cultures at different times, I know of no culture in which male virginity was or is distinguished.) In general, though medieval law could make a distinction between the married and unmarried man, it did not recognize the male virgin in the same way that it did the female virgin. For example, while the question of a girl's virginity could affect the conditions of a marriage contract or negotiations over the dowry, a prospective groom's virginity did not.

Of course, the Church always recognized male bodily and spiritual chastity, but in the hierarchy that developed in the early Church, male celibacy simply acquired a different historical and discursive power than that of female virginity.[11] When we talk about male virginity and its status in the medieval Church, it is important to make a distinction between the history of clerical continence (that is, chastity in the context of a Christian priesthood for which compulsory virginity became the norm), and the personal commitment to virginity that any Christian layperson may choose to make. Granted, such a distinction artificially separates the private and public functions and valences of virginity, which in reality are very much intertwined. However, this distinction allows us to see that, while clerical continence continued to be a subject of debate within the early Church, consecrated virginity was universally praised, even though its realization might take different forms at various historical moments. John Bugge furnishes us with an example of the different ways virginity has been figured at different times. He traces out what he calls the "sexualization" of virginity in the monastic culture of twelfth-century Western Europe. The metaphor of marriage came to symbolize the union of God and humanity, Christ and Church, thus gendering the relationship in a way that still characterizes religious discourse. Bugge argues that:

> It is no coincidence that, at precisely the point that devotional literature for women is said to have become "mystical," the male sex began to be dispossessed of the ideal of virginal perfection. The result of the misapplication of Bernardine mysticism, in other words, was the irretrievable identification of virginity with womankind.[12]

Of course, such a "misapplication" had its beginnings in the earliest patristic texts on virginity, as we saw in the Introduction and in Chapter 2. The continued effort to identify virginity so absolutely with the feminine not only produced a new set of metaphors to live by, but also a whole series of social regulations and rituals dependent upon those metaphors. The question, Do men have a hymen? is a facetious one if we think strictly in terms of anatomy, but it is a serious question in the context of social roles and how such roles have been historically marked, measured, and regulated.

Assaying male virginity

The increased availability of new editions and translations of saints' legends, the interest that feminist scholars have shown in vernacular hagiography, and the influence that cultural studies have exerted on medieval studies have combined in recent years to spark a renascence in the study of hagiography. Female saints' lives have garnered the most attention by far, while male saints' lives have been relatively neglected, making it risky to generalize about hagiography based on gender alone. Research trends notwithstanding, the sheer variety and number of extant saints' lives have always made generalizations problematic. In spite of its repetitive formulae, hagiography is by no means a monolithic genre, a fact made particularly clear when one attempts to study the representation of gender. (Spirituality, for example, takes many forms in hagiography, ranging from a model that absolutely transcends gender to one emphatically predicated upon it.) With such caveats in mind, I nevertheless feel that, with respect to the small subset of the complicated, heteroglossic texts with which I am working, it is safe to say that the representation of the threat to virginity in the hagiography of late antiquity (later recycled in the Middle Ages) is gender-specific. The difference between the treatment of the male virgin and the female virgin is that between rape and seduction, between *assaulted* virginity and *assayed* virginity. As we saw in Chapter 2, we find iterated endlessly the story of the menaced female virgin threatened with the brothel because she refuses to sacrifice to the gods, or threatened with rape after having rejected a would-be seducer or suitor. Yet in the hagiographical corpus, the male virgin is not threatened with rape, but with seduction. "Representation," argues Michel de Certeau, "disguises the praxis that organizes it," and in this case, this difference in representation both conceals and reveals received notions about male and female physiology and psychology, as we shall see.[13]

The few extant legends of the assayed male virgin found in late antiquity were never very popular in the Middle Ages. Though stories of menaced female virgins, such as those of Agatha, Agnes, and Lucy, were recycled over and over in medieval literature and iconography, their male counterparts were relatively unknown. This fact makes Aldhelm's *De Virginitate* (late seventh century) unique. Along with a list of female virgins, and without precedent (and without imitators), Aldhelm also includes a catalogue of male virgins.[14] He explicitly addresses his treatise to the nuns at Barking, though he could have easily made men part of his audience, since Barking was one of the monasteries in England that housed both men and women. One wonders if he meant to address the monks after all, or if he used examples of assayed male virgins as a way to suggest that the maintenance of male virginity/chastity is a burden that women must shoulder along with the responsibility for their own purity – women were supposed to be, as Tertullian said, "the devil's door," in part because it was commonly believed that, since their humors were out of balance, women possessed a greater sexual desire than men.[15]

Aldhelm recounts how the saints Amos, Malchus, and Julian were "threatened" with marriage (though it must be said that threats of marriage were often visited upon the adamant female virgin as well). Borrowing from Jerome, Aldhelm recounts how the parents of Malchus, out of concern for heirs, threatened him with "carnal union" (*carnale consortium*) – that is, marriage. Aldhelm writes: "Forced at the point of a sword into abandoning the glories of the chastity he longed for ... he preferred to die transfixed cruelly by the sword."[16] Aldhelm also includes the story of Chrysanthus, whose own father, upon hearing that his son had become a Christian, imprisons him, not only fearing for his son, but for his fortune as well, since Christians so often gave away their wealth upon conversion.

After starvation and torture failed to change Chrysanthus' mind, the father took him from prison, and

> dressed him in silken garments and sent him into the dining-room where very beautiful girls adorned in sumptuous dresses had prepared the luxurious delights of wine and the sumptuous entertainment of a feast, combining unrestrained shrieks of joy with the light-hearted embraces of sexual play, so that they might soften the iron resolve of the youth with such blandishments.[17]

For a modern reader, this scene can hardly be compared to the scene in the female *passio*, in which laughing, jeering men menace the naked virgin at the door of the *lupanar*. Yet this story of seduction may have been equally horrifying for those nuns and monks at Barking: for the believing Christian looking forward to her or his place in heaven among the elect, the loss of vowed virginity, not the manner in which it was lost, was certainly the greater calamity. Chrysanthus, we are told, "avoids the girls' soft lips as if they were the baleful venom of vipers."[18] Kisses simply do not compare to rape, yet they might lead to consent, and consent, whether arrived at in the midst of rape or of seduction, is precisely what puts the virgin in peril, not the physical act itself.

Voragine's *Legenda Aurea* (which contains a less sensational version of the story of Chrysanthus) includes another example of the assayed male virgin borrowed from Jerome, a story of two unnamed but resolute Christians tortured by the emperor Decius. In this tale, the first young man is coated with honey, left under the hot sun, and stung to death by flies, hornets, and wasps. The other was

> laid upon a downy bed in a pleasant place cooled by soft breezes, filled with the sound of murmuring streams and the songs of birds, redolent with the sweet odor of flowers: he was bound down with ropes entwined with flowers … Then a very beautiful but totally depraved young woman was sent to defile the body of the youth, whose only love was for God. As soon as he felt the disturbance of the flesh [*carne motus contrarios rationi sensisset*], having no weapon with which to defend himself, he bit out his tongue and spat in the face of the lewd woman.[19]

Which is worse: to be stung to death by insects, or to be seduced to death? Anaphylactic shock at least holds no carnal temptation, the pull of which exhausts the will and leads to utter perdition – or, at least, to a demotion in virginal rank. The descriptive language in this passage recalls the sensuousness of the Garden of the Song of Songs, and the outcome the (feminized) evils of Eden. The scene also exploits misogynist medieval stereotypes about the voraciousness of women's sexual appetites. As I would argue about Aldhelm's tale of Chrysanthus, we are so caught up in, if not titillated by, the details of the seduction narrative that Voragine's male virgin fades into the background. Such a shifting of attention away from the male virgin is very different from what we find in tales of near-rape of the female virgin, who is, as I have said, so often stripped, displayed, and tortured, relentlessly fixed in our line of sight.

When we look for examples of the seduction narrative originating in the Middle Ages, we find that such stories have dwindled into anecdote. In the *Gemma Ecclesiastica* (c. 1190), for example, Geraldus Cambrensis collected a number of stories about clerics who resist the advances of wanton women, or the devil in feminine disguise, or, simply, *carnis temptatio*, lust itself. (In fact, a perusal of the *Motif-Index of Folk-Literature* reveals that the majority of tales of assayed male chastity collected there involve monks and priests. The story of Potiphar's unnamed wife and Joseph may well be the first recorded example of assayed priesthood.) We can read about St. Benedict in the *Gemma Ecclesiastica*, who threw himself naked into stinging nettles in order to exorcise his lustful thoughts, and about St. Godric, who plunged into an icy river in order to put out the fires of lust.[20] Geraldus also includes the story of St. Bernard, who, while staying at an inn, woke to find his hostess embracing him and kissing him. He protected himself by shouting, "Thief! Thief!" – for, as he is supposed to have said, "She who endeavors to steal my chastity ... wishes to make a great theft indeed" ("Furtum ... magnum facere volebat, quæ castitatem meam mihi surripere molita est").[21] As far as I am aware, except for these stories in the *Gemma Ecclesiastica* and similar stories elsewhere, there are no tales of the male virgin under assault in medieval hagiography; by this I mean no full-blown, autonomous life, as opposed to a series of brief anecdotes.[22]

The tales of Chrysanthus and of the unnamed martyr who bit off his own tongue rather than submit to seduction reflect certain received ideas about the body that circulated in both medical treatises and patristic writings. For example, it was believed that sexual arousal could be precipitated by food and wine and other sensual pleasures: in classical humoral theory, eating and drinking were thought to heat the body, and once the body was heated, the will to resist intercourse was that much weaker. (As we know, alcohol indeed lowers inhibitions, no matter what the paradigm.) Jerome acknowledges the dangers of sensual indulgence when he cautions against "deliciis fruitur" ("enjoyment of luxuries"), declaring: "First the belly is swollen, then the other members are roused."[23] Augustine also puts the burden of chastity on the will when he says that "no one, however magnanimous and shamefast, has it always in his power to decide what shall be done with his flesh, having power only to decide what he will in his mind accept or refuse."[24] While both Jerome and Augustine speak generally, in a way relevant to both male and female virgins, Jerome specifically addresses his remarks to the female virgin Eustochium, and Augustine makes his statement in the context of his discussion of the female virgins raped during Alaric's taking of Rome in 410. I think that both Jerome and Augustine would agree that a woman could be just as easily seduced as a man – perhaps more easily, given her humoral constitution and predilections – yet this is not the story that gets told in the hagiography of late antiquity. Perhaps we can turn to humoral theory once again to account for what story gets told about whom. Men, though hotter than women, were thought to be slower to arouse than women. On the other hand, women, because of their putative cold (and thus imperfect) bodies, were thought to long for union with the hotter (and thus perfect) bodies of men. As Joan Cadden notes in "Western Medicine and Natural Philosophy," it was believed that women were "always ready" for intercourse – and thus, I would add, "always ready" for rape (a pernicious idea that still circulates today).[25] According to the Galenic model, men, on the other hand, had to wait for various "spirits" to fill them up before being ready for coitus.[26] We no longer look to humoral theory to account for the physiology of sex, but no matter which paradigm we apply, the fact remains that, for a man to consummate heterosexual intercourse, he must have an erection. It seems quite obvious to say – and dangerously, tautologically so – that women, while certainly susceptible to seduction, do not "need" seduction to lose their heterosexual virginity. Rape will suffice. The correlative to this belief is that men *have* to be seduced – that is, aroused, cajoled, or coerced into an erection – in order to lose their heterosexual virginity. (I will return shortly to the issues raised by the qualifier *heterosexual*.) I am suggesting that we read the difference between the rape narrative and the seduction narrative as the result of the way in which certain bodily "facts" about men and women were socially expressed in late antiquity. The understanding of anatomy and physiology – what constitutes the deep structure, as it were – becomes mystified and aestheticized on the surface structure in the hagiographical narrative. Biology (both effect and cause of culture) cannot be represented on its own terms (it does not exist "on its own terms"), but must somehow be transformed into an intelligible social narrative.

Jerome, Augustine, and others may have accepted and perpetuated the dominant ideology that constructed the body in late antiquity, but they were also busy working out an ideology of their own. Besides relying on humoral theory for their constructs of gender difference, patristic writers also combined classical ethical and natural philosophy with theology to create a gendered psychology in which men were associated with soul or spirit, reason, and strength, and women with matter or body, emotion, and weakness.[27] Jerome takes this binary as a given in his famous comment on virginity:

> as long as woman is for birth and children, she is different from men as body is from soul. But if she wishes to serve Christ more than the world, she will cease to be woman and be called man.[28]

Women, here reduced to pregnant, maternal bodies, must somehow transcend their weak natures in order to rank with the first tier of heavenly virgins. Whether Jerome actually believed in the performativity of gender – that women could actually "change" their status as dictated by their sex – is probably not worth pursuing here, but not all of the architects of the early Church entertained the idea, however rhetorically, that women could change their nature. Approximately a century and a half later in Syria, Severus of Antioch (d. 538) writes:

> As to John the scribe who threw himself into a river and departed from this life, I am in doubt, and I have no sure decision to give. Know that since the

times of Christ's coming in the flesh we find in church histories that this is allowed to women, to remove themselves I mean from this life, and throw themselves on to rocks or into water: on account of the weakness of their nature, and the fact that they are exposed to double danger, that of the pollution of the body I mean, and that of denial of the faith: but in the case of men we have nowhere known this principle to have been accepted or sanctioned.[29]

As Eusebius and others record, many Christian women killed themselves during the time of the Christian persecutions, leaving such champions of virginity as Ambrose and Augustine in a quandary: bound by the laws of God to condemn suicide, they nevertheless praised the courage of women who chose to take their own life rather than suffer rape. In this passage, Severus makes it very clear that Church "policy" on the subject of suicide was in part driven by a notion of gender difference: women were thought to be too physically weak to fight off rape. Moreover, if Severus were familiar with humoral theory as detailed by Aristotle and others, perhaps he also believed that, because of their sexual appetites, women were too *morally* weak to resist rape. Better death than dishonor. Such a distinction between the sexes results in a number of problems for women, of course, but it also has serious implications for John the scribe and his masculinity. Perhaps one of the reasons Severus hesitates to condone John's suicide is that John, by killing himself, behaved in a womanly fashion. While it may have been a compliment for a woman to be re-categorized as an honorary man, it was no compliment to be thought a *vir effeminatus*. What may be so troubling is John's switching of social categories, which served to destabilize both male and female gender roles. If this is so, the horror of the seduction narrative for its immediate audience may be a bit more recoverable for a modern audience. Read in this way, the seduction narrative tells a tale of enforced male passivity that would have contradicted both patristic/theological and medical constructs of masculinity, in which men were expected to assume the active role, and women, in spite of their hotter lust, were relegated to the passive role. The seductress usurps male prerogatives through her overt sexual advances, while the male virgin (helplessly bound to the bed, say) is made to behave like a woman in that he is acted upon, not acting. No longer a desiring subject – even if his desire is focused on keeping his virginity – the assayed male virgin becomes a desired object. At this moment, male subjectivity is as much at risk as is male virginity.

Severus' letter opens up another intriguing possibility as well: did John commit suicide in order to avoid betraying his faith, and/or to avoid the threat of seduction, or to avoid rape? After all, Severus avers that Christian women killed themselves during the persecutions in order to preserve their virginity: would a man in the same position choose to do the same? Severus obviously believes that men are stronger than women, but does he really believe that men were never "exposed to double danger"? – that is, forced to deny one's faith *and* to endure rape? Or does Severus seek to deny the very possibility that a man may be raped – by a woman or a man?

Of all the hagiographers and historians of late antiquity, perhaps Eusebius comes closest to suggesting that men might had been sexually assaulted or raped. Indeed, he mentions that some men were castrated as part of their torture.[30] Yet this sort of sexualized suffering is more equivalent to a female saint's having her breasts cut off than to rape itself. At one point, however, Eusebius notes that both men and women

> endured sufferings horrible to hear. Their fingers were pierced with sharp reeds under their nails. Melted lead, bubbling and boiling with the heat, was poured down the backs of others, and they were roasted in the most sensitive parts of the body. Others endured on their bowels and privy members shameful and inhuman and unmentionable torments.[31]

We may never be able to determine if these "torments" included sodomy. I suspect that they did. It is possible that Eusebius' reports of mutilation and torture were indeed coded references or euphemisms for rape, intended as a substitute for a taboo narrative. In other words, in the rhetoric of torture that characterizes the hagiography of late antiquity, sexual assault and rape may well have been taken as givens, with no need for articulation. Modern readers are usually surprised by the amount of graphic violence found in hagiography, and have been hard put to explain its presence. Reading hagiographical legends through Elaine Scarry's *The Body in Pain* goes a long way in explaining the obsession with torture that we find in these legends, but it does not account for the possibility that the narrativization of torture may actually displace a more graphic and socially threatening story.

Even if we read accounts of torture as literary displacements of stories of actual rape, we must still contend with its articulated absence, as it were. Such an aporia in the historical record, I would argue, cannot be dismissed simply as a matter of "taste" or "aesthetics" – which is not to say that taste or aesthetics did not play a role in structuring these texts. To open up such a discussion (perhaps a tasteless one by academic standards, or at least rendered tasteless, if not downright misguided, by an empirical method which disallows such speculation) leads us to consider what sort of sexual assault can and cannot be effected upon the male body, which is perhaps a question that few in the time of Severus were willing to contemplate, let alone narrate. It is one thing to set up an elaborate scene in which a man must be "seduced" by a woman into an erection and therefore into losing his virginity, and quite another to tell a blatant story of forcible rape. Thus the female seduction narrative has its uses, for it may well forestall any suggestion that a rape narrative involving a male virgin *requires* a male perpetrator. It seems to me that rape is a very good reason for a claustrophilic narrative, given what it might have meant to narrate rape directly: Eusebius and other historians and hagiographers would have had to make explicit the vaginal, oral, or anal rape of a female virgin, and the anal rape or forced fellatio of a male. As we saw in Chapter 2, only the threat of rape, but never rape itself, is narrated in the female virgin martyr's tale. It seems that in the male virgin's tale, not even the *threat* of rape can be admitted.[32]

In the *Commedia*, Dante thoroughly illustrates the medieval idea that everything in Nature strives for perfection; that is, toward Godhead. It would have been a natural assumption, then, that a woman could and should transcend her biological destiny and become socially and culturally "like" a man, and thus one step closer to God in the grand hierarchy. Conversely, a man could lose status and his social identity if he behaved, or was forced to behave, "like" a woman. Seduction in the hagiographical narrative has precisely this effect, and is as threatening to masculine subjectivity as rape is to feminine subjectivity.

The case of Pelagius

In 925 or 926, at the age of thirteen, the virgin Pelagius was tortured, dismembered, and martyred in Cordoba by the caliph 'Abd al-Rahmân III. While details vary somewhat in the handful of extant versions of the legend, it seems that at one point the caliph made sexual advances toward Pelagius, and, because the saint categorically rejected these advances, he was punished forthwith.

An Iberian priest, Raguel, first recorded the story sometime before 967.[33] Raguel tells us that after the caliph attempts to touch Pelagius in a sexual way, Pelagius strikes him and asks: "Numquid me similem tuis effeminatum existimas?" ("Do you think me like one of yours, an effeminate?")[34] Pelagius then makes a strange gesture: he casts off the rich garments that the caliph has provided, and stands naked before the court. As Mark Jordan says in *The Invention of Sodomy*, Pelagius "expos[es] the body that is the object of desire," and that he does so "to show the king what he cannot have."[35] This dramatic moment recalls but revises the motif of the stripping of the female virgin found in the hagiography of late antiquity. Such a humiliation foregrounds the female saint's bodiliness, creating a tension between *pudicitia*, the "natural" modesty of the virgin, and *pudenda*, the shame that the tormentors intend the virgin to feel under the pressure of their gaze. Quite often, a miracle protects the virgin from the invasive gaze – as in, for example, the striking story of the Persian martyr Anahid, who is stripped, spread-eagled and attached to stakes, and finally smeared with honey to attract stinging insects. However, the horde of wasps that descend upon her leave her untouched, instead creating "a canopy above her body," preventing anyone from coming close enough to view her.[36] In contrast, Pelagius overtly invites the gaze of the caliph and his court. By publicly rejecting the caliph's gift of finery, Pelagius rejects the giver; perhaps more important, he also rejects the feminine role in which the caliph has attempted to place him, asserting his own active masculinity in a show of pride, the opposite of feminine shame. In his nakedness, Pelagius reminds everyone that he is indeed a man, not an *effeminatus* subject to the caliph's will. Like Chrysanthus and the other unnamed martyr confronted by a "beautiful but totally depraved young woman," Pelagius faces the perils of seduction, not rape, in this singular legend in which the seducer is male. While Raguel engages with the complications of same-sex desire in extremely allusive ways, he most clearly identifies the homoerotic as a characteristic of ethnic and religious otherness. In many respects, the story of Pelagius reflects medieval Western European prejudices against Muslims, who were often accused of engaging in any number of non-normative sexual practices. In effect, the Caliph's desire functions as a marker of his Muslim identity. One might argue that Pelagius not only rejects the Caliph's desire to colonize his body, but also 'Abd al-Rahmân's desire to colonize his Christianity and his Westernness. Indeed, in addition to the binaries of Christian/Muslim, West/East, sodomite/virgin that are present here, we also find that the opposition between human/not human comes into play when the caliph reaches out to touch Pelagius, and he responds unequivocally: "Tolle, canis" (Away, dog).[37] Pelagius' virginity seemingly functions as a metonym, as a cover, for a multifaceted identity that Pelagius represents and successfully defends – successfully, that is, according to the logic of Christian martyrdom. Such a representation of male virginity is consistent with later representations of male virginity in vernacular romance in that virginity by itself (except, perhaps, in the case of Galahad) is never enough to define a man, but is one attribute among many.

Perhaps within a few years of Raguel's account, Hrotswit composed a metrical *vita*, naming an eyewitness to the event as her source.[38] Her *Pelagius* is quite a florid, dramatic tale indeed. I quote the seduction passage in full:

> Now when [Pelagius] stood in the midst of the courtiers, his appearance surpassed in splendor that of all his companions. Toward him all directed their gaze, at one time admiring his countenance, at another, the charming utterance of his lips. The king also, attracted to him at first sight, was passionately inflamed by the amiable beauty of that royal youth. At length he ordered that Pelagius, for whom he entertained such an excessive infatuation, be now placed on the throne of the realm with him, so that he might give expression to his affection. And then he sought in his frenzy to bend his head and kiss the youth he loved, embracing him the while.[39]

While Raguel never puts a name to the caliph's desire, Hrotswit notes that the entire court knows that Abdrahemen ('Abd al-Rahmân) has been "corrupted by Sodomitic vices" ("Corruptum vitiis cognoscebant Sodomitis").[40] There is no casting off of garments in this version, but Pelagius just as firmly turns aside Abdrahemen's advances, saying that it is not fitting for a Christian to accept such a "barbarous" embrace, or to be kissed by "a lewd slave of the demon" ("Daemonis oscillum spurci captare famelli").[41] He tells the king that he should pursue other pagan idol-worshippers instead, finally hitting Abdrahemen in the face to deter his embraces. (The otherness of ethnicity is much more explicit in Hrotswit's version.) The King, now angry, orders Pelagius to be thrown over the wall with a catapult: so is Pelagius "hurl[ed] from a sling to martyrdom."[42] However, Pelagius, like many a martyr before him, is miraculously unharmed, and finally decapitated. Pelagius thus relies on a brand of muscular Christianity, not divine intervention, to protect his virginity until his death. Pelagius' active, physical resistance is one aspect of this legend that sets it apart from the legends of menaced female virgin martyrs.

On the other hand, the legend of Pelagius in Hrotswit's hands has much in common with the female saints' lives of late antiquity, in which beauty, bravery and eloquence prevail in the face of powers hostile to Christianity. (The story of Jeanne d'Arc demonstrates that she is heir to both traditions.) For example, Hrotsvit tells us that Pelagius, in the "first flower of manhood" ("primos flores iuvenilis") is noble, "endowed with every charm that bodily comeliness could afford ... resplendent in person, prudent in counsel, glorious in all virtue."[43] Abdrahemen's courtiers, who hear of Pelagius before the caliph sees him, report that Pelagius is both beautiful and eloquent, with "a comely countenance" ("vultum ... speciosum") and "sweet lips" ("praedulcis ... oris").[44] Such language induces the reader to look, to admire, to focus on the bodily from outside the text. Once Pelagius arrives at the caliph's court, he becomes the object of an overtly erotic regard *within* the text: "Toward him all directed their gaze, at one time admiring his countenance, at another, the charming utterance of his lips."[45] These and other details of Pelagius' physicality rely upon a semiotic system in which women have traditionally been the object of the gaze.[46] It strikes me that the less Pelagius is represented as a manly man, the more the representation of same-sex desire or rape – mutually exclusive, but not absolutely so – is made less threatening. Feminizing Pelagius, which we can identify as a strategy of "heterosexualizing" homosexuality (as Jonathan Goldberg puts it in a different context[47]) and/or homosexual acts vitiates the destabilizing effects of a story in which the desiring male subject is made into the desired object. We do not know if the historical Pelagius, as opposed to his textual representation, suffered rape as part of his final torture, by the caliph himself or perhaps by one of his dungeon keepers. I wonder about the possibility of a lacuna in the legend of Pelagius, the only hagiographical legend from the Middle Ages, if not the entire extant corpus to the present day that I know of, that includes a male virgin martyr and a villain "[c]orruptum vitiis cognoscebant Sodomitis."

The legend of Pelagius represents a cul-de-sac in the hagiographical tradition, for Pelagius' cult is much limited in scope and influence when compared to other saints and their cults. In fact, as Mark Jordan compellingly demonstrates, the textual representation of Pelagius as a young, vulnerable, beautiful boy is revised in the iconography of the eleventh and twelfth centuries so that he appears as a "triumphant military saint." For example, in a sculpture from the former cathedral of León (where Pelagius' cult took hold), Pelagius' naked body acquires an armored breastplate. I think Jordan is right when he says that "the transformation from ephebe to glorious captain is also a curious sublimation of homoerotic desire."[48] Moreover, we can read the armor – an obvious cover – as a projected, physical sign of male subjectivity. Pelagius' nakedness, his vulnerability to male desire, is put under cover, suppressed in these visual narratives. As we saw in Chapter 2, we are often made voyeurs in the tale of the menaced female virgin, and this is certainly true of Hrotsvit's account. Yet later representations of Pelagius seem intent on avoiding any such opportunity.

Just as Dinshaw argues for *Sir Gawain and the Green Knight*, Jordan argues that "[s]ame-sex desire has to be invoked and then contained, made possible but implausible" in the legend of Pelagius.[49] Precisely how this is done, I have been arguing, is through a claustrophilic narrative in which Pelagius is made less a man and more a woman – a sister to the many female virgins who were martyred before him. We do not know what else Raguel wrote, but we do know that Hrotswit wrote a number of female saints' legends: when we compare her charismatic, beautiful heroines with Pelagius, we can see how closely he is positioned on a continuum with these women.[50] Raguel's and Hrotswit's versions of the legend may well lack the vocabulary for a full articulation of same-sex desire (however negatively portrayed in the person of the caliph), but both are still capable of registering anxiety about such desire, and do so by re-inscribing it in the feminine mode.

Whose body?

I have been arguing that the male virgin never takes center stage in the saint's life, reading this phenomenon as a strategy to protect masculine subjectivity from the objectifying gaze. I find a similar strategy in Malory's *Morte Darthur*. In this poem (which so problematizes late medieval codes of knighthood), the masculine body, in its function as a metonym for the social body chivalric, must be preserved intact and inviolate at all costs. I argue that, when the male body is threatened with penetration and fragmentation (words taken from the rhetoric of menaced female virginity) a feminine and feminized body takes its place within the narrative frame. Nor is substitution the only strategy activated to protect the male body: we can also discern a pattern of transformation of the masculine into the feminine for precisely the same reason: the feminized masculine body preserves the body chivalric from any real threat or critique.

Moreover, not only are we encouraged to look *at* the female body and *away* from the male body, we can also look *through* the male body to discover another man. As I read it in the *Morte Darthur*, this homosocial/homoerotic line of sight is a feminizing gaze, and thus implicated in the bait-and-switch game to which I have alluded.[51] (I should note that I am using the terms *female body* and *male body* to denote an essentialized notion of sex, and I reserve the terms *feminine body* and *masculine body* to describe gender as a social category; that is, positions that are not naturalized and fixed but negotiable and unstable. However, I should add that both ways of looking at bodies may be realized in a given text – sometimes simultaneously.)

Malory's shell game

In the story of the menaced female virgin, whether in hagiography or romance, one cannot avoid "looking." Yet when we consider the various temptations and seductions that the Knights of the Round Table face in the *Morte Darthur*, it is the female body that once again captures our attention – this time, not as menaced virgin, but as menacing seductress. Under cover of the feminine, the male virgin/ male body fades into the background. For example, after Gareth (disguised under the name of Beawmaynes) arrives at Persaunte's castle, Persaunte commands his (unnamed) daughter to visit Gareth in bed. He gives her very specific instructions: "'And lye downe by his syde and make hym no strange chere but good chere, and take hym in your armys and kysse hym and loke that this be done, I charge you, as ye woll have my love and my good wylle'" (314).[52] Gareth awakens to find Persaunte's daughter beside him. She tells him that her father sent her. He asks, "'Be ye a pusell [maiden] or a wyff?'" (315). His own behavior, apparently, will depend on her answer – *her body* – and not on any commitment to his own chastity.

In fact, when Persaunte's daughter says that she is indeed "'a clene maydyn,'" Gareth asks her to leave. She then reports his behavior to her father. His response: "'Truly … whatsomever he be he is com of full noble bloode'" (315). Obviously, it is not chastity, or, more accurately, it is *more* than chastity that is being tested here. Larry Benson would call this episode an example of "proof-of-knighthood," in which the term "knighthood" subsumes a number of different qualities, of which chastity is only one.[53] (In this light, one might conclude that the subject of this "test" is Gareth's allegiance to the guest-host relationship.) However, if we look again, we might detect Persaunte lurking behind his daughter's body in Gareth's bed. Using a paradigm quite different from Benson's, we can read this scene as an enactment of homosociality, in which male-male desire is "conducted" through the body of Persaunte's daughter.

Malory is always circumspect when it comes to scenes in which women and men lie "abed togydirs," and this scene is no exception.[54] Yet while the bedroom scene has no erotic content, the same cannot be said of Persaunte's speech to his daughter. Persaunte's words have a certain forbidden and ambiguous allure: he seems to commit a kind of verbal incest on the one hand, and to express a homo-erotic desire on the other. And how are we to interpret the order to make "no strange chere but good chere"? We can translate this to mean simply "do not be shy" (that is, reserved, distant, aloof). Yet in Malory's English, as in modern English, *strange* also connotes that which is alien, foreign, unfamiliar, even abnormal.

I am not saying that Persaunte's interest lies in incest or sodomy, to use the language of fifteenth-century England. However, this episode has the effect of destabilizing the normative relationships between daughter and father, guest and host, man and maid. And in this murkiness what gets lost is Gareth. His body, his virginity, remains invisible, unreadable, while Persuante's daughter's virginity is openly displayed – though refused. And Gareth's refusal opens up a line of sight through her to Persaunte, away from his own body, and thus to another relationship altogether, a relationship between men.

The female body diverts the gaze elsewhere in the *Morte Darthur*, in two parallel episodes involving Bors and Percivale as they seek the Grail. An unnamed lady begs Bors to lie with her, saying, "'I have loved you longe for the grete beauté I have sene in you and the grete hardynesse that I have herde of you'" (965). When he refuses, she threatens suicide – and murder, for she will take her twelve ladies with her. In spite of the women's pleas and threats, Bors remains steadfast. The women cast themselves down from a tower. As they do so, Bors "blysse[s] hys body and hys vysayge"; that is, he blesses the very thing that we ought to be looking at, but aren't – and everything disappears in a great rush of noise (966). Apparently, that was no lady.

Percivale meets a woman who claims that she is a "'jantillwoman ... diseryte'" (917). She invites him to her pavilion for a feast. After drinking strong wine with the lady, Percivale

> was chaffett [heated] a lityll more than he oughte to be. With that he behylde that jantilwoman, and hym thought she was the fayryst creature that ever he saw ... [Percivale] profird hir love and prayde hir that she wolde be hys. Than she refused hym in a maner whan he requyred her, for cause he sholde be the more ardente on hir. And ever he sesed nat to pray hir of love. (918)

She makes him promise to be her "trew servaunte." He swears, appropriately enough, "by the feythe of my body." She has a bed made up, and lies down "unclothed." Percivale also lies down "naked," which may mean that he removes all of his clothes, or, simply, that he disarms (918). He happens to glance at his sword, which is also "naked"; that is, out of its scabbard. As he gazes upon the crucifix in the pommel, he begins to have regrets, and makes the sign of the cross. The lady, the devil in disguise, departs on the wind, "rorynge and yellynge" (919).

Both episodes represent a well-known and well-documented misogynist intertext in which female desire is demonized, here literally. Moreover, in both instances, the devil, indicated as masculine in the text, is the real body in woman's dress and flesh – the homoerotic with a whiff of brimstone. More important is the larger "body" that is being tested by Percivale and Bors: the secular body chivalric, the code that bonds knights in service to another man: namely, Arthur. And, of course, the sacred body chivalric is at stake in the Grail Quest, undertaken on behalf of Jesus Christ himself.

When I first began to look closely at these and other episodes, it seemed to me that my own line of sight – *my* temptation, perhaps – was directed toward the female body and away from the male body.[55] As the passages I cite reveal, it is not anything overt in the text that would cause me to read this way. Instead, I had assumed that the appropriate point of view was a naturalized male one, and therefore I looked *with* Gareth, Bors, and Percivale.[56] Such an alignment with the masculine is a classic example of what Judith Fetterley calls an immasculated reading.[57] It would be wrong, of course, to attribute such an experience to all women reading the *Morte Darthur*, either in the fifteenth century or at the end of the twentieth. At the same time, no matter what one's position is to the text, it is clear that masculinity and its maintenance is a central concern of the *Morte Darthur*, and that women play a secondary role, either facilitating the masculine project or, like Bors' and Percevale's seductresses, interfering in it.

Menacing Launcelot

Jeanne d'Arc's virginity was satisfactorily established at her trial through a series of physical examinations predicated upon her sex. Yet though her virginity was a precondition for her military victories, her victories were also interpreted as proof of her virginity. How could she have triumphed on the battlefield unless she had been sanctioned by God? And how could she have received God's blessing unless she had been pure? Jeanne's imaginary compatriot, Launcelot, inspires the same sort of questions about his chastity in the *Morte Darthur*, but unlike Jeanne, provides very equivocal answers. Jeanne was first measured against a feminine, bodily standard of virginity, and then measured against a masculine standard in which valor and victory on the battlefield were made synonymous with virginity. Launcelot, because his virginity is finally unverifiable and unknowable, actually undermines this latter standard as it is realized in Malory's text.

As we saw in the previous chapter, tests and ordeals of female chastity are clearly labeled as such and foregrounded in the romance plot. As a result, the reader cannot avoid thinking about and imagining the female body and its purported secrets, as in the case of Jeanne d'Arc, whose very private examinations were made public to all. There are no parallel narratives in which the male body is subject to such speculation. I would argue, however, that there are many narratives in which the questioning or proofing of male virginity is implicit. Launcelot, for example, is "tested" many times throughout the *Morte Darthur*, in one-to-one combat and in various encounters with ardent maidens. Both kinds of tests bear similarities to the more fully articulated chastity tests to which women in romance are subjected. Yet while women invariably fail, Launcelot always succeeds when it would appear to the reader that he shouldn't. The *Morte Darthur* oscillates between demonstrating that Launcelot is invincible because he is pure and furnishing us with evidence that he is not so pure. It has been argued that Launcelot remains a virgin until he is tricked into having intercourse with Elayne (approximately halfway through the *Morte Darthur*), and that the first time that he has intercourse with Gwenyver is after Mellyagaunce abducts her.[58] However, I believe that the *when* and the *how* of Launcelot's virginity is deliberately left ambiguous in the *Morte Darthur*.[59] Recall that Launcelot, like many a consecrated virgin before him, possesses certain healing powers. Launcelot cures the wounded Melyot de Logrys in the adventure of the Chapel Perelus. Later, Launcelot is the only knight who is able to heal Sir Urré. In fact, as if to emphasize Launcelot's unique gift, Malory lists the names of one hundred and ten knights, including Arthur, who had attempted to cure Urré, but were unable – or unworthy – to do so.[60] This episode, apparently original with Malory, follows immediately after "The Knight of the Cart," – that is, after Launcelot clearly and explicitly has had intercourse with the Queen.

Consider further that Launcelot is able to defend Gwenyver against numerous accusations, regardless of the status of his bodily and "social" virginity (and regardless of the status of the Queen's fidelity, of course). Launcelot never fails Gwenyver; as Bors reproachfully puts it to the Queen, "in youre ryght nother in youre wronge" (1052). First, Launcelot defeats Sir Mador in a judicial trial-by-combat after Gwenyver is accused of poisoning Sir Patryse. While Gwenyver is indeed innocent of this crime, she and Launcelot *are* guilty of adultery. In theory, Launcelot lacks the ritual purity necessary for such a trial-by-combat. Second, Launcelot (fresh from the Queen's bed, as it were) triumphs over Mellyagaunce in another trial-by-combat, a battle that he should have lost by reason of his adultery. Finally, and most spectacularly, Launcelot saves Gwenyver from burning after he is ambushed in her bedchamber. In the latter two episodes, Launcelot makes a series of equivocal statements about his and Gwenyver's innocence that, while they may be technically true, reveal a distinct gap between *verbum* and *res*. Consider what Launcelot says after the ambush: "I shall … prove hit uppon ony knyght … that my lady, quene Gwenyver, ys as trew a lady unto youre person *as ys ony lady lyvynge unto her lorde*, and that woll I make good with my hondis" (1188, emphasis mine). Does this mean that Gwenyver is faithful absolutely? Or simply as faithful as anyone might expect; that is, faithful in comparison to other women? It then follows that Launcelot is *just as* "trew" as Gwenyver.

Nacien the hermit is the first critic to supply us with a (postmodern) reading of Launcelot, telling Gawayn that Launcelot "ys nat stable" (948). Nacien seems to recognize that "Launcelot" is a site of contradictory and often ironic meanings, whether he happens to represent the man who is Arthur's best knight or the very ideals of knighthood. He is both chaste and an adulterer; he is worthy enough to see the Grail and yet not. Launcelot's virginity is both affirmed and denied in the *Morte Darthur*, and this single contradiction illustrates in small not only how the text resists any sort of closure, but also how virginity itself resists final resolution.

In the previous chapter, we saw that the chastity test or ordeal, initially threatening to the social order, actually reaffirms social bonds and hierarchies when men choose to reject the "evidence" the ordeal provides. If women cannot pass the test, then the test must be rejected. According to the same logic, if men cannot "pass" the test of knighthood, if Launcelot were not able to furnish proof-of-knighthood upon demand, then the threat to Arthur's Round Table and what it stands for would be too great to bear. The male body (like a woman's virginity) is of value only in paradox: when it is at once inviolate *and* sacrificable. Extremes, such as the absolutely unassailable body or the irreparably wounded and broken body, would leave no game to be played at all. What is needed is a body that breaks and heals, breaks and heals over and again, and Launcelot becomes the paradigm for such a body.

Throughout the *Morte Darthur*, it seems that Launcelot's prowess is not tied to the "fact" of his virginity, but nevertheless his prowess can be interpreted as "proof" of his virginity. It is not that Launcelot is exempt from the rules, secular *and* sacred, that seem to govern chivalric behavior in the *Morte Darthur*; rather, chivalry and its realizations are always already flawed, contradictory, and relative. Perfected knighthood, like perfected virginity, resists representation.[61]

The pleasures of the homoerotic

As the knights of the Round Table make their vows to find the Grail, Arthur says:

> "nevyr shall I se you agayne *holé togydirs*, therefore ones shall I se you *togydir* in the medow, all *holé togyders*! Therefore I woll se you all *holé togyder* in the

medow of Camelot, to juste and to turney, that aftir youre dethe men may speke of hit that such knyghtes were here, such a day, *holé togydirs.*" (864, emphasis mine)[62]

The Grail Quest will indeed sunder the body chivalric, fragmenting it irrecoverably. Arthur's lament emphasizes the importance of communal integrity and, through its very excess of repetition, reveals its fragility.

The word *togydirs* also links this passage with two distinct but parallel moments repeated over and again throughout the *Morte Darthur:* first, the times a knight and a lady lie "abed togydirs," and second, the times when two knights, spears at the ready, rush "togydirs" at one another in the first heat of battle.[63] Fellowship, sexual intercourse, and the *pas d'armes* become points on a circle, part of a tautological tangle.

While seduction troped as battle is overt enough in medieval texts (the assault on the Rose in the *Roman de la Rose* comes immediately to mind), battle troped as seduction is a subtler phenomenon. Still, it is possible to recover moments when spears and swords substitute for, and perhaps extend, the phallus/penis. We can discern a pattern in Malory (and in other medieval romances) in which bed and battlefield stand in chiastic relation to each other. There is, however, one difference: on the battlefield, the Other – so often figured as female – is male.[64] In the clash between the hero and this male Other, "virginity" of a different sort appears to be at stake, while the imagery remains essentially the same: the imagery of submission, penetration, and triumph.[65] Such imagery underwrites a common discourse that constructs descriptions of one-to-one combat *and* sexual intercourse, a discourse in this instance that figures the homoerotic in terms of heterosexual coupling. Thus the more threatening end of the homosocial bond, that is, male-male desire, is suppressed in one part of the text only to surface elsewhere, in the ritualized "courtship" of battle.

We find a rather bizarre enactment of the homosocial/homoerotic (in which blood takes on a feminine valence) in the triangle that develops between Tristram, the unnamed wife of Segwarydes, and King Mark. Mark attacks Tristram out of jealousy – he himself is attracted to Segwarydes' wife – and seriously wounds him. Tristram rides from this encounter to tryst with Segwarydes' wife, and "eyther halsed other in armys" (394). (Tristram puts down one set of arms to take up another.) However, "in hys ragynge [Tristram] toke no kepe of his grene wounde that kynge Marke had gyffyn hym, and so ... bledde bothe the over-shete and the neyther-shete, and the pylowes and the hede-shete" (394). Segwarydes comes home to find "hys bedde troubled and brokyn." Segwarydes concludes (though the text does not explain how) that only a wounded knight could have left such blood, the sheets serving, then, as a sort of knightly Veronica's veil.

In a comparable episode, Launcelot enters Gwenyver's chamber in Mellya-gaunce's castle. In his eagerness, he lays hold of the iron bars and cuts his hand "thorowoute to the bone." He goes "to bedde with the quene and toke no force of hys hurte honde, but toke hys plesaunce and hys lykynge" (1131). As a result, "all the hede-shete, pylow, and over-shyte was all bebled of the bloode of sir Launcelot"

(1132). Mellyagaunce, who apparently shares with Segwarydes a talent for reading sheets, assumes Gwenyver has slept with "som" of the wounded knights who lie near her bedchamber – the very knights who were wounded in their heroic attempt to rescue the Queen. Here indeed is an excess of fellowship – or, at least, fellowship as it is imagined by Mellyagaunce, who has already tried, unsuccessfully, to crash the Arthur-Gwenyver-Launcelot triangle.[66]

In "Symbolic Sexual Inversion and the Construction of Courtly Manhood in Two French Romances," Gary Ferguson suggests that the blood on the sheets is multivalent, evocative of menstrual blood, hymeneal blood, circumcision – and even the "blood" of lineage.[67] This is a productive way for us outside the text to "read" this blood. In effect, both Tristram and Launcelot reverse gender roles: no longer readers of feminine bodies, they are instead made read*able* by the bodily fluids they leave behind.[68] Yet I am more interested in how the blood on the sheets is read *within* the text. After all, the significance of the blood seems to be clear to Segwarydes, Mellyagaunce, and, apparently, to all of Gwenyver's knights who crowd her bed for a look. Granted, Gwenyver is surrounded by ten wounded knights, so Mellyagaunce's conclusion makes some sense. But there are no wounded knights in the Tristram episode, apart from Tristram himself. One could explain this episode away by describing it as one of the many instances of doubled plot (here imperfect) that characterizes the *Morte Darthur*. However, what the two episodes have in common is that the interpreters of bloody sheets make the woman – usually conveniently inserted between men – into a conspicuous absence.

I see these two acts of interpretation – reading bloody sheets – as radical examples of slippage in the text. The knights read past the feminine to gaze directly upon the masculine, which is just the opposite of the way in which I was reading the stories of Bors and Percivale earlier. The knights cannot "see" the woman in these scenes because in the homosocial relationship, she has no originary power or agency. The blood on the sheets is read *by* men as saying something *about* men because they have so completely appropriated the feminine that it is reconstituted as the sign of the homoerotic.[69] Just for a moment, the true relationship between men is exposed. Gwenyver is then hastily reinserted into the story, charged with treason, and consigned to burning at the stake. As we have seen, Launcelot passes a test he ought to fail when he successfully rescues the Queen, in spite of both their guilt.

The case of Segwarydes' wife is more complicated. The episode is apparently designed to highlight Mark's enmity and jealousy, and furnishes yet another reason for the craven Cornish King to hate Tristram. Yet the episode also sends ripples through the text in quite another direction. The triangle, in which the (unnamed) lady finds herself between Mark and Tristram, expands to a quadrangle when the lady's lawful husband sees the sheets. Then the quadrangle becomes a pentagon when sir Bleoberys comes to court and asks Mark to give him "'the fayreste lady in your courte,'" who turns out to be, in Bleoberys' estimation, Segwarydes' wife (396). Tristram decides to stay out of any rescue attempt (it's a matter of honor, he says [397]) until he hears how badly Bleoberys has beaten Segwarydes. He then rides after Bleoberys. They meet and fight to a standoff. The wife of Segwarydes is told to choose between the two combatants, and she picks Bleoberys, for, she says, Tristram had abandoned her. He is therefore a shameful knight. Bleoberys and Tristram himself agree with this assessment, and Bleoberys decides to give the lady back to her husband. Now I think that one would be hard put to find a more blatant example of the commodification of women or of the primacy of the homosocial bond anywhere in the *Morte Darthur*. (At first, the wife of Segwarydes appears to have a say in the matter; after all, she is asked to choose between the men. However, I would argue that Segwarydes' wife chooses according to a paradigmatic masculine code, not according to her own desires, here obscured, suppressed, or illegible.) This sequence of exchanges – in which the lady is so speedily passed from one knight to another – seems to parody homosociality, not to affirm it, thus opening up a space for a critique of the body chivalric within the text.

In the world of the *Morte Darthur*, social roles are radically constrained by gender, and are continually reproduced as binarized, exclusionary positions. As Joan Cadden puts it, "in spite of the possibility of middle terms admitted by medical theory" in the European Middle Ages, we find a relentless drive toward a "binary typology."[70] In other words, one "must" be either masculine or feminine – which is not to say that the *Morte Darthur* succeeds in realizing such an imperative, but only to acknowledge the resulting tensions from any attempt to do so. This dynamic allows for the possibility that it is not two "men" who are engaged in battle, but, finally, one "man" (the triumphant knight) and one "woman" (the defeated knight). The body chivalric remains intact, because once again, "women" are consigned to its margins.

Hymeneal performances

I want to return to a scene that I have suppressed in my reading until now: what Percivale does after his diabolical lady vanishes. At this point, Percivale moves clearly into our line of sight as he draws his sword, declaring "'Sitthyn my flessh woll be my mayster I shall punyssh hit'" (a comment original with Malory). The narrator takes over at this point: "And therewith he rooff hymselff thorow the thygh, that the blood sterte aboute hym" (919). As the blood flows from his wound, Percivale laments: "'How nyghe I was loste, and to have lost that I sholde never have gotyn agayne, that was my virginité, for that may never be recoverde aftir hit ys onys loste'" (919).[71] The thigh is a common enough euphemism for the genitals; thus it seems that Percivale intended to make an eunuch of himself "for the sake of the kingdom of heaven" (Matthew 19:12). However, taking a cue from Peter Brown in his discussion of Origen's reputed self-castration,[72] I'd like to suggest that castration is too dangerous and too extreme a remedy, for it calls into question what it means to be a man, and therefore destabilizes the premises of the homosocial bond. Within the context of a homoerotic constructed by a feminine/masculine binary that consistently feminizes the "other" knight, a different reading of this self-mutilation is possible.[73] Percivale enacts on his own body what an Other, a demon lover, would have done, effectively taking his own "maidenhead" in a ritualized enactment of intercourse. Being feminized (or feminizing oneself) assures social and sexual difference more safely than castration, which consigns the castrated to a place outside difference.

Thaïs E. Morgan's remarks on transvestite female impersonation have relevance here:

> I regard female impersonation in any context as suspect *for women* – potentially misogynist because it too often turns out, upon closer analysis, to be a mockery and expulsion of the feminine in men by men ... At the same time, I see female impersonation as liberating *for men* – potentially disruptive of normative heterosexual masculinity.[74]

Morgan adds, "the sex-gender system ... often operates not despite but through gender crossing."[75] In other words, when the strict binaries of feminine/masculine, female/male are to some degree destabilized and subverted, such subversions do not free up these polarities, but lock them into place. It might be said that, when a knight is defeated on the battlefield and forced to take a submissive posture, he switches social categories and is feminized. He simply cannot "be" masculine *and* "be" defeated simultaneously. Such a transformation guarantees the working of the body chivalric by keeping at least one man on top.

Galahad "ys a mayde"

In his essay, "The Double Session," in a now notorious move, Derrida appropriates the hymen, which he describes as "a closeness and a veil," as

> first of all a sign of fusion ... It is not only the difference (between desire and fulfillment) that is abolished, but also the difference between difference and nondifference.[76]

Derrida, of course, is fully aware of the masculine/feminine binary that he has created. He goes on to collapse the masculine/feminine together in order to arrive at hymen, and then reconstitutes the binary *in* hymen. One result is that the hymen functions as (is figured as) both an opening and a cover. In Malory's *Morte Darthur*, this contradiction is embodied by Galahad.

When we compare Galahad to the other knights of the Round Table, we see that he is the only man whose virginity is foregrounded. A hermit tells Gawayne that Galahad "'ys a mayde and synned never, and that ys the cause he shall enchyve where he goth'" (891). And Mordrayns says to Galahad: "'For thou arte a clene virgyne above all knyghtes, as the floure of the lyly in whom virginité is signified. And thou arte the rose which ys the floure of all good vertu, and in colour of fyre'" (1025). He makes a well stop boiling, described as "a sygne of lechory that was that tyme muche used. But that hete myght nat abide [Galahad's] pure virginité" (1025). He also heals Mordrayns, who is said to have waited four hundred years for the Grail Knight – and, of course, he heals the Maimed King. Most important, and most famously, he is the only knight who is able to behold the Grail without impediment.

Yet in spite of these accomplishments, Malory's Galahad remains a curiously static character. The battles he fights do not help Galahad grow into knighthood in any way (as, say, Gareth's adventures do by helping him enter into homosociality). Alone among the knights of the Round Table, Galahad is not tested: he is simply affirmed in his monumental monologism. From start to finish, Galahad escapes penetration and dismemberment; he dies intact, his soul translated into heaven.

In short, Galahad never enters into the homosociality that so often drives Malory's *Morte Darthur*. He does not participate in any exchange; he never circulates or is circulated. Galahad exists outside *any* sociality; in fact, he prevents sociality from ever becoming fully realized, even before he comes to Camelot: the Syege Perelous is a rupture, a site that predicts the final destruction of the Round Table. Galahad's very place at the Round Table (itself rather like the hymen) is a breach.[77]

Galahad is the "sygne" *par excellence* of the threatening feminine that Arthur's knights work so hard to suppress. More accurately, he is in excess of this sign, more feminine than the feminine itself in his inviolateness. Virginity, constructed as it is in the realm of the social, always carries within it the potential for its own loss, a paradox not lost upon the early Church Fathers. As we have seen, they were so concerned about the fragility of chastity that they insisted on sequestering the virgin to protect her from prying eyes and lascivious thoughts, either of which could lead to the loss of her chastity/virginity. Similarly, Malory's Galahad is shielded from bodily and spiritual penetration, both within the text, in that he remains unscathed by sword and temptation, and outside the text, in that he resists any final or complete reading.

So far, I have tried to imagine how the hymen – a phantom body part – might serve as a sign for the male virgin. Yet, as the figure of Galahad demonstrates, the male virgin seems to have no place in the *Morte Darthur*'s system of signification; he is an impossibility, just as a male virgin equipped with a hymen is an absurdity. However, it is necessary to invoke such a figure in order to make visible a narrative in which masculinity and virginity are equally threatened by the feminine. (Why else do Jerome, Ambrose, and others masculinize the virgin in the first place, if not to save her from her own nature?) Menaced masculinity in the *Morte Darthur* looks very much like imperiled virginity, because at the moment of crisis on the battlefield, loss is gain: as the masculinity of the weaker knight begins to destabilize, it reemerges in a new, more powerful form in the figure of the triumphant knight.

The case of Gawain

The hagiographic scenes of assayed chastity discussed above (the legend of Pelagius excepted) may have reminded the reader of perhaps the most famous seduction scenes in English romance: the unnamed Lady's exchanges with Gawain in *Sir*

Gawain and the Green Knight (c. 1400). I do not wish to argue that the story of Chrysanthus or of the bound boy in the *Legenda Aurea* ought to be identified as sources for these scenes in *Gawain*; in fact, such stories only remotely qualify as analogues. What ties these saints' legends (and in this respect I include the legend of Pelagius) to *Gawain*, however, is a similar claustrophilic resistance to representing the male body and masculinity in object position. I locate this resistance in the conventions of both the chastity test and the ordeal that have left their traces on the poem, as in, most notably, the meeting at the Green Chapel, which is reminiscent of the juridical ordeal in that Gawain must submit to a physical test and be judged accordingly. Just *what* is being tested is a fundamental issue in *Gawain* scholarship, and the poem has proved capacious enough to allow for a variety of answers, most recently framed as having to do with heteronormativity, homosociality, and masculinity.[78] Of course, the testing of Gawain is not just a testing of his virginity/chastity, but I think that the way in which his virginity in the poem emerges as dependent on a model of female virginity/chastity is integral to how male subjectivity is represented in *Sir Gawain and the Green Knight*.

Yet I must say that using the word *virginity* is misleading here. *Sir Gawain and the Green Knight* makes a distinction between virginity; that is, physical integrity, and chastity; that is, spiritual purity. We are told in the arming scene that Gawain "vsed ... clannes" ("practiced ... cleanness"[79]), which may assure us that Gawain practiced *continentia*, but not necessarily that he was a virgin. The idea of *continentia* returns us to Tertullian and *De virginibus velandis*, who says that, if anyone should be honored for virginity, it is the male virgin, first on the "authority of sex" ("sexus auctoritatem": that is, on the authority of masculinity), and second on the "ground of continency." Tertullian continues:

> The more their sex is eager and warm toward females, so much the more toil does the continence of (this) greater ardour involve ... For is not continence withal superior to virginity ... For constancy of virginity is maintained by grace; of continence, by virtue.[80]

In other words, women, for whom virginity is constructed as an *a priori* condition, maintain their chastity by grace alone. On the other hand, continence is a matter of *manly* virtue; that is, of conscious maintenance, because once one knows the pleasures of the flesh, it is even harder to give them up. And Tertullian should know: he himself was married before choosing celibacy. It may be that Gawain also knows what he is giving up by practicing *clannes* – or perhaps we should say "Gawain," whose textual/sexual dossier is apparently well-known at Bertilak's castle. Following a fruitful suggestion of Carolyn Dinshaw's, we might say that both the Lady in the tale and the reader outside of the tale suffer from a sort of intertextual interference, as it were, when it comes to deciding if the Gawain that we find in bed is "really" Gawain.[81] When the Lady first enters Gawain's bedchamber, she says, "'For I wene wel, iwysse, Sir Wowen ȝe are,'" (I know well, certainly, that Sir Gawain you are, 1226). He responds: "'Þaȝ I be not now he þat ȝe of speken'" (though I am not now he of whom you speak, 1242). On the surface, this is a gracious, modest reply to her compliments, but the *now* suggests a change, a break with the past, either the immediate past in the poem (the reader knows, even if the Lady doesn't, that Gawain has recently renewed his chivalric vows, including a vow of chastity), or the past chronicled in other texts, outside of Cotton Nero A.x. Later, the Lady exclaims: "'Bot þat ȝe be Gawan hit gotz in mynde!'" (But I cannot conceive that you are Gawain, 1293), because the "real" Gawain "'Couth not lyȝtly haf lenged so long wyth a lady / Bot he had craued a cosse bi his courtaysye'" (Could not lightly have lingered so long with a lady, unless he had craved a kiss for his courtesy, 1299–1300). The Gawain of this poem, caught between his vow of "cortaysye" and that of "clannes" (courtesy, cleanness, 653) is reluctant to play the game of *fine amor*, denying his "Continental" past as an experienced lover, if not as an outright womanizer.[82] I am suggesting that part of the problem in determining Gawain's virginity lies in the impossibility of determining who *Gawain* is. In a way, the many images of enclosure that scholars have noted within the poem are paralleled but reversed on a meta-level, for Gawain, or "Gawain," actually exceeds the confines of the poem.

Early on in the poem, one can discern a series of images of containment that, in effect, draw a veil (a metaphorical hymeneal covering) over Gawain and his body, protecting him from both the reader's gaze and the Lady's advances. Gawain is repeatedly set apart and enclosed in either a physical or rhetorical space, and his body exposed or opened, only to be covered or closed up again. For example, in the arming scene, a silk tapestry is ceremoniously spread on the floor. Gawain's armor is placed on the "tulé tapit," and then Gawain himself steps onto it (568). The tapestry marks off a literal *and* metaphorical space, separating Gawain from the world and rhythms of Arthur's court. This *tapit*, a deliberately-constructed threshold or liminal space between the ordinary and the sacred or magical, pre-figures the series of thresholds, both geographical and psychological, that Gawain must traverse on his way to the Green Chapel. In fact, Gawain's own body functions as a threshold that the Lady attempts to cross and that the Green Knight succeeds in crossing.

We are told that Gawain comes to his arming in a silk doublet and a "crafty capados, closed aloft" (well-made cape, closed at the top, 572). His legs are then "lapped in stel" (enclosed in steel, 575), his thighs "coyntlych closed" in armor (skillfully closed, 578). Gawain's coat of mail "[v]mbeweued" (enveloped, 581) him; he is "hasped in armes" (fastened in arms, 590), his helmet "stapled stifly" (securely fastened), "hasped," and "bounden" (606, 607, 609); even his horse is "gurd" (girded), "barred," and "bounden" (597, 600). The next image of contain-ment is Gawain's shield with its pentangle, each line of which "vmbelappeȝ and loukeȝ in oþer" (overlaps and locks with the other, 628), the famous "endeles knot" of which chastity is but one of five chivalric virtues. The shield itself is, of course, a very material cover; the pentangle, a highly symbolic cover (and remin-der). Most important, Gawain comes under the special grace and protection of the Virgin, whose image he has had painted on the inside of his shield (647–49). Gawain's body thus disappears under layers of garments, armor, and talismans. As Clare Kinney puts it, in *Sir Gawain and the Green Knight*, while women are described in "emphatically fleshly terms ... real men ... don't have bodies."[83] Compare this description of armored Gawain – the only physical description that we get – to that of the Lady, whose breast and throat are "bare displayed," her body open and available (955). This detail may capture the fashion of the time, but it also registers a gendered difference in what can and cannot be exhibited. Gawain, on the other hand, only possesses the outlines of a body, a carapace, a simulacrum of his real body. Once fully dressed in his armor, Gawain represents a highly stylized masculine physicality. His molded armor both exaggerates and obscures the lineaments of the fleshly body enclosed within it, covering the body and drawing attention to its function as a cover and the *need* for a cover.

Once fully encased in his armor, Gawain moves from the closed, protective cocoon of Arthur's court into the fastness of Bertilak's castle. The containment images now take on a more claustrophobic turn. The castle is described as located in "a park al aboute / With a pyked palays pyned ful þik" (a park all around / fenced in by a spiked palisade), surrounded by trees (768–70). Gawain stands before its gates "stoken faste" (closed shut, 782), but soon finds himself on the other side, locked within. Once inside the castle, Gawain is led to an enclosed, curtained "boure" (853), where he is "dispoyled"; that is, undressed (860) and then (like Chaucer's Grisilde) redressed, a symbolic exchange of one sort of sartorial protection for another. This dressing also foreshadows his donning of the green girdle, itself an obvious symbol of containment. As the reader may recall, the Lady visits Gawain in his bedroom three times, winning one kiss on the first day, two kisses on the second, and three on the third. In these encounters, the Lady and Gawain spar delicately, wielding a language that is courtly and flirtatious, oblique but pointed, and founded on an eroticized image of enclosure. The Lady greets him on the first morning with a jest: "'Now ar ȝe tan astyt! ... I schal bynde yow in your bedde'" ("now are you soon taken . . I shall hold you in you bed," 1211), telling him that the door is locked and the bolt drawn (1233). Gawain calls himself her "prysoun" (prisoner, 1219), and attempts to rise – and perhaps to dress himself; given the sleeping customs of the time, Gawain most likely lies naked in his "boure." He is thus at his most vulnerable, both to sexual seduction and violent assault.

On the morning Gawain arms to go to the Green Chapel, he wraps the girdle twice and tightly around his body ("Bi he hade belted þe bronde vpon his balȝe haunchez / Þenn dressed he his drurye double hym aboute, / Swyþe swepled vmbe his swange, swetely, þat knyȝt" (after belting his sword over his smooth hips, he tied his love-token twice around himself, wrapped it completely around his waist, 2032–34). The girdle is a woman's garment (and a woman's gift), and, like a man's armor, both covers and reveals. Designed to wrap around a woman's waist and hips, it also calls attention to the body that it hides. The girdle is, in fact, a gift that cuts both ways: while it promises a "zone" of protection, the girdle *actually delivers Gawain into danger, not only to his life, but also to something more permanent: his honor and his reputation.* Moreover, by asking Gawain to promise not to tell about the gift of her girdle, the Lady "binds" them both in a secret ("And besoȝt hym for hir sake disceuer it neuer / bot to lelly layne for hir lorde" (and beseeched him, for her sake, to never reveal it, but to carefully hide it from her lord, 1862–64).[84] The girdle thus represents a kind of substitute deception: the exchange of such a "drurye" (love-token, 2033), underscores the fact that, while Gawain never breaks his vow of chastity, never commits adultery with the Lady, he does indeed have something to hide.

While Gawain's various covers may have protected him from the act of intercourse with the Lady – and, perhaps, intercourse with Bertilak in turn – they are useless in that they cannot prevent Gawain's final meeting with the Green Knight, cannot prevent his receiving a nick in the neck. He flinches from the first blow, causing the Green Knight to say: "þou art not Gawayn ... is so goud halden" (you are not Gawain, who is thought so good, 2270). Gawain's reputation as a lover has already been interrogated by Bertilak's Lady; here, his reputation as a courageous knight is now called into question. Gawain's choice of the girdle over a dalliance with the Lady suggests which identity is more important to him. The Green Knight stops short on the second blow, re-testing Gawain's bravery, and finally "snyrt hym on þat on syde, þat seuered þe hyde" (nicked him on the side, breaking the skin, 2312), until Gawain sees his own blood "blenk on þe snawe" (shining on the snow, 2315). I do not want to insist on a parallel between this wound, this breaking open, this blood, and the "wound" of sexual penetration and loss of virginity. But consider how Western, Judaeo-Christian culture has made a woman's first experience of heterosexual intercourse into a liminal, transitional event that affects her social identity (girl to woman, innocence to experience). Gawain is similarly changed in this encounter, his breaking open revealing the "inner" man. Gawain passes over, becomes wiser, more experienced, less prideful (though given the ending of the poem, it is questionable whether he retains his new identity), and this experience is figured in feminized, physical imagery of penetration and blood. In this context, Gawain's famous misogynist tirade might be read as a ritual rejection of his feminization, designed to regain and secure his masculine subjectivity by publicly identifying against the Other upon whom he projects his own failings.

Let us return to the girdle, a polysemous sign even within the poem, for it takes on different meanings in different hands: the Lady calls it a "symple" silk (1847) – surely an ironic understatement. The narrator glosses the girdle as a "luf-lace" (love-lace, 1874) and "drurye" (love-token, 2033); by doing so, the narrator suggests that it functions as a symbol not only of the many things that lovers exchange in bed, but also as a sign of their love and loyalty out of bed, according to the conventions of *fin amor*. However, the girdle is actually a sign of a sexual consummation that never happened, a Derridian present absence. The Green Knight calls the girdle a "pure token" (2398) – an emblem of chastity? A symbol of chivalric behavior? A commentary on sign theory? An impossible desire for an absolute sign untainted by culture? Gawain himself calls it a "sygne of my surfet" (sign of my transgression, 2433), which nicely elides the exact nature of his *surfet*.[85] However, Gawain loses control of this "interpretation" once he returns to court and everyone good-humoredly chooses to wear the girdle, thus effectively and famously deconstructing Gawain's attempt to betoken himself.

The community, then, makes the final determination of meaning for Gawain and of Gawain; in essence, the community gives us a social, disembodied Gawain. Yet I would argue that such a Gawain is actually more useful to the community of knights than an abjected Gawain whose subjectivity has been threatened, if not breached, and who would come to serve as a constant reminder that any knight might be put at similar risk. In the end, Gawain's body and his virginity are made unavailable for interpretation (consumption?), but absorbed back into the community under the protection of the green girdle.

I have been arguing that male virginity is unable to generate its own representation (because it lacks a history of representation), but can only be discerned according to the conventions of the representation of female virginity, both in the saint's life and the romance. The absence of male virginity as a signifier in the sex-gender system of antiquity and the Middle Ages is both curious and predictable. It is curious in that the hymen and what I have called its cultural analogues – the various magical objects and tests designed to verify its presence or absence in women – disrupts the tidy homology between male and female anatomy, in which primary and secondary sex characteristics are paralleled and mirrored, though hierarchized by gender. What is predictable, however, is that the hymen and its analogues come to be used as a sign of woman's difference and as an instrument of control. Because it is "there" it must be safeguarded; because it is safeguarded, it must be "there." In the case of the hymen, anatomy does indeed dictate destiny, however tautological. Though this thin ridge of venous tissue may be the one thing a woman has got that a man has not, the possession of it does not confer any status on a woman beyond that which the Law of the Father bestows.

In the end, however, I would say that yes, men do have a "hymen," a social cover that effectively shields, not the individual man, but the idea of manhood. The hymen that culture has imposed on the feminine body, on the other hand, reveals an obsession with (or perhaps a fear of) fragments and fragmentation. It is a metonym that reduces a woman to less than the sum of her parts. The masculine hymen (an anatomical impossibility, but a social necessity), however, is generalized to cover the entire body chivalric; as such, it is metaphoric, and greater than the sum of his – their – parts.

5 Multiple virgins and contemporary virginities

The simple joys of maidenhood

In his 1942 dedication of his *Preface to Paradise Lost* to his friend the poet and critic Charles Williams, C. S. Lewis remembers a lecture given by Williams at Oxford's Divinity School:

> There we elders heard (among other things) what we had long despaired of hearing – a lecture on *Comus* which placed its importance where the poet placed it – and watched "the yonge fresshe folkes, he or she," who filled the benches listening first with incredulity, then with toleration, and finally with delight, to something so strange and new in their experience as the praise of chastity. … of those who heard you in Oxford many will understand henceforward that when the old poets made some virtue their theme they were not teaching but adoring, and that what we take for the didactic is often the enchanted.[1]

I have read or recalled this anecdote of Lewis' quite often through the years. The first time that I encountered it, in my teens in the late 60s (my Tolkien and Lewis phase: I was reading everything that I could find by both), I felt nothing but rage at what I then characterized as Lewis' oppressive rectitude. Rage, I came to see in retrospect, really masked my disappointment that the promises and delights of virginity extolled in my Roman Catholic education had remained out of my reach. (After all, at my Confirmation, I had chosen to be named for Jeanne d'Arc because I had been taught to admire her chastity and her bravery.) Later, in the 70s, the promises and delights of sexual experience were to prove equally elusive. When I reread *Preface to Paradise Lost* in graduate school in the 80s, it struck me that I could have used a little less bravery and a little more chastity – and a good deal more enchantment.

Today, and in the context of a scholarly project (which nevertheless has its roots in the personal), I recognize the above story as quintessential Lewis, more revealing of his brand of neo-Platonic Christianity than it is of Williams, of *Comus*, or of the "old poets." Lewis' point, that a decidedly disenchanted group of young people could find meaning in a lecture in praise of chastity, takes on new resonance fifty-odd years later at the end of the twentieth century, as disillusionment with the 60s sexual revolution as well as the late 80s' response to the AIDS crisis have made abstinence (or, at least, selective abstinence) more attractive than ever. Virginity is enjoying quite a renascence these days. The P.C. term for *virgin*, according to Cher's friend in *Clueless* (1995; Amy Heckerling), is "hymeneally challenged." "Is that a bad thing?" asks Cher, and we know that the answer ought to be "no." As proof, a male character on MTV's pseudo-chronicle *The Real World* maintains that he is a virgin; pop singer Julianna Hatfield says she is as well, and before he got married, Phoenix Suns forward A. C. Greene said that he had always planned to wait until marriage. Such statements are not sad or desperate confessions (as they would have been construed in previous decades), but announcements of a positive life choice.

These days, people not only flaunt their virginity, but reclaim it once it is gone, for virginity is often constructed as subject to revision: some Gen-Xers insist that one can recover one's virginity if one remains celibate for a period of time (though how long it is supposed to take is not specified). "True Love Waits," a fundamentalist organization that promotes abstinence, welcomes back the prodigal virgin – what it calls the "recycled" or "secondary" virgin.[2] The Website BAVAM! – Born-Again Virgins of America – publishes a quarterly newsletter, sells t-shirts, and dispenses jokey but serious advice to virgins post- and demi-.[3] The Website for the Society for the Recapture of Virginity ("Feeling melancholy? Coffee doesn't taste good in the morning anymore? Then GET IT BACK") advertises that one can revirginize if one wears a "Virginator" – a wristband with a microchip attuned to one's biorhythms.[4]

Spoof that the Society for the Recapture of Virginity is, it represents an important thread in the contemporary tangle of attitudes toward sexuality. These days, abstinence, for a while or for a lifetime, is often constructed not in opposition to sexuality, but as a point on an erotic continuum. (An 80s techno-pop band, Frankie Goes to Hollywood, furnished the signature song for hip celibates: "Relax" – "Don't do it.") Those who practice the new virginity, a flexible enough concept to include the born-again virgin, are not necessarily reading (or misreading) Judith Butler. Rather, the desire to revirginize and/or to discount past sexual activity as a "loss" of virginity arises out of a prevailing popular belief that one can reinvent or construct oneself at will. The foundations of this belief can be found in good old American individualism. *People* magazine has replaced Horatio Alger stories in its chronicling of the newly-rich, the newly-famous, and the newly-reinvented. (Never mind the harsh realities of class and socioeconomic barriers, or the losses people of color and gays and lesbians are now experiencing in the legal arena.) Passing, as white, as straight, has been an option for a long time; why couldn't one pass as a virgin? Who is to know? Who is to *say*?

The concept of the writable – and revisable – body takes many forms in contemporary American culture. Consider the flexibility and variety in hair styles and colors for both men and women; modern eclectic fashion (albeit often tyrannical, but less rule-based than in the past); the reworking of bodies through intensive diet and exercise regimes; the low cost and easy availability of cosmetic surgery; the spread of tattooing and body-piercing; the visibility, if not the fad, of male cross-dressing and celebrity transvestites; the freedom the Internet has offered to many (captured in the now-famous New Yorker cartoon with the line, "On the Internet, nobody knows you're a dog"); the science (and the science fiction) of cybernetics; the public discussion of (though not necessarily understanding or acceptance of) gender difference as existing on a continuum rather than as a binary; the difficulties in fixing racial boundaries (contra *The Bell Curve*'s assumptions – or nostalgia – about discrete genetic pools);[5] the ongoing and increasingly more complicated debate about when life begins; medical technologies that call into question such categories as "dead" and "alive." For the most part, popular praxis is not driven by theory, but by consumerist capitalism (and to say so is a theory); nevertheless, theory often takes praxis as its subject, working along a continuum on which the transgressive is located at one end, and the wholly interpellated at the other. Tattoos and transvestites may well be signs of the postmodern times, but they have also been domesticated by fashion. Virginity performed and/or regained may well be evidence of a sense that bodily identities are more fluid than fixed, but it may also be symptomatic of a capitulation to conservative mores and rigid gender-typing, or of a nostalgia for a non-existent, *a priori* innocence or Imaginary.

In this final chapter, I take up these issues as I turn to the construction of and the anxieties about virginity and its verifications in *fin de siècle* America. As we shall see, some of the notions about virginity and the testing of virginity that we saw at work in the Middle Ages continue to circulate through both high and low culture today. By saying so, I am not making a claim for an unbroken chain of theories and practices from the Middle Ages to the present. (Though others have done so: for example, before and after Diana's marriage to Prince Charles, the media made many a sly reference to the custom of conducting a physical examination of a bride who is about to marry into the royal house, often referring to the practice as "medieval.") However, I do take as my premise that the idea of virginity and its proofs transcends historical bounds: virginity may not be constructed as the same over time and according to place, but it is continually constructed all the same. Though the answers are always historically specific and local, the question of the ontology of virginity remains a constant in Western culture.

Consider the following scenes in contemporary American culture: an *X-Files* episode exploits the trope of the sacrificial virgin, as teenagers scare themselves with stories about a satanic cult that is rumored to torture and murder blonde virgins as part of their rituals. One blonde young woman blurts: "But how do they know you are really a *virgin?*" (How do they know you are really a *blonde?*). Steve Guttenberg says that he is "technically" a virgin in *Diner* (1982; Barry Levinson). Valeria Golino declares that she is a virgin but "not very good at it" in *Hot Shots* (1991; Jim Abrahams); Ben Stiller describes himself as a "non-practicing virgin" in *Reality Bites* (1994; Ben Stiller). "My man is satisfied," says Cher's best friend in *Clueless*, "but technically, I am a virgin – you know what I mean." Such vignettes from TV and film suggest that contemporary American culture is perfectly capable of imagining/representing virginity as located in the social realm rather than as lodged in the physical body. Virginity is constructed, consciously or unconsciously, as existing at the point at which the body and the social meet and intermingle, resulting in a kind of mixed metaphor or confusion of categories. *Verifying* virginity is compromised by the possibilities of *performing* virginity; performing virginity both leads to and is caused by interrogating virginity. By grappling with what it means to be a virgin, one must also come to terms with the fact that virginity is, for the most part, beyond proof. The bar, the either/or of virginity, dissolves in the face of such a paradox.

As we have seen in earlier chapters, virginity was usually inflected as feminine in the Middle Ages, as it has been in every subsequent age in Western culture. In the early modern period, after heated debate over its existence, the hymen, a real but variable and unstable physiological phenomenon, came to function as the primary sign of virginity from which all others were derived. The signifier *hymen* has many more signifieds than that of mere physical intactness, and takes on a number of highly-charged meanings as it is constituted within and by the social. The hymen is a sign of difference that reinforces the binaries of "feminine" and "masculine" and is intelligible only within a dominant heterosexual paradigm. Thus I suggest in what follows that the figure of the virgin – female and feminine – often functions as an icon of normative (and compulsory) heterosexual behavior in contemporary culture. Virginity is a concept founded upon a model of sexuality predicated upon penetration of a vagina by a penis (which may or may not result in loss of blood). Yet there are other stories to be told about coming into sexual experience, stories that fall outside the paradigm of heterosexual description and metaphor, and as such, have been rendered as untellable and unreadable. Such narratives and the experiences on which they are based undermine the construction of virginity as feminine and the "loss" of virginity as heterosexual. Gay and lesbian sex questions the importance and "use" of the verification of virginity, and renders visible the illusory nature of virginity as knowable and verifiable. To suppress such stories, to privilege heterosexual virginity, is to shore up heterosexuality and to deny the possibility of homosexuality.

In this chapter, I have chosen to focus on contemporary popular culture because its discursive boundaries are so much more permeable than those of high culture; popular culture often includes the set that is high culture – or, at least, its effects, whether full strength, diluted, or transformed. I also want to emphasize the difference between what is available to us for analysis in our own, modern culture and what remains of the Middle Ages for study: the ephemera of gestures, conversation, jokes, rumors, and pictures that variously shaped people's daily lives at court and in courtyard, in town and in country, is almost impossible to reconstruct. Such a study as this, concerned with representations of virginity/ chastity and its verifications in medieval culture, can only be partial insofar as the signs and habits of daily life are irrecoverable. However, if I can capture something about the range of attitudes toward virginity and its verifications as they are expressed in contemporary popular culture, then perhaps by analogy I can suggest how multi-dimensional medieval experience of and knowledge about virginity must have been.

Moreover, as a subject and as a phenomenon, popular culture has the potential for breaching the bar between our academic or professional selves and our lived experience. As I was writing this book, friends, students, and colleagues would often ask me what I was working on. When I described this final chapter, saying that I was gathering information about modern myths about verifying virginity, I invariably received the same reaction: the person I was talking to would get slightly embarrassed, and even take on a mildly alarmed look. Was I going to ask her or him for an anecdote? Was I going to disclose my own virginal or non-virginal status? *Was I going to get personal?* Some would interrupt me and ask about the "sources" I had found, as if documented materials would legitimate my project. Some would hurriedly start listing films, or bits of books, usually fiction, which I should consider, as if such a discussion would steer me away from their private lives.

The group of people with whom medievalists discuss medieval literary texts is relatively small, and the ways in which we talk about them extremely prescribed. We bring many tools and strategies to interpreting such texts, but our experience and personal histories, even if they figure in our readings, are not to be counted among them. On the other hand, a variety of forums exist in which we can discuss the latest bestseller, from conferences to elevator talk. Elevator gatherings prompt anecdotes and reminiscences and allow us to express our feelings in ways that academic talk does not. This chapter is an attempt to bridge the gap between what we recognize as legitimate "evidence" and the evidence of experience. The "texts" that I cite here contain traces of my personal history, of serendipitous encounters with TV, film, and current fiction, and anecdotes collected from the Internet and from friends. As I was finishing this book, I set up a Web site in order to gather current myths about verifying virginity, and a few of the responses that I received appear here as well.[6]

Having said that, I also want to acknowledge that to take personal experience or anecdote as "evidence" without examining how that experience is constituted and expressed is potentially dangerous and distorting. Joan Scott has made this point most compellingly in "The Evidence of Experience." "It is not individuals who have experience," argues Scott, "but subjects who are constituted through experience."[7] She adds: "The project of making experience visible precludes analysis of the workings of [a system structured according to presence and lack] and its historicity; instead, it reproduces its terms."[8] Scott quotes Michel de Certeau, who argues that the

> authorized appearance of the "real" serves precisely to camouflage the practice which in fact determines it. Representation thus disguises the praxis that organizes it.[9]

In other words, we may be seduced, as de Certeau says, into accepting the surface "truth" of a given narrative precisely and tautologically because it is represented as a true history. Yet all histories, writ large or small and personal, are shaped and produced by culture. Thus Scott critiques the appeal to experience as evidence, an appeal which she sees as underwriting various histories of difference, as if experience (specifically, gay/lesbian experience) and its attestation is somehow immune from the workings of the dominant ideology that shapes all experience. Scott's critique is precisely where I want to begin in this chapter, for examining how personal narratives about virginity are constrained (and contained) by narrative and cultural convention reveals the degree to which they are driven by a dominant heterosexual ideology – and propelled into the same rhetorical grooves as a result.

Two books, both journalistic in style and popular in intent, illustrate this point extremely well: *The First Time: What Parents and Teenage Girls Should Know about "Losing Your Virginity"*, a series of interviews conducted by Karen Bouris, and *Losing It: The Virginity Myth*, a collection of first-person narratives edited by Louis M. Crosier.[10] Bouris collected narratives from women, both lesbian and straight, in which women reveal feelings of deep shame or embarrassment (such anecdotes are sometimes humorously told), or tell of family abuse and date rape, of experiences that were flat and unemotional or exhilarating and life-changing. Crosier's narratives were written by both men and women, gay, lesbian, and straight. Contributors to both books struggle with defining and recognizing virginity, with attempting to fix the "before" and "after" of the experience. Most conclude that the actual physical "first time," accompanied by the breaking of the hymen, pain, or some other sign, does not always correlate with a sense of themselves as sexual beings. *The First Time* – which tips its ideological hand in such chapter titles as "Pressure from all Directions," "Just Get it Over With," and "The Romantic Minority" – includes this rather typical story:

> "I didn't really think sex was a big deal, but it is ... last year, when I was thirteen, I lost my virginity to a sixteen-year-old boy I had been friends with for three years. He was pretty drunk, and I had just broken up with my boyfriend and was upset. We went on a walk in the woods and lay down on his sweater. It hurt, and I bled a lot. I regretted it later and wished it had been with someone whom I was really in love with. I felt sad because losing my virginity should have been a wonderful experience, but instead it was meaningless."[11]

When we compare this to other first-time narratives, a pattern quickly emerges, for such tales usually include the following elements: 1) a description of the partner and an analysis of one's feelings for the partner; 2) a description of the place and time; 3) a description of the actual act; 4) a meditative coda or discussion of the lesson to be drawn from the experience. We find the same elements in more polished, belletristic narratives, such as in Naomi Wolf's *Promiscuities: The Secret Struggle for Womanhood*, in which she recounts the story of her own loss of virginity, supplementing it with stories that her friends shared as she was researching and writing. Wolf's story is more interesting reading than the accounts in *The First Time* and *Losing It*, in part because she is a known public figure – a neo-feminist spokesperson to boot. (I found myself voyeuristically entertained by her story, frankly, because she is made – or makes herself – so available for consumption: one may examine her glossy, studio-produced photograph on the inside back cover and freely fantasize about her fifteen-year-old, virginal self.) In addition, Wolf's awareness and exploitation of her own self-fashioning undermines the authenticity, or the effect of authenticity, of her experiences. A much more self-conscious social constructionist than the narrators in *The First Time* and *Losing It*, Wolf refers to the "*normatively shocking* narrative" of female sexual initiation and desire, the often-angry stories that she believes constitute the genre.[12] For example, Wolf tells us that, as her younger self rode the streetcar toward her rendezvous, she thought: "this is not the way my fantasies want it to be. It is not a Rod Stewart song."[13] (She was thinking of "Tonight's the Night.") Wolf works the tension between needing to particularize and thus validate her own narrative and desiring to aestheticize it for a public audience, between writing a "true" story and the weight of convention that shapes such a story. At one point, she says: "When we made love, it hurt, but only a little. It was nice, but strange. I realize my good luck with every disastrous loss-of-virginity story I hear."[14] Her experience of pain, of *niceness*, is immediately framed within a tradition, as it were, of women's stories about heterosexual intercourse that regularly include references to the initial awkwardness of intercourse, to pain, and, often, to lack of orgasm. These elements are often narrativized as "proof" of virginity in *The First Time* and *Losing It*, and have a long history as such. The author of the thirteenth-century *De secretis mulierum*, as we have already seen, notes that a lack of pain indicates that the woman is not a virgin. A virgin experiences pain, he says, because the vagina must be "enlarged and disposed for coitus," and because of the breaking of the hymen.[15] Pain in particular is a persistent element in loss-of-virginity narratives, true or fictional. In Sylvia Plath's *The Bell Jar*, for example, Esther Greenwood's first sexual experience is conflated with an experience of pain – and disappointment: "I lay, rapt and naked, on Irwin's rough blanket, waiting for the miraculous change to make itself felt. But all I felt was a sharp, startling bad pain."[16] Wolf's relative lack of pain correlates with her rather "nice" experience, proof that her first lover, Martin – whose most attractive attribute seems to have been his level-headedness – was indeed a "sensitive, respectful teacher."[17] Yet for the fictional Esther (transparently Plath herself), her experience of a "sharp, startling, bad pain" functions as a compressed narrative of oppression, emblematic of all the pain that Esther Greenwood had already suffered in her relations with men. Assuredly, many women do experience pain with first heterosexual intercourse, but it is the consistent *narrativization* of pain that I find so fascinating, especially given the fact that faking pain is a way to fake virginity.

On the whole, though occasionally sad, funny, and/or erotic, the narratives in *The First Time* and *Losing It* are not very interesting because they are so conventional. The narratorial "I" drops easily into clichéd expressions of sincerity. Gender difference is often expressed and reproduced through stereotypes: women often discussed their virginity as tied into their sense of self-esteem; many described virginity as a burden. On the other hand, men frequently said that they felt pressured to have intercourse by their peers and through popular macho-guy images. It seems that one of the most intimate experiences of one's life, presumably and potentially the most pleasurable, resists language, falls into triteness and cliché, suggesting the degree to which the experience of virginity is culturally scripted and commodified. Indeed, the Society for the Recapture of Virginity exploits the formulaic nature of virginity narratives at its Web site. One "tells" the story of one's first time by answering a multiple-choice questionnaire: I was a) at my parents' house b) outdoors c) in the back seat of a car ... the sounds within earshot included a) a dog barking b) television c) a party d) birds ... and so on. Perhaps the only interesting "first time" narrative is one's own – or one's lover's.

Multiple versions

One way into contemporary American attitudes about verifying virginity is to go elsewhere, to non-Western cultures, and explore how their constructions of virginity have returned to the West as exaggerated and exoticized myth. If we examine the history of Western travel literature and modern ethnography and anthropology (which owe much to travel literature, as these disciplines both deny and acknowledge), we find a good deal of interest in, if not to say obsession with, the sexual beliefs, mores, and practices of other cultures. Alternative sexual practices and their resulting social organizations have held a great deal of fascination for Western observers: the possibilities call into question the naturalness of Western practices and organizations, or, conversely, confirm the superiority of Western culture. Often, the historical veracity of anthropological observations has been less important than their *usefulness* for Westerners. A case in point is Freud and his essay, "The Taboo of Virginity." Predictably, Freud uses "primitive" peoples (of Africa, Australia, Malaysia, the Philippines, and Sumatra) as a foil for the more "civilized" attitudes of his contemporaries toward virginity. Freud begins his essay by saying:

> Few details of the sexual life of primitive peoples are so alien to our own feelings as their estimate of virginity, the state in a woman of being untouched [*der weiblichen Unberührtheit*]. The high value which her suitor places on a woman's virginity seems to us so firmly rooted, so much a matter of course, that we find ourselves almost at a loss if we have to give reasons for this opinion.[18]

According to Freud's reading of turn-of-the-century anthropology, many primitive peoples place little or no value on female virginity; indeed, they turn the first penetration of a virgin into a ritual in which anyone else *but* the intended husband takes part: an old woman of the tribe, an elder or priest, even her father. Freud believes that he has identified a mark of civilized society: the high value placed on virginity. Freud projects his own (euphemistic) definition of (gendered) virginity on primitive peoples: a woman *Unberührtheit*. Yet difference returns as civilized sameness when Freud advances his thesis about the menacing virgin: "with the taboo of virginity primitive man is defending himself against a correctly sensed, though psychical, danger" – that is, fear of castration from a hostile, most likely frigid, woman.[19]

Freud goes on to perpetuate one of the great clichés about a virgin's desire and the consequences of her first sexual experience with a man:

> Whoever is first to satisfy a virgin's desire for love, long and laboriously held in check ... that is the man she will take into a lasting relationship ... This experience creates a state of bondage in the woman which guarantees that possession of her shall continue undisturbed and makes her able to resist new impressions and enticements from outside.[20]

Like a duck, a woman imprints herself on her first lover; she remains forever in thrall. If a woman does not so bind herself to her husband, would he conclude that he was not her first lover? Would such "bondage" serve as proof of virginity? Freud does not say. Freud never raises the issue of verifying virginity; rather, he seems to assume that the hymen is the incontrovertible sign of virginity, and that it is always "there" to be ruptured. By universalizing every bride as a virgin (and every virgin as a bride), Freud refuses to acknowledge that a woman may be sexually experienced before marriage.

Freud's observations in "The Taboo of Virginity" (which have their vivid analogues in Gauguin's exotic and erotic visions of Tahiti and the Marquesas) are part of a larger, enduring myth about the promiscuity of various non-Western, non- or pre-Christian societies that anthropologists such as Bronislaw Malinowski and Margaret Mead studied.[21] This myth (since revised and/or amended by later anthropologists) is repeated over and over in popular culture, in, for example, the film *South Pacific* (1958; Joshua Logan; based on the James Michener novel), and, more recently, in episodes of *Star Trek: The Next Generation* set on the tropical pleasure-planet Risa. At the same time, another, contrasting idea about non-Western sexual practices circulates in contemporary popular culture: that else-where, in less "civilized" countries, women's sexual activities before marriage are rigidly proscribed, grounds for punishment and death if discovered. In such locales, proofs of virginity are taken to extremes for obvious economic reasons. In "Status, Property, and the Value on Virginity," anthropologist Alice Schlegel correlates the value of virginity with the type of marriage transaction that obtains in a given society; that is, those societies that practice gift and dowry exchange value virginity more than those which do not, even when it is the bride's family that gives the dowry.[22] In such societies, "proofs" of virginity are demanded as a matter of course. If so-called promiscuous cultures allow Westerners to take the moral high ground, the knowledge that certain other cultures ostracize and punish sexual transgressions committed by women (commodities in a system of exchange) enables Westerners to congratulate themselves for their understanding and liberality – and to feel superior about their record on women's rights to boot.

Many observations made by anthropologists and others about the centrality of female virginity in various Middle Eastern cultures have trickled down into popular Western culture, there to become a subject for titillation and mockery as well as a rallying point in the continuing vilification of Arabs and Muslims. The story of examining the sheets for traces of blood on the wedding night, apparently an ancient practice among certain peoples of the Mediterranean, North Africa, and the Middle East, is a case in point. (See the discussion of Deuteronomy 22: 13–20 in Chapter 1). The bloody sheet is the subject of a tale in *The Arabian Nights* that actually calls into question its veracity as proof of virginity. In fact, it could be argued that anxiety about ascertaining chastity – that is, regulating marital fidelity – motivates the entire plot of *The Arabian Nights*. In the frame story, we read how King Shahriyar, after he and his friend Shahzaman are betrayed by their wives, resolves to sleep with a virgin every night and then have her killed. In this way, the King makes sure that his wife will never be unfaithful to him. Sheherazade, of course, interrupts this project, and one of the many stories she tells raises the issue of the proofs of virginity. In "The Story of Qumar al-Zaman and His Two Sons," the Princess Budur disguises herself as a man after her husband Qumar al-Zaman disappears. While in her disguise, events force her to marry the Princess Hayat. Budur spends the wedding night and the next in prayer in order to protect her secret. On the third night, she confesses her true identity to Hayat, and the two stage a fake consummation scene:

> Hayat ... got up, and, taking a chicken, slaughtered it and smeared herself with its blood. Then she took off her pants, and cried out. The women of her family went in to her, and her waiting women let out trilling cries of joy.[23]

Here, the narrative of faking virginity in a situation in which virginity is actually maintained invokes and interrogates the many narratives in which virginity is said to have been "taken." The irony lies in the fact that, if a virgin bride may fake *loss* of virginity, so may a sexually-experienced bride fake *virginity*. Moreover, the "consummation" of the marriage and its bloody proof (which is no proof at all), may well begin as a private act, but takes on significance only after Hayat's women witness to the "proof." In Lacanian terms, what was once in/of the Imaginary has crossed over into the Symbolic order, there made subject to the Law of the Father, here actually and ironically represented by the testimony of women. It is a paradox in that there is "nothing" there (the proof is fake) yet there is "something" (still) there – the hymen, or, at least, the blood of virginity.

Contemporary anthropologists, Western and non-Western, as well as Arab women themselves, attest to the fact that in some parts of the Arab world, families still require the evidence of the bloody sheets. Geraldine Brooks, in *Nine Parts of Desire: The Hidden World of Islamic Women*, quotes a manager at a hotel in Baghdad which is a popular spot for wedding parties. He says: "[A]lmost all of them [the new brides] check out with a stolen sheet in their bag, you know ... Their older relatives still insist on seeing it."[24] In their study of the semi-rural town of Zawiya, Morocco, anthropologists Susan Schaefer Davis and Douglas Davis report that public proof of virginity is obligatory at the wedding ceremony. If the bloody sheets or garments are not produced, the wedding contract can be declared void and the bride sent away.[25] One of Davis and Davis' informants reports that quite often, the brothers of the bride, knowing that their sister is not a virgin, will "stay close to the bridal chamber to calm or threaten the unsuspecting groom" in order to prevent a public scandal; he adds that he had heard of brides who were known to have had premarital intercourse, yet bloody garments were produced at the strategic moment on the wedding night.[26] This informant also describes certain deceptions practiced by husbands-to-be who have already slept with their betrothed, including cutting themselves to avoid public humiliation on the wedding night.[27] (As we saw in Chapter 3, in *Guillaume de Dole*, the mark of female virginity is so unstable that even a man can carry it; here, a man is actually able to *fake* female virginity.) Davis and Davis report that their informants described the ubiquity of such practices as heavy petting, inter-femoral intercourse, shallow penetration, and withdrawal – that is, sexual activities that would not rupture the hymen.[28] One of my Web site correspondents, an Arab man, told me that he has heard about certain Arab women who only have anal intercourse in order to "protect" their virginity.[29] These anecdotes attest to a prevailing awareness of the slip between theory and practice, and of the consequences of not adhering to theory in practice.

The motif of the bloody sheets has its current fictional representations as well. In a short story by Egyptian Alifa Rifaat, "Honor," the narrator, Bahiya, tells the story of her sister Sophia, who has lost her virginity to a lover, but is contracted in marriage. The village midwife, bribed with a gold bracelet, promises to come to Sophia on her wedding night in order to "bring some powdered glass to smear" in the girl's vagina.[30] The groom takes his new bride into his house, where the midwife waits while everyone gathers outside, shooting their guns off and singing, but quieting so that they can hear "the shouts mixed with pride and elation" from inside. Then the midwife emerges, her face "tensed with joy" as she hands Sophia's father the "bloodstained silk handkerchief and clutched the sweet reward of good news in her palm" (that is, the tip that he gives her).[31] As we saw in Chapter 1, there are many ways to fake the blood of virginity. Whatever its foundation in actual practice, the use of ground glass in this story gives one pause. Besides causing the necessary blood, the glass seems to serve as a sort of penance for the bride. She is to endure the pain as a punishment. In fact, the use of ground glass ensures that even the groom will have an opportunity to shed virginal blood.

Along with exotic tales of harems and eunuchs, these and other stories return to the West as "truths" against which Westerners measure their own beliefs and desires about sexuality and how it should be practiced and organized. However, many Westerners who denounce the display of the bloodstained wedding sheets as a "barbaric" and "medieval" practice are willing enough to accept the theory behind the practice – that public and incontestable proof of virginity is possible and desirable. What is suppressed is the fact that hymeneal blood is not unequivocal proof; what persists is the idea that somewhere, elsewhere in the world, fathers and husbands have a way of ascertaining virginity. Seeking elsewhere – and apparently finding – an answer to the conundrum of virginity further mystifies the workings of culture and how it is complicit in constructing the signs of virginity as invariable from body to body. The story of the bloody sheets and its reception in the West reproduces both difference (culture is variable) and sameness (anatomy, not culture, is universal).

Performing virgins

Within the semiotics of cinematic sex, intercourse has been represented in an endless number of ways. Some signs, through their very repetition, have now become conventional, including fuzzy dissolves, fades, or unusual cuts. Burt Lancaster and Deborah Kerr on the beach in *From Here to Eternity* (1953; Fred Zinnemann) immediately come to mind: as they embrace in the shallows, the camera slowly pans outward, until all we see are crashing waves and all we hear is the roar of the surf. These signs and others are parodied in *Naked Gun* (1988; David Zucker): in a series of MTV-inspired cuts set to the music of "I'm into Something Good" by 60's pop band Herman's Hermits, Frank Drebin (Leslie Nielson) and Jane Spencer (Priscilla Presley) cavort in the surf, squirt ketchup and mustard at each other, and ride a bull at a rodeo. Other cinematic signs of loss of virginity are more idiosyncratic, but are certainly still readable. For example, in *Love in the Afternoon* (1957; Billy Wilder), when luminous Arianne Chavasse (Audrey Hepburn) and playboy Frank Flannagan (Gary Cooper) become lovers, the signs of loss of virginity are particularly subtle. Though Arianne/Hepburn appears as virginal at the end of the film as she did at the beginning, we learn that she has had intercourse through several elegant and indirect scenes: when Arianne and Frank first embrace, the camera cuts slowly to a man playing the violin, then to a shut door, and finally to Arianne combing her hair in the bathroom mirror. The process of sexual initiation itself is gracefully elided, but its post-coital sign, the primping ritual, is eloquent enough. (We find a parallel scene in *Scream* [1997; Wes Craven], at the point at which the camera cuts from Sydney [Neve Campbell] embracing Billy [Skeet Ulrich] on a bed to her dreamily brushing her hair.) In another scene in *Love in the Afternoon*, Arianne hunts for one of her shoes under the furniture in Frank's suite, from bedroom to living room. Frank, who does not want her to leave, hides her shoe in the pocket of his dressing gown. He embraces her, and Arianne finds the shoe, rapping him teasingly on the head with it before leaving. The shoe, lost, hidden, and then recovered, has a double valence: it not only signifies Arianne's new-found sexuality, but also Frank's "lost" heart. Properly contextualized, any sign is capable of signifying virginity and its presence or absence. (At one point, a man cuckolded by Flannagan tells him: "A girl may look as innocent as the freshly fallen snow and then suddenly you find the footprints of hundreds of men." This remark captures the anxiety that drives the desire for verification in the first place: the signs of virginity are multiple in order to answer to such fears.)

Along with Audrey Hepburn (who managed to appear perpetually virginal in real life as well, even after two marriages and a long-term live-in relationship), Doris Day and Sandra Dee are perhaps the great iconic American virgins of the 50s. (And if Doris Day was the blonde virgin *par excellence* of the decade, then Jayne Mansfield was the supreme blonde anti-virgin. Both women's images were carefully controlled on screen and off. Hairstyle, makeup, and the cut of a dress were signs made readable to all.) It would be facetious to compare Doris Day and Sandra Dee to the virgin martyrs of antiquity and the Middle Ages, "known" to be virgin through their modest looks, dress, and behavior; however, it is worth noting that, just as Ambrose and Jerome constructed a semiotics of virginal behavior for the early Church, so did the PR machine of 50s Hollywood create their version of the virginal. In what follows, I focus on two films made twenty years apart in which the signs of virginity drive the plot, reproducing a materialized and naturalized version of virginity. *A Summer Place* (1959; Delmer Daves) and *Hair* (1979; Milos Forman) may register what a difference twenty years can make, but they also draw upon the same set of assumptions about virginity and its presence or absence.

I first saw the film *A Summer Place* when I was around twelve, then a few times on cable over the years, and then again when I began this study. I did not understand a good deal of the film the first time that I saw it: I was already pretty sure that teenage pregnancy was not a good thing, and this film confirmed that fact – though it also suggested that if Troy Donahue were your boyfriend and Richard Egan your father, teenage pregnancy would probably work out OK. (*A Summer Place* generated a good deal of controversy when it was first released, though the focus of the attention was on the film's frank treatment of teenage pregnancy, not on the proofs of virginity.) On the whole, I was left feeling rather uneasy at age twelve, and it was only years later that I was able to locate the source of my discomfort in the scene in which Sandra Dee's mother forces her to undergo a physical examination for virginity.

A plot summary is in order: the recently rich, handsome, and patient Ken Jorgenson (Richard Egan), (mis)married to the masculine, dominating, and sexually-repressed Helen (Constance Ford), takes his wife and daughter Molly (Sandra Dee) to the resort hotel where he used to work as a lifeguard on an island off the coast of Maine. He meets his first love Silvia (Dorothy McGuire), now married to a sensitive, aristocratic drunk, Bart Hunter (Arthur Kennedy), who has fallen on hard times and is reduced to running the hotel where he once used to visit with his friends and snub the lifeguard. They have a son John (Troy Donahue).

Ken and Silvia realize that they still love each other, and begin to meet clandestinely in the boathouse. Molly and John fall in love, but Helen, who thinks sex is "filthy," continually interferes. When the teenagers go sailing one afternoon and are overtaken by a storm, they are wrecked on a small island where they must spend the night. When they are rescued and return to the hotel, Helen is enraged. She has a doctor waiting, who examines Molly in order to ensure that she is still a virgin. Helen forbids Molly to see John again. Ken and Silvia's affair is finally exposed, a huge scandal ensues, and the two divorce their respective spouses and marry. Molly, sent off to a girl's finishing school, and John, now at college, correspond secretly. They meet again at Ken and Silvia's beach house and make love for the first time. Molly becomes pregnant. They run away to get married, but cannot because they are underage. They finally turn to Ken and Silvia for help, and all are reconciled.

That Molly is examined in order to determine the status of her virginity is never stated in the film. The scene is set up in this way: the young couple, cold, wet, and wrapped in blankets, return to the hotel. We see them nervously peering up the long front staircase, where Helen glares down at them, an avenging harpy. Molly begins to ascend slowly, never removing her eyes from her mother's. As violins and piano crash discordantly in the background, Helen says roughly, "Come with me," and pulls Molly along into her room. As the camera looks over Helen's shoulder, Helen says, "Here she is, doctor," and we see a dark-suited, severe man rising from his chair in the sitting-room. We are pulled into the room with Molly, and the door shuts behind her. "I haven't done anything wrong," says Molly, her voice rising in panic. Helen says, "Take off every stitch you've got on and let him examine you completely and make his own report." Molly is in absolute terror as the doctor approaches, who says, "Leave me alone with your child; you're being of less than no help." Molly begins to cry: "I want my father ... I've been a good girl, I've been a good girl," over and over again. We watch as the doctor drops a claw-like hand on her shoulder, and he begins to unbutton Molly's top. She screams, and the scene dissolves to John. He faces his father, who leers drunkenly, asking about what he "did" to Molly.

The scene between Molly and the doctor is Hitchcockian in its menace: it looks like a prelude to a classic rape scene in which the rape itself occurs off-screen. When I was twelve, it was mystifying, inexplicable and terrifying. The subsequent dissolve to John seems to suggest that he is the evil perpetrator of the "rape." Only after, when Helen must answer to a furious Ken, do we get a partial explanation: "obviously I had to find what happened out there. I had to be sure the examination revealed nothing wrong." But again, virginity is not mentioned, though the possibility of something being "wrong" is. Always there as a subtext, the subject of virginity is finally made explicit much later in the film, when Ken says that he doesn't want his daughter to be a "half virgin ... to just go half way in the back seat ... is there no completely honest answer I can give her?"

One of my Web site correspondents told a story about returning home one night at curfew and then climbing out the window in order to rejoin the party. She made it back to the house a few hours later, only to find her father running around the backyard with a baseball bat, furiously looking for the boy that he was convinced was hiding in the bushes. He then drove her to the hospital, and demanded that the doctor test her for alcohol, drugs, and the possibility of intercourse. The doctor tried to explain that no such test could ever be conclusive, and her father finally gave in – on the virginity test, at least. My correspondent said that her initiation into sexual responsibility was very different from her younger brother's, who was laughingly told to "keep it in his pants" one night over dessert.[32] Life imitates art in part because of a lack of imagination: our society provides only so many options when a parent must confront the possibility of a daughter's sexuality (and, apparently, a son's as well). Both Molly's mother in *A Summer Place* and my correspondent's father believe that the physical body can be trusted to give up its sexual secrets precisely because the body can *not* be trusted; that is, any girl who spends the night with a boy, no matter the circumstances, ought to be suspect. In *A Summer Place*, a 50s idiom is employed that forces us to read between the lines in order to discover virginity and its verifications; in this real-life anecdote, a daughter and her father are less concerned with representationality, of course, than they are with the exigencies of the situation. However, virginity proves equally allusive in both contexts; like quarks and other theorized particles of matter, virginity can not be examined directly, and so must be approached obliquely. Neither a doctor's examination nor a baseball bat can discover – or recover – something that counts only when it is thought lost. Perhaps allusiveness is the only mode available when it comes to virginity, for one might argue that virginity always exists between the lines, between the scenes, becoming visible only after it is gone – as a nostalgic backward glance, as a present pregnancy. Such allusiveness is not confined to effects of Hollywood censorship (which in the 50s decreed that even married couples could not be shown sharing the same bed, but only side-by-side in twin beds), but can also be found in more contemporary contexts, as in the counter-cultural film *Hair*, based on the popular musical of the early 70s.

Long after the 60s had its brief shining moment, *Hair* purported to tell its story. It never caught on as a mainstream film, but played over and over at art houses where stoned audiences would get high on the music and visual effects. There are other films that attempt to capture the so-called sexual revolution of the 60s (for example, Paul Mazursky's *Bob & Carol & Ted & Alice*, 1969), but no film quite matches *Hair* in its portrayal of the transformative powers of music, sex, and drugs. No film could be more different from *A Summer Place* than *Hair* ; yet, as in *A Summer Place*, a virgin is found at the center of the story: a Sandra Dee-like deb named Sheila (Beverley D'Angelo).

We first meet Sheila as she rides horse-back through Central Park. She becomes the object of the curious and insolent gaze of a group of hippies. George Berger (Treat Williams), the leader (and marked as the most sexually potent of the group), stares at her and sings, "Looking for Donna, for Madonna, a sixteen-year-old virgin." Seventeen centuries earlier, Tertullian had declared that "every public exposure of an honourable virgin is (to her) a suffering of rape."[33] George's gaze is a deliberate, clichéd figuring of penetration, precisely the sort of gaze Tertullian was so anxious about. (George's gaze crosses boundaries of class as well as gender: Sheila is obviously a rich and privileged deb, while George makes a living by panhandling.) As Sheila gallops off, the rise and fall of her buttocks on the horse's rump explicitly imitates the movement of sexual intercourse. "Mounting" and "riding," of course, are common enough metaphors for intercourse: references to horseback riding are central to many a crude joke. There is another allusion here as well, to "accidental" loss of virginity through injury to the hymen. Young girls are often cautioned against strenuous exercise – such as horseback riding and bicycling – precisely because of injury. (As I mentioned in Chapter 2, it was said by her examining doctors that Jeanne d'Arc may have damaged herself on horseback).

Crashing waves and violins tell us in *A Summer Place* that Molly (and John, also a virgin) finally have intercourse; in *Hair*, we know that Sheila has lost (is losing) her virginity through tracking her sartorial transformation from scene to scene, as she exchanges her preppie wardrobe piece by piece for hippie gear and her long, blonde, hair-sprayed flip turns into wild locks. The "proof" of Sheila's lost virginity is to be located in her outward appearance. Another example of such proof can be found in the film version of *Grease* (1978; Randal Kleiser) in which bad girl Rizzo (Stockard Channing) mocks Sandy (Olivia Newton-John) by singing, "Look at me, I'm Sandra Dee, lousy with virginity." Rizzo has in mind Sandy's severe ponytail, pastel angora sweater, and white ankle socks. In the final scene of the movie, Sandy transforms herself, and appears in teased hair, heavy makeup, high heels, and tight pants, apparently signaling to Danny (John Travolta) that she is ready for a change in their heretofore chaste relationship.

One of the contributors to the book, *Losing It*, reflecting on her own loss of virginity, sums up popular lore about the correlation between outward appearance and virginity: "Virgins are pure, kind, beautiful, clear-skinned ... non-virgins are selfish, cheap, loud, bad-skinned."[34] Such an idea predates our mothers' admonishments: recall that the thirteenth-century *De secretis mulierum* lists a modest demeanor as a sign of virginity. However, the correlation between behavior and virginity is much older. In *Ab urbe condita* (c. 25–29 BC), Livy tells the tale of the Vestal Postumia, who, because of her "pretty clothes and unmaidenly freedom of her wit," was thought to have lost her chastity. She was found innocent, and was told to dress more modestly – and to curb her wit.[35] Livy also mentions another Vestal, Minucia, who was found guilty of unchastity and buried alive – she was "suspected in the first instance because of her dress, which was more ornate than became her station."[36] It may be a tenuous thread that connects classical ideas about appearance and behavior to modern ideas, particularly as represented by Sheila's and Sandy's metamorphoses, yet the belief that the secrets of the body are to be discovered in dress and speech is certainly a persistent one.

While *A Summer Place* and *Hair* employ very different vocabularies for representing virginity and its verifications, both films accept the idea that virginity is a verifiable, testable condition. Even though *A Summer Place* depicts conflicting attitudes and mores about female sexuality and autonomy, and, through Molly's mother's insistence on a medical examination, locates virginity in the body, both films attempt to work out how the consequences of the body take on meaning – or, more accurately, are assigned meaning – in the social realm. It is finally culture, not nature, which writes the body in these films.

Equivocal virginity

One of the commentators on *De secretis mulierum* declares that "when the male and female have sexual intercourse, they should not do it standing up, because then the seed is projected upwards and afterwards falls down, because what goes up must come down."[37] This was the same wisdom that I received from my Catholic school girlfriends, who had an altogether different end in mind: vertical intercourse as contraception. Another notion that circulated among my friends was that if one had intercourse with a boy, but was not in love, one remained a virgin. I also learned at Mount St. Mary's that one could verify virginity by looking at a girl's legs, for a virgin's legs met at ankle, knee, and inner thigh. (Years later, I realized that this "test" was the same that teen magazines periodically offered to young girls so that they could determine if they had "perfect" legs – perfect in that one ought to possess three diamond-shaped spaces, the first between ankle and calf, the second between calf and knee, and the third between the knee and the top of the thigh.) Part wishful thinking, part earnest belief, such myths about intercourse and virginity endure for a number of reasons. Such myths suggest that one can be found out, that one's sexual history can be read on the body, exposed to all. As such, these and other beliefs can serve as effective deterrents, particularly for the naive and inexperienced. On the other hand, to believe that one might actually practice vertical birth control or experience loveless sex without loss of virginity has its advantages, if not unexpected consequences. Moreover, one might take comfort in the idea that, since so many tests of virginity tests seem to exist, one could find a way to fake virginity if it were necessary. As we have seen, hymeneal blood is easy enough to fake, either through substituting animal blood or menstrual blood – or performing self-mutilation.

These days, modern medicine has made it much less dangerous to fake virginity. In "Intimate Surgery: The Surprising Answer to Sexual Problems," author Catie Meyer describes surgical procedures for vulvaplasty (removal of excess tissue of the labia minora, which can sometimes protrude beyond the labia majora), mons pubic liposuction, tightening the vagina after childbirth, and hymen reconstruction. One woman interviewed who had opted for hymen reconstruction, Arlene (no last name given, but described as "a successful New York attorney") says her hymen

> was ruptured in a junior-high gym class ... and it's bothered me ever since. I know what you're going to say. All my friends have already said it – "a little flap of skin doesn't make or break a virgin." And I know they're right. Technically, I'm still a virgin. The trouble is I don't feel like a virgin.[38]

Dr Darrick E. Antell, who has been performing hymen reconstructions for fifteen years, says that the women who undergo hymen reconstruction

> are either victims of rape or have lost their virginity [through non-sexual activity] and would like to be a virgin by every definition. ... women want

hymen reconstruction for the psychological benefits – not to pretend they're something they're not.[39]

The more cynical reader may find Arlene's and Antell's remarks rather disingenuous. Meyer also describes the procedure: "The surgeon cuts the healed membrane ... to create a 'fresh' edge. Then it is pulled back over and reattached with dissolvable sutures." Surgically restoring virginity costs around three to four thousand dollars.[40] The hymen is now available as a prosthesis.

Such surgery is not just a 90s phenomenon. In *The Janus Report on Sexual Behavior*, Samuel S. Janus and Cynthia L. Janus describe the "lover's knot," which they describe as a "poignant piece of medical history." Saying that the lover's knot was popular between 1920–1950, Janus and Janus describe this surgical procedure as adding several stitches in the labia of brides-to-be. "On their wedding night, when consummating their marriages, these women would feel pain, and bleed, convincing their new husbands that they were pure and virginal."[41] Once again, we encounter the idea that pain is somehow necessary to the construct of virginity. And now, one can actually guarantee it through surgery. The herbs, ointments, and dove's bladder filled with blood of the medieval gynecological treatise may have been replaced by modern medical techniques, but the impulse for going to such lengths has not changed much.

If modern medicine can help a woman fake virginity, it can also complicate the question of virginity. In Chapter 1, I discussed a story found in Averroës' *Colliget*, about a young girl who was impregnated after bathing in water in which a man had ejaculated. One of the commentators on *De secretis mulierum* wanted to know if the woman was still a virgin. The answer was an equivocal *sic et non*. What follows is a modern analogue:

Dear Abby:

I have a problem that is probably unlike any you have ever received. I am a twenty-six-year-old woman who is about to be married. I have never had sex, but when I was 24 years old, I agreed to be artificially inseminated and gave birth to a child for a couple who wanted one, but the woman was not able to have a child.

Now here is my question: Am I still a virgin? My husband-to-be is well aware that I want to wait until our wedding night to make love, so he has never pressured me. I need to know if I am still a virgin.

Yes or No

Dear Yes or No:

Since you have never had sexual intercourse, you are still a virgin. If your fiancé is not aware that you have given birth to a child, I suggest that you tell him.[42]

The answer is pure Dear Abby. She expresses no doubt about the ontological status of the young girl in a way that is designed to be most reassuring. At the same time, she displays her command of ironic understatement when she "suggests" that the young woman inform her fiancé about the child.

These anecdotes suggest that the continued preoccupation with female virginity is founded upon the premise, not that it *is* absolutely verifiable, but that it *should* be so verifiable. Ultimately, such verification is impossible, and is apparently getting more impossible. It seems that to say that one is "not exactly" a virgin or that one is "technically" a virgin is not so odd after all. "Guilty, with explanation," is one way to plead in traffic court; "virgin, with explanation," seems to be more of an option than ever.

Default setting

TV Guide, hyping a night-time soap opera called *Savannah*, displayed the three female leads of the show on the cover, labeling them "Victim, Virgin, and Vixen." Even at the end of the 90s, the convenient alliterative phrase is as resonant as ever; moreover, it seems as if the alliteration confers some sort of indisputable reality on these (and only these) categories of femininity. In discussing what she calls "the myth of Virginity," Simone de Beauvoir says that the virgin, "[n]ow feared by the male, now desired or even demanded ... would seem to represent the most consummate form of the feminine mystery. She is therefore its most disturbing and at the same time its most fascinating aspect."[43] Luce Irigaray sums up the cultural stereotype of the female virgin when she writes that, for men,

> in their system ... "virgin" means one as yet unmarked by them, for them. Not yet a woman in their terms ... Not yet penetrated or possessed by them ... A virgin is but the future for their exchanges, their commerce, and their transports. A kind of reserve for their explorations, consummations, and exploitations.[44]

Such an image of the virgin may represent masculine desires, says Irigaray, "[b]ut not ours." And if the virgin chooses to opt out of this exchange, this future? To remain outside of the heterosexual relation? She becomes the figure of "the sterile virgin," as Kathy Newman says, "the impotent old maid, the dried-up and ineffectual maiden aunt ... the poisonous, vampire lesbian teacher or the monstrous female artist."[45] These avatars of the virgin have long histories in Western culture, constructed as figures to be feared and vilified and as examples to be avoided.[46] On the other hand, the *TV Guide* virgin is the preferred version, a virgin in a holding pattern destined to bestow her virginity on the right man at the right time. Such a virgin is an advertisement for the proper functioning of the sex/gender system, inspiring women to be her and men to have her. And, I would argue, it seems that she is most visible – and most definitively heterosexual – when her virginity is endangered; that is, when we are forced to contemplate loss of virginity.

The menaced virgin's tale is retold over and again in Western (and world) literature: its form, content, and audience may change, but the motif itself has enormous vitality. I am suggesting that the many and varied textual and visual representations of women under assault – such as the Sabine women raped by the Romans, Agnes threatened by the consul Quintianus, Gwenyver abducted by Mellyagaunce, Clarissa harrassed and finally raped by Lovelace, Fay Wray sacrificed to King Kong, Nell tied to the tracks by Snidely Whiplash (a fascinating displaced image of rape) – help to produce what appears to be an inexorable, inevitable heterosexuality through a series of identifications and counter-identifications. Sexual difference in these tales is predicated upon rape or the possibility of rape, transitively gendered in that it is something that men do to women. (Certainly men rape other men, but such rape must be qualified as "male-male rape.") Perversely enough, it seems that the narrative in which a woman is threatened with rape or actually raped reproduces sex/gender roles. In this story, the menaced virgin functions as a paragon for women and as a prize or reward for men, either for the villain who rapes her, or for the hero who rescues her. As such, the virgin is a charismatic figure within patriarchal discourse, the star of an sensational narrative that asserts and confirms male heterosexual hierarchical prerogatives while attempting to suppress alternative narratives, both of female autonomy and of homosexual desire. In *Invisible Lives: The Truth about Millions of Women-Loving Women*, Martha Barron Barrett says that: "Because two women together are incapable of the central act [copulation], their existence as lovers has been denied, downgraded to harmless play, or viewed as a perverted obsession."[47] Barrett unreflectively accepts heterosexual intercourse as the norm (lesbians are "incapable") while struggling to find different grounds for writing and validating lesbian experience. The fact is, heterosex is "central" only to patriarchy, central to a sex-gender system that privileges (in full force or vestigially) procreation as the ultimate end of sex and sexual pleasure.

Representations of virginity, its verifications, and its perils in pop culture are especially interesting because they rely on such a crude set of correspondences and signs. Such representations tend to go unexamined, because they are so pervasive and ubiquitous – in part, the secret of their power to mystify. Consider the role and function of TV virgin Donna Martin (Tori Spelling) on *Beverly Hills 90210* in its early days. Donna is one of several media virgins, both male and female, who must confront the moral, social, and logistical problems of virginity. A thread running through several episodes of *90210* was devoted to Donna and the fact that she was "still" a virgin. A good Catholic girl, Donna is embarrassed by her virginity, and she and all of her friends discuss her feelings endlessly, supporting her decision to wait until marriage. Donna finally begins to feel proud about her unique virginal status. (It was at this point that the media made Donna/Tori the most famous virgin in TV history.) She falls in love with David Silver (David Austin Green), also a virgin, who decides he can not wait for Donna. They break up after she discovers him with another girl in a scene in which his loss of virginity is signified by the camera lingering on an open condom package. Donna then must endure several attempted seductions by a string of types: the fraternity boy who deceives her into thinking that he is understanding and sensitive, the construction worker/musician who does the same, and so on. She finally reunites with David, and the 1996–97 season ends with Donna telling David that she is finally ready. (The actual consummation happens off-screen, and the 1997–98 season begins by assuming that Donna's virginity is in the past.) In many ways, Donna's predicament furnishes viewers with an opportunity to revisit their own virginal past or to contemplate their post-virginal future. Whatever the emotions attendant upon such imaginings – fear, regret, tenderness, elation – such emotions are validated as normal because they are expected to be experienced within a heterosexual paradigm. Whether we choose the lesson or not, media virgins teach us how to behave according to a script in which virginity is described as something "given" or "lost" or "taken." A virgin such as Donna Martin, blonde, wide-eyed, and innocent (in spite of her hip and sexy wardrobe), is intended to be the object of a curious, titillated male gaze – she would fail as a character if she were not. She and other such virgins are designed to attract male heterosexual interest, which runs the gamut from a desire to conquer and steal to a desire to serve and protect.

Jane Halliday on *L.A. Law* was another media virgin who became the object of predatory interest. A 50s retro blonde who wore her hair like a helmet, Jane was a lawyer who was also a fundamentalist Christian. Sexual shark Arnie Becker (Corbin Bernsen) "naturally" takes Jane on as a challenge to his powers of persuasion, arranging all the standard arguments against virginity for Jane's and the viewer's edification. In several episodes, Arnie manages to embrace and kiss Jane. We are to gather from these encounters that such caresses begin to weaken her determination; simultaneously, Arnie begins to rethink his promiscuous position, seeing his desires as shallow and selfish. The series ended before this subplot was resolved; Jane remains forever irresolute in syndicated reruns.

The virgin pursued is capable of generating endless plot lines and complications – whether the setting is the ancient Aegean, the Roman court, the medieval countryside, or modern Los Angeles. For example, Donna Martin allowed the writers of *90210* to create dream episodes in which she works out her anxieties about her virginity – in one she is dressed in her Confirmation dress; in another, she is mocked by a Howard Stern-like character. Loss of virginity, after all, signals the end of the story – traditionally, within the happily-ever-after of marriage. What matters is that virginity must be kept in play as long as possible in order to sustain interest in the narrative, thus generating viewer/reader pleasure in one direction – and sales in another.

The tale of menaced virginity also has a socializing function in that men are taught that sexual assault and rape will not be condoned. This is the essence of the plot of Richardson's *Pamela*, in which the heroine finally tames "Mr. B" by her virtuous example. We find a similar plot in play at the end of the TV series, *Blossom*, when Blossom (Mayim Bialik) had grown up enough to date. One night, she goes out with a young man and they end up in his car. After a few kisses, he puts the car seat down, a clear signal to the audience that he expects sex. Blossom refuses, and he strikes her. She tries to hide her bruises from her father, but when he finally sees them, he convinces her to file charges. The last scene of the last episode follows her out the school door after she tells the boy that she is going to the police. The didactic and worthy lesson is clear enough: date rape, or attempted date rape, could happen to anyone, and should not be tolerated. Doogie Howser is another example of a TV character whose virginity at one point drives the plot, though there is nothing menaced or menacing about his situation. Doogie and his girlfriend, both virgins, are "naturally" attracted to each other; no other alternative is offered except the heterosexual. After much discussion among their friends and family, they agree that they care enough about each other to have intercourse. Part of this discussion involves talk about safe sex (Doogie is a genius kid who earned his M.D. while still a teenager, and so is especially knowledgeable in a sort of infomercial style). Doogie proceeds to turn his adolescent bedroom into a romantic candle-lit setting. However, when the time comes, both decide that they are not ready for sex. This lesson, comforting as it may be for anxious parents and for even more anxious teenagers, assumes what Harriet Malinowitz calls the "default setting" of heterosexuality.[48] It seems that both respecting and transgressing the boundaries of the female virgin body are actions and ideologies that attempt to fix identities through biological and social difference, while sanctioning the "opposite" sex as the object of desire. These two distinct and contradictory narratives – one in which female virginity is praised and revered, the other in which female virginity is "lost" or "taken" – valorize heterosex while suppressing gay and lesbian constructions of sex and desire.

Lesbians and gays have inherited the template of heterosexual virginity – imitating it, adapting it, rejecting it in favor of an alternative virginity, or even rejecting the concept entirely, but nevertheless always having to react to the idea of the virgin and what she stands for. "[W]hat exactly constitutes losing 'lesbian virginity,'" says one respondent whom Karen Bouris interviewed for *The First Time*, "is a debate among many lesbians I have talked with. For me, it is a matter of having oral sex in which both participants give pleasure to each other." Other lesbians she talked to, says Bouris, felt "technically, according to society, they were still virgins, although they were complete sexual beings."[49] Many gays and lesbians assert that it is the coming out narrative, not the fact that one has had sex, that is the core of the gay/lesbian "virginity" story.[50] For example, in *Losing It*, a gay man recalls "losing it" with another boy, but says that he was too young for that sexual experience to "count." Now that he is older and identifies as gay, he says that he has had another "first time."[51] Another man says: "many people (mostly ignorant) assume that all gays and lesbians are so very sexually promiscuous, yet we can't even lose our virginity!" He identifies the moment that he lost his virginity as when he was with a man he loved, and they were just talking and laughing: "In a wave of warmth, I felt whole ... as if I would never be alone."[52]

The relationship of Celie and Shug in Alice Walker's *The Color Purple* challenges the dominant heterosexual narrative of the virgin and what it means to be a virgin. We know that Celie has had heterosex. Her children are the proof of that. (Celie is a menaced virgin who has been forced to pay a terrible price for her youth and inexperience – and physical unattractiveness.) However, Celie has never experienced sexual pleasure. Shug, upon learning that Celie had never had an orgasm, exclaims: "Why Miss Celie ... you still a virgin."[53] It is Shug who introduces her to the pleasures of the body, lesbian pleasures centered on Celie's "button," pleasures which have nothing to do with a penis. In *The Color Purple*, "virginity" is reconfigured as a pre-pleasurable condition, as it were; loss of virginity, as initiation into orgasm by another. To imagine virginity and its loss in such a way defies the binarized construction of bodies, sex, and gender upon which heteropatriarchy depends. On the other hand, virginity defined as a condition conferred upon a woman but surrendered to a man shores up such binaries, dis-allowing the possibility of a scale or spectrum of acts and/or identities, and reaffirms the power of the penis/phallus.

Judith Butler argues that "the gendered body is performative," which "suggests that it has no ontological status apart from the various acts which constitute its reality."[54] Yet the day-to-day experience of the body as such rarely involves a sense of a conscious performance, but takes for granted the beingness of the body. Culture mystifies performance, resulting in an effect of "ontologizing" the body. Virginity and its verifications challenge such an ontology, making visible the workings of culture that have hitherto remain hidden. As we have seen throughout this book, the female virgin is a vastly overdetermined sign, capable of proliferating meanings in many directions. She has functioned, and functions, as a metonym for the inviolability of the Christian Church, the figure of spirituality *sine qua non*, the lynchpin in patrilinear cultures, a commodity to be exchanged between men, a blank page on which male desires, sexual and otherwise, are to be inscribed – and, as I am arguing here, the guarantee of as well as the reward for conforming to the heterosexual imperative. The idea of virginity in the Middle Ages was not monologic and therefore unproblematic, but heteroglossic, conflicted, and conditional. The same can be said of virginity at the end of the twentieth century.

Notes

Introduction: Castitas/Virginitas

1   Robertson Davies, *The Rebel Angels*, Harmondsworth, England, Penguin, 1983, p. 52.

2   For a survey of the literature on theories about the body (with extensive bibliography), both medieval and modern, see Caroline Walker Bynum, "Why All the Fuss about the Body? A Medievalist's Perspective," *Critical Inquiry*, Autumn 1995, vol. 22, pp. 1–33. More than a survey, however, this essay takes issue with current discussions of the body in medieval scholarship. For a fascinating study of the body as an effect of diagnostic narratives, see Julia Epstein, *Altered Conditions: Disease, Medicine, and Storytelling*, New York and London, Routledge, 1995.

3   John Bugge's *Virginitas: An Essay in the History of a Medieval Ideal*, The Hague, Martinus Nijhoff, 1975, remains an important starting point for an understanding of virginity in Western Europe. Vern L. Bullough's and James Brundage's work, such as their collection of essays, *Sexual Practices and the Medieval Church*, Buffalo, Prometheus Books, 1982; Peter Brown's *The Body and Society: Men, Women, and Sexual Renunciation in Early Christianity*, New York, Columbia University Press, 1988; and Pierre J. Payer's *The Bridling of Desire: Views of Sex in the Later Middle Ages*, Toronto and Buffalo, University of Toronto Press, 1993; provide valuable insights into the psychology of medieval sexuality. See Joyce Salisbury, *Church Fathers, Independent Virgins*, London and New York, Verso, 1991, who furnishes a superb analysis of patristic positions on virginity.

4   Davies, *The Rebel Angels*, pp. 52–53.

5   Patristic writers usually identified three distinct states of female chastity: virginity, widowhood, and marriage. However, later writers sometimes formulated their own models. Aldhelm, for example, in *De virginitate* (late seventh century), replaces this tripartite scheme with another: *virginitas* ("spontaneous desire for celibacy"), *castitas* (continent marriage) and *iugalitas* (accession to the necessity of procreation). Aldhelm goes on to compare the three states in an elaborate set of metaphors: "virginity is the sun, chastity a lamp, conjugality darkness ... virginity is a queen, chastity a lady, conjugality a servant ... virginity is the royal purple, chastity the re-dyed fabric, conjugality the undyed wool." *Aldhelm: The Prose Works*, Michael Lapidge and Michael Herren (trans.), Cambridge, England, D. S. Brewer/Totowa, NJ, Rowman & Littlefield, 1979, XIX, p. 75; Latin, *PL* 89.116–7.

6   See Brown, *Body and Society*, pp. 306–22, for a different interpretation. He argues that Chrysostom's emphasis on virginity "elevated the Christian household so as to eclipse the ancient city," p. 313.

7   John Chrysostom, *De Virginitate*, in *On Virginity, Against Remarriage*, Sally Rieger Shore (trans.), Studies in Women and Religion 9, New York and Toronto, Edwin Mellen Press, 1983, p. 8.

8   Mary D'Angelo, in "Veils, Virgins, and the Tongues of Men and Angels: Women's Heads in Early Christianity," makes a similar point about Tertullian's polemical *De Virginibus Velandis* (c. 211; usually translated as "On the Veiling of Virgins"; D'Angelo prefers the more literal "That Virgins Must be Veiled"). She argues that this text represents a moment in the struggle for power in the formation of the early church between the Montanists (who were ultimately judged as heretics, and believed in a rigid sexual and ascetic code) and their "orthodox" opponents. Though Tertullian

rejected the Montanist idea that women had a right to preach, he was influenced by other tenets of the sect, such as the requirement that virgins cover themselves in public. Tertullian argues that virgins must be veiled because they can be both corrupted (by the male gaze) and corrupting (by sexually arousing those men who look upon them). Chastity constructed as so vulnerable (and so powerful), one might conclude, begs for institutional protection. D'Angelo says of Tertullian, and of Paul before him, that both "write in the context of communities which are trying to establish themselves, and both must deal with the issue of religious innovation in a culture in which antiquity is the test of truth," p. 132. In Howard Eilberg-Schwartz and Wendy Doniger (eds) *Off with Her Head!: The Denial of Women's Identity in Myth, Religion, and Culture*, Berkeley and London, University of California Press, 1995, pp. 131–64.

9 John Chrysostom, *De Virginitate*, pp. 8, 115.

10 For a helpful introduction to the *subintroductae*, as the virgins who shared households with men were called, see Elizabeth A. Clark, "John Chrysostom and the *Subintroductae*," *Church History* 1977, vol. 46, pp. 171–85.

11 John Chrysostom, *On the Necessity of Guarding Virginity*, Elizabeth A. Clark (trans.), in *Jerome, Chrysostom, and Friends: Essays and Translations*, New York and Toronto, Edwin Mellen, 1979, p. 242. Reprinted in Clark, *Women in the Early Church*, Wilmington, DE, Glazier, 1983, p. 147. This translation is based on *Comment Observer la Virginité*, in *Saint Jean Chrysostome: Les Cohabitations Suspectes et Comment Observer la Virginité*, Jean Dumortier (ed. and trans.), Paris, Bude, 1955, pp. 133–34.

12 *The Principal Works of St. Jerome*, trans. W. H. Fremantle [1893], Nicene and Post-Nicene Fathers 6, 2nd series, Peabody, MA, Hendrickson, reprinted 1994, p. 346. Latin: "evangelico atque apostolico vigore conterrerem," *PL* 23.221.

13 See R. Howard Bloch, *Medieval Misogyny and the Invention of Western Romantic Love*, University of Chicago Press, 1991, pp. 97–100. Courtly love, argues Bloch, contains "a contradiction every bit as powerful as the paradox of virginity: that love only exists to the degree that it is secret; that secret love only exists to the degree that it is revealed; and revealed, it is no longer love," p. 123.

14 Ambrose, *De Virginitate [On Virginity]*, Daniel Callam (trans.), Toronto, Peregrina, 1980, reprinted 1989, IV.15, p. 13. Latin: "Videte quod meritum non sola carnis virginitas facit, sed etiam mentis integritas," *PL* 16.284.

15 Jerome, *On the Perpetual Virginity of the Blessed Mary Against Helvidius*, in *Saint Jerome: Dogmatic and Polemical Works*, John N. Hritzu (trans.), The Fathers of the Church 53, Washington, D.C., Catholic University of America Press, 1965, p. 43. Latin: "quæ institorias exercet artes, nescio an corpore quod scio, spiritu virgo non permanet," *PL* 23.215. Cf. Song of Songs, 3: 1–2; Ambrose expresses similar sentiments about the marketplace in *On Virginity* VIII.46, p. 26; Latin: *PL* 16.292.

16 Augustine, *De Civitate Dei*, George E. McCracken (ed. and trans.), Loeb Classical Library, Cambridge MA, Harvard University Press/London, William Heinemann, 1957, I.xviii. Latin: "nullus autem magnanimus et pudicus in potestate habeat, quid de sua carne fiat, sed tantum quid adnuat mente vel renuat."

17 *Aldhelm: The Prose Works*, Lapidge and Herren (trans.), XVI, p. 72; Latin: "nequaquam carnalis integritas comprobatur, nisi consors spiritualis castimonia comitetur," *PL* 89.115.

18 Bugge, *Virginitas*, p. 136; also see pp. 80ff.

19 See Chapter 6, "The Virtue of Temperance," and Chapter 7, "Continence, Chastity, and Virginity" in Payer, *Bridling of Desire*, and p. 161.

20 Payer, *Bridling*, p. 7. Payer also notes that some twelfth- and thirteenth-century scholastic thinkers departed from the traditional threefold division of virgins, widows, and married persons in order to propose that "the three states of chastity are (1) those who never have and who propose never to experience sex willingly (virgins); (2) those presently unmarried who have experienced sex willingly and who propose never more to experience it ('widows'); (3) those who are married and who legitimately exercise their rights to sex," p. 161. Payer puts scare quotes around *widows* to indicate that this category was not restricted to widows, but could also include those who had not married but still experienced intercourse, pp. 162–61.

21 Payer, *Bridling*, p. 162.

22   Payer summarizes the four kinds of virginity in *Bridling*, p. 162. See Albertus Magnus, *De Bono, Quaestio III: De Castitate, Opera Omnia*, H. Kühle, C. Feckes, B. Geyer., and W. Kübel, (eds), Münster, Aschendorff, 1951, vol. 28, art. 5, pp. 157–60. Tertullian includes a similar, but less elaborate, scheme in *De Exhortatione Castitatis, PL* 2.963–94.

23   Payer, *Bridling*, p. 163.

24   Thomas Aquinas, *Summa Theologiæ*, Thomas Gilby (ed. and trans.), Blackfriars, in conjunction with New York, McGraw Hill/London, Eyre and Spottiswoode, 1968, 2a2æ.151,2, p. 161. Latin: "Dicendum quod nomen castitatis dupliciter accipitur. Uno modo proprie, et sic est quædam specialis virtus habens specialem materiam, scilicet concupiscentias delectabilium, quæ sunt in venereis. Alio modo nomen castitatis accipitur metaphorice," p. 160.

25   Aquinas, *Summa Theologiæ* 2a2æ.151, 2, pp. 160–61.

26   Aquinas, *Summa Theologiæ* 2a2æ.152, 1, pp.168–69.

27   Mary Wack, *Lovesickness in the Middle Ages: The Viaticum and its Commentaries*, University of Pennsylvania Press, 1990.

28   R. Howard Bloch, *Medieval French Literature and Law*, Berkeley and Los Angeles, University of California Press, 1977, p. 242.

29   Ellen Ross and Rayna Rapp, "Sex and Society: A Research Note from Social History and Anthropology," in Ann Snitow, Christine Stansell, and Sharon Thompson (eds) *Powers of Desire: The Politics of Sexuality*, New York, Monthly Review Press, 1983, p. 51.

30   For an overview of chastity tests found in medieval vernacular languages and their possible sources, see Tom Peete Cross, "Notes on the Chastity-Testing Horn and Mantle," *Modern Philology*, January 1913, vol. X.3, pp. 1–11; Edmund Karl Heller, "The Story of the Magic Horn: A Study in the Development of a Mediaeval Folk Tale," *Speculum*, 1934, vol. 9, pp. 38–50; F. J. Childs' introduction to *The Boy and the Mantle* in *The English and Scottish Popular Ballads* I, 1882–84; reprinted New York, Dover, 1965, pp. 257–71; and Marianne Kalinke, Introduction, *Möttul's Saga*, Editiones Arnamagnaeanae, Series B, vol. 30, Copenhagen, C. A. Reital, 1987. For a critical treatment of chastity tests, see Bloch, *Medieval Misogyny*, pp. 94ff.

31   *Floris and Blauncheflur*, Franciscus Catharina de Vries (ed.), Groningen, Druk. V.R.B., 1966, ll. 618–22. All quotations are taken from this edition of the Egerton MS; henceforth, line numbers will be given in the body of the text in parentheses. In the Old French version, if a virgin attempts to cross a rivulet from the fountain, the water will run clear, but it turns muddy when an unchaste woman crosses it. *Floire et Blancheflor*, Margaret M. Pelan (ed.), Paris, Société d'édition, 1937, rev. 1956, ll.1830–35.

32   *Gray's Anatomy* states that, in the neonate, "the orifice of the vagina is surrounded by a thick elliptical ring of connective tissue, the hymen. During childhood the hymen becomes a membranous fold along the posterior margin of the vaginal lumen," *Gray's Anatomy: The Anatomical Basis of Medicine and Surgery*, 38th ed., New York/Edinburgh, Churchill Livingstone, 1995. p. 351.

33   *American Medical Association Encyclopedia of Medicine*, New York, Random House, 1989, p 551. Compare to OED: "The virginal membrane, a fold of mucus membrane stretched across and partially closing the external orifice of the vagina." *Random House*, 2nd ed.: "a fold of mucus membrane partly closing the external orifice of the vagina in a virgin." *American Heritage*, 3rd ed.: "a membranous fold of tissue that partly or completely occludes the external vaginal orifice."

34   See Abbey Berenson, Astrid Heger, and Sally Andrews, "Appearance of the Hymen in Newborns," *Pediatrics*, April 1991, vol. 87.4, p. 459; Abbey Berenson, Astrid Heger, Jean M. Hayes, Rahn K. Bailey, and S. Jean Emans, "Appearance of the Hymen in Prepubertal Girls," *Pediatrics*, March 1992, vol. 89.3, pp. 387–94; and S. Jean Emans, Elizabeth R. Woods, Elizabeth N. Allred, and Estherann Grace, "Hymenal Findings in Adolescent Women: Impact of Tampon Use and Consensual Sexual Activity," *Journal of Pediatrics*, 1994, vol. 125.1, pp. 153–60. Also see Astrig Heger and S. Jean Emans, et.al., *Evaluation of the Sexually Abused Child: A Medical Textbook and Photographic Atlas*, New York, Oxford UP, 1992, for photographs of different kinds of hymens.

35   See *The New Our Bodies Our Selves: A Book By and For Women*, New York, Simon and Schuster/ Touchstone, 1992, which contains illustrations of "some hymen variations," as the caption for the illustration puts it, p. 244. Also see Ruth Bell, *et.al, Changing Bodies, Changing Selves*, New York,

Random House, 1980, pp. 26–27. In *You're in Charge: A Teenage Girl's Guide to Sex and Her Body*, New York, Fawcett Columbine, 1993, Niels H. Lauersen defines the hymen as "a thin tissue that covers the vaginal opening," and acknowledges that appearances of the hymen may vary; that, in fact, a girl may not be born with one, or may lose it "during activities like horseback riding or cycling," pp. 100, 101. (A point contested by Emans, *et. al*, cited above, n34.) Lauresen on tampon use: "If a girl has a thick hymen ... she may have difficulty using a tampon, but most of the time the tissue of the hymen is thin and a girl can comfortably insert a tampon"; moreover, Lauersen notes that one may destroy the hymen with a tampon, p. 101. Lauersen also notes the trope of the "bloody sheet," which I discuss in Chapter 5.

36 Giulia Sissa, *Greek Virginity* [1987], Arthur Goldhammer (trans.), Cambridge, MA, Harvard University Press, 1990, p. 2.

37 Sissa, *Greek Virginity*, pp. 1, 2.

38 Ambrose, *De Virginitate*, Callam (trans.), XI.66, p. 34. Latin: "Claude integritatis clave," *PL* 16.296; *De Institutione Virginis*, "aperi mentem, serva signaculum," *PL* 16.321. Cf. "you have heard that you are an enclosed garden," *De Virginitate*, Callam (trans.), XII.69, p. 36. Latin: "audisti quia hortus es conclusus," *PL* 16.297. And cf. Jerome, *Ad Jovinianum*, when he speaks of "That which is shut up and sealed reminds us of the mother of our Lord who was a mother and a Virgin" ("Quod clausum est atque signatum, similitudinem habet Matris Domini, matris et virginis"). In *The Principal Works of St. Jerome*, W. H. Fremantle (trans.) [1893], Nicene and Post-Nicene Fathers 6, Second Series, Peabody, MA, Hendrickson, reprinted 1994, p. 370; Latin: *PL* 23.265.

39 Mary Louise Pratt, "Interpretive Strategies/Strategic Interpretations," *Boundary 2*, Fall-Winter 1982–83, vol. 11.1–2, p. 228.

40 Donna Haraway, "A Cyborg Manifesto: Science, Technology, and Socialist-Feminism in the Late Twentieth Century," in *Simians, Cyborgs, and Women: The Reinvention of Nature*, New York, Routledge, p. 164.

41 I am influenced here by E. Jane Burns' discussion of repetition as a sign of textuality in *Arthurian Fictions: Rereading the Vulgate Cycle*, Columbus, published for Miami University by the Ohio State University Press, 1985.

42 Jacques Derrida, "The Double Session" [1970], in *Dissemination*, Barbara Johnson (trans.), Chicago, University of Chicago Press, 1981, p. 180.

43 Chapter 1 builds on and synthesizes the research of a number of historians of medicine to whose work I am heavily and happily indebted. A full accounting of the history of gynecological and medical knowledge and practices in antiquity and the Middle Ages is yet to be written, and only then will we be able to reconstruct fully the history of the hymen and its analogues. See Chapter 1, note 67.

44 Eusebius, *Ecclesiastical History*, Philip Schaff and Henry Wace (trans.) [1890], Nicene and Post-Nicene Fathers vol. 1, Second Series, Peabody, MA, Hendrickson, reprinted 1994, VI.XLI, p. 284.

45 Judith Butler, *Bodies that Matter: On the Discursive Limits of "Sex"*, London and New York, Routledge, 1993, p. ix.

Chapter 1 Hymenologies: the multiple signs of virginity

1 According to Jean Pasquerel, Jeanne's gender was also under interrogation; she was examined early on in order to determine "if she were a man or a woman, corrupt or virgin; she was found to be a woman, virgin and maid" ("si esset vir vel mulier, et esset corrupta vel virgo; et intenda fuit mulier, virgo tamen et puella.") *Procès de Condamnation et de Réhabilitation de Jeanne D'Arc dite La Pucelle*, 5 vols, Jules Quicherat (ed.) [Paris, 1841–49], New York, Johnson, reprinted 1965, III.102.

2 My translation. French: "[P]ar lesquelles icelle Pucelle fut veue, visitée et secrètement regardée et examinée ès secrètes parties de son corps; mais, après ce qu'ilz eurent veu et regardé tont ce que faisoit à regarder en ce cas, ladicte dame dist el relata au roy qu'elle et sesdictes dames trouvoient certainement que c'estoit une vraye et entière pucelle, en lacquelle n'apparroissoit aucune corrupcion on violence," Quicherat, III.209–10.

3 Assessor Jean Fabri testified to Jeanne's willingness to submit to an examination by the English, Quicherat, III.175. Bailiff Jean Massieu says: "I know very well that she was examined to see whether she was a virgin or not by some matrons and midwives at the Duchess of Bedford's orders"; "bene scit quod fuit visitata an esset virgo vel non per matronas seu obstetrices, et hoc ex ordinatione ducissæ Bedfordiæ," Quicherat, III.155. This and the following English translations of the records of Jeanne d'Arc's Rehabilitation are from Régine Pernoud's *The Retrial of Joan of Arc: The Evidence at the Trial for Her Rehabilitation 1450–1456*, J. M. Cohen (trans.), New York, Harcourt, Brace, 1955, p. 203.

4 Scribe Guillaume Colles (also known as Boisguillaume) testified that "the Duke of Bedford concealed himself in a place from which he could watch Joan's examination." Pernoud, p. 203; "dux Bedfordiæ erat in quodam loco secreto, ubi videbat eamdem Johannam visitari," Quicherat, III.163.

5 Quicherat, III.63.

6 Pernoud, p. 203. "[E]t scit ipse loquens, prout percipere potuit secundum artem medicinæ, quod erat incourrupta et virgo, quia eam videt quasi nudam ... et eam palpavit in renibus, et erat stricta, quantum percipere potuit ex aspectu," Quicherat, III.50.

7 Pernoud, p. 111. "[Q]uod eam pluries vidit in balneo et stuphis, et, ut percipere potuit, credit ipsam fore virginem," Quicherat III.88.

8 In this chapter, I would have liked to discuss a few cases of miraculous "revirgination" – the story of the Nun of Watton comes immediately to mind – but have deferred this subject to another time because of its complexity. One would have to begin with Peter Damien's "test question" for the omnipotence of God: could he restore virginity if he chose? Another fascinating example of the association of virginity with the miraculous is the story of the "doubting midwife" at the Nativity, who put her finger into the vagina of the Virgin in order to examine her. Because of the midwife's lack of faith, her hand is withered, but restored to health after she comes to believe.

9 *Hali Meiðhad*, Bella Millet (ed.), London, E.E.T.S. O.S. 284, 1982, p. 5.

10 Tertullian, *De virginibus velandis*, Sydney Thelwall (trans.) [1885], Ante-Nicene Fathers 4, Peabody, MA, Hendrickson, reprinted 1994, p. 33. Latin: *PL* 2.950.

11 John Chrysostom, *De Virginitate*, in *On Virginity, Against Remarriage*, Sally Rieger Shore (trans.), Studies in Women and Religion 9, New York and Toronto, Edwin Mellen Press, 1983, p. 1. Chrysostom's intention is to condemn the Jews for rejecting Christ as the Messiah; he says that they "have dishonored Christ himself, born of a virgin."

12 Part of the subtext to this passage in Deuteronomy is the monetary value of virginity: a virgin is worth more than a nonvirgin and/or a widow when a marriage contract is to be negotiated. For biblical references to brideprice, see Exodus 22: 16–67, Deuteronomy 22: 28–29. For a sampling of discussions on brideprice in the Babylonian Talmud, see tractate *Kethuboth* (or *Ketubbot*; concerned with legalities related to marriage): 10a, p. 47; 10b, p. 52; 11a, p. 54; 11a-11b, pp. 56–59. All quotations are taken from *The Soncino Talmud*, translated under the general editorship of Isidore Epstein, London, Soncino Press, 35 vols, 1935–48.

13 *Kethuboth* 9b, p. 46, and passim. Howard Adelman notes that, in the case of a young girl who lost the blood of virginity in early modern Italy, "entries were often made in the public records of Italian Jewish communities based on the testimony of competent witnesses ... so that when she married there would be no suspicions about her conduct and she would be entitled to the rights and privileges of a virgin." Howard Adelman, "Italian Jewish Women," in Judith R. Baskin (ed.) *Jewish Women in Historical Perspective*, Detroit, Wayne State University Press, 1991, pp. 144–45.

14 In his well-received commentary on Deuteronomy, Jeffrey H. Tigay asserts that the *betulim* is indeed hymeneal blood. The *JPS Torah Commentary: Deuteronomy*, Philadelphia and Jerusalem, Jewish Publications Society, 1966, pp. 205, 384, n. 47. Tigay cites the widespread and attested custom of displaying the wedding sheet in Jewish and Arab communities.

15 *Kethuboth* 10b, p. 51.

16 The Rabbi sees that the woman's face is "black" from hunger, and orders her to eat and drink, after which she does bleed when she has intercourse, *Kethuboth* 10b, p. 52.

17 *Kethuboth* 11b, p. 57; cf. pp. 67–68, 88–89. A mature woman who has had intercourse with a small boy is to be treated as if she has "injured herself with a piece of wood"; that is, is to be valued

as a virgin, *Kethuboth* 11a-b, pp. 57–59. *Kethuboth* also says that girl children who are less than three years and one day old and who have had intercourse are to be valued as virgins, 11a, pp. 54–55.

18 *Kethuboth* 10a-b, pp. 50–51. We find another chastity test in tractate *Yebamoth* (or *Yevamot*): women are to pass before the High Priest, who wears the "frontplate" on his forehead; those who turn "sickly green" in its presence are "fit for cohabitation"; that is, they are virgins, 60b, p. 403.

19 *Kethuboth* 10a, pp. 49–50.

20 *Kethuboth* 9b, p. 46; see also 10a, pp. 47, 49.

21 According to classical medical knowledge, the "female's natural tendency," says Marilyn A. Katz, is "to revert to a state of closure and impenetrability; sexual intercourse, menstruation, and childbirth, construed as processes that cause or result from the opening of the body, aids her in retaining a state of 'dilation.'" "Sexuality and the Body in Ancient Greece," *Trends in History*, 1990, vol. 4.4, p.118.

22 For comprehensive overviews of classical and medieval medical and gynecological knowledge, including the varied and complicated relationships among texts, see Monica Green, "The Transmission of Ancient Theories of Female Physiology and Disease through the Early Middle Ages," Ph.D. dissertation, Princeton University, 1985. See Joan Cadden, *Meanings of Sex Difference in the Middle Ages: Medicine, Science, and Culture*, Cambridge, Cambridge University Press, 1993, Part I; Monica Green, "Female Sexuality in the Medieval West," *Trends in History*, 1990, vol. 4.4, pp. 127–58; Danielle Jacquart and Claude Thomasset, *Sexuality and Medicine in the Middle Ages* [1985], Matthew Adamson (trans.), Princeton University Press, 1988. See also John W. Baldwin's *The Language of Sex: Five Voices from Northern France around 1200*, University of Chicago Press, 1994; in Chapter 5, "Coitus," Baldwin provides a useful overview of classical learning and attitudes toward virginity.

23 In *Christianity, Social Tolerance, and Homosexuality*, Chicago, University of Chicago Press, 1980, John Boswell says of the ancient world that: "People were thought of as 'chaste' or 'unchaste,' 'romantic' or 'unromantic,' 'married' or 'single'... but no one thought it useful or important to distinguish on the basis of genders alone," p. 59.

24 Galen, *On the Usefulness of the Parts*, 2 vols, Margaret Tallmadge May (trans., with Introduction and Commentary), Ithaca, Cornell University Press, 1968, p. 623.

25 Galen, *Usefulness*, pp. 628–9.

26 Thomas Laqueur, *Making Sex: Body and Gender from the Greeks to Freud*, Cambridge MA, Harvard University Press, 1990.

27 Gail Kern Paster, "The Unbearable Coldness of Female Being: Women's Imperfection and the Humoral Economy," paper delivered at the Center for Literary and Cultural Studies, Harvard University, 1996.

28 Laqueur argues that "the dominant discourse construed the male and female bodies as hierarchically, vertically, ordered versions of one sex," p. 9. And "there was only one [sex] to pick from and it had to be shared by everyone, from the strongest warrior to the most effeminate courtier to the most aggressive virago to the gentlest maiden," p. 124. While I have found Laqueur's study often useful and stimulating, such categorical statements are not supported by the evidence. One can turn to Cadden's *Meanings of Sex Difference* for a more balanced presentation. Cadden is more interested in the implications of the two-sex model for the construction of gender in the Middle Ages, and, by focusing on the medical treatises in the Middle Ages, she is able to show in much more detail how different theories contradict each other. For a critique of Laqueur's "one-sex" model, see Katharine Parks and Robert A. Nye, "Destiny is Anatomy," *The New Republic*, 18 February 1991, pp. 53–58. Also see Gail Kern Paster, *The Body Embarrassed: Drama and the Discipline of Shame in Early Modern England*, Ithaca, Cornell University Press, 1993, a study of how early modern humoral theory encodes and reproduces physiological and social difference, and how this difference is realized in literary texts. Paster criticizes Laqueur for creating a narrative of the history of the body that blurs sexual difference. See pp. 16–17, 82–83, 166–67.

29 As Green notes, what the physicians of the classical period described as female "seed" was most likely the fluids excreted by the Bartholin glands during arousal, "Transmission," p. 67, n. 106. While both the one-seed and two-seed theories described the female body as an inferior homologue

to the male body, the two-seed theory at least allowed for the female to take a more active role in procreation.

30 *Women's Secrets: A Translation of Pseudo-Albertus Magnus'* De secretis mulierum *with Commentaries,* Helen Rodnite Lemay (trans.), Albany, New York, State University of New York Press, 1992, p. 129. Latin: "signum uerissimus si uir sentit sperma mulieris uenire in magna copia," Venice 1508, caput II. While scholarship on the history of classical and medieval medicine has increased dramatically over the past ten years, there is still much work to be done. Many gynecological and medical treatises remain unedited, and those that have been edited are difficult to obtain. Lemay's translation of *De secretis mulierum* is a welcome resource for non-historians, but it cannot replace or reproduce – nor was it intended to do so – the complex history of transmission, interpellation, and commentary that characterizes this text and the majority of medical texts of antiquity and the Middle Ages.

31 Giulia Sissa, *Greek Virginity* [1987], Arthur Goldhammer (trans.), Cambridge, MA, Harvard University Press, 1990, pp. 53ff. Galen mentions the labia as "formed for the sake of ornament" and as "a covering to keep the uteri from being chilled," *Usefulness,* p. 660. (*Uterus* is pluralized because it was thought to be multi-chambered.)

32 Sissa, *Virginity,* 194–95, n1, n2.

33 Sissa, *Virginity,* pp. 36, 44ff.

34 Ann Ellis Hanson, "The Medical Writer's Woman," in David Halperin, John J. Winkler, and Froma I. Zeitlin (eds) *Before Sexuality: The Construction of Erotic Experience in the Ancient Greek World,* Princeton, NJ, Princeton University Press, 1990, p. 325. Also see Helen King, "Producing Woman: Hippocratic Gynecology," in Léonie J. Archer, Susan Fischler, and Maria Wyke (eds) *Women in Ancient Societies: An Illusion of the Night,* New York and London, Routledge, 1994, p. 108. In *The Corinthian Body,* New Haven, CT, and London, Yale University Press, 1995, Dale B. Martin says: "The usual term for 'veil' is *krēdemnon,* the ambiguity of which is important for the multivalent significations of unveiling. In Homeric texts *krēdemnon* can refer to the stopper, seal, or cover of a wine jug .... *krēdemnon* could also connote the 'closed' (in common opinion) uterus of a virgin; 'to loose the *krēdemnon*' could refer either to the breaking of the seal and unstopping of a wine jug or the defloration of a virgin.... For ancient Greeks, then, the veil ... not only symbolized but actually effected a protective barrier guarding a woman's head and, by metonymic transfer, her genitals," p. 234.

35 Hanson, "Medical," p. 324. Hanson says that "Soranos' sophisticated description of defloration relies on an image of pleats or folds, drawn together at one end by retraining cords or vessels, and his picture may ultimately depend upon the pursed lips of an earlier anatomy," p. 325.

36 In Brussels MS. 3701–15, a text attributed to Muscio, who translated Soranus' *Gynaikeia* into Latin by the fifth or sixth century. Reproduced in *Soranus' Gynecology,* Owsei Temkin (trans.), Baltimore, John Hopkins University Press, 1956, p. 9. Though Soranus compares the uterus to a "medicinal gourd," he does not describe this vessel as sealed or stoppered, p. 10.

37 Hanson, "Medical," p. 330.

38 Peter Brown, *The Body and Society: Men, Women, and Sexual Renunciation in Early Christianity,* New York, Columbia University Press, 1988. Also see Sissa's final chapter in *Greek Virginity,* "Toward a Sealed Fountain."

39 Galen, *Usefulness,* p. 623.

40 Galen, *Usefulness,* p. 624. Greek physicians were aware that the urethra (Galen calls it the "neck" of the bladder) was separate from the vaginal canal; Galen describes this neck as very short, opening up at the anterior side of the vagina, p. 660. However, Galen says that men used the same channel for the expulsion of sperm and the excretion of urine. For a different account, see Esther Lastique and Helen Rodnite Lemay, "A Medieval Physician's Guide to Virginity," in Joyce Salisbury (ed.) *Medieval Sexuality: Essays,* New York, Garland, 1991, pp. 61–63.

41 See Soranus, Temkin (trans.), p. 9; Hanson, p. 325. Galen says that the penis ought to be "perfectly tensed in coitus" so that (in a manner similar to the straightened-out uterus) the semen can be best expelled, pp. 659–60.

42 Trans. Hanson; quoted by Monica Green in "Transmission," p. 18.

43 Green, "Transmission," p. 20.

44 *De secretis mulierum*, Lemay (trans.), p. 66; Latin: Lyons, 1580, caput I, p. 18. In the medical texts of late antiquity, the word *vulva*, as Jacquart and Thomasset point out, "tended, depending on the authors, to designate either the woman's external genital apparatus taken as a whole, or ... the womb," *Sexuality and Medicine*, p. 24.

45 "The Nature of Wommen" (British Library MS Egerton 827), quoted in Monica Green, "Obstetrical and Gynecological Texts in Middle English," *Studies in the Age of Chaucer*, 1992, vol. 4, pp. 86–87. As Green notes, an adaptation of Muscio's *Gynaecia* (c. late thirteenth century) is the source for Egerton 837.

46 Jacquart and Thomasset, *Sexuality and Medicine*, pp. 173–77. For an overview of the nosology of women's diseases in antiquity and its far-reaching cultural implications, see Helen King, "Once Upon a Text: Hysteria from Hippocrates," in Sander L. Gilman, Helen King, Roy Porter, G. S. Rousseau, and Elaine Showalter (eds) *Hysteria Beyond Freud*, Berkeley and Los Angeles, University of California Press, 1993, pp. 3–90.

47 *The Medieval Woman's Guide to Health: The First English Gynecological Handbook*, Beryl Rowland (ed. and trans.), Kent, OH, Kent State University Press, 1981, pp. 90–91. Rowland identifies this early fifteenth-century MS, Sloane 2463, as the earliest gynecological treatise in English. But see Green, "Texts."

48 *Commentary on the Sentences*, quoted and trans. in Jacquart and Thomasset, *Sexuality and Medicine*, p. 176. Latin text edited in Josef Löffler, "Die Störungen des geschlechtlichen Vermögens in der Literatur der autoritativen Theologie des Mittelalters," Mainz, Akademie der Wissenschaften und der Literatur, 1958, vol. 6, p. 350.

49 Albertus Magnus, *De Bono, Quaestio III: De Castitate*, in *Opera Omnia*, H. Kühle, C. Feckes, B. Geyer, and W. Kübel (eds), Münster, Aschendorff, 1951, vol. 28, art. 5, pp. 160–63.

50 *Soranus' Gynecology*, Temkin (trans.), p. 15. For the text on which this translation is based and from which I take the Greek, see *Sorani Gynaeciorum Libri IV, De Signis Fracturarum, De Fasciis, Vita Hippocratis Secundum Soranum*, Johannes Ilberg (ed.), in *Corpus Medicorum Graecorum IV*, Leipzig and Berlin, B. G. Teubner, 1927, pp. 11–12.

51 Soranus' *Gynecology*, Temkin (trans.), p. 15.

52 Aline Rousselle, *Porneia: On Desire and the Body in Antiquity* [1983], Felecia Pheasant (trans.), Oxford, Blackwell, 1988, pp. 32–33, 36–37, 72.

53 Soranus' *Gynecology*, Temkin (trans.), p. 15.

54 Ann Ellis Hanson and Monica Green, "Soranus of Ephesus: *Methodicorum princeps*," in Wolfgang Haase and Hildegard Temporini (eds) *Aufstieg und Niedergang der römischen Welt*, Teilband II, Band 37.2, Berlin and New York, Walter de Gruyter, 1994, p. 1003, n123.

55 Soranus' *Gynecology*, Temkin (trans.), p. 15. Soranus argues that virginity is the ideal healthy state for both men and women. This idea, firmly grounded in Soranus' belief in the importance of achieving a proper balance in the body, was not widely held in antiquity, and seems not to have circulated in the medieval West, pp. 27–30. See Joan Cadden, *Meanings*, pp. 30, 45; see Jacquart and Thomasset, *Sexuality and Medicine*, pp. 48ff.

56 Soranus, *Gynecology*, Temkin (trans.), p. 8, p. 11.

57 Rhazes, *Liber ad Almansorem ... continens*, Tractatus Primus, Cap xxxvi: "Vulve autem orificium in virgine constrictum est et rugosum. In rugis autem ipsius colli virginalis quinque vene contexuntur subtiles, que quando corrumpitur virgo abrumpuntur, et predicte dilantur ruge" ("The opening of the vulva in virgins is constricted and wrinkled. Five fragile veins are woven into these folds of the virginal neck, which are broken when the woman is corrupted; these aforesaid wrinkles are spread smooth"), quoted and translated in Lastique and Lemay, "Guide," p. 74, n23.

58 Avicenna, "Et ante violationem puelle virginis sunt in ore matricis *panniculi* contexti ex venis et ligamentis subtilibus valde ortis ex omni membro eius quod destruit violator et currit quod in eis ex san. est" ("Before the violation of a virgin girl, certain *membranes* exist in the mouth of the womb woven from veins and extremely fragile ligaments issuing from every member, which the violator destroys and the blood in them runs out"), *Liber canonis*, Liber III, fen xxi, caput i, folio 360v, 1507; reprinted Hildesheim, G. Olms, 1964, my emphasis. Also quoted in Lastique and Lemay, "Guide," p. 74, n. 24.

59 Averroës, "Et orificium vulue virginis est crispuz," *Colliget*, Venice, 1514, caput xxxv. Lastique and Lemay cite a 1549 Venice edition, folio 49v, for the same remark.

60 Guilielmus de Saliceto, *Summa conservationis*, Venice 1489, f. i3r, col a.

61 Albertus Magnus, "ante corruptionem in collo et ore matricis virginum sunt panniculi contexti ex venis et ligamentis subtilibus valde, quae sunt signa virginitatis per aspectum probata, et haec destruuntur per concubitum aut etiam per immissionem digitorum, et parum sanguinis quod est in illis tunc effluit." *De Animalibus libri XXVI*, Hermann Stadler (ed.), Münster, Aschendorff, 1916, 1920, p. 164.

62 See Green, who has traced the transmission of the Latin texts of Soranus, "Transmission," pp. 315–16, and Hanson and Green, *"Methodicorum,"* pp. 1043–61, which updates Green's earlier work. Both scholars demonstrate how Soranus' remarks on virginity were in fact edited out of the medieval tradition of translations and abridgements. Also see G. E. R. Lloyd, *Science, Folklore, and Ideology: Studies in the Life Sciences in Ancient Greece*, Cambridge University Press, 1983, for an overview of the Greek medical framework within which women were diagnosed and treated, and how Soranus departed from this framework.

63 *De secretis mulierum*, Lemay (trans.), p. 127. Latin: Lyons, 1580, caput IX, p. 117.

64 *De secretis mulierum*, Lemay (trans.), p. 127. Latin: "omnibus uirginibus cum primum commiscentur uiris corrumpitur quædam pellicula quæ vocatur himen & cum custos uirginitatis & locatur circa uisicam & orificium matricis supra uuluam. ... omnibus fœminis cum primum corrupuntur." Commentary B, Venice, 1508, caput II.

65 *De secretis mulierum*, Lemay (trans.), p. 127. Latin: "Et quanto plus coëunt, tanto plus in tali ludo fortificantur," Lyons, 1580, caput IX, p 118.

66 Galen, *Usefulness*, pp. 628–29.

67 A question that I have only partially been able to answer in the course of this study remains: how did the Greek word ὑμένα originally and generically denoting any "membrane" of the body, come to narrow in meaning to denote a *membrana virginalis* by the early modern period? I must defer to the historian of medicine to answer this question satisfactorily, for not only do we need a full account of the word ὑμένα, but also of Latin *himen* and related words, such as *membranas, panniculus,* and *pellicula*. (These various terms were commonly used to describe parts of human anatomy in the Middle Ages; most of the major organs, in fact, were described as being enveloped in some sort of membrane.) We should also consider the development of "hymeneal" metaphors, such as *nodus virginitatis* (the knot of virginity), as Guilielmus de Saliceto puts it. (And see note 34, above, on *krēdemnon*, "veil.") In what follows, I list what I have found to be the earliest appearances and transformations of the word *hymen*, with the understanding that this etymological exercise is subject to further calibration, particularly since I confine myself to the earliest English appearances of the word. (An intriguing question: at what point does a technical, specialized word borrowed from one language become less "foreign" and thoroughly incorporated into the target language? Consider the word *glasnost*, for example, which first appeared in print in English accompanied by a gloss. Once the word became more familiar to Americans, *glasnost* then appeared in italics or with quotation marks. Now, while most people can identify *glasnost* as a Russian word, it has achieved the status of a "native" word, and appears without italics – in fact, my use of italics here may be considered rather pedantic. Linda Voigts furnishes a partial answer to this question about the gradual evolution of the vocabulary of a learned language into that of the vernacular. Voigts is not interested in lexical borrowing *per se*; she is engaged in studying how various writers and redactors of medical and scientific treatises switch or mix codes. While I am thinking in terms of a particular word moving from Latin to English [via French and possibly Italian; see below], she sees it the other way, as the "movement of vernacular languages into domains of written language that were formerly the exclusive preserve of Latin." "What's the Word? Bilingualism in Late-Medieval England," *Speculum*, October 1996, vol. 71, p. 813.)

We have already seen how Soranus uses ὑμένα, and how his use does not correspond to our modern notion of the hymen. After Soranus, we find a few scattered examples of the Latin word *himen*, denoting either the membrane in which the fetus is held, or a *membrana virginalis*. In the latter case, *himen* often has more of a metaphorical sense than an anatomical one. Yet this sense –

probably, but not conclusively so – related to the lore associated with the god Hymen (discussed below), seems not to have been carried over into medieval medical texts. (See Sissa, *Greek Virginity*, on the Christian contributions – if not confusions – to the evolving meaning of the word *hymen*, pp. 172–77.)

If we move to the Middle Ages, we find that Roger Bacon glosses ὑμένα with the Latin *matrix* ("uterus") in his Greek Grammar (thirteenth century). See *Greek Grammar of Roger Bacon and a Fragment of His Hebrew Glossary*, Edmond Nolan and S.A. Hirsch (eds), Cambridge University Press, 1902, p. 67. The MED records this meaning in its only entry for *hymen*: "þe hyme that þe childe liþe jn" ("the membrane, or hymen, surrounding the fetus"). This citation, from an English herbal dated c. 1425, found in MS Sln 5, is identified as a translation of Macer Floridus' *De Viribus Herbarum* (a Latin poem dated c. 849–1112). (However, Gösta Frisk, who edited a late fourteenth-century English translation of Macer's text, says that MS Sln 5 is not a Macer text, but that he has not, however, been able to identify its source. *A Middle English Translation of De Viribus Herbarum*, Uppsala, Lundequistska bokhandeln, Cambridge, Harvard University Press, 1949, p. 135.) The English-Latin lexicon known as the *Catholicon Anglicum* (1483) includes the same definition: *himen* is the "skyn yat ye chylde is lappyd in jn ye moder wame" ("the skin which wraps around the child in the mother's uterus"), p. 342.

As far as I have been able to determine, the earliest use of the word *hymen* as "virginal membrane" in English can be found in Thomas Elyot's *Dictionary*, (London, 1538) in which *hymen* is glossed as "a skinne in the secrete place of a maiden, which whanne she is defloured is broken," Menston, Yorkshire, Scolar Press, facsimile, 1970. The same definition is given in Thomas Cooper's 1584 *Thesaurus*: "a skinne in the secreate partes of a maiden broken when she is defloured," London, 1584. After these initial glosses, in the early modern period (perhaps not coincidentally, just as Greek language and learning became more widespread), the word *hymen* came to denote the "virginal membrane" almost exclusively (that is, outside of botany), while disputes over its existence proliferated (see the following note).

Part of the puzzle of the shift in meaning of the word ὑμένα/*hymen* is to note where it is *not* found in medieval medical texts. The hymen as a concept or structure (disputed or not) cannot be found in the late antique Latin translations of Soranus, such as Caelius Aurelianus' *Gynaecia* (late fourth century, or first half of the fifth century?) and Muscio's *Gynaecia* (fifth century). (See Hanson and Green, "*Methodicorum princeps*," pp. 1042–61, for a thorough discussion of translations of Soranus' *Gynaikeia* into Latin.) The hymen is not mentioned in Constantinus Africanus' influential *Pantegni* (eleventh century; a translation of al-Majusi's *Kitab as-Sina'a*); nothing is found in the corpus of Salernitan anatomical texts of the twelfth and thirteenth centuries.

Of course, a full etymology of the word *hymen* – indeed, a full history of the concept – would have to range beyond the limits of English. I want to mention a few Latin sources that, while they do not specifically use the word *hymen*, suggest the structure or concept of one: the Norman surgeon Henry de Mondeville writes in his *Chirurgie* (c. 1306–20): "Towards the middle of the cervix one can find, in virgins, veins which are torn at the moment of flowering," quoted in Jacquart and Thomasset, *Sexuality and Medicine*, p. 44. In my next two examples, the image of a covering or seal dominates, and may be more metaphorical than anatomical: Mondino de'Luzzi (d. 1326), who actually dissected at least two female cadavers, writes that the surface of the entrance to the womb "in virgins is covered by an intact subtle and venous 'covering'; when broken, women bleed on that account" ("[I]n uirginibus est uellatum uellamine subtili uenoso et inuiolantur rumpitur et ideo sanguinantur"). *Anatomies de Mondino dei Luzzi et de Guido de Vigevano*, Ernest Wickersheimer (ed.), Paris, E. Droz, 1926, p. 26. And consider the following, written by Niccolò Falcucci in *De passionibus mulierum* (fifteenth century): "Before defloration ... the mouth of the womb is covered with a membrane woven with veins and arteries which are broken when she is deflowered and as a result the woman bleeds" ("Quoniam ante deflorationem ... os matricis est velatum panniculo contexto venis arteriis qui cum defloratur rumpitur et inde sanguis emittitur"), edited and translated by Lastique and Lemay in "Guide," pp. 59 and 72. However, Michael Savonarola, in his *Practica Maior* (fifteenth century), does use the word *hymen*: "The cervix is covered by a subtle membrane called the *hymen*, which is broken at the time of deflowering, so that the blood flows," as translated in Jacquart and Thomasset, *Sexuality and Medicine*, p. 44. Given the provenance of these writers, and the fact that Mondeville is particularly important for bringing Italian innovations to the attention of French physicians and surgeons, perhaps the key to a full history of the etymology of the hymen lies in an Italian "tradition," so to speak.

Finally, the reader may be wondering about Hymen (Ὑμήν), the Greek god who presides over the marriage ceremony and the nuptial bed, and his association with the "virginal membrane." According to Sissa in *Greek Virginity*, any etymological or figurative connection between *Hymen* and *hymen* was usually disputed by ancient writers; modern classicists continue to disagree on the question of a connection. "Despite the apparent and plausible proximity," says Sissa, "the relation between the hymeneal song and the hymen of histology remains 'obscure,'" p. 109; cf. pp. 106–109. Jane Chance outlines a medieval link between Hymen and hymen in her monumental *Medieval Mythography: From Roman North Africa to the School of Chartres, AD 433–1177*, Gainesville, University Press of Florida, 1994. Here, we discover an elaborate allegory in which Hymen presides not only over weddings – that is, literal and figurative unions, both between the sexes and among the disparate elements of the universe – but also over what follows such unions: conception. The writer known as the Second Vatican Mythographer (c. ninth-tenth century) describes Hymen as responsible for "garlanding thresholds … at which 'inner' and 'outer' converge,'" as Chance puts it, p. 261; see pp. 260–62, 344–45, 432–39. Such an image is highly suggestive with respect to virginity and the hymen, yet it does not seem to have been exploited in the works of these mythographers: Hymen and hymen are not linked to suggest a "virginal membrane," but an "amniotic membrane."

68 See my "The Hymen has a History: Early Modern Doubts about and Disputations on the *Claustrum Virginitatis*," delivered at "Attending to Early Modern Women: Crossing Boundaries," Center for Renaissance and Baroque Studies, University of Maryland, November 1997, College Park, MD. Marie H. Loughlin thoroughly covers the subject of the hymen in early modern medical texts in the first chapter of *Hymeneutics: Interpreting Virginity on the Early Modern Stage*, Lewisburg, PA, Bucknell University Press/London, Associated University Presses, 1997.

69 de Saliceto, *Summa conservationis*: "sanguinis corruptionis virginitatis minimum est comperatione temporis menstruorum & quantitatis minima etiam color vero sanguinis qui erit hora corruptionis virginitatis clarus & non fusens est," f. i3ra. Niccolò Falcucci makes similar observations; see Lastique and Lemay, "Guide," pp. 60 and 72.

70 Cf. Lastique and Lemay, "Guide," p. 175.

71 *De secretis mulierum*, Lemay (trans.), p. 126. Latin: Venice, 1508, caput II.

72 *De secretis mulierum*, Lemay (trans.), p. 127. Latin: "quod vulua virginis semper est clausa," London, 1625, p. 107.

73 *De secretis mulierum*, Lemay (trans.), p. 128. Latin: "[C]lara & lucida, quandoque alba, quandoque glauca," Lyons, 1580, caput X, p. 119.

74 *De secretis mulierum*, Lemay (trans.), p. 129. Latin: "Corruptæ enim mulieres habent vrinam turbidam per fracturam pelliculæ præcedentem, & sperma viri apparet in fundo vrinæ talis mulieris," Lyons, 1580, caput X, p. 119.

75 de Saliceto, *Summa conservationis*, folio i3ra.

76 Niccolo borrows this test from Gilbertus Anglicus (d. 1250), Lastique and Lemay, "Guide," p. 63; Latin, p. 72. See also *De secretis mulierum*, Lemay (trans.), p. 127.

77 *De secretis mulierum*, Lemay (trans.), p. 127. Latin: "Nota, si vis experiri, utrum virgo sit corrupta, pulveriza fortiter flores lilij crocei que sunt inter flores, & da ei comedere de illo puluere, si est corrupta, statim mingit," London, 1625, p. 107.

78 For a different interpretation, see Lastique and Lemay, "Guide" p. 61.

79 *De secretis mulierum*, Lemay (trans.), p. 67. But Averroës goes on to say that the girl "ought to engage in the venereal act, and have intercourse with men." It is if by doing so, she will somehow erase the paradox of pregnancy without intercourse.

80 *De secretis mulierum*, Lemay (trans.), p. 67.

81 Jacquart and Thomasett, *Sexuality and Medicine*, pp. 61–70.

82 *De secretis mulierum*, Lemay (trans.), p. 128. Latin: Lyons, 1580, caput X, p. 119.

83 Albertus Magnus, *De Mineralibus*, Dorothy Wyckoff (ed.), Oxford, Clarendon Press, 1967, p. 93.

84 John of Trevisa, *On the Properties of Things, John of Trevisa's Translation of Bartholomæus Anglicus De Proprietatibus Rerum*, 3 vols, M.C. Seymour (ed.), Oxford, Clarendon, 1975–1988, XVI.lxii. And

compare the entry for *gagate*: it "warneþ of maydenhode, for if a mayde drynkeþ of þe water þerof sche pisseþ nought; and if sche is no mayde and drynkeþ þerof sche pisseþ anon and also aȝens hire will" (indicates virginity, for if a virgin drinks of the water [in which the gem is steeped], she will not urinate; if she is not a virgin and drinks of it, she urinates immediately and against her will), XVI.xlvii.

85 The Latin, "Aiohel. Deomedius. Eugenius. Probatus. Sabatus. Stephanus. Quiriacus. Hec nomina scripta in carta uirginia. inter mamillas pone dormienti. omni adulteros nominat." Quoted in Lucille B. Pinto, "The Folk Practice of Gynecology and Obstetrics in the Middle Ages," *Bulletin of the History of Medicine*, 1973, vol. 47, p. 523.

86 Translated by Helen Rodnite Lemay in "The Stars and Human Sexuality: Some Medieval Scientific Views," *Isis*, 1980, vol. 71, p. 130. Her text is Abenragel's *Liber in iudiciis astrorum*, Venice 1485, folio 27.

87 John of Seville, *De interrogationibus*, Venice, 1493, folio130rb. Qtd. in Lemay, "Stars," n. 13. Original Arabic text attributed to Zahel.

88 Guido Bonatti, "[F]uit tentata, sed non acquieuit uerbis tentatorum. ... fuit tentata, & adhuc tentatur ... iam amplexatus est eam, & osculatus quidam ... tetigit ille pudibunda mulieris," *Astronomiæ Tractatus X*, Basel, 1550, pars II, caput IV, p. 268. See Lemay, "Stars," pp. 130–31.

89 Bonatti, *Astronomiæ*, p. 269. See Lemay, "Stars," p. 131.

90 The "proof" of pregnancy may underpin one chastity test that came to be known in England through its depiction on the late twelfth-century Hereford Map. The Hereford illustration is based on a story related by Solinus, who says an Ethiopian people known as the Psylli tested their wives' chastity by exposing their infants to serpents. An "unfaithful" wife had to watch her child be stung to death – presumably, the child born of the illicit union. Inscribed on the Hereford Map: "Philli pudicitiam uxorum probant objectu nobiter natorum serpentibus." See W. L. Bevan and H. W. Phillott, *Medieval Geography: An Essay in Illustration of the Hereford Map*, London, 1873, p. 103. See also Solinus, *Collectanea Rerum Memorabilium*, Th. Mommsen (ed.) [1895], reprinted Berlin, Weidman, 1958: "recens etiam editos serpentibus offerebant: si essent partus adulteri, matrum crimina plectebantur interitu parvulorum: si pudici, probos ortus a morte paterni sanguinis privilegium tuebatur: sic originis fidem probabant venenis iudicantibus," pp. 124–25.

91 *De secretis mulierum*, Lemay (trans.), p. 129. Latin: "si mammillæ puellæ tendant dorsum signum est corruptionis ... menstrua mouentur sursum uersus mamillas & tunc mamillæ tendunt deorsum propter grauedinem menstruorum," Venice, 1508, caput II. Diagnoses of pregnancy in the Middle Ages were not always reliable; in fact, it was not until late in the nineteenth century that physicians developed a reliable pregnancy test. In "A Jury of Matrons," *Medical History* 32, 1988, pp. 23–33, Thomas R. Forbes read legal records to find examples of women who were ordered to be examined for pregnancy. This usually occurred when a woman's husband had died, and a dispute arose over the disposal of the estate. If the woman were indeed pregnant at the time of her husband's death, she would inherit more of, or all of, the estate. As Forbes notes, the expert witness (a physician, midwife, or respectable matron of the community) was not always correct in her or his diagnosis.

92 *De secretis mulierum*, Lemay (trans.), p. 128.

93 See Helen Lemay, "William of Saliceto on Human Sexuality," *Viator*, 1981, vol. 12, pp. 165–81, who paraphrases the text: "wash the mouth of the vulva, sit in a hot bath, rub on certain prescribed ointments, and place in the vulva a dove's intestine that she has filled with blood," p. 176. A mention of ointments designed to contract the vagina is found in *De secretis mulierum*, Lemay (trans.), p. 129.

94 The English translation, somewhat revised here, can be found in Julia O'Faolain and Lauro Martines (eds) *Not in God's Image: Women in History from the Greeks to the Victorians*, New York, Harper and Row, 1973, p. 143, and is based on a text in *Collectio Salernitana*, 5 vols, Salvatore de Renzi (ed.), Naples, 1852–59, vol. IV (1856), p. 23:

> Indiget istius etiam medicamine libri
> Quam secretus amor veneris furibunda voluptas
> Perlargam dederant ut amicis crura relaxans

Nubere cum sit opus, ignoret ut ista vir ejus,
Excecabit eum sic virgo sophistica caute.
Pulvere contritum zucarinum sumat alumen
Ovi commiscens albumen aqua pluviali
In qua decocta sint pulegium, calamentum
His quoque consimilies herbe quas scripsimus ante;
His pannum rarum tingat bis terve quaterve;

...

Omnibus est melius quibus hunc deludere possit:
Sanguisugam vulve pridie quam nubat, in ore
Cautius immittat, vulvam ne forte subintret;
Exeat hinc sanguis et crustula fiat ibidem
Sanguinis ob fluxum vulve strictumque meatum.
Sic coeundo virum deludet virgo sophista (caput 45)

This verse translation, found in a unique thirteenth-century MS (which is not attributed to Trotula in the manuscript), is typical of the recipes for vaginal constrictives found in the prose versions of the Trotula text – except, as I said, for the tone. See Monica Green, "The Development of the *Trotula*," *Revue d'Histoire des Textes*, 1996, vol. 26, pp. 118–203; the two recipes cited here correspond to what she lists as 190 and 195.

95 Cited in Jacquart and Thomasset, *Sexuality and Medicine*, p. 153.
96 Giovanni Boccaccio, *The Decameron*, G. H. McWilliam (trans.), Harmondsworth, England, Penguin Books, 1972, p. 191. R. A. Shoaf compares Chaucer's Custance to Boccaccio's Alatiel in that Custance remains "unwemmed" in spite of her trials. See "'Unwemmed Custance': Circulation, Property, and Incest in the Man of Law's Tale," *Exemplaria*, 1990, vol. 2.1, p. 296; pp. 301–02, n18. The Italian: "Ed essa che con otto uomini forse diecemilia volte giaciuta era, allato a lui si coricò per pulcella, e fecegli credere che così fosse." *Decameron*, Natalino Sapegno (ed.), Turin, Fratelli Fabbri Editori, 1975, p. 179.
97 Cyprian, *De Habitu Virginis*; Tertullian, *De virginibus velandis* and *Ad Uxorem*; Jerome, *Ad Eustochium*; Ambrose, *De Virginibus ad Marcellinam* (which includes a catalog of female virgins), *De Virginitate*, and *De Institutione Virginis*; Augustine, *De Sancta Virginitate*. John Chrysostom's *De Virginate* is meant for women, but also addresses men, albeit in an abstract way, and Tertullian's *Exhortatione Castitatas* is addressed to a friend who has recently lost his wife. The Wife of Bath made famous the *Liber de nuptiis* attributed by Jerome to Theophrastus in *Adversus Jovinianum* (c. 393; *PL* 23.221–352). See also the 13th-century satirical poem *De coniuge non ducenda* – no doubt aimed at a clerical audience, and found in no fewer than fifty-five MSS. In *Gawain on Marriage: the Textual Tradition of the* De coniuge non ducenda, with critical edition and translation by A. G. Rigg, Toronto, Pontifical Institute of Mediaeval Studies, 1986. And see, of course, the antifeminist sections of Guillaume de Lorris' and Jean de Meun's *Le Roman de la Rose* (thirteenth century), Daniel Poirion (ed.) Paris, Garnier-Flammarion, 1974.
98 Michel Foucault, *Discipline and Punish: The Birth of the Prison* [1975], Alan Sheridan (trans.), New York, Vintage Books, 1977, p. 135. Foucault speaks of "asceticism and 'disciplines' of a monastic type, whose function was to obtain renunciations rather than increases of utility and ... had as their principal aim an increase of the mastery of each individual over his own body," p. 137. True enough, but Foucault neglects how renunciations as acts can indeed be useful; that is, as a model, literal or metaphorical, for the behavior of others.
99 Jerome, "Ad Eustochium" (Epistola XXII), in *Select Letters of St. Jerome*, T. E. Page, E. Capps, and W. H. D. Rouse (eds), F. A. Wright (trans.), Cambridge, MA, Harvard University Press/Loeb Classical Library, 1933, pp. 87, 115, 125.
100 Ambrose, "Letter to Syagrius," in *Saint Ambrose: Letters*, Sister Mary Melchior Berenka (trans.), New York, Fathers of the Church, 1954, p. 159; *PL* 16.934.
101 Augustine, *De Civitate Dei*, George E. McCracken (ed. and trans.), Loeb Classical Library, Cambridge MA: Harvard University Press/London, William Heinemann, 1957, I.XVIII.

102 Cyprian, "Ad Pomponium, Ad Virginibus" (Epistola LXII), in *Saint Cyprian: Letters 1–81*, Sister Rose Bernard Donna (trans.), Washington, Catholic University of America Press, 1964, p. 13. Latin: *PL* 4.370.

103 Cyprian, "Ad Pomponium," p. 12. Latin: "cum et manus obstetricum et oculi sæpe fallantur, et si incorrupta inventa fuerit virgo ea parte sui qua mulier potest esse, potuerit tamen ex alia corporis parte peccasse quæ corrumpi potest et tamen inspici non potest," *PL* 4.367–68.

104 Ambrose, "Letter to Syagrius," p. 154. Latin: "cum probatione destiterint, patebit ut genitalium secretorum petant inspectionem, et addicentur semper sacræ virgines ad hujusmodi ludibria, quæ et visu et auditu, horrori et pudori sunt?" *PL* 16.931.

105 Ambrose, "Letter to Syagrius," pp. 154, 155–56. Latin: "vile mancipium, procacem vernulam, cur non abutaris pudibundo ministerio, et exponas ejus modestiam," *PL* 16.931; "peritissima et locupleti femina hujusmodi artis," *PL* 16.932.

106 Ambrose, "Letter to Syagrius," p. 155. Latin: "Virgo Domini suis est nixa fulcris ad sui probationem ... et nec abditorum, occultorumque inspectio, sed obvia omnibus modestia astipulatur integritati," *PL* 16.931.

107 Jerome, "Ad Laeta," pp. 344–45.

108 Jerome, "Ad Laeta," p. 345. Latin: "ne, quod mali didicerint, peius doceant" p. 344.

109 Ambrose, "Letter to Syagrius," p. 155. Latin: "Quid, quod etiam ipsi archiatri dicunt non satis liquido comprehendi inspectionis fidem et ipsis medicinæ vetustis doctoribus id sententiæ fuisse?" *PL* 16.932.

110 Ambrose, "Letter to Syagrius," p. 157. Latin: "Quid igitur suspecta et dubia captamus; cum majora sint alia examinandæ veritatis documenta et testimonia," *PL* 16.933.

111 Ambrose, "Letter to Syagrius," p. 162. Latin: *PL* 16.936.

112 John Chrysostom, *On the Necessity of Guarding Virginity*, Elizabeth A. Clark (trans.), in *Jerome, Chrysostom, and Friends: Essays and Translations*, New York and Toronto, Edwin Mellen, 1979, pp. 133–34. Reprinted in Clark, *Women in the Early Church*, Wilmington, DE, Glazier, 1983. This translation is based on *Comment Observer la Virginité*, in *Saint Jean Chrysostome: Les Cohabitations Suspectes et Comment Observer la Virginité*, Jean Dumortier (ed. and trans.), Nouvelle Collection de textes et documents, Paris, Bude, 1955, p. 100.

113 Augustine, *De Civitate Dei*, I.xviii. Since Augustine apparently read Soranus (either in a Latin translation or in the original Greek; he calls him "medicinae auctor nobilissimus," [that most famous medical author] in *Contra Julianum*, *PL* 44.813), it is tempting to think that he might have known what he was talking about; however, it seems that he did not read Soranus until after writing *De Civitate Dei*. Of the four extant Latin translations of Soranus' works, three were produced in North Africa, and two by contemporaries of Augustine. See Green, "Transmission," pp. 134–35. Also see Pierre Courcelle, *Late Latin Writers and their Greek Sources* [1943; rev. 1948], Harry E. Wedeck (trans.), Cambridge, MA, Harvard University Press, 1969, pp. 194–96.

114 See Forbes, "A Jury of Matrons."

115 James Brundage, *Law, Sex, and Christian Society in Medieval Europe*, Chicago and London, University of Chicago Press, 1987, p. 385 and n296.

116 Henry de Bracton, *De Legibus et Consuetudinibus*, George E. Woodbine (ed.) (1915–42), Samuel E. Thorne (trans.), Cambridge, MA, Harvard University Press/Belknap Press, 1968, vol. 2, pp. 344–45.

117 Bracton, *De Legibus*, p. 201; and see pp. 202, 203.

118 Brundage, *Law*, p. 224; also see 322, 413.

119 James Brundage, "The Problem of Impotence," in Vern L. Bullough and James Brundage (ed.) *Sexual Practices and the Medieval Church*, Buffalo, Prometheus Books, 1982, p. 136.

120 Richard Helmholz cites the *Liber Extra* in *Marriage Litigation in Medieval England*, Cambridge Studies in English Legal History, Cambridge, 1974, p. 88. See also A. Esmein, *Le Mariage en Droit Canonique*, 2nd ed., Paris, R Génestal, 1929, pp. 282–85.

121 Jacqueline Murray, "On the Origins and Role of 'Wise Women' in Causes for Annulment on the Grounds of Male Impotence," *Journal of Medieval History*, 1990, vol. 16, p. 239.

122 Murray, "Origins": "The report being heard of trustworthy matrons being sworn before us in this matter and examined and being expert in these matters, p. 245; "audita relatione matronarum fide

dignarum juratarum super hoc coram nobis et examinatarum et expertarum in talibus," p. 248, n9. For what an "inspection" of the male would entail, see Brundage, *Law* p. 457, and Helmholz, *Marriage*, p. 89.

123 Froissart, *Chronicles*, (Geoffrey Brereton, trans.), Harmondsworth, England, Penguin, rev. 1978, p. 253. For the French text, see *Chroniques de J. Froissart*, vol. 11, Gaston Raynaud (ed.), Paris, La Société de l'Histoire de France, 1899, p. 224. I thank Amy Goodwin for directing me to this passage.

124 Froissart, *Chronicles*, (Geoffrey Brereton, trans.), p. 254; French, (Raynaud) p. 226.

125 Froissart, *Chronicles*, (Geoffrey Brereton, trans.), p. 255; for the French, (Raynaud) see p. 228.

126 See Cadden, "Is Sex Necessary? The Problem of Sexual Abstinence," in *Meanings*, pp. 259–77; Michael M. Sheehan, *Marriage, Family, and Law in Medieval Europe: Collected Studies*, Toronto and Buffalo, University of Toronto Press, 1996, especially "The Formation and Stability of Marriage in Fourteenth-Century England: Evidence of an Ely Register," pp. 38–76; and Georges Duby, *The Knight The Lady and the Priest: The Making of Modern Marriage in Medieval France* [1981], Barbara Bray (trans.), New York, Pantheon Books, 1983.

127 Cadden, *Meanings*, p. 264. She adds, "in their attention solely to female virginity, medical texts reveal an involvement with secular interests rather than with the increasingly tenuous gender neutrality of ecclesiastical values." Secular interests are certainly represented in medieval medical texts, but I do not agree that the Church was evolving gender-neutral values in their treatment and regulation of virginity.

128 For a fine discussion of the tradition of the eloquent virgin, see Maud Burnett McInerney, "Rhetoric, Power and Integrity in the Passion of the Virgin Martyr," in Kathleen Coyne Kelly and Marina Leslie (eds) *Menacing Virgins: Representing Virginity in the Middle Ages and Renaissance*, Newark, University of Delaware Press/London, Associated University Presses, 1999, pp. 50–70.

Chapter 2 "Armour of proof": the virgin and the church in hagiography

1 Jules Quicherat (ed.) *Procès de Condamnation et de Réhabilitation de Jeanne D'Arc dite La Pucelle*, 5 vols [Paris, 1841–49], New York, Johnson, reprinted 1965, III.100.

2 In Régine Pernoud, *The Retrial of Joan of Arc: The Evidence at the Trial for Her Rehabilitation 1450–1456*, J. M. Cohen (trans.), New York, Harcourt, Brace, 1955, p. 107; Latin: "[U]ltra quod nunquam habuerant concupiscentiam carnalem," Quicherat, III.77.

3 Pernoud, p. 154; French: "[E]t aucunes foiz les jambes toutes nues, en la faisant apareiller de ses plaies; et que d'lle approuchoit souventes foiz, et aussi qu'il feust fort, jeune et en sa bonne puissance … ne s'esmeut son corps á nul charnel désir vers elles, ne pareillement ne faisoit nul autre quelconque de ses gens et escuiers, ainsi qu'il qui parle leur a oy dire et relater par plusieurs foiz," Quicherat, III.219.

4 Sherry B. Ortner, "The Virgin and the State," *Feminist Studies*, 1978, vol. 4, p. 22. Ortner was criticized for overgeneralizing the value of virginity in all cultures, and has since modulated her position as a result. See, for example, her "Gender and Sexuality in Hierarchical Societies: The Case of Polynesia and Some Comparative Implications," in Sherry B. Ortner and Harriet Whitehead (eds) *Sexual Meanings: The Cultural Construction of Gender and Sexuality*, Cambridge University Press, 1981, pp. 359–409, as well as her introduction to this volume.

5 Geraldine Brooks, *Nine Parts of Desire: The Hidden World of Islamic Women*, New York, Doubleday Anchor Books 1994, p. 32.

6 Thomas Heffernan, *Sacred Biography: Saints and Their Biographers in the Middle Ages*, New York and Oxford, Oxford University Press, 1988, p. vii and *passim*. Heffernan defines sacred biography as "a narrative text of the *vita* of the saint written by a member of a community of belief," p. 16.

7 Hayden White, "The Question of Narrative in Contemporary Historical Theory," in *The Content of the Form*, Baltimore and London, Johns Hopkins University Press, 1987, p. 44.

8 White, "The Question of Narrative," p. 45.

9 Michel Foucault, *Discipline and Punish: The Birth of the Prison* [1975], Alan Sheridan (trans.), New York, Vintage Books, 1977, p. 137.

10 Jerome, Letter XXII, "Ad Eustochium," in T. E. Page, E. Capps, and W. H. D. Rouse (eds), F. A. Wright (trans.) *Select Letters of St. Jerome*, Cambridge, MA, Harvard University Press/Loeb Classical Library, 1933, p. 105. Latin: "Neque enim aureum vas et argenteum tam carum Deo fuit, quam templum corporis virginalis," p. 104. Ambrose, *De Virginibus ad Marcellinam*, PL 16.225.

11 Ambrose, Epistola LXIII, "Letter to the Church at Vercelli," in Sister Mary Melchior Berenka (trans.) *Saint Ambrose: Letters*, New York, Fathers of the Church, 1954, pp. 333–334. "Christus hoc dicit ad Ecclesiam, quam vult esse virginem, sine macula, sine ruga.... Nec potest dubitare quisquam quod Ecclesia virgo sit," PL 16.1250.

12 Brown, *Body and Society*, p. 356. Later on, such canonists as Tancred (1078?–1112) and Innocent IV (1200–1254) quite explicitly work out the metonymic relationship of the female virgin to the institutionalized Church in order to explain why it is necessary to monitor a woman's behavior and control her desires. See James A. Brundage, *Law, Sex, and Christian Society in Medieval Europe*, Chicago and London: University Chicago Press, 1987, pp. 350–351, 427.

13 Foucault, *Discipline*, p. 136.

14 Gravdal mentions in passing the topoi of forced prostitution and forced marriage in which divine intervention is featured. See *Ravishing Maidens: Writing Rape in Medieval French Literature and Law*, University of Pennsylvania Press, 1991, pp. 22–24.

15 According to Sherry Reames in *The Legenda Aurea: A Reexamination of Its Paradoxical History*, Madison and London, University of Wisconsin Press, 1985, p. 4. Reames approaches hagiography from a historian's point of view, and in doing so, finds Voragine's text wanting. She is quick to point out that, contrary to what many modern readers have thought of the text, it is not the sum of what medieval people thought about hagiography, or even "a splendid representative of its genre, or even a very adequate one," p. 7. Nevertheless, as an influential text in the Middle Ages, it is ideal for my purposes. I follow Reames on dating here.

16 Simon Gaunt, *Gender and Genre*, Cambridge University Press, 1996, p. 183.

17 Hayden White, *Metahistory: The Historical Imagination in Nineteenth-Century Europe*, Baltimore and London, Johns Hopkins University Press, 1973, pp. 34–35.

18 Jocelyn Wogan-Browne, "Saints' Lives and the Female Reader," *Forum for Modern Language Studies*, 1991, vol. 27.4, p. 317. Wogan-Browne asks, "Did twelfth- and thirteenth-century girls *need* to develop wills capable of withstanding floggings, flesh-hooks and lighted tapers?" p. 316. She argues for a "potential relation between model virgin lives and the experience of the women who read them," for the possibility that many young women "might have to develop a will capable of withstanding ... emotional and social pressures," p. 321. Wogan-Browne's point is vividly supported by Jane Tibbets Schulenberg, in "The Heroics of Virginity: Brides of Christ and Sacrificial Mutilation," in Mary Beth Rose (ed.) *Women in the Middle Ages and the Renaissance*, Syracuse, Syracuse University Press, 1986, discussed below.

   Many fine studies exist that historicize how and why the saints' legends in the Middle Ages were written and read. In addition to Wogan-Browne's and Shulenberg's work, see Sheila Delany's introduction to *A Legend of Holy Women: A Translation of Osbern Bokenham's* Legends of Holy Women, Notre Dame and London, University of Notre Dame Press, 1992, who takes great pains to contextualize the first audience (the nuns of the Clare Priory in Suffolk, England) for Osbern Bokenham's *Legendys of Hooly Wummen* (after 1447), the first all-female hagiography. This contains a number of stories about virgin martyrs who managed to keep their vow of chastity against all odds, from an unwelcome marriage proposal to rape. Wogan-Browne and Brigette Cazelles (in her introduction to *The Lady as Saint: A Collection of French Hagiographic Romances of the Thirteenth Century*, Philadelphia, University of Pennsylvania Press, 1991), in their respective examinations of vernacular hagiography of the twelfth and thirteenth centuries, show that the story of the menaced virgin was very popular in England and France at this time, and cite specific circumstances for this popularity.

19 *Acts of Paul and Thecla*, in *New Testament Apocrypha*, vol. 2, Wilhelm Schneemelcher (German ed.), R. M. Wilson (English ed.), A. J. B. Higgins and others (trans), Philadelphia, Westminster Press, rev. 1993, pp. 239–246. The story of the attempted rape at the end of Thecla's life is not preserved

in all MSS; it can be found in *The Apocryphal New Testament*, J. K. Elliott (ed.), Oxford University Press, 1993, p. 372.

20 *Acts of St. John*, in *New Testament Apocrypha*, vol. 2, Schneemelcher (ed.), pp. 194–201. Drusiana is later resurrected, and her would-be seducer reformed. She is the subject of a play by Hrotsvit, titled *Callimachus*.

21 R.G. Collingwood, *The Idea of History* (1946), Jan van der Dussen, (ed. with introduction), Oxford, Clarendon Press, rev. ed., 1993, p. 275.

22 *Acts of Paul and Thecla*, p. 278.

23 See George Hicks, *The Comfort Women: Japan's Brutal Regime of Enforced Prostitution in the Second World War*, New York, Norton, 1995. In their introduction to *Holy Women of the Syrian Orient*, Berkeley, University of California Press, 1987, a collection of saints' lives, Sebastian P. Brock and Susan Ashbrook Harvey say: "While historians have generally viewed the extent of ... violence to be a literary exaggeration, our experience of torture in the twentieth century has taught us the extremes that can in fact be administered and suffered." They go on to say: "Still, in these martyr's stories a religious motive is present ... The hagiographer's stylized portrayal of the martyr's interrogation, torture, and death represents these events as containing a greater significance than their physical occurrence would indicate ... literarily the violence is such that it moves all the participants beyond the realm of humanity," p. 17.

24 Eusebius, *Ecclesiastical History* VIII.XIX, p. 337. Eusebius adds: "Many others, unable even to listen to the threat of violation from the heathen rulers, endured every form of tortures, and rackings, and deadly punishment," p. 337. G. E. M. de Ste. Croix's "Aspects of the 'Great' Prosecution," *Harvard Theological Review*, January 1954, vol. XLVII.1, pp. 75–113, is still the definitive introduction to the Great Persecutions. For the historical background to the persecutions, as well as an assessment of Eusebius' works, see Timothy D. Barnes, *Constantine and Eusebius*, Cambridge, MA, Harvard University Press, 1991. Compare the *Acts of the Edessan Martyrs*, in which it is said that "priests and deacons were being tormented with bitter burdens, and Daughters of the Covenant were standing in bitter exposure, and Christians were all in afflictions and anguish," and that "chaste women [were] exposed and Daughters of the Covenant despised, or believers persecuted and women carried away captive." "Martyrdom of Shmona and Guria, Confessors of Edessa," in *Euphemia and the Goth, with the Acts of Martyrdom of the Confessors of Edessa*, F. C. Burkitt (ed.), London, Williams and Norgate, 1913, pp. 90, 109.

25 Eusebius, *Ecclesiastical History* VIII.IX, p. 329.

26 Eusebius, *Ecclesiastical History* VIII.XII, p. 332; also told by Chrysostom in his homily, "Saints Bernice and Prosdoce," *PG* 50.629–640.

27 Eusebius, *Martyrs of Palestine* V, p. 347.

28 Eusebius, *Ecclesiastical History* VI.V, p. 253. Palladius tells the story of Potamiæna in his *Historia Lausiaca* (early fifth century). In the *Historia*, she is a slave whose master could not convince her to yield to his advances. The master accuses her of being a Christian, and, worse, critical of the Emperors and their policy of persecution. He bribes the judge to break her, or, failing that, to kill her so that she might not accuse him before the world. *Acta et temperantia Potamiæna*, *PG* 34.1014. English translation by Robert T. Meyer, *Palladius: The Lausiac History*, Westminster, MD, The Newman Press/London, Longmans, 1965, pp. 34–35.

29 Eusebius, *Martyrs of Palestine* VI, p. 252.

30 As Timothy Barnes suggested in a letter to the author, 3 January 1996.

31 Eusebius, *Ecclesiastical History* VIII.II, p. 324.

32 As quoted in Aline Rousselle, *Porneia: On Desire and the Body in Antiquity* [1983], Felicia Pheasant (trans.), Oxford, Blackwell's, 1988, p. 192. See Brown, *The Body and Society*, pp. 267–269. Brown says: "Basil's extraordinarily frank treatise was written ... as a call to precise and anxious vigilance. By being fully aware of her sexuality and its continued dangers, the virgin would take greater care in fashioning herself as a living icon, whose severely drawn and luminous features, glimpsed in the local church, would instill awe into the Christian community," p. 269.

33 Ambrose, *De Virginibus ad Marcellinam*, in *St. Ambrose: Select Works and Letters*, H. de Romestin (trans.) [1890], Nicene and Post-Nicene Fathers 10, 2nd series, Peabody, MA, Hendrickson, reprinted 1994, p. 377. "Christi virgo prostitui potest, adulterari non potest. Ubicunque virgo Dei

est, templum Dei est: nec lupanaria infamant castitatem, sed castitas etiam loci abolet infamiam," *PL* 16.225. Also in the *Legenda Aurea*, LXII.

34 Ambrose, *De Virginibus ad Marcellinam*, p. 377. "Discite martyrum miracula, sanctæ virgines, dediscite locorum vocabula," *PL* 16.225.

35 Ambrose, *De Virginibus ad Marcellinam*, *PL* 16.201.

36 Augustine, *De Civitate Dei*, George E. McCracken (ed. and trans.), Loeb Classical Library, Cambridge MA: Harvard University Press/London, William Heinemann, 1957, I.XVI. Latin: "An stupris, quae etiam sacrarum forte virginum est passa captivitas, contaminari poterit virtus animi sine voluntatis assessu."

37 Augustine, *De Civitate Dei*, I.XVI. Latin: "Nec tantum hic curamus alienis responsionem reddere, quantum ipsis nostris consolationem."

38 Augustine, *De Civitate Dei*, I.XVIII. Latin: "[Q]uidqiuid alius de corpore vel in corpore fecerit quod sine peccato proprio non valeat evitari praeter culpam esse patiens"; "Si autem animi bonum est, etiam oppresso corpore non amittitur," I.XVI. See Jerome, "Ad Eustochium": "Virginity therefore can be lost even by a thought. Those are the evil virgins, virgins in the flesh, but not in the spirit" ("Perit ergo et mente virginitas. Istae sunt virgines malae, virgines carne, non spiritu," pp. 62–63).

39 Pope Leo, "Epistola XII," in *Correspondence*, Edmund Hunt (trans.), New York, Fathers of the Church 34, 1957, pp. 54–55. Latin: "Illæ autem famulæ Dei quæ integritatem pudoris oppressione barbarica perdiderunt, laudabiliores erunt in humilitate ac verecundia sua si se incontaminatis non audeant comparare virginibus. Quamvis enim omne peccatum ex voluntate nascatur, et potuerit corruptione carnis mens invicta non pollui, minus tamen hoc eis oberit si quod potuerunt animo non amittere, doleant se vel corpore perdidisse," *PL* 54.653.

40 Brundage, *Law*, p. 46.

41 Aldhelm, *De Virginibus*, Callam (trans.), p. 364, Latin: *PL* 16.201.

42 Tacitus, "Tradunt temporis eius auctores, quia triumvirali supplicio adfici virginem inauditum habebatur, a carnifice laqueum iuxta conpressam." *The Annals of Tacitus*, John Jackson (trans.), Loeb Classical Library, Cambridge MA: Harvard University Press, 1937, reprinted 1951, VI.v.9, pp. 150–151.

43 Suetonius, "Immaturae puellae, quia more traditio nefas esset virgines strangulari, vitiatae prius a carnifice, dein strangulatae." *Suetonius: The Lives of the Caesars*, J. C. Rolfe (trans.), Loeb Classical Library, New York, Macmillan/London, William Heinemann, 1924, Book III, *Tiberius*, 61, pp. 380–81

44 D. A. Miller, *The Novel and the Police*, Berkeley and Los Angeles, University of California Press, 1988, pp. 205–207.

45 Tertullian, in *Tertullian: Apologeticum and De Spectaculis [and Minucius Felix]*, T. R. Glover (trans.), Loeb Classical Library, Cambridge MA, Harvard University Press/London, William Heinemann, 1977, pp. 226–227.

46 Prudentius, *Works*, 2 vols, H. J. Thomson (ed. and trans.), Harvard University Press, 1949–53, p. 339, ll. 23–25. Latin: "vita vilis spernitur, at pudor / carus dicatae virginitatis est. / hanc in lupanar trudere publicam," p. 338.

47 Seneca the Elder, *Controversiae*, Michael Winterbottom (ed.), Loeb Classical Library, Cambridge MA, Harvard University Press/London, William Heinemann, 1975, 1.2, pp. 58–59.

48 See Gail Paterson Corrington, "The 'Divine Woman'? Propaganda and the Power of Celibacy in the New Testament Apocrypha: A Reconsideration," *Anglican Theological Review*, 1988, vol. 70, pp. 207–220. Reprinted in Everett Ferguson (ed.) *Studies in Early Christianity: A Collection of Scholarly Essays*, New York, Garland, 1993, pp. 169–182. Also see Tomas Hägg, *The Novel in Antiquity* [Swedish, 1980], Berkeley and Los Angeles, University of California Press, 1983, rev. 1991, 154ff., and "The *Parthenope Romance* Decapitated?" *Symbolae Osloenses*, 1984, vol. LIX, pp. 61–92.

49 The dates of these texts are taken from *Collected Ancient Greek Novels*, B. P. Reardon (trans.), Berkeley and Los Angeles, University of California Press, 1989. In *The Novel in Antiquity*, Hägg notes that the legend of Thecla has much in common with the Greek novel, but he is cautious when it comes to ascribing influence, pp. 160–161. He speculates that "the same readership which provided a market for the Hellenistic novel was now devouring stories about apostles, martyrs, and

saints," p. 161, and argues that "a new historical situation, with new demands, gave rise to a new literary form, which borrowed freely from predecessors and contemporaries," p. 161. Hägg argues that chronology, the actual production and dissemination of the Greek novel as represented by Chariton and Xenophon, seems to taper off in the second century. These texts were followed by the so called Sophistic novels (by Tatius, Longus, and Heliodorus); thus Hägg sees a break between the earlier Greek novel, which may have had an impact on the Apocryphal Acts, while the Sophistic novel did not. Also see Kate Cooper, *The Virgin and the Bride: Idealized Womanhood in Late Antiquity*, Harvard University Press, 1996, who describes the Apocryphal Acts as a "penumbral manifestation of the romance phenomenon," p. 44, and notes the "uncanny" resemblance between Leukippe and the Christian heroine, p. 30; and see Reardon, Introduction, *Collected Ancient Greek Novels*, pp. 3–9. Simon Goldhill's *Foucault's Virginity: Ancient Erotic Fiction and the History of Sexuality*, Cambridge, Cambridge University Press, 1995, is a particularly witty and insightful reading of the Greek novel.

50 Achilles Tatius, *Leucippe and Cleitophon*, John J. Winkler (trans.), in *Collected Ancient Greek Novels*, p. 259.

51 See Ian Donaldson, *The Rapes of Lucretia: A Myth and its Transformations*, Oxford, Clarendon Press, 1982.

52 Ortner, "The Virgin," p. 23.

53 Robertson Davies, *Fifth Business*, Harmondsworth, England, Penguin Books, 1993, p. 136.

54 See, for example, Schulenberg, "Heroics of Virginity," especially p. 46, as well as her essay, "Saints' Lives as a Source for the History of Women, 500–1100," in Joel T. Rosenthal (ed.) *Medieval Women and the Sources of Medieval History*, Athens, University of Georgia Press, 1990, pp. 285–320, and Evelyne Patlagean, "Ancient Byzantine Hagiography and Social History," in Stephen Wilson (ed.) *Saints and Their Cults: Studies in Religion, Sociology, Folklore and History*, Cambridge University Press, 1983, pp. 101–121.

55 I owe this citation and translation to Donald Weinstein and Rudolph M. Bell, *Saints and Society: The Two Worlds of Western Christendom, 1000–1700*, Chicago, University of Chicago Press, 1982, pp. 88–89. Latin: "Quid tamen ageret? Quo se verteret? Si fugere vellet, non erat fugiendi locus: si resistere, fortior erat vir: si clamare, timebat notam infamiæ, quæ tam illi, quam sibi ad perpetuam confusionem cedere posset, si fama rei prodiret in publicum," *Acta Sanctorum*, 13 January, p. 867.

56 *Gemma Ecclesiastica*, in *Giraldi Cambrensis opera: Gemma Ecclesiastica*, J. S. Brewer (ed), Rerum Britannicarum MediÆvi Scriptores, Rolls Series 21, London [1861–91], Kraus reprinted 1964, vol. II, Book I, Caput XXXIV, pp. 106–09. English translation by John J. Hagen, *The Jewel of the Church*, Leiden, The Netherlands, Brill, 1979, pp. 82–84.

57 See *The Life of Christina of Markyate: A Twelfth-Century Recluse*, C. H. Talbot (ed.), Oxford, Clarendon, 1959, reprinted 1987.

58 *De. S. Liberata Alias Wilgeforte Virgine et Martyre*, Acta Sanctorum, 5 July: 50–70 (20 July). Gregory the Great tells a story about a young widow named Galla who did not want to remarry, but who had, Gregory says, "a very passionate nature." Doctors warned her that she would grow a beard if she did not marry again – presumably, if she did not engage in intercourse. She withdrew into a convent, undismayed by her beard, "since her body was not the object of her heavenly spouse's love." *Dialogues*, Odo John Zimmerman (ed.), New York, Fathers of the Church 39, 1959, p. 206.

59 Schulenberg, "Heroics of Virginity," p. 55. In her fine and widely-influential essay, Schulenburg attributes this mutilation to "the rather effective conditioning of ... ecclesiastical doctrines [on virginity] along with the Germanic values of the age," p. 29.

60 *An Alphabet of Tales*, M. M. Banks (ed.), London, E.E.T.S. O.S. 126, 127, 1904, reprinted one vol., 1973, CXXXVI, "Castitatis amore eciam membra corporis contempnuntur," p. 95.

61 H. Delehaye, *The Legends of the Saints* [1905, rev. 1927, reprinted 1955], Donald Attwater (trans.), New York, Fordham University Press, 1962, p. 31.

62 Graham Pechey, "Bakhtin, Marxism and Post-Structuralism," in Francis Barker, Peter Hulme, Margaret Iversen, and Diana Loxley (ed.) *Literature, Politics, and Theory*, London and New York, Methuen, 1986, p. 123.

63 Ambrose, *De Virginibus ad Marcellinam*, de Romestin, p. 364. Latin: "Quanto terrore egit carnifex ut timeretur, quantis blanditiis ut suaderet! quantorum vota ut sibi ad nuptias perveniret! ... virgo permansit, et martyrium obtinuit," *PL* 16.201–202.

64 A.J. Denomy, *The Old French Lives of Saint Agnes and Other Vernacular Versions of the Middle Ages*, Cambridge, Harvard University Press, 1938, p. 3. See also Anne-Marie Palmer, *Prudentius on the Martyrs*, Oxford, Clarendon, 1989, pp. 250–253. I am particularly indebted to Denomy's discussion of the origin of the legend of St. Agnes and of the various problems concerning dates and influences, pp. 3–32.

65 See Denomy, *Lives of Saint Agnes*, p. 154.

66 Jody Enders, "Medieval Snuff Drama," *Exemplaria*, Spring 1998, vol. X.1, 171–206, p. 179.

67 Haraway, "A Cyborg Manifesto," p. 164.

68 *The Golden Legend*, 2 vols, William Granger Ryan (trans.), Princeton, NJ, Princeton University Press, 1993, p. I.102. Henceforth, page numbers will appear in the body of the text. The Latin will be given in the notes, taken from *Legenda Aurea* 3rd ed., T. Graesse (ed.) [1890], Osnabrück, Zeller, photo rep. 1965. "[D]iscede a me fomes peccati, nutrimentum facinoris, pabulum mortis, quia jam ab alio amatore praeventa sum," pp. 113–114. Voragine says the young man fell in love with Agnes, promising her great riches if she would marry him ("si consensum ejus conjugio non negaret," p. 113.

69 "[U]t melius capillis quam vestibus tegretur," p. 115. See Eusebius, *Martyrs of Palestine* IX, for the story of the virgin Ennathas who is stripped and exhibited in the city of Caesarea. Philip Schaff and Henry Wace (trans.), and found between Book VIII and IX of the *Ecclesiastical History*, Nicene and Post-Nicene Fathers 1, 2nd ser., [1890], Peabody MA, Hendrickson, reprinted 1994, pp. 350–351. See also *Holy Women of the Syrian Orient*, trans. with an introduction by Sebastian P. Brock and Susan Ashbrook Harvey, Berkeley and London, University of California Press, 1987, the legends of Anahid, p. 94; Elizabeth, p. 106; Mahya, p. 110; and Febronia, p. 165.

70 *Legenda Aurea*, Graesse (trans.), "[E]os prius ad ipsam invitavit," p. 115.

71 *Legenda Aurea*, Graesse (trans.), "[A]d eam furens intrans cum eam vellet contingere," p. 115.

72 *Legenda Aurea*, Graesse (trans.), "[S]ed illa viriliter reluctante manum ejus virtus divina contraxit. Tunc putans se incantatum praepositum domus suae ad ipsam direxit, ut multa promitteret, si eam faceret consentire. Sed ille carcerem clausum nec clavibus aperire potuit nec securibus frangere, donec a daemone arreptus clamans et se ipsum dilanians vix evasit," p. 621.

73 *Legenda Aurea*, Graesse (trans.), "[Q]ui tamdiu eam illuderent, donec fatigata deficeret," p. 621.

74 *Legenda Aurea*, Graesse (trans.), "[I]nter quatuor magnos lapides sicut oliva constringeretur," p. 621. Elizabeth Petroff, in "Eloquence and Heroic Virginity in Hrotsvit's Verse Legends," argues that Hrotsvit's heroic virgins "must be killed with heroic weapons, the weapons of personal combat." In Katharina M. Wilson (ed.) *Hrotsvit of Gandersheim: Rara Avis in Saxonia?*, Ann Arbor, University of Michigan/MARC, 1987, p. 236. Susan Ashbrook Harvey makes the point that "the deed must be done by human hands"; that is, not by some force of nature, such as fire or wild beasts. "Violence, Gender, and God: Male and Female Martyrs in the Early Church," paper presented at Amherst College, December, 1989.

75 For the legends of Candida and Febronia, see Brock and Harvey, pp. 181 and 168.

76 *Legenda Aurea*, Graesse (trans.), "[B]eatam Agatham comprehendere nitebatur, ut quia erat ignobilis, comprehendendo nobilem timeretur, quia libidinosus, ejus pulchritudine frueretur, quia avarus, ejus divitias raperet, quia ydololatra, Diis eam faceret immolare, fecitque eam ad se adduci," p. 170.

77 *Legenda Aurea*, Graesse (trans.), "[F]acilius possunt saxa molliri et ferrum in plumbi mollitiem converti, quam ab intentione christiana mens istius puellae converti seu revocari" p. 170.

78 *Legenda Aurea*, Graesse (trans.), "[I]nvitate ad eam omnem populum et tamdiu illudatur, donec mortua nuntietur," p. 31.

79 *Legenda Aurea*, Graesse (trans.), "Videntes autem amici Paschasii eum angustiari, in gutture ejus gladium immerserunt," p. 32.

80 Ann Hanson and David Armstrong, "The Virgin's Voice and Neck: Aeschylus, *Agamemnon* 245 and Other Texts," *Bulletin of the Institute of Classical Studies*, 1986, vol. 33, pp. 97–100. Hanson and Armstrong read allusions to an enlarged neck in Greek literary texts as a reference to loss of virginity. The neck in these texts functions as a homology to the neck of the uterus, which, according to Greek medical lore, widens for the first time after first intercourse. And, since it was thought that one acquired a deeper voice when the neck was made wider, a change in voice was considered an index of chastity.

81 Eva Cantarella, "Dangling Virgins: Myth, Ritual and the Place of Women in Ancient Greece," *Poetics Today*, 1985, vol. 6.1–2, p. 92. I quote Cantarella's paraphrase of Pacatus, p. 95.

82 Patricia Klindienst Joplin, "The Voice of the Shuttle is Ours," *Stanford Literature Review*, 1984, vol. 1, p. 38.

83 I echo Luce Irigaray here, who, in discussing another topic altogether – the rich possibilities and circularities of lesbianism – asks, "*But what if the 'goods' refused to go to market at all?*" "When the Goods Get Together" [1977], Claudia Reeder (trans.), reprinted in Elaine Marks and Isabelle de Courtivron (ed.) *New French Feminisms*, New York, Schocken Books, 1981, p. 110.

84 Simone de Beauvoir, *The Second Sex* [1952], H. M. Parshley (trans. and ed.), New York, Random House/Vintage Books, 1989, p. 131.

85 *De Venerabili Oda, Acta Sanctorum*, 2 April: 770–778 (April 20), 776. I owe this citation to Schulenberg, "Heroics of Virginity," pp. 48–49.

86 Thomas Aquinas, *Summa Theologiæ*, Thomas Gilby (ed. and trans.), Blackfriars, in conjunction with New York, McGraw Hill/London, Eyre and Spottiswoode, 1968, 2a2æ.124, 4, pp. 50–51.

87 Thomas Aquinas, *Summa Theologiæ* 2a2æ.124,4, p. 51. Latin: "[P]ro integritate carnis servanda aliquæ mulieres legunter laudabiliter vitam suam contempsisse ... Sed quandoque ipsa integritas carnis aufertur, vel auferri intentatur, pro confessione fidei christianæ ... Ergo videtur quod martyrium magis debeat dici si aliqua mulier pro fide Christi integritatem carnis perdat, quam si etiam vitam perderet corporalem," p. 50.

88 Thomas Aquinas, *Summa Theologiæ* 2a2æ.124, 4, p. 53. Latin: "Et ideo ad perfectam rationem martyrii requiritur quod aliquis mortem sustineat propter Christum," p. 52.

89 Thomas Aquinas, *Summa Theologiæ* 2a2æ.124, 4, pp. 52–53.

90 R. Howard Bloch, *Medieval Misogyny and the Invention of Western Romantic Love*, Chicago, University of Chicago Press, 1991, p. 108.

91 Allon White, "Bakhtin, Sociolinguistics and Deconstruction," in Frank Gloversmith (ed.) *The Theory of Reading*, New York, Barnes and Noble/Sussex, England, Harvester Press, 1984, 123–46, p. 130.

92 Mary Douglas, *Purity and Danger* [1966], London and New York, Routledge, 1991, p. 115.

93 Thomas More scoffs at the veneration of Wilgefortis. She is honored with oats, he says, "bycause she shold prouyde an horse for an euyll housbonde to ryde to the deuyll vpon." He continues, "women ... call her saynt Vncumber bycause they reken that for a pecke of otys she wyll not fayle to vncumber theym of theyr housbondys." In Thomas M. C. Lawler, Germain Marc'Hadour, and Richard C. Marius (eds) *A Dialogue Concerning Heresies*, in *The Complete Works of St. Thomas More*, vol. 6, part I, New Haven and London, Yale University Press, 1981, p. 227. I owe this citation to David Hugh Farmer, *The Oxford Dictionary of Saints*, 2nd ed., 1987, reprinted 1991, p. 437.

94 *Legenda Aurea*, Graesse (trans.), 620, *The Golden Legend*, Ryan (trans.), II. 181.

95 *Legenda Aurea*, Graesse (trans.),170; *The Golden Legend*, Ryan (trans.), I. 154.

96 On the other hand, when Aldhelm says that one Melanthia "deceitfully tried to force upon ... Eugenia the false debauchery of the bawdy-house and the wickedness of the polluted brothel," he plays upon the etymology of her name, which is Greek for "black": "nominis præsagio traducta," *De virginitate* XLIV, Lapidge and Herren (trans.), p. 111; *PL* 89.145. Dorothea is another virgin, Aldhelm tells us, who was given over to women to be corrupted ("tradidit depravandam.") However, she convinces the two apostate women so "recently shipwrecked in their faith" to repent and renew their faith, *De virginitate* XLVII, Lapidge and Herren (trans.), p. 114; *PL* 89.147.

97 Mikhail Bakhtin, "Discourse in the Novel," in *The Dialogic Imagination*, Caryl Emerson and Michael Holquist (trans.) Michael Holquist (ed.), Austin, University of Texas Press, 1981, p. 343. The monologic, Bakhtin says, permits no "zone of contact," p. 345.

98 See, for example, the story of Febronia in *Holy Women of the Syrian Orient* (Brock and Harvey), pp. 150–176. In this Syriac legend (late sixth- early seventh-century, translated from a MS of the ninth century), Febronia is told by her older female companions that the tyrants "will grab you, seeing that you are young and beautiful, and they will upset you with their advances and words of seducement" p. 159. But *they* do much worse. She is stripped, whipped with rods, her intestines burned with fire, her torso raked with iron nails, her teeth pulled out, her breasts cut off (in spite of the crowd's pleading for mercy), and her chest burned with fire. Her right foot and her hands are cut off, and finally she is decapitated. In a fifth-century Persian legend in the Brock and Harvey

collection, one Anahid has her breasts torn off by having string tied around them and pulled together, p. 95.

99 See Joplin, "Voice," p. 42.

100 Elizabeth A. Castelli, "Visions and Voyeurism: Holy Women and the Politics of Sight in Early Christianity," in Christopher Ocker (ed.) *Protocol of the Colloquy of the Center for Hermeneutical Studies*, December 1992, New Series 2, pp. 1–27, p. 8.

101 *Legenda Aurea*, Graesse (trans.), "[I]llum amo, qui longe te nobilior est ... cujus amor castitas est, tactus sanctitas, unio virginitas ... Jam amplexibus ejus castis adstricta sum; jam corpus ejus corpori meo sociatum est," p. 114.

102 Clifford Geertz, "Deep Play: Notes on the Balinese Cockfight," in *The Interpretation of Cultures*, New York, Basic Books, 1973, p. 448.

103 Adrienne Auslander Munich, "What Lily Knew: Virginity in the 1890s," in Lloyd Davis (ed.) *Virginal Sexuality and Textuality in Victorian Literature*, Albany, University of New York Press, 1993, p. 145.

Chapter 3 "Love's traces": the lady and the test in vernacular romance

1 See Leonard Swidler, *Women in Judaism: The Status of Women in Formative Judaism*, Metuchen, NJ, Scarecrow Press, 1976, pp. 151–54, for a discussion of the bitter waters; Robert Bartlett also mentions this ordeal in *Trial by Fire and Water: The Medieval Judicial Ordeal*, Oxford, Clarendon, 1986, pp. 84–85. The motif of the bitter waters is found in *The Trial of Mary and Joseph*, a play in the cycle known as the *N-Town Play* (c. 1460–80). It is the Virgin Mary and Joseph, no less, who are accused of unchastity before the magistrate and the *Episcopus*. The Bishop decrees that Joseph and Mary must drink a potion – "þe drynge of vengeawns" – and ritually circle the altar. If the accused "be gylty, sum maculacion / Pleyn in his face xal shewe it owth." *The Trial of Mary and Joseph*, in *The N-Town Play: Cotton MS Vespasian D.8*, Stephen Spector (ed.), E.E.T.S. S.S. 11, Oxford, Oxford University Press, 1991, ll. 233, 240–241.

2 Herodotus, *Histories*, Aubrey de Sélincourt (trans.) [1954], Penguin, reprinted 1984, IV.180, p. 331.

3 Valerius Maximus, *Facta et dicta memorabilia*, Venice, 1471, VIII.1.5.

4 Aelian, *De natura animalium*, A. F. Scholfield (trans.), Loeb Classical Library, Cambridge, MA, Harvard University Press/London, William Heinemann, 1958, XI.16.

5 Achilles Tatius' *Leucippe and Clitophon*, John J. Winkler (trans.), pp. 275–81; Heliodorus' *An Ethiopian Story*, J. R. Morgan (trans.), pp. 563–564. In *Collected Ancient Greek Novels*, B. P. Reardon (ed.), Berkeley and Los Angeles, University of California Press, 1989.

6 As recounted in John Bowers' "Ordeals, Privacy, and the *Lais* of Marie de France," *Journal of Medieval and Renaissance Studies*, Winter 1994, vol. 24.1, p. 4. Bowers notes that this story was most likely invented in the twelfth century.

7 See Bartlett, *Trial*, pp. 16–18, for the story of Cunegunda, along with other stories of calumniated Queens who choose the ordeal to prove their chastity or marital fidelity. John Baldwin, in "the Crisis of the Ordeal: Literature, Law, and Religion around 1200," *Journal of Medieval and Renaissance Studies*, Fall 1994, vol. 24.3, pp. 327–353, and Bowers in "Ordeals" also discuss the story of Cunegunda. These two excellent essays furnish not only valuable readings of the ordeal, but also survey and summarize the secondary literature.

8 This anecdote is told by Baldwin, "Crisis," pp. 343–344. Jacques de Vitry tells a story (unusual because it is about a man rather than about a woman) about a monk who could pick up a hot iron while he was a virgin, but was unable to do so after his seduction – a seduction which was, apparently, the result of his own innocence when it came to *eros*. *The Exempla or Illustrative Stories from the Sermones Vulgares of Jacques de Vitry*, Thomas Frederick Crane (ed.) [1890], Millwood, New York, Kraus reprinted, 1967, CCXLVII, pp. 103–104.

9 See, for example, E. Jane Burns, *Bodytalk: When Women Speak in Old French Literature*, Philadelphia, University of Pennsylvania Press, 1993, Chapter 5, "Why Beauty Laughs: Iseut's Enormous Thighs."

10 See R. Howard Bloch, *Medieval French Literature and Law*, Berkeley and Los Angeles, University of California Press, 1977, in which he links the suppression of trial by combat to the formation of the state, p. 119. Bloch also notes the "thematic and stylistic commingling" of the legal and literary representation of the ordeal, observing that, "in perusing the customal, the reader frequently has the impression of a distinctly literary legal document; and in studying the more conventional poetic forms, he becomes aware of the documentary nature of the literary text," pp. 4, 5.

11 John F. Benton's "Clio and Venus: An Historical View of Medieval Love," in F. X. Newman (ed.) *The Meaning of Courtly Love* [1968], Albany, NY, State University of New York Press, 1973, 19–42, is still useful for a general discussion of medieval ideas about marriage and attitudes toward adultery. See p. 24 for a discussion of the penalties for premarital sex and adultery – erring daughters and adulterous wives, that is. As Benton notes, the fact that penalties such as burning and hanging existed did not mean that men availed themselves of them.

12 Allen Frantzen, "Between the Lines: Queer Theory, the History of Homosexuality, and Anglo-Saxon Penitentials," *Journal of Medieval and Early Modern Studies*, Spring 1996, vol. 26.2, p. 272.

13 Bowers, "Ordeals," p. 3. In discussing Marie de France's *Chaitivel* and the ambiguous outcome of the tournament of the four equally matched knights, Bowers says: "Because its judicial goals in this case were not made explicit, the function of the viewing public as an 'interpretive community' was eliminated, with the result that the act of interpretation itself was permanently deferred," p. 15.

14 Robert Stoller, *Observing the Erotic Imagination*, New Haven, CT, Yale University Press, 1985, p. 155.

15 Tertullian, *De virginibus velandis* [*On the Veiling of Virgins*], Sydney Thelwall (trans.) [1885], Ante-Nicene Fathers 4, reprinted Peabody, MA, Hendrickson, 1994, XI, p. 34. I have removed the translator's italics in this passage. *PL* 2.953.

16 Hayden White, "The Value of Narrativity in the Representation of Reality," in *The Content of the Form*, Baltimore and London, Johns Hopkins University Press, 1987, pp. 20–21.

17 R. Howard Bloch, *Medieval Misogyny and the Invention of Western Romantic Love*, University of Chicago Press, 1991, p. 114. "The abstraction virginity implies is destroyed by its articulation … there is no way of talking about virginity that does not entail its loss," p. 109.

18 Bartlett, *Trial*, pp. 4–12. Also see Henry C. Lea, *Superstition and Force: Essays on the Wager of Law, the Wager of Battle, the Ordeal, and Torture*, 2nd. ed. [rev. 1870], Westport, CT, Greenwood Press, reprinted 1968, pp. 28–31, 90–93, 223. See Margaret H. Kerr, Richard D. Forsyth, and Michael J. Plyley, "Cold Water and Hot Iron: Trial by Ordeal in England," *The Journal of Interdisciplinary History*, Spring 1992, vol. XXII.4, pp. 573–595.

19 Paul Hyams, "Trial by Ordeal: The Key to Proof in the Early Common Law," in Morris S. Arnold et al. (ed.) *On the Laws and Customs of England: Essays in Honor of Samuel E. Thorne*, Chapel Hill, University of North Carolina Press, 1981, p. 98.

20 Hyams, "Trial," p. 95; cf. p. 97. See also Peter Brown, "Society and the Supernatural: A Medieval Change," *Daedalus*, 1975, vol. 104, pp. 133–51, reprinted in *Society and the Holy in Late Antiquity*, Berkeley and Los Angeles, University of California Press, 1982, pp. 302–332. Brown argues that the ordeal not only functions as an "instrument of consensus," but as "a theatrical device by which to contain disruptive conflict," p. 137.

21 Bartlett, *Trial*, pp. 36ff.

22 Bartlett, *Trial*, p. 77; see pp. 39–40, 70ff. See Brown, "Supernatural," p. 139. "[T]he supernatural," says Brown, "becomes the depository of the objectified values of the group," p. 140.

23 Brown, "Supernatural," p. 139.

24 Bartlett, *Trial*, pp. 19–20.

25 Baldwin, "Crisis," p. 329.

26 Achilles Tatius, *Leucippe and Cleitophon*, John J. Winkler (trans.), in *Collected Ancient Greek Novels*, B. P. Reardon (ed.), Berkeley and Los Angeles, University of California Press, 1989, p. 279.

27 *Leucippe and Cleitophon*, Winkler (trans.), p. 279.

28 The motif of the equivocal oath in the Tristan legend is first found in Béroul's *Le Roman de Tristan* (c. 1170), but not in Malory's *Morte Darthur*, where the episode of the drinking horn has replaced the oath. See Ernest C. York, "Isolt's Ordeal: English Legal Customs in the Medieval Tristan Legend," *Studies in Philology*, January 1971, vol. 68.1, pp. 1–9, in which he argues that the ordeal in some of

these texts reflect actual Anglo-Saxon or English practice. Also see Elaine Newstead, "The Equivocal Oath in the Tristan Legend" for a comparison of the treatment of the ordeal by Béroul and Thomas, and possible sources and analogues, in *Mélanges offerts á Rita Lejeune* (introduction by Fred Duthier), Gembloux, Duculot, 1969, 2: 1077–1085. See Bartlett, *Trials*, pp. 18–19. "[H]ow natural it was," says Bartlett, "for medieval story-tellers to move their plot from accusations of adultery to the drama of the ordeal. This charge and this form of proof belonged together," p. 19.

29 Gottfried von Strassburg, *Tristan*, A. T. Hatto (trans.) [1960] Penguin Books, 1984, p. 240. German text edited by Peter Ganz, *Gottfried von Strassburg's Tristan*, Wiesbaden, F. A. Brockhaus, 1978, l. 15120.

30 Hatto translates *minnen spor* as "Love's guilty traces," p. 242; Ganz (ed.), l. 15259.

31 *Tristan*, Hatto (trans.), p. 242; Ganz (ed.), "und vant dehéinéz dervor. / Hie mite was ime diu wârheit / beidlu geheizen unde verseit," ll. 15260–62.

32 See Baldwin, "Crisis," p. 335.

33 *Tristan*, Hatto (trans.), p. 247; Ganz (ed.), "gegeben durch gotes hulde, / daz got ir wâren schulde / an ir iht gedæhte," ll.15651–53.

34 *Tristan*, Hatto (trans.), p. 246; Ganz (ed.), "So twanc si daz verholne leit, / dass ir unwarheit / solte warbaeren," ll.15543–45; "einen list ir herzen vür geleit / vir verre uf gotes höfscheit," ll.15555–56.

35 *Tristan*, Hatto (trans.), pp. 247–248; Ganz (ed.), "daz mînes lîbes nie kein man / deheine künde nie gewan / nch mir ze keinen zîten / weder z' árme noch ze sîten / ân' iuch nie lebende man gelac / wan der, vür den ich niht enmac / gebieten eit noch lougen, / den ir mit iuwern ougen / mir sâhet an dem arme, / der wállære der árme," ll. 15711–20.

36 *Tristan*, Hatto (trans.), p. 248; Ganz (ed.), "[D]a wart woll goffenbæret / und al der werlt bewæret, / daz der vil tugenhafte Krist / wintschaffen alse ein ermel ist: / er füeget unde suochet an, / dâ man'z an in gesuochen kan, / alsô gefüege unde alse wol / als er von allem rehte sol. / er'st allen hérzén bereit, / ze durnáhte und ze trügeheit. / ist ez ernest, ist es spil, / er ist ie, swie sô man wil," ll.15737–48.

37 For a useful summary of critical interpretations through 1975, see Ralph J. Hexter, *Equivocal Oaths and Ordeals in Medieval Literature*, Cambridge, MA, Harvard University Press, 1975, pp. 20–26.

38 *The Continuations of the Old French* Perceval *of Chrétien de Troyes* 2 vols, William Roach (ed.), Philadelphia, University of Pennsylvania Press, 1949, I. 234.

39 Jean Renart, *The Romance of the Rose or Guillaume de Dole*, Patricia Terry and Nancy Vine Durling (trans), Philadelphia, University of Pennsylvania Press, 1993, p. 64. The French: "'Ja mes nuls hom qui parler puisse / ne verra si fete merveille / come de la rose vermelle / desor la cuisse blanche et tendre," ll. 3362–65. *Le Roman de la Rose ou de Guillaume de Dole*, Félix Lecoy (ed.), Paris, Champion, 1962.

40 *Guillaume de Dole*, Terry and Durling (trans.), p. 67; Lecoy (ed.), "qu'il a eü son pucelage," l. 3586.

41 *Guillaume de Dole*, Terry and Durling (trans.), p. 83; Lecoy (ed.), "'Ja mes Dex ne me doint cest sueil / passer, se onques mes la vi!,'" ll. 4806–07.

42 *Guillaume de Dole*, Terry and Durling (trans.), p. 86; Lecoy (ed.), "Cë ont bien veü li baron / que li juïses l'en sauva, / et moi et lui, et qu'il ne m'a / despucelee ne honie," ll. 5084–87.

43 Laurence de Looze, "The Gender of Fiction: Womanly Poetics in Jean Renart's *Guillaume de Dole*," *The French Review*, March 1991, vol. 64.4, p. 597.

44 Norris J. Lacy, "'Amer par oïr dire': *Guillaume de Dole* and the Drama of Language," *The French Review*, May 1981, vol. 54.6, pp. 779–87.

45 de Looze, "Gender," p. 604.

46 Helen Solterer, "At the Bottom of Mirage, a Woman's Body: *le Roman de la Rose* of Jean Renart," in Linda Lomperis and Sarah Stanbury (eds) *Feminist Approaches to the Body in Medieval Literature*, Philadelphia, PA, University of Pennsylvania Press, 1993, p. 224. As Solterer notes, the rose has many names, depending upon who speaks it: the mother refers to it as *l'afaire* (3360); the senechal as *mehaig* ("wound" 3552), and, when about to undergo his ordeal, makes a legalism out of it: *veraie ensaigne* ("true evidence" 3589). Says Solterer: "Introducing multiple terms for the rose, this

narrative challenges the audience to interrogate the status of the figure of the rose. That is, it focuses our attention specifically on the process of figuration," p. 225.

47 Solterer, "Mirage," p. 228. She adds: "That the male body is forced to discredit lies about the female body reveals the ultimate irony of this narrative," p. 229.

48 Jean Baudrillard distinguishes between the terms *fetish* and *fetishist metaphor*, arguing that it is mistaken to theorize, as he accuses Marx of having done, that a fetish resides in an object – a signifier. By locating power in an object, Marx perpetuates "magical thinking," a belief that objects are capable of having power. Thus, according to Baudrillard, the Marxist idea of "fetish commodity" reproduces a system it was designed to critique. (However, it must be said that Marx privileges process over product in his conception of the dialectic.) *For a Critique of the Political Economy of the Sign*, Charles Levin (trans.), St. Louis, Telos Press, 1981, p. 89.

49 Michel Foucault, "Nietzsche, Genealogy, History" [1971], in *Language, Counter-Memory, Practice: Selected Essays and Interviews*, Donald F. Bouchard (ed.), Ithaca, Cornell University Press, 1977, p. 153.

50 Georges Duby, *The Knight, The Lady and the Priest: The Making of Modern Marriage in Medieval France* [1981], Barbara Bray (trans.), New York, Pantheon Books, 1983, pp. 18–19. Also: "the function of marriage was to ensure that the manly virtue of valor was passed on in honor from one generation to the next, that blood was propagated in such a way that it did not, as they said then, degenerate," p. 37.

51 Robert Biket, *Lai du Cor*, Fredrik Wulff (ed.), Paris, 1888, ll. 193–194. Henceforth, line numbers will be given in the body of the text.

52 *The Works of Sir Thomas Malory* 3rd. ed., Eugène Vinaver (ed.), P. J. C. Field (rev.), Oxford, Clarendon, 1990, p. 430. Hereafter, all quotations will be cited in the body of the text by page number.

53 We find a similar episode in *The French Prose Romance of Tristan* (1230). Available in P. J. C. Field's partial text of one MS of this romance (MS Bibliotheque Nationale fr.103, ff.27r, col.1–91r) in *Romance and Chronicle*, Bloomington, Indiana University Press, 1971, pp. 168–73. Malory adds: "So there were many knyghtes made their avowe that and ever they mette wyth Morgan le Fay that they wolde shew her shorte curtsey," p. 430.

54 Italian: *La Tavola Ritonda*, 2 vols, F. L. Polidori (ed.), Bologna, 1864–65, pp. 158–159; English: *Tristan and the Round Table*, Ann Shaver (trans.), Binghamton, New York, Medieval and Renaissance Texts & Studies, 1983, p. 103. All quotations taken from these two editions.

55 *La Tavola Ritonda*, "Ma credo che al paese ciò addivenisse per cagione che le dame vi sono molte grandi bevitrici, bugiarde e ghiotte, e bene pacchianti di roba, più che altre dame lussuriose: gli uomini begli, e vili di loro persone, e poco atanti nelle armi e poco valorosi; ma molto erano arroganti, avarissimi," p. 159.

56 *La Tavola Ritonda*, "Monsignore, a me non pare ragione che le nostre dame siano arse per gli corni incantati, fatti e formati per distruggere alcuna dama a grande torto e a falsitade.... Ma la reina Isotta, bene ch'ella non sia in colpa, da poi che voi volete o vi diletta, sia arsa e divampata," p. 159.

57 Lewis Jillings, *Diu Crône of Heinrich von dem Türlin: The Attempted Emancipation of Secular Narrative*, Göppingen, Kümmerle Verlag, 1980, p. 12.

58 The glove test, according to Heinrich/the narrator, will identify "any man or woman whose heart has been corrupted by inconstancy and whose life has been dishonored by the mark of shame" (259). As Jillings notes, the glove test is both a repeat and an extension of the tankard test; moreover, the choice of object and its effects (turning invisible all but the transgressing parts of the body) is, says Jillings, original with Heinrich, pp. 23–26.

59 Jillings, *Secular Narrative*, says the cup "disclose[s] the conduct of the specific individual ... [and] permits a comprehensive scrutiny of the morals of each and every literary model of courtly chivalry, male and female alike," p. 22. See also p. 22 and p. 33, n. 11. For a similar but more detailed view, see Ann G. Martin, *Shame and Disgrace in King Arthur's Court: A Study in the Meaning of Ignominy in German Arthurian Literature*, Göppingen, Kümmerle Verlag, 1984.

60 *The Crown: A Tale of Sir Gawein and King Arthur's Court*, J. W. Thomas (trans.), Lincoln, University of Nebraska Press, 1989, p. 13. Hereafter, all page numbers will appear in the body of the text. For

the German text, see *Diu Crône von Heinrich von dem Türlin*, G. H. F. Scholl (ed.), Stuttgart, 1852. The tankard episode begins at l. 917 and runs to l. 3131.

61 Jacques Lacan, "The Function and Field of Speech and Language in Psychoanalysis" [1953], in *Écrits*, Alan Sheridan (trans.), New York and London, Norton, 1977, p. 86.

62 As Annette Kuhn explains: "According to the Lacanian model, the human subject is not only a speaking subject with an Unconscious, but also a masculine or feminine subject in relation to the Oedipus complex. Sexual difference is seen as structured by the subject's relation to the phallus, the signifier which stands in for the play of absence and presence that constitutes language. Because the oedipal moment inaugurates sexual difference in relation to the phallus as signifier, men and women enter into language differently, and Lacan's argument is that the female entry into language is organized by lack, or negativity." "Introduction to Hélène Cixous's 'Castration or Decapitation?'" *Signs*, Autumn 1981, vol. 7.1, p. 37.

63 As Jillings observes in his discussion of the glove test in *Diu Crône*, "Keii offers an unsympathetic interpretation of each lady's conduct … an interpretation which has, lacking refutation, the effect of appearing to be true since each lady is indeed found wanting," *Secular Narrative*, p. 28.

64 See Jillings, *Secular Narrative*, pp. 27–30 and 34, n. 17.

65 *Wigalois*, J. W. Thomas (trans.), Lincoln and London, University of Nebraska P, 1977, p. 118.

66 Susann Samples discusses how Gasozein is re-integrated into society in "The Other? A Critical Study of the Rapist-Knight Gasozein in Heinrich von dem Turlin's *Diu Crône*," paper delivered at the XVIIIth International Congress of the Arthurian Society, 1996.

67 Jacques Lacan, "Agency of the Letter in the Unconscious or Reason Since Freud" [1957], in *Écrits*, Alan Sheridan (trans.), New York and London, Norton, 1977, p. 150.

68 M. M. Bakhtin, *Discourse in the Novel*, in *The Dialogic Imagination*, Caryl Emerson and Michael Holquist (trans), Michael Holquist (ed.), Austin, University of Texas Press, 1981, pp. 304–305.

69 Carolyn Dinshaw, "A Kiss is Just a Kiss: Heterosexuality and its Consolations in *Sir Gawain and the Green Knight*," *Diacritics*, Summer-Fall 1994, vol. 24.2–3, p. 222.

70 Eve Kosofsky Sedgwick, *Between Men: English Literature and Male Homosocial Desire*, New York, Columbia University Press, 1985, p. 1.

71 Georges Duby, *William Marshal: The Flower of Chivalry* [1984], Richard Howard (trans.), New York, Pantheon Books, 1985, p. 8.

72 As Duby translates the *Histoire* in *William Marshal*, p.8. Maréchal was finally persuaded to leave Anselm one hundred and forty pounds per annum to outfit him.

73 Duby, *William Marshal*, p. 85; and see Dinshaw, p. 222.

74 Georges Duby, *The Chivalrous Society*, Cynthia Postan (trans.), Berkeley, University of California Press, 1977, p. 119.

75 See Laurie Finke, "The Rhetoric of Desire in the Courtly Lyric," in *Feminist Theory, Women's Writing*, Ithaca, Cornell University Press, 1992, pp. 29–74.

76 Duby, *Society*, p. 122.

77 Duby, *Marshal*, p. 128.

78 *L'histoire de Guillaume le Maréchal*, 3 vols, Paul Meyer (ed.), Paris, Société de l'histoire de France, 1891–1901, II.13533–44. See Duby's translation for lines 13533–36: "I beg you all to care for her kindly and by nature, since she is your lady," *Marshal*, p. 129.

79 As quoted and translated by David Crouch in *William Marshal: Court, Career and Chivalry in the Angevin Empire, 1147–1219*, London and New York, Longman, 1990, p. 6. While accepting a good deal of the *Histoire* as accurate, Crouch also notes that there is an "element of identifiable fiction" in the poem; certainly its status as a mixed-genre text compromises its "truthfulness."

80 Hayden White, "The Value of Narrativity in the Representation of Reality," in *The Content of the Form*, p. 4.

Chapter 4 Oxymoronic bodies: male virgins in hagiography and romance

1 Tertullian, *De virginibus velandis* [*On the Veiling of Virgins*] Sydney Thelwall (trans.) [1885], Ante-Nicene Fathers vol. 4, Peabody, MA: Hendrickson, reprinted 1994, p. 28; *PL* 2.939.

2 Tertullian, *Veiling*, p. 35. "Impone velamen extrinsecus, habenti tegumen intrinsecus," *PL* 2.995.

3 Tertullian, in full: "it were sufficiently discourteous, while females, subjected as they are throughout to men, bear in their front an honourable mark of their virginity [that is, display their veiling], whereby they may be looked up to and gazed at on all sides and magnified by the brethren, so many men-virgins, voluntary eunuchs, should carry their glory in secret, carrying no token to make them, too, illustrious," *Veiling*, p. 33. Latin: "Cæterum satis inhumanum, si feminæ quidem per omnia viris subditæ, honorigeram notam virginitatis suæ præferant, qua suspiciantur et circumspiciantur et magnificentur a fratribus, viri autem tot virgines, tot spadones voluntarii, cæco bono suo incedant, nihil gestantes, quod et ipsos faceret illustres," *PL* 2.951.I have deleted the italics from the translation.

4 See Joan Cadden, *Meanings of Sex Difference in the Middle Ages: Medicine, Science, and Culture*, Cambridge: Cambridge University Press, 1993, pp. 260–261, for a brief discussion of the word *virgo* and its eventual use as a masculine form by patristic writers.

5 Monique Wittig, "The Mark of Gender," *Feminist Issues*, Fall 1985, vol. 5.2, pp. 3–12.

6 Thomas Laqueur, *Making Sex: Body and Gender from the Greeks to Freud*, Cambridge MA: Harvard University Press, 1990, p. 22. Carol Clover draws on Laqueur's arguments in "Regardless of Sex: Men, Women, and Power in Early Northern Europe," *Speculum*, April 1993, vol. 68.2, pp. 363–387. She describes "a world in which a physical woman could become a social man, a physical man could ... become a social woman," p. 387.

7 Quoted in Kirstin Hastrup, "The Semantics of Biology: Virginity," in *Defining Females: The Nature of Women in Society*, Shirley Ardener (ed.), New York: Croom Helm, 1978, 49–65, p. 64, n. 10.

8 Laqueur, *Making Sex*, p. 22.

9 Paul Smith, *Discerning the Subject*, Minneapolis: University of Minnesota Press, 1988; reprinted 1989, p. 98.

10 In *Women's Bodies in Classical Greek Science*, Oxford: Clarendon Press/New York: Oxford University Press, 1994, Lesley Dean-Jones cites a Hippocratic text that states that adolescent boys may bleed at first intercourse, or even when their voice breaks. However, she notes that this notion "would seem to be another attempt at correlating male and female puberty," p. 53.

11 In *The Body and Society*, Brown says that, in the early church, "perpetual virginity ... never acquired the unambiguous association with specifically female chastity that it achieved in other ages, both in the pagan world and in later forms of Catholic Christianity," p. xv. Also see pp. 60–61, 66–72.

12 John Bugge, *Virginitas: An Essay in the History of a Medieval Ideal*, The Hague: Martinus Nijhoff, 1975, p. 135.

13 Michel de Certeau, "History: Science and Fiction," in *Heterologies: Discourse on the Other*, Brian Massumi (trans.), Minneapolis: University of Minnesota Press, p. 203.

14 Aldhelm includes the stories of visionaries and miracle-workers Elijah, Elisha, Jeremiah, Daniel, John the Baptist, John, and Luke; ecclesiastics Clement, Silvester, Martin of Tours, Gregory of Nazianzus, Basil; ascetics Paul the Hermit, Hilarion, John the Hermit; and virgin martyrs Malchus, Babilas, Cosmas, Damianus, Chryanthus, and Julian. See *Aldhelm: The Prose Works*, Michael Lapidge and Michael Herren (trans.), Cambridge, England, D. S. Brewer/Totowa, NJ, Rowman & Littlefield, 1979, pp. 76–101. Lapidge and Herren say: "One looks in vain ... for a structural principle informing the catalogues of virgins," p. 57. One text in which male virginity is the chief subject should be noted here: Eustache Deschamps' defense of male celibacy, the *Miroir de mariage* (c. 1380–90). Unique in its interest in male chastity, the *Miroir* is utterly predictable in its arguments against marriage. See Eustache Deschamps, *Miroir de mariage*, vol. 9 in *Œuvres complètes d'Eustache Deschamps* 11 vols, Le Marquis de Queux de Saint-Hilaire and Gaston Raynoud (eds) Paris, 1878–1903. For an overview and analysis, see Laura Kendrick, "Transgression, Contamination, and Woman in Eustache Deschamps's *Miroir de mariage*," *Stanford French Review*, Spring-Fall 1990, vol. XIV, 1–2, pp. 211–30.

15 See James A. Brundage, *Law, Sex, and Christian Society in Medieval Europe*, Chicago and London: University of Chicago Press, 1987, pp. 426–27, for a discussion of women's sexual appetites, and pp. 64–65 on Origen's and Tertullian's condemnations of women as temptresses.

16 *Aldhelm: The Prose Works*, Lapidge and Herren (trans.), XXXI, p. 91; Latin: *PL* 89.129. Also see Jerome, *Vita S. Malchi, PL* 23.55–62.

17 *Aldhelm: The Prose Works* XXXV, p. 97; Latin: "olosericis et bombycinis indutum vestibus misit in triclinium, ubi pulcherrimæ virgines pretiosis comptæ cycladibus delicatas defruti delicias et sumptuosa ferculorum convivia præparent, effrenatos lætitiæ cachinnos, et jocosos ludorum amplexus miscentes, ut in talibus blandimentis ferrea juvenis præcordia mollescerent," *PL* 89.134. Chrysanthus' father finally marries him to the vestal virgin Daria, but Chrysanthus converts her, and they live together chastely until both are martyred.

18 *Aldhelm: The Prose Works* XXXV, p. 97; Latin: "sed mollia puellarum labra, ut nociva viperarum venena declinat," *PL* 89, 134.

19 *Legenda Aurea*, English trans., p. 84. Latin: "Alter vero mollissimo lecto imponitur et in loco amoenissimo collocatur, ubi aëris erat temperies, rivorum sonitus, cantus avium et florum olfactus; funibus tamen floreis coloribus obtectis sic juvenis cingitur ... Adest quaedam juvencula corpore pulcherrima et impudica ac impudice tractat juvenem Dei amore repletum. Cum autem ille in carne motus contrarios rationi sensisset, non habens arma, quibus ab hoste se eruat, linguam propriam dentibus suis incidit et in faciem impudicae exspuit," p. 94.

20 Giraldus Cambrensis, *The Jewel of the Church*, John J. Hagen (trans.), Leiden, The Netherlands, Brill, 1979, pp. 163, 164; *Gemma Ecclesiastica*, in *Giraldi Cambrensis opera: Gemma Ecclesiastica*, J. S. Brewer (ed.) Rerum Britannicarum MediÆvi Scriptores 2 vols [Rolls Series 21, 1861–91], Millwood, New York, Kraus, reprinted 1964–66, pp. 213–15.

21 *The Jewel of the Church*, Hagen (trans.), pp. 169–170. *Gemma Ecclesiastica*, p. 222.

22 For example, in the *Confessio Amantis*, John Gower tells us that one Phyryns thrust out his eyes so that he might avoid temptation – and, because he was beautiful, cease to be a source of temptation to women: "And thus his maidehede he boghte." *The English Works of John Gower* 2 vols, G. C. Macaulay (ed.) [1900–1901], London, E.E.T.S. E.S. 81, 82, reprinted 1978, V, ll. 6384ff., p. 121.

23 "Prius venter et statim cetera." Jerome, "Ad Eustochium" (Epistola XXII), in *Select Letters of St. Jerome*, T. E. Page, E. Capps, and W. H. D. Rouse (eds), F. A. Wright (trans.), Cambridge, MA: Harvard University Press/Loeb Classical Library, 1933, pp. 68–69, 70–71. See Joyce Salisbury, *Church Fathers, Independent Virgins*, London and New York: Verso, 1991, p. 20, for a discussion of the domino effect of the appetites.

24 Augustine, *De Civitate Dei*, George E. McCracken (ed. and trans.), Loeb Classical Library, Cambridge MA: Harvard University Press/London, William Heinemann, 1957, I.XVIII. Latin: "nullus autem magnanimus et pudicus in potestate habeat, quid de sua carne fiat, sed tantum quid adnuat mente vel renuat."

25 Joan Cadden, "Western Medicine and Natural Philosophy," in Vern L. Bullough and James A. Brundage (ed.) *Handbook of Medieval Sexuality*, New York: Garland, 1996, 51–80, p. 57. Cadden cites Albertus Magnus's *De animalibus* for the phrase, "semper parata."

26 For a general discussion of the construction of female and male desire, see Cadden, *Meanings*, p. 138; on the erection, see Danielle Jacquart and Claude Thomasset, *Sexuality and Medicine in the Middle Ages* [1985], Matthew Adamson (trans.), Princeton University Press, 1988, pp. 31, 79.

27 See Salisbury, "The Early Fathers on Sexuality: The Carnal World," pp. 11–38, in *Church Fathers, Independent Virgins*, for a discussion of patristic writings on the spiritual and psychological differences between men and women.

28 Jerome, "Commentariorum in epistelam ad ephesios," Lib. III, caput V. Latin: "[Q]uandiu mulier partui servit et liberis, hanc habet ad virum differentiam, quam corpus ad animam. Sin autem Christo magis voluerit servire quam sæculo, mulier esse cessabit, et dicetur vir," *PL* 26.567. We can trace such rhetoric to Galatians 3. 28: "There is neither Jew nor Greek, there is neither slave nor free, there is neither male nor female; for you are all one in Christ Jesus." See also Clement of Alexandria, *Stromaton* VI.12: "Souls are neither male nor female, when they no longer marry nor are given in marriage. And is not woman translated into man, when she is become equally unfeminine, and manly, and perfect?", A. Cleveland Coxe, (trans.) [1885], Ante-Nicene Fathers 2,

Peabody, MA: Hendrickson, reprinted 1994, p. 503. In the *Martyrs of Palestine*, when Eusebius speaks of one virgin martyr who, though "in body a woman," was "in understanding a man ... endowed with an understanding superior to her body," he means that she has attained the perfection of manliness in her virginity. Found at the end of Book VIII of the *Ecclesiastical History*, Arthur Cushman McGiffert (trans.) [1890], Nicene and Post-Nicene Fathers 1, Second Series, Peabody MA: Hendrickson, reprinted 1994, p. 349. As Eusebius demonstrates elsewhere, "manliness" is not necessarily a sex-typed trait: "And the women were not less manly than the men in behalf of the teaching of the Divine Word" *Ecclesiastical History*, p. 337. And Ambrose says that "she who believes, comes to perfect manhood ... She then does without worldly name, [without] gender of body." "[N]am quae credit, occurrit in virum perfectum ... carens jam nomine sæculi, corporis sexu." In "Expositio Evangeliis in Secundum Lucam," *PL* 15.1844. Laqueur cites classical analogues to this notion, including a statement by Pliny: "Ex feminis mutari in mares non est fabulosum" ("Transformation of females into males is not an idle story"), in his *Natural History* vol. 2, H. Rackham (ed.), Loeb Classical Library, Cambridge MA: Harvard University Press/London, William Heinemann, 1942, reprinted 1947, 7.4.36–38.

29 Severus of Antioch, Letter VIII.5, in *The Sixth Book of Select Letters of Severus, Patriarch of Antioch*, 2 vols, E. W. Brooks (ed. and trans.), London: Williams and Norgate, 1903, 1904, pp. 413–414.

30 Eusebius, *Martyrs of Palestine* VII, p. 348.

31 Eusebius, *Ecclesiastical History* VII.XIII, p. 333. He adds: "And new tortures were continually invented, as if [the judges] were endeavoring, by surpassing one another, to gain prizes in a contest."

32 There is much more work to be done on the representation of the male virgin and rape, both in the hagiographical narrative of antiquity and in the Middle Ages. One might begin with E. Jane Burns, "Devilish Ways: Sexing the Subject in the *Queste del Saint Graal*," *Arthuriana* Summer 1998, vol. 8.2, pp. 11–32, and David L. Boyd, "Sodomy, Misogyny, and Displacement: Occluding Queer Desire in *Sir Gawain and the Green Knight*," *Arthuriana*, Summer 1998, vol. 8.2, pp. 77–113. For an instructive example of how one might go about examining male-male rape in hagiography, see Robert Richmond Ellis, "Reading through the Veil of Juan Francisco Manzano: From Homoerotic Violence to the Dream of a Homoracial Bond", *PMLA*, May 1998, vol. 113.3, pp. 422–435, in which he argues that, in his *Autobiografía*, Cuban slave Juan Francisco Manzano veils references to rape under graphic descriptions of floggings and other physical tortures.

33 For factual details, I rely on Mark D. Jordan's insightful and impressive first chapter, "The Passions of St. Pelagius," in *The Invention of Sodomy in Christian Theology*, University of Chicago Press, 1997, pp. 10–28.

34 *La pasión de S. Pelayo: Edición crítica, con traducción y comentarios*, Rodríguez Fernández Celso (ed.), Santiago de Compostela, Spain, Universidade de Santiago de Compostela, 1991, 1.93. I quote Jordan's translation. The Bollandists, on the other hand, have: "Numquid me similem tuis effeminat*is* existimas?," "Do you think me like one of your effeminates?", p. 13, n. 11. On the sexual nature of the caliph's touch, see Jordan, p. 12.

35 Jordan, *Invention*, pp. 15–16.

36 "Anahid," in *Holy Women of the Syrian Orient*, Sebastian P. Brock and Susan Ashbrook Harvey (trans, with an introduction), Berkeley and London, University of California Press, 1987, p. 97.

37 *La pasión de S. Pelayo*, l. 92.

38 One of Hrotswit's editors, Sister M. Gonsalva Weigand, notes that Hrotswit indeed may have heard the story of Pelagius from an eyewitness, since Otto I had trade relations with the caliphs of Cordova. See "The Non-Dramatic Works of Hrosvitha: Text, Translation, and Commentary," Ph.D. Dissertation for St. Louis University, St. Louis MI, 1936, p. 154. All quotations are from this edition.

39 Hrotswit, *Pelagius*, Weigand (trans.), p. 143. Latin, p. 142, ll. 231–237:

> Aspectu primo quoque rex suspensus in illo
> Ardebat formam regalis stirpis amandam
> Tandem Pelagium nimium mandavit amandum
> In solio regni secum iam forte locari,
> Ignis ut ipsius fieret sibi sedulo iunctus;

Fronteque summisso libaverat oscula caro
Affectus causa, complectens utpote colla.

40 Weigand omits the word *Sodomitis* in her translation of Hrotswit's *Pelagius*, (l.205, pp. 140–41) but goes on to translate the somewhat explicit "Formosos facie iuvenes ardentur amare / Hos et amicitiae propriae coniungere velle": "he ardently loved youths of handsome appearance and desired to join them to friendship with himself," pp. 140–41, ll. 206–207. Also see the lines, "Non patitur talem Christi nam miles amorem / Regis pagani luxu carnis maculati": "But the soldier of Christ would not endure such advances from a pagan king tainted with the lust of the flesh," pp. 142–143, ll. 238–239.

41 Hrotswit, *Pelagius*, Weigand (trans.), pp. 142–3, l. 246.

42 Hrotswit, *Pelagius*, Weigand (trans.), p. 145.

43 Hrotswit, *Pelagius*, Weigand (trans.), pp. 136–137, l. 148. Latin: "Omni praenitida compostus corpore forma, / ... formae splendore decorus, / Concilio prudens, tota bonitate refulgens," ll. 144–146.

44 Hrotswit, *Pelagius*, Weigand (trans.), pp. 140–41, ll. 199, 200. Also see ll. 201–02, 210–17.

45 Hrotswit, *Pelagius*, Weigand (trans.), pp. 143. Latin: "In quem conversis omnes mirantur ocellis / Tum faciem iuvenis, tum dulcia verbula fantis," p. 142, ll. 229–230.

46 Mark Jordan suggests provocatively that, in Hrotswit's version, the "unburned head of Pelagius is much like a female martyr's hymen. It is the physical evidence of his virginity, his innocence of Sodomitic kisses," *Invention*, p. 22.

47 Jonathan Goldberg, *Sodometries: Renaissance Texts, Modern Sexualities*, Stanford, Stanford University Press, 1992, p. 173.

48 Jordan, *Invention*, pp. 25–27.

49 Jordan, *Invention*, p. 27.

50 Elizabeth Petroff argues that for Hrotswit, virginity is not linked to gender; it is, rather, "Christ-like and prophetic" and "beautiful ... heroic or victorious, and ... eloquent." "Eloquence and Heroic Virginity in Hrotswit's Verse Legends," in *Hrotswit of Gandersheim: Rara Avis in Saxonia?*, Katharina Wilson (ed.), Medieval and Renaissance Monograph Series VII, University of Michigan: MARC, 1987, p. 230.

51 I do not attempt to distinguish between those instances in the *Morte Darthur* when the homosocial is "merely" an act of bonding and those instances when it may have a homoerotic valence. In *Between Men: English Literature and Male Homosocial Desire*, New York: Columbia University Press, 1985, Eve Kosofsky Sedgwick argues that "desire" is "a structure ... the affective or social force, the glue ... that shapes an important relationship. How far this force is properly sexual (what, historically, it means for something to be 'sexual') [is] an active question," p. 2. She also argues that "the place of drawing the boundary between the sexual and the not-sexual ... *is* variable but is *not* arbitrary," p. 22. Thus, the homosocial as male-male desire is not fixed at any one point in a narrative. It is a "modern supposition," says Jonathan Goldberg in *Sodometries*, "that a line can be drawn between homosocial and homosexual relations," p. 163. One reason that such a buffer can be so easily inserted is that in current criticism, the homoerotic has been strongly coded as male. That is, the term *homoerotic* is almost invariably used to describe male-male desire. I would go so far as to say that the term is in danger of losing its generic meaning, and is becoming gender-specific. Recently, however, this trend in criticism has been challenged by scholars who are exploring what I call the "lesboerotic." For a general discussion that privileges female-female desire, see Bonnie Zimmerman, "Perverse Reading: The Lesbian Appropriation of Literature," in *Sexual Practice, Textual Theory: Lesbian Cultural Criticism*, Susan J. Wolfe and Julia Penelope (eds), Cambridge, MA and Cambridge, England: Blackwell, 1993, pp. 135–49. In medieval studies, Carolyn Dinshaw takes Geraldine Heng's essay, "Feminine Knots and the Other *Sir Gawain and the Green Knight*," *PMLA*, 1991, vol. 106.3, pp. 500–14, to its lesboerotic conclusion in a paper delivered at the MLA in 1994: "When the Goods Get Together: *Sir Gawain and the Green Knight*." Also see Dinshaw, "Kiss," p. 209, n. 8.

52 See my "Malory's Body Chivalric," *Arthuriana*, Winter 1996, vol. 6.4, pp. 52–71, which covers some of the same ground that I discuss here, but focuses on subjectivity, masculinity, and violence in the *Morte Darthur*.

53   Larry Benson, *Malory's* Morte Darthur, Cambridge: Harvard University Press, 1976, p. 88. Joan Cadden cites Bernard of Gordon, who "placed chastity tenth on a list of things a tutor should teach a young man and first on the list of traits to be encouraged in young women," *Meanings*, pp. 262–263.

54   For example, Malory says of Launcelot and Elayne: "Now we leve them kyssynge and clyppynge, as was a kyndely thynge," p. 804.

55   In the episode in which Gareth and Lyoness attempt to become lovers, Lyonett directs our attention to the matter of Lyoness' honor and integrity, not Gareth's, though it is Gareth who is wounded in the thigh as punishment, pp. 333ff.

56   In her prefatory remarks to a paper ("Lancelot: Ladies' Man or Lady-Man?") delivered at the 1994 International Congress on Medieval Studies at Kalamazoo MI, E. Jane Burns describes a situation in reverse: she started out to write about the Queen, but Lancelot kept getting in the way. This paper has since been expanded and published as "Refashioning Courtly Love: Lancelot as Ladies' Man or Lady/Man?" in Karma Lochrie, Peggy McCracken, and James A. Schultz (ed.) *Constructing Medieval Sexuality*, Minneapolis and London: University of Minnesota Press, 1997, pp. 111–134.

57   Judith Fetterley, *The Resisting Reader: A Feminist Approach to American Fiction*, Bloomington, IN, Indiana University Press, 1978, pp. xx–xxii.

58   Beverly Kennedy argues most vigorously for constructing a chronology of Launcelot's sexual experience in *Knighthood in the* Morte Darthur, Cambridge, England, D. S. Brewer, 1985. R. M. Lumiansky constructs a chronology of his own in "'The Tale of Launcelot': Prelude to Adultery," in R. M. Lumiansky (ed.) *Malory's Originality*, Baltimore, Johns Hopkins University Press, 1964, pp. 91–98.

59   Malory/the narrator is reluctant to commit himself on the issue of Launcelot's virginity. When Launcelot is trapped in Gwenyver's bedchamber, Malory says in a famous passage, "whether they were abed other at other maner of disportis, me lyste nat thereof make no mencion" (1165). See Kevin T. Grimm, "The Reception of Malory's *Morte Darthur* Medieval and Modern," *Quondam et Futuris*, 1992, vol. 2.3, pp. 1–14, for an appreciation of the ambiguities in the Launcelot and Gwenyver relationship. Stephen C. B. Atkinson argues that Malory leaves the question of adultery "stubbornly unanswerable" in "Malory's Lancelot and the Quest of the Holy Grail," in James W. Spisak (ed.) *Studies in Malory*, Kalamazoo, MI, Western Michigan University, Medieval Institute Publications, 1985, p. 130.

60   Mark Lambert reads this episode as "the measurability of knightliness," and as a moving celebration of knightliness, in *Malory: Style and Vision in* Le Morte Darthur, New Haven, CT, Yale University Press, 1975, p. 57. He argues for humility as the chief lesson to be learned, along with the idea that the demands of the body chivalric take precedence over the individual: "for Malory knightliness is one soul in one hundred and forty bodies," p. 59. The famous catalog of knights, Lambert argues, emphasizes fellowship, p. 62. Robert L. Kelly takes up the ambiguities of the Urré episode in "Wounds, Healing, and Knighthood in Malory's Tale of Lancelot and Guenevere," in *Studies in Malory*, pp. 173–197.

61   See my "Malory's Body Chivalric" for a discussion of the blood on the sheets.

62   In "Malory's Ideal of Fellowship," *Review of English Studies*, 1992, vol. n.s. XLIII.171, Elizabeth Archibald observes that the word *fellowship* functions in a "double sense" as "the bond between members of the Round Table as well as the friendship between individual knights," p. 317. The term, she argues, takes on an importance and resonance that are not found in Malory's sources. Jill Mann, though her interest is not the homosocial per se, suggests that the words *hole, body,* and *togidir*, among others, are particularly crucial to our understanding of the poem; see her remarks on the knightly body as a "testing ground of … validity … a repository of truths" in "Malory: Knightly Combat in *Le Morte D'arthur*," in Boris Ford (ed.) *Medieval Literature: Chaucer and the Alliterative Tradition*, Harmondsworth, England, Penguin, 1984, reprinted 1991, 331–339, p. 338. Also see Lambert, *Malory*, pp. 63–65.

63   A few examples: when Launcelot is with Elayne ("they lay togydir" 795; "in bedde togydyrs" 804); when Launcelot is with Gwenyver ("For, as the Freynshhe booke seyth, the quene and sir Launcelot were togydirs" 1165).

64   In *Gender and Romance in Chaucer's* Canterbury Tales, Princeton University Press, 1994, Susan Crane explores the "analogies that connect … the demands of courtship and male friendship." She

argues that "the heterosexual relation imitates the chivalric one, expanding and complicating knightly identity" and "heterosexual interaction patterns itself on male relations," pp. 47, 52, n. 29. How one conducts oneself on the battlefield is translated to courtship behavior, and this reifies both masculine and feminine roles. However, according to Crane, the influence flows in only one direction, pp. 21, 23. By norming behavior according to a heterosexual blueprint, Crane suppresses what I see as a two-way, sometimes homoerotic flow. I would not argue for a cause-effect relation so much as for a parallel development.

65 See Anne Clark Bartlett, "Cracking the Penile Code: Reading Gender and Conquest in the *Alliterative Morte Arthure*," *Arthuriana*, Summer 1998, vol. 8.2, pp. 56–76, for a homosocial reading of the battle between Gawain and Priamus in the *Alliterative Morte Arthure*.

66 The Tristram-Mark-Isode triangle is also supplemented, first by Palomydes, and then by Keyhydns, brother to Isode le Blaunche Maynys.

67 Gary Ferguson, "Symbolic Sexual Inversion and the Construction of Courtly Manhood in Two French Romances," *Arthurian Yearbook III*, 1993, pp. 203–213. Ferguson is reading Chrétien de Troyes' *Chevalier de la Charrete* and Béroul's *Roman de Tristan*.

68 Both Lumiansky (*Malory's Originality*, pp. 227ff.) and Lambert point to Arthur's silence: he never asks whose blood it is. Launcelot, Arthur, and Gwenyver, says Lambert, are "concerned with the Queen's shame rather than her guilt"; he sees the episode as a "loose end," p. 188. The knights are also ashamed because Mellyagaunce has Gwenyver at his mercy, and not because of any evidence of adultery, p. 189, n. 79.

69 In "Arthurian Literature and the Rhetoric of 'Effeminacy,'" Ad Putter argues that "effeminacy" is a "label … attached – quite gratuitously – to whatever or whoever happens to be despised at different historical moments." The "feminine" – defined as that which is despised transhistorically, as it were – remains an unexamined and naturalized constant. According to Putter, the signs of effeminacy in the vernacular romance include beardlessness, a preference for peace over battle, an interest in fashion and a concern for one's looks, and an interest in courtly and romantic dalliance. In Friedrich Wolfzettel (ed.) *Arthurian Romance and Gender/Masculin/Feminin dans le roman arthurien medieval/ Geschlechterrollen in mittelalterlichen Artusroman*, Amsterdam: Rodopi, 1995, p. 34.

70 Cadden, *Meanings*, p. 205.

71 Malory's version of this scene in the *Queste de Saint Graal* is much less lurid; in the original, or at least in the standard edition that we have now, Percivale's remorse and suffering are more drawn out. See Vinaver's notes on this passage, pp. 1543 and 1556.

72 Brown, *Body and Society*, p. 169.

73 See Jerome Mandel, "The Idea of Coherence and the Feminization of Knights in Malory's 'Alexander the Orphan,'" *Arthurian Yearbook III*, 1993, pp. 91–105, in which he argues that Alexander regularly feminizes the knights he defeats.

74 Thaïs E. Morgan, "Two Conversations on Literature, Theory, and the Question of Genders," in Thaïs E. Morgan (ed.) *Men Writing the Feminine: Literature, Theory, and the Question of Genders*, Albany NY, State University of New York Press, 1994, p. 193.

75 Morgan, *Men Writing the Feminine*, p. 193.

76 Jacques Derrida, "The Double Session" [1970], in *Dissemination*, Barbara Johnson (trans.), Chicago, University of Chicago Press, 1981, pp. 208, 209. The "hymen is the structure of *and/or*, between *and* and *or*," p. 261.

77 Galahad's analogue is the Virgin Mary. She is also an opening and a cover, embodying the contradiction of the maternal virgin. In "Stabat Mater," Julia Kristeva asks, "what is it about the representation of the Maternal in general, and about the Christian or virginal representation in particular, that enables it … to calm social anxiety and supply what the male lacks?" In Susan Rubin Suleiman (ed.) *The Female Body in Western Culture: Contemporary Perspectives*, Cambridge, Harvard University Press, 1986, p. 101.

78 See Carolyn Dinshaw, "A Kiss is Just a Kiss: Heterosexuality and its Consolations in *Sir Gawain and the Green Knight*," *Diacritics*, Summer-Fall 1994, vol. 24.2–3, pp. 205–226; Clare R. Kinney "The (Dis)Embodied Hero and the Signs of Manhood in *Sir Gawain and the Green Knight*," in Clare Lees (ed.) *Medieval Masculinities: Regarding Men in the Middle Ages*, Minneapolis: University

of Minnesota Press, 1994, 47–57. Kinney emphasizes the importance of "continuous and ultimately equivocal negotiation" of "chivalric manhood," p. 47.

79 *Sir Gawain and the Green Knight*, in *The Poems of the Pearl Manuscript*, Malcolm Andrew and Ronald Waldron (eds), Berkeley and Los Angeles: University of California Press, 1978, ll. 651, 653. Henceforth, all line numbers will appear in the body of the text in parentheses.

80 Tertullian, *Veiling*, p. 33. I have removed the translator's italics in this passage. "[Q]uorum quanto sexus avidior et calidior in feminas, tanto continentia majoris ardoris laboratior ... Non enim et continentia virginitati antistat ... Nam virginitas gratia constat, continentia vero virtute," *PL* 2.952.

81 Dinshaw, "Kiss," p. 212.

82 See Keith Busby, *Gauvain in Old French Literature*, Amsterdam, Rodolpi, 1980, for a thorough treatment of the development and variations of the Gawain-character in Old French romances. Busby speaks of the many "women who have fallen in love with his reputation," p. 14. As Busby points out, Gawain/Gauvain may bed the maiden, but does not always enjoy the "soreplus," p. 252. He partakes in casual love affairs, but is rarely associated with any one lady.

83 Kinney, "Hero," p. 49.

84 Like the Lady, Gawain's guide offers the comfort of a secret to the knight: no one ever has to know if Gawain never goes to the Chapel ("Þat I schal lelly yow layne and lauce neuer tale / Þat euer ȝe fondet to fle for freke þat I wyst" (I shall absolutely never reveal that you thought to flee on account of any man that I know of, 2124–25).

85 I am influenced here by a similar observation that Helen Solterer ("Mirage") makes about the sign of the rose in Jean Renart's *le Roman de la Rose*. See Chapter 3, n. 46.

Chapter 5 Multiple virgins and contemporary virginities

1 C. S. Lewis, *Preface to Paradise Lost*, Oxford University Press, 1942, p. v.

2 Erica Werner, "The Cult of Virginity," *Ms.* March/April 1997, vol. VII.5, p. 41.

3 Born-Again Virgins of America (BAVAM!): http://www.sexless.com.

4 The Society for the Recapture of Virginity: http://www/thebluedot.com/srv. This Web site is occasionally revised and updated, and therefore what I have quoted here may not correspond to its latest incarnation.

5 *The Bell Curve* is Richard J. Hernstein and Charles Murray's controversial book in which they argue for a correlation between race and intelligence, and the resulting implications for social policy. New York, Free Press, 1994.

6 See http://www.dac.neu.edu/english/kakelly/forth/virsite.html

7 Joan Scott, "The Evidence of Experience," in Henry Abelove, Michèle Aina Barele, and David M. Halperin (eds) *The Lesbian and Gay Studies Reader*, New York and London: Routledge, 1993, p. 401.

8 Scott, "Evidence," p. 401. Scott also says: "The evidence of experience ... becomes evidence for the fact of difference, rather than a way of exploring how difference is established, how it operates, how and in what ways it constitutes subjects," pp. 399–400.

9 Quoted in Scott, p. 399; original in Michel de Certeau, "History: Science and Fiction" [1983], in *Heterologies: Discourse on the Other*, Brian Massumi (trans), Minneapolis: University of Minnesota Press, 1986, p. 203.

10 Karen Bouris (ed.), *The First Time: What Parents and Teenage Girls Should Know about "Losing Your Virginity"*, Berkeley, CA: Conari Press, 1993, and *Losing It: The Virginity Myth*, Louis M. Crosier (ed.), Washington, D.C., Avocus, 1993.

11 Bouris, *The First Time*, p. 18.

12 Naomi Wolf, *Promiscuities: The Secret Struggle for Womanhood*, New York: Random House, 1997, p. xvi.

13 Wolf, *Promiscuities*, p. 121.

14 Wolf, *Promiscuities*, p 124.

15 *Women's Secrets: A Translation of Pseudo-Albertus Magnus' De secretis mulierum with Commentaries*, Helen Rodnite Lemay (trans.), Albany, NY: State University of New York Press, 1992, pp. 126–127. Latin: "ampliatur in coitu," Venice 1508, caput II.

16 Sylvia Plath, *The Bell Jar* [1963, under a pseudonym, 1966 under her own name], New York, Bantam Books, 1981, p. 187.
17 Wolf, *Promiscuities*, p 124.
18 Sigmund Freud, "The Taboo of Virginity," in *On Sexuality: Three Essays on the Theory of Sexuality*, James Strachey (gen. ed.), Angela Richards (ed.), Penguin Freud Library, vol. 7 [1953] 1977, p. 265. "Das Tabu der Virginität," in *Sigmund Freud: Gesammelte Werke, Chronologisch Geordnet, Werke aus den Jahren 1917–1920*, vol. XII, London, Imago, 1947, p. 161.
19 Freud, "The Taboo of Virginity," p. 274.
20 Freud, "The Taboo of Virginity," p. 265.
21 Bronislaw Malinowski, for example, whose famous studies of the Trobriand Islanders (Melanesia) persist in the popular imagination, said in 1922: "Chastity is an unknown virtue among these natives ... As they grow up, they live in promiscuous free-love." *The Sexual Life of Savages in Northern Melanesia: An Ethnographic Account of Courtship, Marriage and Family Life Among the Natives of the Trobriand Islands*, British New Guinea, 2 vols, New York, Horace Liveright/London, Routledge, 1929, vol. 1, p. 53.
22 Alice Schlegel, "Status, Property, and the Value on Virginity," *American Ethnologist*, November 1991, vol. 18.4, pp. 719–34.
23 "The Story of Qumar al-Zaman and His Two Sons," in *The Arabian Nights II: Sinbad and Other Popular Stories*, Hussain Haddawy (trans.), New York, Norton 1995, pp. 209–210.
24 Geraldine Brooks, *Nine Parts of Desire: The Hidden World of Islamic Women*, Doubleday Anchor Books 1994, p. 57. Brooks reports that women regularly use blood-soaked sponges or splinters of glass to fake the blood of virginity. She also mentions that if the husband does not get an erection, the bride may repudiate him, p. 57.
25 Susan Schaefer Davis, "Changing Gender Relations is a Moroccan Town," in Judith E. Tucker (ed.) *Arab Women: Old Boundaries, New Frontiers*, Bloomington: Indiana University Press 1993, pp. 209–210.
26 Susan Schaefer Davis and Douglas Davis, "Dilemmas of Adolescence: Courtship, Sex, and Marriage in a Moroccan Town," in Donna Lee Bowen and Evelyn Early (eds) *Everyday Life in the Muslim Middle East*, Bloomington, Indiana University Press, 1993, pp. 87–88.
27 According to Douglas Davis' field notes, "Dilemmas," pp. 87–88.
28 Susan Schaefer Davis, "Changing Gender," pp. 214–215.
29 Cited with permission, though the correspondent wishes to remain anonymous.
30 Alifa Rifaat, "Honor," Elise Goldwasser and Miriam Cooke (trans), in Margot Badran and Miriam Cooke (eds) *Opening the Gates: A Century of Arab Feminist Writing*, Bloomington, Indiana University Press, 1991, p. 81.
31 Rifaat, "Honor," p. 83.
32 Cited with permission, though the correspondent wishes to remain anonymous.
33 Tertullian, *De virginibus velandis*, PL 2.892.
34 Sybil Joy, in Crosier, *Losing It*, p. 104.
35 Livy, *Ab urbe condita*, B. O. Foster (trans.), London, William Heinemann/New York, Putnam, 1926. Latin: "[C]ultum amoeniorem ingeniumque liberius," IV.xliv.11.
36 Livy, *Ab urbe condita*, "[S]uspecta primo propter mundiorem iusto cultum," VIII.xv.7.
37 *De secretis mulierum*, Lemay (trans.), p. 67.
38 Catie Meyer, "Intimate Surgery," *First*, 1 August 1994, p. 48.
39 Meyer, "Intimate," p. 48.
40 Meyer, "Intimate," p. 48.
41 Samuel S. Janus and Cynthia L. Janus, *The Janus Report on Sexual Behavior*, New York, John Wiley, 1993, pp. 43–44.
42 Reproduced in *Losing Your Virginity*, pp. 184–185.
43 Simone de Beauvoir, *The Second Sex* [1952], H. M. Parshley (trans. and ed.) New York: Random House/Vintage Books, 1989, p. 152.
44 Luce Irigaray, "When Our Lips Speak Together," *Signs*, Autumn 1980, vol. 6.1, p. 74.
45 Kathy Newman, "Re-membering an Interrupted Conversation: the Mother/Virgin Split," *TRIVIA*, Spring 1983, vol. 2, p. 47.

46 Marilyn Frye wants to recuperate this aspect of the virgin within a feminist/lesbian paradigm, and insists on a rather willful history for the word *virgin*: "The word "virgin" did not originally mean a woman whose vagina was untouched by any penis, but a free woman, one not betrothed, not married, not bound to, not possessed by any man. It meant a female who is sexually and hence socially her own person. In any universe of patriarchy, there are no Virgins in this sense. ... Hence Virgins must be unspeakable, thinkable only as negations, their existence impossible. Radically feminist lesbians have claimed positive Virginity and have been inventing ways of living it out, in creative defiance of patriarchal definitions of the real, the meaningful." *Willful Virgin: Essays in Feminism 1976–1992*, Freedom, CA, The Crossing Press, 1992, p. 133.

47 Martha Barron Barrett, *Invisible Lives: The Truth about Millions of Women-Loving Women*, New York, William Morrow 1989, p. 258.

48 Harriet Malinowitz, *Textual Orientations: Lesbian and Gay Students and the Making of Discourse Communities*, Portsmouth, NH, Boynton/Cook 1995, p. 357.

49 Bouris, *The First Time*, p. 141.

50 Cited with permission, though the correspondent wishes to remain anonymous.

51 Braxton Brittle, in Crosier, *Losing It*, pp. 31–39.

52 Jack Watson, in Crosier, *Losing It*, pp. 73, 74.

53 Alice Walker, *The Color Purple* [1982], New York, Simon and Schuster/Pocket Books/Washington Square Press, 1983, p. 79.

54 Judith Butler, *Gender Trouble: Feminism and the Subversion of Identity*, New York and London, Routledge, p. 136.

Bibliography

Abenragel, *Liber in iudiciis astrorum*, Venice, 1485.

Achilles Tatius, *Leucippe and Cleitophon*, John J. Winkler (trans.), in *Collected Ancient Greek Novels*, B. P. Reardon (ed.), Berkeley and Los Angeles, University of California Press, 1989.

Acts of Paul and Thecla, in *New Testament Apocrypha*, vol. 2, Wilhelm Schneemelcher (German ed.), R. McL. Wilson (English ed.), A. J. B. Higgins and others (trans), Philadelphia, Westminster Press, rev. 1993.

Acts of St. John, in *New Testament Apocrypha*, vol. 2, Wilhelm Schneemelcher (German ed.), R. McL. Wilson (English ed.), A. J. B. Higgins and others (trans), Philadelphia, Westminster Press, rev. 1993.

Adelman, Howard, "Italian Jewish Women," in Judith R. Baskin (ed.) *Jewish Women in Historical Perspective*, Detroit, Wayne State University Press, 1991, pp. 135–158.

Aelian, *De natura animalium*, A. F. Scholfield (ed. and trans.), Loeb Classical Library, Cambridge MA, Harvard University Press/London, William Heinemann, 1958.

Albertus Magnus, *De Animalibus libri XXVI*, Hermann Stadler (ed.), Münster, Aschendorff, 1916, 1920.

——, *De Bono, Quaestio III: De Castitate*, in *Opera Omnia*, vol. 28, H. Kühle, C. Feckes, B. Geyer, and W. Kübel (eds), Münster, Aschendorff, 1951.

——, *Commentary on the Sentences*, edited by Josef Löffler in "Die Störungen des geschlechtlichen Vermögens in der Literatur der autoritativen Theologie des Mittelalters," Mainz, Akademie der Wissenschaften und der Literatur, 1958, vol. 6, pp. 296–380.

——, *De Mineralibus*, Dorothy Wyckoff (ed.), Oxford, Clarendon Press, 1967.

Aldhelm, *De Virginitate*, PL 89.

——, *De Virginitate*, in *Aldhelm: The Prose Works*, Michael Lapidge and Michael Herren (trans), Cambridge, England, D. S. Brewer/Totowa, NJ, Rowman & Littlefield, 1979.

Ambrose, "Expositio Evangeliis in Secundum Lucam," *PL* 15.

——, *De Institutione Virginis*, PL 16.

——, "Ad Syagrius" (Epistola V), *PL* 16.

——, "Letter to Syagrius," in *Saint Ambrose: Letters*, Sister Mary Melchior Berenka (trans.), New York, Fathers of the Church, 1954.

——, "Ad Vercelli" (Epistola LXIII), *PL* 16.

——, "Letter to the Church at Vercelli," in *Saint Ambrose: Letters*, Sister Mary Melchior Berenka (trans.) New York, Fathers of the Church, 1954.

——, *De Virginibus ad Marcellinam*, PL 16.

——, *Concerning Virgins*, in *St. Ambrose: Select Works and Letters*, H. de Romestin (trans.) [1890], Nicene and Post-Nicene Fathers 10, Second Series, Peabody, MA, Hendrickson, reprinted 1994.

——, *De Virginitate*, PL 16.

——, *On Virginity*, Daniel Callam (trans.), Toronto, Peregrina, 1980, reprinted 1989.

An Alphabet of Tales, M. M. Banks (ed.), London, E.E.T.S. O.S. 126, 127, 1904, reprinted one vol., 1973.

Apocryphal New Testament, J. K. Elliott (ed. and trans.), Oxford University Press, 1993.

Aquinas, Thomas, *Summa Theologiæ*, Thomas Gilby (ed. and trans.), Blackfriars, in conjunction with New York, McGraw Hill, London, Eyre and Spottiswoode, 1968.

Arabian Nights II: Sinbad and Other Popular Stories, Hussain Haddawy (trans.), New York, Norton, 1995.

Archibald, Elizabeth, "Malory's Ideal of Fellowship," *Review of English Studies*, 1992, New Series XLIII.171, pp. 311–328.

Atkinson, Stephen C. B., "Malory's Lancelot and the Quest of the Holy Grail," in James W. Spisak (ed.) *Studies in Malory*, Kalamazoo, MI, Western Michigan University, Medieval Institute Publications, 1985, pp. 129–152.

Augustine, *De Civitate Dei*, George E. McCracken (ed. and trans.), Loeb Classical Library, Cambridge MA, Harvard University Press/London, William Heinemann, 1957.

——, *Contra Julianum*, PL 44.

——, *De Sancta Virginitate*, PL 40.

Averroës, *Colliget*, Venice, 1514.

Avicenna, *Liber canonis* [1507], Hildesheim, G. Olms, reprinted 1964.

Bacon, Roger, *Greek Grammar of Roger Bacon and a Fragment of His Hebrew Glossary*, Edmond Nolan and S. A. Hirsch (eds), Cambridge University Press, 1902.

Bakhtin, M. M., "Discourse in the Novel," in *The Dialogic Imagination*, Caryl Emerson and Michael Holquist (trans), Michael Holquist (ed.), Austin, University of Texas Press, 1981.

Baldwin, John W., *The Language of Sex: Five Voices from Northern France around 1200*, University of Chicago Press, 1994.

——, "The Crisis of the Ordeal: Literature, Law, and Religion around 1200," *Journal of Medieval and Renaissance Studies*, Fall 1994, vol. 24.3, pp. 327–353.

Barnes, Timothy D., *Constantine and Eusebius*, Cambridge MA, Harvard University Press, 1991.

——, letter to the author, 3 January 1996.

Barrett, Martha Barron, *Invisible Lives: The Truth about Millions of Women-Loving Women*, New York, William Morrow, 1989.

Bartlett, Anne Clark, "Cracking the Penile Code: Reading Gender and Conquest in the Alliterative Morte Arthure," *Arthuriana*, Summer 1998, vol. 8.2, pp. 56–76.

Bartlett, Robert, *Trial by Fire and Water: The Medieval Judicial Ordeal*, Oxford, Clarendon, 1986.

Baudrillard, Jean, *For a Critique of the Political Economy of the Sign*, Charles Levin (trans.), St. Louis, Telos Press, 1981.

Bell, Ruth, et al. (ed.), *Changing Bodies, Changing Selves*, New York, Random House, 1980.

Benson, Larry, *Malory's Morte Darthur*, Cambridge, Harvard University Press, 1976.

Benton, John F., "Clio and Venus: An Historical View of Medieval Love," in F. X. Newman (ed.) *The Meaning of Courtly Love* [1968], Albany, NY, State University of New York Press, 1973, pp. 19–42.

Berenson, Abbey, Astrid Heger, and Sally Andrews, "Appearance of the Hymen in Newborns," *Pediatrics*, April 1991, vol. 87.4, pp. 458–465.

——, Astrid Heger, Jean M. Hayes, Rahn K. Bailey, and S. Jean Emans, "Appearance of the Hymen in Prepubertal Girls," *Pediatrics*, March 1992, vol. 89.3, pp. 387–394.

Bevan, W. L., and H. W. Phillott, *Medieval Geography: An Essay in Illustration of the Hereford Map*, London, 1873.

Bloch, R. Howard, *Medieval French Literature and Law*, Berkeley and Los Angeles, University of California Press, 1977.

——, *Medieval Misogyny and the Invention of Western Romantic Love*, University of Chicago Press, 1991.

Boccaccio, Giovanni, *Decameron*, Natalino Sapegno (ed.), Turin, Fratelli Fabbri Editori, 1975.

——, *The Decameron*, G. H. McWilliam (trans.), Harmondsworth, England, Penguin Books, 1972.

Bonatti, Guido, *Astronomiæ Tractatus X*, Basel, 1550.

Born-Again Virgins of America: BAVAM!. http://www.sexless.com.

Boswell, John, *Christianity, Social Tolerance, and Homosexuality*, Chicago, University of Chicago Press, 1980.

Bouris, Karen (ed.), *The First Time: What Parents and Teenage Girls Should Know about "Losing Your Virginity,"* Berkeley, CA, Conari Press, 1993.

Bowers, John, "Ordeals, Privacy, and the *Lais* of Marie de France," *Journal of Medieval and Renaissance Studies*, Winter 1994, vol. 24.1, pp. 1–31.

Boyd, David L., "Sodomy, Misogyny, and Displacement: Occluding Queer Desire in *Sir Gawain and the Green Knight*," *Arthuriana*, Summer 1998, vol. 8.2, pp. 77–113.

de Bracton, Henry, *De Legibus et Consuetudinibus*, 2 vols, George E. Woodbine (ed.) [1915–42], Samuel E. Thorne (trans.), Cambridge, MA, Harvard University Press/Belknap Press, 1968.

Brock, Sebastian P. and Susan Ashbrook Harvey (trans, with an introduction), *Holy Women of the Syrian Orient*, Berkeley and London, University of California Press, 1987.

Brooks, Geraldine, *Nine Parts of Desire: The Hidden World of Islamic Women*, New York, Doubleday Anchor Books, 1994.

Brown, Peter, "Society and the Supernatural: A Medieval Change," *Daedalus*, 1975, vol. 104, pp. 133–51. Reprinted in *Society and the Holy in Late Antiquity*, Berkeley and Los Angeles, University of California Press, 1982, pp. 302–332.

Brown, Peter, *The Body and Society: Men, Women, and Sexual Renunciation in Early Christianity*, New York, Columbia University Press, 1988.

Brundage, James, *Law, Sex, and Christian Society in Medieval Europe*, Chicago and London, University of Chicago Press, 1987.

——, "The Problem of Impotence," in Vern L. Bullough and James Brundage (ed.) *Sexual Practices and the Medieval Church*, Buffalo, Prometheus Books, 1982, pp. 135–140.

Bugge, John, *Virginitas: An Essay in the History of a Medieval Ideal*, The Hague, Martinus Nijhoff, 1975.

Bullough, Vern L. and James Brundage, *Sexual Practices and the Medieval Church*, Buffalo, Prometheus Books, 1982.

Burns, E. Jane, "Lancelot: Ladies' Man or Lady-Man?," paper delivered at the International Congress on Medieval Studies at Kalamazoo MI, 1994. Revised and published as "Refashioning Courtly Love: Lancelot as Ladies' Man or Lady/Man?," in Karma Lochrie, Peggy McCracken, and James A. Schultz (eds) *Constructing Medieval Sexuality*, Minneapolis and London, University of Minnesota Press, 1997, pp. 111–134.

——, "Devilish Ways: Sexing the Subject in the *Queste del Saint Graal*," *Arthuriana*, Summer 1998, vol. 8.2, pp. 11–32.

——, *Bodytalk: When Women Speak in Old French Literature*, Philadelphia, University of Pennsylvania Press, 1993.

——, *Arthurian Fictions: Rereading the Vulgate Cycle*, Columbus, OH, published for Miami University by the Ohio State University Press, 1985.

Busby, Keith, *Gauvain in Old French Literature*, Amsterdam, Rodolpi, 1980.

Butler, Judith, *Bodies that Matter: On the Discursive Limits of "Sex,"* London and New York, Routledge, 1993.

——, *Gender Trouble: Feminism and the Subversion of Identity*, London and New York, Routledge, 1990.

Bynum, Caroline Walker, "Why All the Fuss about the Body? A Medievalist's Perspective," *Critical Inquiry*, Autumn 1995, vol. 22, pp. 1–33.

Cadden, Joan, "Western Medicine and Natural Philosophy," in Vern L. Bullough and James A. Brundage (eds) *Handbook of Medieval Sexuality*, New York, Garland, 1996, pp. 51–80.

——, *Meanings of Sex Difference in the Middle Ages: Medicine, Science, and Culture*, Cambridge, Cambridge University Press, 1993.

Cantarella, Eva, "Dangling Virgins: Myth, Ritual and the Place of Women in Ancient Greece," *Poetics Today*, 1985, vol. 6.1–2, pp. 91–101.

Castelli, Elizabeth A., "Visions and Voyeurism: Holy Women and the Politics of Sight in Early Christianity," in Christopher Ocker (ed.) *Protocol of the Colloquy of the Center for Hermeneutical Studies*, December 1992, New Series 2, pp. 1–27.

Cather, Willa, letter of 23 November 1927 to the editor of *Commonweal*, reprinted in *On Writing: Critical Studies on Writing as an Art*, New York, Knopf, 1949.

Catholicon Anglicum, Sidney J. H. Herrtage (ed.) [1881], E.E.T.S. O. S. 75.

Cazelles, Brigette (ed.), *The Lady as Saint: A Collection of French Hagiographic Romances of the Thirteenth Century*, Philadelphia, University of Pennsylvania Press, 1991.

Chance, Jane, *Medieval Mythography: From Roman North Africa to the School of Chartres*, AD 433–1177, Gainesville, University Press of Florida, 1994.

Chaucer, Geoffrey, *Troilus and Criseyde*, in *The Works of Geoffrey Chaucer* 3rd ed., L. D. Benson (ed.) Boston, Houghton, 1987.

Childs, F. J., Introduction, *The Boy and the Mantle*, in *The English and Scottish Popular Ballads* I [1882–84], reprinted New York, Dover, 1965, pp. 257–271.

Cixous, Hélène. "The Laugh of the Medusa," Keith Cohen and Paul Cohen (trans), in Elaine Marks and Isabelle de Courtivron (eds) *New French Feminisms*, New York: Schocken Books, 1981, pp. 245–264.

Clark, Elizabeth A., "John Chrysostom and the *Subintroductae*," *Church History*, 1977, vol. 46, pp. 171–185.

Clement of Alexandria, *Stromaton*, A. Cleveland Coxe (trans.) [1885], Ante-Nicene Fathers 2, reprinted Peabody, MA, Hendrickson, 1994.

Clover, Carol, "Regardless of Sex: Men, Women, and Power in Early Northern Europe" *Speculum*, April 1993, vol. 68.2, pp. 363–387.

Collingwood, R. G., *The Idea of History* (1946), Jan van der Dussen, (ed. with introduction), Oxford, Clarendon Press, rev. ed., 1993.

Continuations of the Old French Perceval of Chrétien de Troyes, 2 vols, William Roach (ed.), Philadelphia, University of Pennsylvania Press, 1949.

Cooper, Kate, *The Virgin and the Bride: Idealized Womanhood in Late Antiquity*, Harvard University Press, 1996.

Cooper, Thomas, *Thesaurus*, London, 1584.

Corrington, Gail Paterson, "The 'Divine Woman'? Propaganda and the Power of Celibacy in the New Testament Apocrypha: A Reconsideration," *Anglican Theological Review*, 1988, vol. 70, pp. 207–220. Reprinted in Everett Ferguson (ed.) *Studies in Early Christianity: A Collection of Scholarly Essays*, New York, Garland, 1993, pp. 169–182.

Courcelle, Pierre, *Late Latin Writers and Their Greek Sources*, [1943; rev. 1948] Harry E. Wedeck (trans.) Cambridge, MA, Harvard University Press, 1969.

Crane, Susan, *Gender and Romance in Chaucer's* Canterbury Tales, Princeton University Press, 1994.

Crosier, Louis M. (ed.), *Losing It: The Virginity Myth*, Washington, D.C., Avocus, 1993.

Cross, Tom Peete, "Notes on the Chastity-Testing Horn and Mantle," *Modern Philology*, January 1913, vol. X.3, pp. 1–11.

Crouch, David, *William Marshal: Court, Career and Chivalry in the Angevin Empire, 1147–1219*, London and New York, Longman, 1990.

Cyprian, "Ad Pomponium, Ad Virginibus" (Epistola LXII), *PL* 4.

——, "Ad Pomponium, Ad Virginibus,"in *Saint Cyprian: Letters 1–81*, Sister Rose Bernard Donna (trans.), Washington, Catholic University of America Press, 1964.

——, *De Habitu Virginis, PL* 4.

D'Angelo, Mary, "Veils, Virgins, and the Tongues of Men and Angels: Women's Heads in Early Christianity," in Howard Eilberg-Schwartz and Wendy Doniger (eds) *Off with Her Head!: The Denial of Women's Identity in Myth, Religion, and Culture*, Berkeley and London, University of California Press, 1995, pp. 131–164.

Davies, Robertson, *Fifth Business*, Harmondsworth, England, Penguin Books, 1993.

——, *The Rebel Angels*, Harmondsworth, England, Penguin, 1983.

Davis, Susan Schaefer, "Changing Gender Relations in a Moroccan Town," in Judith E. Tucker (ed.) *Arab Women: Old Boundaries, New Frontiers*, Bloomington, Indiana University Press 1993, pp. 208–223.

——, and Douglas Davis, "Dilemmas of Adolescence: Courtship, Sex, and Marriage in a Moroccan Town," in Donna Lee Bowen and Evelyn Early (eds) *Everyday Life in the Muslim Middle East*, Indiana University Press 1993, pp. 84–90.

de Beauvoir, Simone, *The Second Sex* [1952], H. M. Parshley (trans. and ed.), New York, Random House/Vintage Books, 1989.

de Certeau, Michel, "History: Science and Fiction" [1983], in *Heterologies: Discourse on the Other*, Brian Massumi (trans.), Minneapolis, University of Minnesota Press, 1986, pp. 199–221.

Deschamps, Eustache, *Miroir de mariage*, vol. 9 in *Œuvres complètes d'Eustache Deschamps*, 11 vols, Le Marquis de Quex de Saint-Hilaire and Gaston Raynoud (eds), Paris, 1878–1903.

De coniuge non ducenda, in *Gawain on Marriage: the Textual Tradition of the* De coniuge non ducenda, with critical edition and translation by A. G. Rigg, Toronto, Pontifical Institute of Mediaeval Studies, 1986.

Delooz, Pierre, *Sociologie et Canonizations*, Liège: Faculté de Droit, 1969.

de Looze, Laurence, "The Gender of Fiction: Womanly Poetics in Jean Renart's *Guillaume de Dole*," *The French Review*, March 1991, vol. 64.4, pp. 596–606.

De Secretis mulierum, London, 1625.

De Secretis mulierum, Lyons, 1580.

De Secretis mulierum, Venice, 1508.

De Secretis mulierum, Women's Secrets: A Translation of Pseudo-Albertus Magnus' De Secretis Mulierum with Commentaries, Helen Rodnite Lemay (trans.), Albany NY, State University of New York Press, 1992.

de Ste. Croix, G. E. M., "Aspects of the 'Great' Prosecution," *Harvard Theological Review*, January 1954, vol. XLVII.1, pp. 75–113.

De Venerabili Oda, Acta Sanctorum, 2 April (20 April).

De S. Liberata Alias Wilgeforte Virgine et Martyre, Acta Sanctorum, 5 July (20 July).

Dean-Jones, Lesley, *Women's Bodies in Classical Greek Science*, Oxford, Clarendon Press/New York, Oxford University Press, 1994.

Delany, Sheila, *A Legend of Holy Women: A Translation of Osbern Bokenham's* Legends of Holy Women, Notre Dame and London, University of Notre Dame Press, 1992.

Delehaye, H., *The Legends of the Saints* [1905, rev. 1927, reprinted 1955], Donald Attwater (trans.), New York, Fordham University Press, 1962.

Denomy, A. J., *The Old French Lives of Saint Agnes and Other Vernacular Versions of the Middle Ages*, Cambridge, Harvard University Press, 1938.

Derrida, Jacques, "The Double Session" [1970], in *Dissemination*, Barbara Johnson (trans.), Chicago, University of Chicago Press, 1981, pp. 183–286.

Dinshaw, Carolyn, "A Kiss is Just a Kiss: Heterosexuality and its Consolations in *Sir Gawain and the Green Knight*," *Diacritics*, Summer-Fall 1994, vol. 24.2–3, pp. 205–226.

——, "When the Goods Get Together: *Sir Gawain and the Green Knight*," paper delivered at the Modern Language Association, San Diego, 1994.

Donaldson, Ian, *The Rapes of Lucretia: A Myth and its Transformations*, Oxford, Clarendon Press, 1982.

Douglas, Mary, *Purity and Danger* [1966], London and New York, Routledge, 1991.

Duby, Georges, *The Knight, The Lady and the Priest: The Making of Modern Marriage in Medieval France* [1981], Barbara Bray (trans.), New York, Pantheon Books, 1983.

——, *The Chivalrous Society* [1976], Cynthia Postan (trans.), Berkeley, University of California Press, 1977.

——, *William Marshal: The Flower of Chivalry* [1984], Richard Howard (trans.), New York, Pantheon Books, 1985.

Ellis, Robert Richmond, "Reading through the Veil of Juan Francisco Manzano: From Homoerotic Violence to the Dream of a Homoracial Bond," *PMLA*, May 1998, vol. 113.3, pp. 422–435.

Elyot, Thomas, *Dictionary* (London, 1538) Menston, Yorkshire, Scolar Press, facsimile, 1970.

Emans, S. Jean, Elizabeth R. Woods, Elizabeth N. Allred, and Estherann Grace, "Hymenal Findings in Adolescent Women: Impact of Tampon Use and Consensual Sexual Activity," *Journal of Pediatrics*, 1994, vol. 125.1, pp. 153–160.

Enders, Jody, "Medieval Snuff Drama," *Exemplaria*, Spring 1998, vol. X.1, pp. 171–206.

Epstein, Julia, *Altered Conditions: Disease, Medicine, and Storytelling*, New York and London, Routledge, 1995.

Esmein, A., *Le Mariage en Droit Canonique*, 2nd ed., Paris, R. Génestal, 1929.

Eusebius, *Ecclesiastical History*, Philip Schaff and Henry Wace, (trans) [1890], Nicene and Post-Nicene Fathers vol. 1, Second Series, Peabody, MA, Hendrickson, reprinted 1994.

Eusebius, *Martyrs of Palestine*, Philip Schaff and Henry Wace (trans.) [1890], included between Book VIII and IX of the *Ecclesiastical History*, Nicene and Post-Nicene Fathers 1, Second Series, Peabody MA, Hendrickson, reprinted 1994.

Falcucci, Niccolò, "De defloratione seu violatione virginis" [Chapter 30, *De passionibus mulierum*], Esther Lastique and Helen Rodnite Lemay (eds and trans), in "A Medieval Physician's Guide to Virginity," in Joyce Salisbury (ed.) *Medieval Sexuality: Essays*, New York, Garland, 1991, pp. 56–79.

Farmer, David Hugh, *The Oxford Dictionary of Saints*, 2nd ed., Oxford University Press, 1987, reprinted 1991.

Ferguson, Gary, "Symbolic Sexual Inversion and the Construction of Courtly Manhood in Two French Romances," *Arthurian Yearbook III*, 1993, pp. 203–213.

Fetterley, Judith, *The Resisting Reader: A Feminist Approach to American Fiction*, Bloomington, Indiana University Press, 1978.

Finke, Laurie, "The Rhetoric of Desire in the Courtly Lyric," in *Feminist Theory, Women's Writing*, Ithaca, Cornell University Press, 1992, pp. 29–74.

Floire et Blancheflor, Margaret M. Pelan (ed.), Paris, Société d'édition, 1937, rev. 1956.

Floris and Blauncheflur, Franciscus Catharina de Vries (ed.), Groningen, Druk. V.R.B., 1966.

Forbes, Thomas R., "A Jury of Matrons," *Medical History*, 1988, vol. 32, pp. 23–33.

Foucault, Michel, "Nietzsche, Genealogy, History" [1971], in *Language, Counter-Memory, Practice: Selected Essays and Interviews*, Donald F. Bouchard (ed.), Ithaca, Cornell University Press, 1977, pp. 139–164.

——, *Discipline and Punish: The Birth of the Prison* [1975], Alan Sheridan (trans.), New York, Vintage Books, 1977.

Frantzen, Allen, "Between the Lines: Queer Theory, the History of Homosexuality, and Anglo-Saxon Penitentials," *Journal of Medieval and Early Modern Studies*, Spring 1996, vol. 26.2, pp. 255–296.

Freud, Sigmund, "Das Tabu der Virginität," in *Sigmund Freud: Gesammelte Werke, Chronologisch Geordnet, Werke aus den Jahren 1917–1920*, vol. XII, London, Imago, 1947.

——, "The Taboo of Virginity," in James Strachey (gen. ed.) and Angela Richards (ed.) *On Sexuality: Three Essays on the Theory of Sexuality*, Penguin Freud Library, vol. 7, 1953, reprinted 1977.

Frisk, Gösta (ed.), *A Middle English Translation of De Viribus Herbarum*, Uppsala, Sweden, Lundequistska bokhandeln/Cambridge, Harvard University Press, 1949.

Froissart, Jean, *Chroniques*, in *Chroniques de J. Froissart*, vol. 11, Gaston Raynaud (ed.), Paris, La Société de l'Histoire de France, 1899.

——, *Chronicles*, (Geoffrey Brereton, trans.), Harmondsworth, England, Penguin, rev. 1978.

Frye, Marilyn, *Willful Virgin: Essays in Feminism 1976–1992*, Freedom, CA, The Crossing Press, 1992.

Galen, *On the Usefulness of the Parts*, 2 vols, Margaret Tallmadge May (trans. with introduction and commentary), Ithaca, Cornell University Press, 1968.

Gaunt, Simon, *Gender and Genre*, Cambridge University Press, 1996.

Geertz, Clifford, "Deep Play: Notes on the Balinese Cockfight," in *The Interpretation of Cultures*, New York, Basic Books, 1973, pp. 412–453.

Giraldus Cambrensis, *Gemma Ecclesiastica*, in *Giraldi Cambrensis opera: Gemma Ecclesiastica*, 2 vols, J. S. Brewer (ed.) Rerum Britannicarum MediÆvi Scriptores [Rolls Series 21, 1861–91], Millwood, New York, Kraus reprinted 1964–66.

——, *The Jewel of the Church* [*Gemma Ecclesiastica*], John J. Hagen (trans.), Leiden, Brill, 1979.

Goldberg, Jonathan, *Sodometries: Renaissance Texts, Modern Sexualities*, Stanford, Stanford University Press, 1992.

Goldhill, Simon, *Foucault's Virginity: Ancient Erotic Fiction and the History of Sexuality*, Cambridge, Cambridge University Press, 1995.

Gower, John, *Confessio Amantis*, in *The English Works of John Gower*, 2 vols, G. C. Macaulay (ed.) [1900–1901], London, E.E.T.S. E.S. 81, 82, reprinted 1978.

Gravdal, Kathryn, *Ravishing Maidens: Writing Rape in Medieval French Literature and Law*, Philadelphia, University of Pennsylvania Press, 1991.

Gray's Anatomy: The Anatomical Basis of Medicine and Surgery, 38th ed., New York/Edinburgh, Churchill Livingstone, 1995.

Green, Monica, "The Development of the *Trotula,*" *Revue d'Histoire des Textes,* 1996, vol. 26, pp. 118–203.

——, "Female Sexuality in the Medieval West," *Trends in History,* 1990, vol. 4.4, pp. 127–158.

——, "The Transmission of Ancient Theories of Female Physiology and Disease through the Early Middle Ages," unpublished Ph.D. Dissertation, Princeton University, 1985.

Gregory the Great, *Dialogues,* Odo John Zimmerman (trans.), New York, Fathers of the Church 39, 1959.

Grimm, Kevin T., "The Reception of Malory's *Morte Darthur* Medieval and Modern," *Quondam et Futuris,* 1992, vol. 2.3, pp. 1–14.

Hägg, Tomas, "The *Parthenope Romance* Decapitated?" *Symbolae Osloenses,* 1984, vol. LIX, pp. 61–92.

——, *The Novel in Antiquity* [1980], Berkeley and Los Angeles, University of California Press, 1983, rev. 1991.

Hali Meiðhad, Bella Millet (ed.), London, E.E.T.S. O.S. 284, 1982.

Hanson, Ann Ellis, "The Medical Writer's Woman," in David Halperin, John J. Winkler, and Froma I. Zeitlin (eds) *Before Sexuality: The Construction of Erotic Experience in the Ancient Greek World,* Princeton, NJ, Princeton University Press, 1990, pp. 309–337.

——, and Monica Green, "Soranus of Ephesus: *Methodicorum princeps*" in Wolfgang Haase and Hildegard Temporini (eds), *Aufstieg und Niedergang der römischen Welt,* Teilband II, Band 37.2, Berlin and New York, Walter de Gruyter, 1994, pp. 968–1075.

——, and David Armstrong, "The Virgin's Voice and Neck: Aeschylus, *Agamemnon* 245 and Other Texts," *Bulletin of the Institute of Classical Studies,* 1986, vol. 33, pp. 97–100.

Haraway, Donna, "A Cyborg Manifesto: Science, Technology, and Socialist-Feminism in the Late Twentieth Century," in *Simians, Cyborgs, and Women: The Reinvention of Nature,* New York, Routledge, pp. 149–181.

Harvey, Susan Ashbrook, "Violence, Gender, and God: Male and Female Martyrs in the Early Church," paper delivered at Amherst College, Amherst, MA, 1989.

Hastrup, Kirstin, "The Semantics of Biology: Virginity," in Shirley Ardener (ed.) *Defining Females: The Nature of Women in Society,* New York, Croom Helm, 1978, pp. 49–65.

Heffernan, Thomas, *Sacred Biography: Saints and Their Biographers in the Middle Ages,* New York and Oxford, Oxford University Press, 1988.

Heger, Astrig, and S. Jean Emans, et. al., (ed.) *Evaluation of the Sexually Abused Child: A Medical Textbook and Photographic Atlas,* New York, Oxford University Press, 1992.

Heliodorus, *An Ethiopian Story,* J. R. Morgan (trans.), in *Collected Ancient Greek Novels,* B. P. Reardon (ed.), Berkeley and Los Angeles, University of California Press, 1989.

Heller, Edmund Karl, "The Story of the Magic Horn: A Study in the Development of a Mediaeval Folk Tale," *Speculum,* 1934, vol. 9, pp. 38–50.

Helmholz, Richard, *Marriage Litigation in Medieval England,* Cambridge University Press, 1974.

Heng, Geraldine, "Feminine Knots and the Other *Sir Gawain and the Green Knight,*" *PMLA,* 1991, vol. 106.3, pp. 500–514.

Herodotus, *Histories,* Aubrey de Sélincourt (trans.) [1954], Harmondsworth, England, Penguin, reprinted 1984.

Hexter, Ralph J., *Equivocal Oaths and Ordeals in Medieval Literature,* Cambridge, MA, Harvard University Press, 1975.

Hicks, George, *The Comfort Women: Japan's Brutal Regime of Enforced Prostitution in the Second World War,* New York, Norton, 1995.

L'histoire de Guillaume le Maréchal, 3 vols, Paul Meyer (ed.), Paris, Société de l'histoire de France, 1891–1901.

Hrosvit, "Pelagius," in Sister M. Gonsalva Weigand (ed.) "The Non-Dramatic Works of Hrosvitha: Text, Translation, and Commentary," Ph.D. Dissertation, St. Louis University, St. Louis MI, 1936.

Hyams, Paul, "Trial by Ordeal: The Key to Proof in the Early Common Law," in Morris S. Arnold, et. al. (eds) *On the Laws and Customs of England: Essays in Honor of Samuel E. Thorne,* Chapel Hill, University of North Carolina Press, 1981, pp. 90–126.

Irigaray, Luce, "When Our Lips Speak Together," *Signs,* Autumn 1980, vol. 61, pp. 69–79.

——, "When the Goods Get Together" [1977], Claudia Reeder (trans.), in Elaine Marks and Isabelle de Courtivron (eds) *New French Feminisms,* New York, Schocken Books, 1981, pp. 107–110.

Jacquart, Danielle, and Claude Thomasset, *Sexuality and Medicine in the Middle Ages* [1985], Matthew Adamson (trans.), Princeton University Press, 1988.

Janus, Samuel S. and Cynthia L. Janus, *The Janus Report on Sexual Behavior,* New York, John Wiley, 1993.

Jerome, "Ad Eustochium" (Epistola XXII), in *Select Letters of St. Jerome,* F. A. Wright (trans.), Loeb Classical Library, Cambridge MA, Harvard University Press/London, William Heinemann, 1933.

——, "Ad Laeta" (Epistola CVII), in *Select Letters of St. Jerome,* F. A. Wright (trans.), Loeb Classical Library, Cambridge MA, Harvard University Press/London, William Heinemann, 1933.

——, "Commentariorum in epistelam ad ephesios," *PL* 26.

——, *Ad Jovinianum, PL* 23.

——, *Ad Jovinianum,* in *The Principal Works of St. Jerome,* W. H. Fremantle (trans.) [1893], Nicene and Post-Nicene Fathers 6, Second Series, Peabody, MA, Hendrickson, reprinted 1994.

——, *Ad Helvidium, PL* 23.

——, *On the Perpetual Virginity of the Blessed Mary: Against Helvidius,* in *Saint Jerome: Dogmatic and Polemical Works,* John N. Hritzu (trans.), The Fathers of the Church 53, Washington, D.C., Catholic University of America Press, 1965.

——, *Vita S. Malchi, PL* 23.55–62.

Jillings, Lewis, Diu Crône *of Heinrich von dem Türlin: The Attempted Emancipation of Secular Narrative,* Göppingen, Kümmerle Verlag, 1980.

John Chrysostom, "Saints Bernice and Prosdoce," *PG* 50.

——, *De Virginitate,* in *On Virginity, Against Remarriage,* Sally Rieger Shore (trans.), Studies in Women and Religion 9, New York and Toronto, Edwin Mellen Press, 1983.

——, *On the Necessity of Guarding Virginity,* in *Jerome, Chrysostom, and Friends: Essays and Translations,* Elizabeth A. Clark (trans.), Lewiston, NY, Edwin Mellen, 1979. Reprinted in Clark, *Women in the Early Church,* Wilmington, DE, Glazier, 1983.

——, *Comment Observer la Virginité* [*On the Necessity of Guarding Virginity*], in *Saint Jean Chrysostome: Les Cohabitations Suspectes et Comment Observer la Virginité,* Jean Dumortier (ed. and trans.), Paris, Bude, 1955.

John of Seville, *De interrogationibus,* Venice, 1493.

John of Trevisa, *On the Properties of Things,* in *John of Trevisa's Translation of Bartholomæus Anglicus De Proprietatibus Rerum,* 3 vols, M.C. Seymour (ed.), Oxford, Clarendon, 1975–1988.

Joplin, Patricia Klindienst, "The Voice of the Shuttle is Ours," *Stanford Literature Review,* 1984, vol. 1, pp. 25–53.

Jordan, Mark D., *The Invention of Sodomy in Christian Theology*, University of Chicago Press, 1997.

Jutta de Huy, *Acta Sanctorum*, 13 January.

Kalinke, Marianne (ed. and trans.), *Möttul's Saga*, Editiones Arnamagnaeanae, Series B, vol. 30, Copenhagen, C. A. Reital, 1987.

Katz, Marilyn A., "Sexuality and the Body in Ancient Greece," *Trends in History*, 1990, vol. 4.4, pp. 97–125.

Kelly, Kathleen Coyne, "Malory's Body Chivalric," *Arthuriana*, Winter 1996, vol. 6.4, pp. 52–71.

——, Virgins Web site: http://www.dac.neu.edu/english/kakelly/forth/virsite.html.

——, "The Hymen has a History: Early Modern Doubts about and Disputations on the *Claustrum Virginitatis*," paper delivered at "Attending to Early Modern Women: Crossing Boundaries" Center for Renaissance and Baroque Studies, University of Maryland, 1997, College Park, MD.

Kelly, Robert L., "*Wounds, Healing, and Knighthood in Malory's Tale of Lancelot and Guenevere*," in James W. Spisak (ed.) *Studies in Malory*, Kalamazoo, MI, Western Michigan University, Medieval Institute Publications, 1985, pp. 173–197.

Kendrick, Laura, "Transgression, Contamination, and Woman in Eustache Deschamps's *Miroir de mariage, Stanford French Review*, Spring-Fall, 1990, vol. XIV. 1–2, pp. 211–230.

Kennedy, Beverly, *Knighthood in the* Morte Darthur, Cambridge, England, D. S. Brewer, 1985.

Kerr, Margaret H., Richard D. Forsyth, and Michael J. Plyley, "Cold Water and Hot Iron: Trial by Ordeal in England," *The Journal of Interdisciplinary History*, Spring 1992, vol. XXII.4, pp. 573–95.

King, Helen, "Producing Woman: Hippocratic Gynecology," in Léonie J. Archer, Susan Fischler, and Maria Wyke (eds) *Women in Ancient Societies: An Illusion of the Night*, New York and London, Routledge 1994, pp. 102–114.

——, "Once Upon a Text: Hysteria from Hippocrates," in Sander L. Gilman, Helen King, Roy Porter, G. S. Rousseau, and Elaine Showalter (eds) *Hysteria Beyond Freud*, Berkeley and Los Angeles, University of California Press, 1993, pp. 3–90.

Kinney, Clare R., "The (Dis)Embodied Hero and the Signs of Manhood in *Sir Gawain and the Green Knight*," in Clare Lees (ed.) *Medieval Masculinities: Regarding Men in the Middle Ages*, Minneapolis, University of Minnesota Press, 1994, pp. 47–57.

Kristeva, Julia, "Stabat Mater," in Susan Rubin Suleiman (ed.) *The Female Body in Western Culture: Contemporary Perspectives*, Cambridge, Harvard University Press, 1986, pp. 100–18.

Kuhn, Annette, "Introduction to Hélène Cixous's 'Castration or Decapitation?'" *Signs*, Autumn 1981, vol. 7.1, pp. 36–40.

La Tavola Ritonda, 2 vols, F. L. Polidori (ed.), Bologna, 1864–65.

——, *Tristan and the Round Table*, Ann Shaver (trans.), Binghamton, New York, Medieval and Renaissance Texts & Studies, 1983.

Lacan, Jacques, "Agency of the Letter in the Unconscious or Reason Since Freud" [1957], in *Écrits*, Alan Sheridan (trans.), New York and London, Norton, 1977, pp. 146–175.

——, "The Function and Field of Speech and Language in Psychoanalysis," [1953], in *Écrits*, Alan Sheridan (trans.), New York and London, Norton, 1977, pp. 30–113.

Lacy, Norris J., "'Amer par oïr dire': *Guillaume de Dole* and the Drama of Language," *The French Review*, May 1981, vol. 54.6, pp. 779–87.

Lambert, Mark, *Malory: Style and Vision in* Le Morte Darthur, New Haven, CT, Yale University Press, 1975.

Laqueur, Thomas, *Making Sex: Body and Gender from the Greeks to Freud*, Cambridge, MA, Harvard University Press, 1990.

Lauersen, Niels H., *You're in Charge: A Teenage Girl's Guide to Sex and Her Body*, New York, Fawcett Columbine, 1993.

Lea, Henry C., *Superstition and Force: Essays on the Wager of Law, the Wager of Battle, the Ordeal, and Torture*, [2nd. ed., rev. 1870], Westport, CN, Greenwood Press, reprinted 1968.

Legenda Aurea, T. Graesse (ed.) [1890], Osnabrück, Germany, Zeller, 3rd ed., photo rep. 1965.

——. *The Golden Legend*, 2 vols, William Granger Ryan (trans.), Princeton, NJ, Princeton University Press, 1993.

Lemay, Helen Rodnite, "William of Saliceto on Human Sexuality," *Viator*, 1981, vol. 12, pp. 165–181.

——, "The Stars and Human Sexuality: Some Medieval Scientific Views," *Isis*, 1980, vol. 71, pp. 127–137.

Lewis, C. S., *Preface to Paradise Lost*, Oxford University Press, 1942.

Life of Christina of Markyate: A Twelfth-Century Recluse, C. H. Talbot (ed.), Oxford, Clarendon, 1959, reprinted 1987.

Livy, *Ab urbe condita*, B. O. Foster (trans.), London, William Heinemann/New York, Putnam, 1926.

Lloyd, G. E. R., *Science, Folklore, and Ideology: Studies in the Life Sciences in Ancient Greece*, Cambridge University Press, 1983.

de Lorris, Guillaume and Jean de Meun, *Le Roman de la Rose*, Daniel Poirion (ed.) Paris, Garnier-Flammarion, 1974.

Loughlin, Marie H., *Hymeneutics: Interpreting Virginity on the Early Modern Stage*, Lewisburg, PA, Bucknell University Press/London, Associated University Presses, 1997.

Lumiansky R. M., "'The Tale of Launcelot': Prelude to Adultery," in R. M. Lumiansky (ed.) *Malory's Originality*, Baltimore, Johns Hopkins University Press, 1964, pp. 91–98.

de'Luzzi, Mondino, *Anatomia*, in *Anatomies de Mondino dei Luzzi et de Guido de Vigevano*, Ernest Wickersheimer (ed.), Paris, E. Droz, 1926.

Malinowitz, Harriet, *Textual Orientations: Lesbian and Gay Students and the Making of Discourse Communities*, Portsmouth, NH, Boynton/Cook 1995.

Malinowski, Bronislaw, *The Sexual Life of Savages in Northern Melanesia: An Ethnographic Account of Courtship, Marriage and Family Life Among the Natives of the Trobriand Islands, British New Guinea*, 2 vols, New York, Horace Liveright/London, Routledge, 1929.

Malory, Sir Thomas, *The Works of Sir Thomas Malory*, 3rd. ed., Eugène Vinaver (ed.), P. J. C. Field (rev.), Oxford, Clarendon, 1990.

Mandel, Jerome, "The Idea of Coherence and the Feminization of Knights in Malory's 'Alexander the Orphan,'" *Arthurian Yearbook III*, 1993, pp. 91–105,

Mann, Jill, "Malory: Knightly Combat in *Le Morte D'arthur*," in *Medieval Literature: Chaucer and the Alliterative Tradition*, Boris Ford (ed.) Harmondsworth, England, Penguin, 1984, reprinted 1991.

Martin, Ann G. *Shame and Disgrace in King Arthur's Court: A Study in the Meaning of Ignominy in German Arthurian Literature*, Göppingen, Kümmerle Verlag, 1984.

Martin, Dale B., *The Corinthian Body*, New Haven, CT, and London, Yale University Press, 1995.

"Martyrdom of Shmona and Guria, Confessors of Edessa," in *Euphemia and the Goth, with the Acts of Martyrdom of the Confessors of Edessa*, F. C. Burkitt (ed.), London, Williams and Norgate, 1913.

McInerney, Maud Burnett, "Rhetoric, Power and Integrity in the Passion of the Virgin Martyr," in Kathleen Coyne Kelly and Marina Leslie (eds) *Menacing Virgins: Representing Virginity in the Middle Ages and Renaissance*, Newark, University of Delaware Press/London, Associated University Presses, 1999, pp. 50–70.

A Medieval Woman's Guide to Health: The First English Gynecological Handbook, Beryl Rowland (ed. and trans.), Kent, OH, Kent State University Press, 1981.

Meyer, Catie, "Intimate Surgery," *First*, August 1994, vol. 1, pp. 47–50.

de Mondeville, Henry, *Chirurgie*, in *Chirurgie de Maître Henri de Mondeville*, E. Nicaise (ed.), F. Alcan, Paris, 1893.

Miller, D. A., *The Novel and the Police*, Berkeley and Los Angeles, University of California Press, 1988.

More, Thomas, *A Dialogue Concerning Heresies*, in *The Complete Works of St. Thomas More*, vol. 6, part I, Thomas M. C. Lawler, Germain Marc'Hadour, and Richard C. Marius (eds), New Haven, CT, and London, Yale University Press, 1981.

Morgan, Thaïs E., "Two Conversations on Literature, Theory, and the Question of Genders," in Thaïs E. Morgan (ed.) *Men Writing the Feminine: Literature, Theory, and the Question of Genders*, Albany, NY, State University of New York Press, 1994, pp. 189–200.

Munich, Adrienne Auslander, "What Lily Knew: Virginity in the 1890s," in Lloyd Davis (ed.) *Virginal Sexuality and Textuality in Victorian Literature*, Albany, State University of New York Press, 1993, pp. 143–157.

Murray, Jacqueline, "On the Origins and Role of 'Wise Women' in Causes for Annulment on the Grounds of Male Impotence," *Journal of Medieval History*, 1990, vol. 16, pp. 235–249.

"The Nature of Wommen," British Library MS Egerton 827.

The New Our Bodies Our Selves: A Book By and For Women, Boston Women's Healthbook Collective (eds), New York, Simon and Schuster/Touchstone, 1992.

Newman, Kathy, "Re-membering an Interrupted Conversation: the Mother/Virgin Split," *TRIVIA*, Spring 1983, vol. 2, pp. 45–63.

Newstead, Elaine, "The Equivocal Oath in the Tristan Legend," in *Mélanges offerts à Rita Lejeune* (introduction by Fred Duthier), Gembloux: Duculot, 1969, vol. 2, pp. 1077–85.

Ortner, Sherry B., "Gender and Sexuality in Hierarchical Societies: The Case of Polynesia and Some Comparative Implications," in Sherry B. Ortner and Harriet Whitehead (eds) *Sexual Meanings: The Cultural Construction of Gender and Sexuality*, Cambridge University Press, 1981, pp. 359–409.

——, "The Virgin and the State," *Feminist Studies*, 1978, vol. 4, pp. 19–35.

Palladius, *Acta et temperantia Potamiænæ*, in *Historia Lausiaca*, PG 34.

——, *Palladius: The Lausiac History*, Robert T. Meyer (trans.), Westminster, MD, The Newman Press/London, Longmans, 1965.

Palmer, Anne-Marie, *Prudentius on the Martyrs*, Oxford, Clarendon, 1989.

Parks, Katharine, and Robert A. Nye, "Destiny is Anatomy," *The New Republic*, February 1991, vol. 18, pp. 53–58.

La pasión de S. Pelayo: Edición crítica, con traducción y comentarios, Rodríguez Fernández Celso (ed.), Santiago de Compostela, Spain, Universidade de Santiago de Compostela, 1991.

Paster, Gail Kern, "The Unbearable Coldness of Female Being: Women's Imperfection and the Humoral Economy," paper delivered at the Center for Literary and Cultural Studies, Harvard University, 1996.

——, *The Body Embarrassed: Drama and the Discipline of Shame in Early Modern England*, Ithaca, Cornell University Press, 1993.

Patlagean, Evelyne, "Ancient Byzantine Hagiography and Social History," in Stephen Wilson (ed.) *Saints and Their Cults: Studies in Religion, Sociology, Folklore and History*, Cambridge University Press, 1983, pp. 101–121.

Payer, Pierre J., *The Bridling of Desire: Views of Sex in the Later Middle Ages*, Toronto and Buffalo, University of Toronto Press, 1993.

Pechey, Graham, "Bakhtin, Marxism and Post-Structuralism," in Francis Barker, Peter Hulme, Margaret Iversen, and Diana Loxley (eds) *Literature, Politics, and Theory*, London and New York, Methuen, 1986, pp. 104–123.

Pernoud, Régine, *The Retrial of Joan of Arc: The Evidence at the Trial for Her Rehabilitation 1450–1456*, J. M. Cohen (trans.), New York, Harcourt, Brace, 1955.

Petroff, Elizabeth, "Eloquence and Heroic Virginity in Hrotsvit's Verse Legends," in Katharina M. Wilson (ed.) *Hrotsvit of Gandersheim: Rara Avis in Saxonia?*, Ann Arbor, University of Michigan/MARC, 1987, pp. 229–238.

Pinto, Lucille B., "The Folk Practice of Gynecology and Obstetrics in the Middle Ages," *Bulletin of the History of Medicine*, 1973, vol. 47, pp. 513–523.

Plath, Sylvia, *The Bell Jar* [1963, under a pseudonym; 1966, under her own name], New York, Bantam Books, 1981.

Pliny, *Natural History*, vol. 2, H. Rackham (ed. and trans.), Loeb Classical Library, Cambridge MA, Harvard University Press/London, William Heinemann, 1942, reprinted 1947.

Pope Leo, "Epistola XII," in *Correspondence*, Edmund Hunt (trans.), New York, Fathers of the Church 34, 1957.

Pratt, Mary Louise, "Interpretive Strategies/Strategic Interpretations," *Boundary 2*, Fall–Winter 1982–83, vol. 11.1–2, pp. 201–231.

Procès de Condamnation et de Réhabilitation de Jeanne D'Arc dite La Pucelle, 5 vols, Jules Quicherat (ed.) [Paris, 1841–49], New York, Johnson, reprinted 1965.

Prudentius, *Works*, 2 vols, H. J. Thomson (ed. and trans.) Harvard University Press, 1949–53.

Pseudo-Albertus, *De secretis mulierum*, Helen Rodrite Lemay (trans.), in *Women's Secrets: A Translation of Pseudo-Albertus' De Secretis Mulierum with commentaries*, Albany, NY, State University of New York Press, 1992.

Putter, Ad, "Arthurian Literature and the Rhetoric of 'Effeminacy,'" in Friedrich Wolfzettel (ed.) *Arthurian Romance and Gender / Masculin/Feminin dans le roman arthurien medieval / Geschlechterrollen in mittelalterlichen Artusroman*, Amsterdam, Rodopi, 1995.

Reames, Sherry, *The Legenda Aurea: A Reexamination of Its Paradoxical History*, Madison and London, University of Wisconsin Press, 1985.

Renart, Jean, *Le Roman de la Rose ou de Guillaume de Dole*, Félix Lecoy (ed.), Paris, Champion, 1962.

——, *The Romance of the Rose or Guillaume de Dole*, Patricia Terry and Nancy Vine Durling (trans), Philadelphia, University of Pennsylvania Press, 1993.

Rifaat, Alifa, "Honor," Elise Goldwasser and Miriam Cooke (trans), in Margot Badran and Miriam Cooke (eds) *Opening the Gates: A Century of Arab Feminist Writing*, Bloomington, IN, Indiana University Press 1991, pp. 78–83.

Robert Biket, *Lai du Cor*, Fredrik Wulff (ed.), Paris, 1888.

Ross, Ellen, and Rayna Rapp, "Sex and Society: A Research Note from Social History and Anthropology," in Ann Snitow, Christine Stansell, and Sharon Thompson (eds) *Powers of Desire: The Politics of Sexuality*, New York, Monthly Review Press, 1983, pp. 51–73.

Rousselle, Aline, *Porneia: On Desire and the Body in Antiquity* [1983], Felicia Pheasant (trans.), Oxford, Blackwell's, 1988.

Salisbury, Joyce, *Church Fathers, Independent Virgins*, London and New York, Verso, 1991.

de Saliceto, Guilielmus, *Summa conservationis*, Venice, 1489.

Samples, Susann, "The Other? A Critical Study of the Rapist-Knight Gasozein in Heinrich von dem Turlin's *Diu Crône*," paper delivered at the XVIIIth International Congress of the Arthurian Society, Garda, Italy, 1996.

Savonarola, Michael, *Practica Maior*, Venice, 1547.

Schlegel, Alice, "Status, Property, and the Value on Virginity," *American Ethnologist*, November 1991, vol. 18.4, pp. 719–734.

Schulenberg, Jane Tibbetts, "Saints' Lives as a Source for the History of Women, 500–1100," in Joel T. Rosenthal (ed.) *Medieval Women and the Sources of Medieval History*, Athens, University of Georgia Press, 1990, pp. 285–320.

——, "The Heroics of Virginity: Brides of Christ and Sacrificial Mutilation," in Mary Beth Rose (ed.) *Women in the Middle Ages and the Renaissance*, Syracuse, Syracuse University Press, 1986, pp. 29–72.

Scott, Joan, "The Evidence of Experience," in Henry Abelove, Michèle Aina Barele, and David M. Halperin (eds) *The Lesbian and Gay Studies Reader*, New York and London, Routledge, 1993, pp. 397–415.

Sedgwick, Eve Kosofsky, *Between Men: English Literature and Male Homosocial Desire*, New York, Columbia University Press, 1985.

Seneca the Elder, *Controversiae*, in *Oratorum et rhetorum sententiae, divisiones, colore*, Michael Winterbottom (trans.), Loeb Classical Library, Cambridge MA, Harvard University Press/ London, William Heinemann, 1975.

Severus of Antioch, "Letter VIII.5," in *The Sixth Book of Select Letters of Severus, Patriarch of Antioch*, 2 vols, E. W. Brooks (ed. and trans.), London, Williams and Norgate, 1903, 1904.

Sheehan, Michael M., *Marriage, Family, and Law in Medieval Europe: Collected Studies*, Toronto and Buffalo, University of Toronto Press, 1996.

Shoaf, R.A., "'Unwemmed Custance': Circulation, Property, and Incest in the Man of Law's Tale," *Exemplaria*, 1990, vol. 2.1, pp. 287–302.

Sir Gawain and the Green Knight, in *The Poems of the Pearl Manuscript*, Malcolm Andrew and Ronald Waldron (eds), Berkeley and Los Angeles, University of California Press, 1978.

Sissa, Giulia, *Greek Virginity* [1987], Arthur Goldhammer (ed.), Cambridge, MA, Harvard University Press, 1990.

Smith, Paul, *Discerning the Subject*, Minneapolis, University of Minnesota Press, 1988, reprinted 1989.

Society for the Recapture of Virginity, http://www.thebluedot.com/srv.

Solinus, *Collectanea Rerum Memorabilium*, Th. Mommsen (ed.) [1895], Berlin, Weidman, reprinted 1958.

Solterer, Helen, "At the Bottom of Mirage, a Woman's Body: *le Roman de la Rose* of Jean Renart," in Linda Lomperis and Sarah Stanbury (eds) *Feminist Approaches to the Body in Medieval Literature*, Philadelphia, PA, University of Pennsylvania Press, 1993, pp. 213–233.

Soranus, *Sorani Gynaeciorum Libri IV, De Signis Fracturarum, De Fasciis, Vita Hippocratis Secundum Soranum*, Johannes Ilberg (ed.), *Corpus Medicorum Graecorum IV*, Leipzig and Berlin, B. G. Teubner, 1927.

——, *Soranus' Gynecology*, Owsei Temkin (trans.), Baltimore, John Hopkins University Press, 1956.

Stoller, Robert, *Observing the Erotic Imagination*, New Haven, CT, Yale University Press, 1985.

von Strassburg, Gottfried, *Tristan*, in *Gottfried von Strassburg's Tristan*, Peter Ganz (ed.), Wiesbaden, F. A. Brockhaus, 1978.

———, *Tristan*, A. T. Hatto (trans.), Harmondsworth, England, Penguin Books, 1984.

Suetonius, *The Lives of the Caesars*, J. C. Rolfe (ed.), Loeb Classical Library, NY, Macmillan/ London, William Heinemann, 1924.

Swidler, Leonard, *Women in Judaism: The Status of Women in Formative Judaism*, Metuchen, NJ, Scarecrow Press, 1976.

Tacitus, *The Annals*, John Jackson (trans.), Loeb Classical Library, Cambridge MA: Harvard University Press, 1937, reprinted 1951.

Talmud, Babylonian, *The Soncino Talmud*, 35 vols, translated under the general editorship of Isidore Epstein, London, Soncino Press, 1935–48.

Tertullian, *Ad Uxorem*, PL 1.

———, *De Exhortatione Castitatis*, PL 2.

———, *De virginibus velandis*, PL 2.

———, *De virginibus velandis*, Sydney Thelwall (trans.) [1885], Ante-Nicene Fathers 4, reprinted Peabody, MA, Hendrickson, 1994.

———, *Apologeticum*, in *Tertullian: Apology and De Spectaculis [and Minucius Felix]*, T. R. Glover (trans.), Loeb Classical Library, Cambridge MA, Harvard University Press/London, William Heinemann, 1977.

Thompson, Stith, *Motif-Index of Folk-Literature*, Bloomington, Indiana University Press, rev. and enlarged, 1966.

Tigay, Jeffrey H., *The JPS Torah Commentary: Deuteronomy*, Philadelphia and Jerusalem, Jewish Publication Society, 1966.

Trial of Mary and Joseph, in *The N-Town Play: Cotton MS Vespasian D.8*, Stephen Spector (ed.) E.E.T.S. S.S. 11, Oxford, Oxford University Press, 1991.

Tristan [French Prose Romance], partial text edited in P. J. C. Field, *Romance and Chronicle*, Bloomington, Indiana University Press, 1971, pp. 168–173.

Trotula, "De virginitate restituenda sophistice," in Julia O'Faolain and Lauro Martines (ed.) *Not in God's Image: Women in History from the Greeks to the Victorians*, New York, Harper and Row, 1973, pp. 142–143.

———, "De virginitate restituenda sophistice," in *Collectio Salernitana*, 5 vols, Salvatore de Renzi (ed.), Naples 1852–59, vol. IV, 1856.

Valerius Maximus, *Facta et dicta memorabilia*, Venice, 1471.

de Vitry, Jacques, "Exemplum CCXLVII," in *The Exempla, or Illustrative Stories from the Sermones Vulgares of Jacques de Vitry*, Thomas Frederick Crane (ed.) [1890], Millwood, New York, Kraus reprinted, 1967.

Voigts, Linda, "What's the Word? Bilingualism in Late-Medieval England," *Speculum*, October 1996, vol. 71, pp. 813–826.

von dem Türlin, Heinrich, *Diu Crône*, in *Diu Crône von Heinrich von dem Türlin*, G. H. F. Scholl (ed.), Stuttgart, 1852.

———. *The Crown: A Tale of Sir Gawein and King Arthur's Court*, J. W. Thomas (trans.), Lincoln, University of Nebraska Press, 1989.

Wack, Mary, *Lovesickness in the Middle Ages: The Viaticum and its Commentaries*, Philadelphia, University of Pennsylvania Press, 1990.

Walker, Alice, *The Color Purple* [1982], New York, Simon and Schuster/Pocket Books/ Washington Square Press, 1983.

Weinstein, Donald, and Rudolph M. Bell, *Saints and Society: The Two Worlds of Western Christendom, 1000–1700*, Chicago, University of Chicago Press, 1982.

Werner, Erica, "The Cult of Virginity," *Ms.*, March/April 1997, vol. 7.5, pp. 40–43.

White, Allon, "Bakhtin, Sociolinguistics and Deconstruction," in Frank Gloversmith (ed.) *The Theory of Reading*, New York, Barnes and Noble/Sussex, England, Harvester Press, 1984, pp. 123–146.

White, Hayden, "The Question of Narrative in Contemporary Historical Theory," in *The Content of the Form*, Baltimore and London, Johns Hopkins University Press, 1987, pp. 26–57.

——, "The Value of Narrativity in the Representation of Reality," in *The Content of the Form*, Baltimore and London, Johns Hopkins University Press, 1987, pp. 1–25.

——, *Metahistory: The Historical Imagination in Nineteenth-Century Europe*, Baltimore and London, Johns Hopkins University Press, 1973.

Wigalois, J. W. Thomas (trans.), Lincoln and London, University of Nebraska Press, 1977.

Wittig, Monique, "The Mark of Gender," *Feminist Issues*, Fall 1985, vol. 5.2, pp. 3–12.

Wogan-Browne, Jocelyn, "Saints' Lives and the Female Reader," *Forum for Modern Language Studies*, 1991, vol. 27.4, pp. 314–332.

Wolf, Naomi, *Promiscuities: The Secret Struggle for Womanhood*, New York, Random House, 1997.

York, Ernest C., "Isolt's Ordeal: English Legal Customs in the Medieval Tristan Legend," *Studies in Philology*, January 1971, vol. 68.1, pp. 1–9.

Zimmerman, Bonnie, "Perverse Reading: The Lesbian Appropriation of Literature," in Susan J. Wolfe and Julia Penelope (eds) *Sexual Practice, Textual Theory: Lesbian Cultural Criticism*, Cambridge, MA and Cambridge, England, Blackwell, 1993, pp. 135–149.

Index

Lightning Source UK Ltd.
Milton Keynes UK
UKOW030436120112

185229UK00001B/8/A